Published by Pearson Education Limited, Edinburgh Gate, Harlow, Essex, CM20 2JE.

www.pearsonschoolsandfecolleges.co.uk

Units 1, 2, 3, 4, 5 and 6 © Pearson Education Limited 2012, Units 7, 8, 9 10, 11, 12, 13, 14, 15, 16, and 17 © Pearson Education Limited 2013.
Typeset by Phoenix Photosetting, Chatham, Kent, UK
Original illustrations © Pearson Education Limited 2012, 2013
Illustrated by Vicky Woodgate, Phoenix Photosetting and Oxford Designers and Illustrators
Picture research by Harriet Merry and Caitlin Swain
Front cover photos: © Getty Images: OJO Images/Paul Bradbury
Indexing by Indexing Specialists (UK) Ltd.

The rights of Mark Adams, Rob Armstrong, Adam Gledhill, Julie Haines, Julie Hancock, Bob Harris, Pam Phillippo and Alex Sergison to be identified as authors of this work have been asserted by them in accordance with the Copyright, Designs and Patents Act 1988.

Units 1–6 first published 2012.
This full edition published 2013.

17 16 15 14 13
10 9 8 7 6 5 4 3 2 1

British Library Cataloguing in Publication Data
A catalogue record for this book is available from the British Library

ISBN 978 1 446901 61 8

Printed in Slovakia by Neografia

Websites
There are links to relevant websites in this book. In order to ensure that the links are up to date, that the links works, and that the sites aren't inadvertently links to sites that could be considered offensive, we have made the links available on our website at www.pearsonhotlinks.co.uk. Search for the title BTEC First Sport Student Book or ISBN 978 1 446901 61 8.

Copies of official specifications for all Pearson qualifications may be found on: www.edexcel.com

A note from the publisher
In order to ensure that this resource offers high quality support for the associated BTEC qualification, it has been through a review process by the awarding organisation to confirm that it fully covers the teaching and learning content of the specification or part of a specification at which it is aimed, and demonstrates an appropriate balance between the development of subject skills, knowledge and understanding, in addition to preparation for assessment.

While the publishers have made every attempt to ensure that advice on the qualification and its assessment is accurate, the official specification and associated assessment guidance materials are the only authoritative source of information and should always be referred to for definitive guidance.

No material from an endorsed book will be used verbatim in any assessment set by BTEC.

Endorsement of a book does not mean that the book is required to achieve this BTEC qualification, nor does it mean that it is the only suitable material available to support the qualification, and any resource lists produced by the awarding organisation shall include this and other appropriate resources.

SPORT

PEARSON

Contents

The following optional units are available on the Pearson Education website.

Acknowledgements

The publisher would like to thank the following for their kind permission to reproduce their photographs:

(Key: b-bottom; c-centre; l-left; r-right; t-top)

Alamy Images: Aflo Alto 75c, Allstar Picture Library 59c, Corbis Bridge 121t, John Fryer 226b, Jonathan Goldberg 149c, keith morris 289c, PCN Photography 324cr, PhotosIndia.com 221tr, Realimage 244b, Richard G. Bingham II 295tl, Science Photo Library 112c, STEVE LINDRIDGE 107c, Tobias Titz 279tr; **Change4Life:** 316c; **Corbis:** Steve Bardens 56cr, Philip Brown 4bl, Nick Dolding 146c, Elizabeth Kreutz 125t, Erik Isakson / Blend Image 8bl, Gero Breloer 192bl, Gero Breloer / epa 319, Image Source 10cl, Mika 22b, Tim Tadder 110br, Turba 215c; **Crown Copyright Courtesy of the Department of Health in association with the Welsh Government, the Scottish Government and the Food Standards Agency in Northern Ireland.:** 240c; **Getty Images:** 64bl, Adam Pretty 193tr, AFP 65tr, 329tr, Alex Livesey 324cl, Shaun Botterill 91tc, Comstock Images 11tr, David Rogers 100cr, Dean Mouhtaropoulos 329tl, Getty Images 6cr, Getty Images Sport 131cl, 156tl, Giuseppe Bellini 180cl, Bertrand Guay / AFP 89c, Hoch Zwei 211c, Hugh Nutt / Flickr 299, Isaac Koval 172br, Erik Isakson 308b, Chris Jackson 84br, Jupiter 323br, Glyn Kirk / AFP 153br, Laurence Griffiths 156br, 327c, Bryn Lennon 78c, Mike Hewitt 88bc, Hans Neleman 169tc, Nick Clements 288b, Mark Nolan 70cl, Richard Heathcote 312cl, Robert Cianflone 21cr, Ross Kinnaird 334b, Stacy Pearsall 310b, Steve Bardens 223b, Bob Thomas 276br, Andrew Wong 92c; **Glow Images:** Image 100 180cr, 256bl, Image 100. Corbis 94br; **Hawk-Eye Innovations Limited:** 62cl; **Image 100:** 237t; **Imagestate Media:** John Foxx Collection 165t; **John Foxx Images:** Imagestate 38tr; **Jupiterimages:** Brand X / Alamy 248c; **London 2012:** 47; **Pearson Education Ltd:** 27c, 45br, 123tr, David Sanderson 274br; **PhotoDisc:** 193cl, Michael Lamotte. Cole Publishing Group. 238bl; **Photolibrary.com:** BananaStock 161t, Les and Dave Jacobs 19cr, Somos 67r; **Rex Features:** 137tl, Offside 285t; **Salford City Stadium:** 303cr; **Science Photo Library Ltd:** Living Art Enterprises 115c; **Shutterstock.com:** 44tr, AISPIX by Image Source 305br, AlexandreNunes 282tl, alysta 253b, Andresr 132bl, 176tr, Andrey Shadrin 76tl, Ariwasabi 113tr, Auremar 133tr, 325tr, Avava 119c, Diego Barbieri 103, Blazej Lyjak 129b, Blend Images 210bl, Adam Borkowski 101tr, Adrian Britton, Brocreative 236tr, Kris Butler 17c, Herminia Lucia Lopes Serra de Casais 60cr, Catalin Petolea 104tl, Diego Cervo 193br, corepics 77bl, Neale Cousland 193bl, Istvan Csak 111b, Denis Vrublevski 174bl, Dmitry Berkut 5tl, DSPA 224b, Elena Elisseeva 46bl, EpicStockMedia 18bl, eurobanks 232bl, Rod Ferris 195tl, Foodpics 56bl, Foto011 192cr, Fotokostic 151b, 163tl, Galina Barskaya 131c, Gelpi 48tl, Herbert Kratky 131cr, 193cr, Margrit Hirsch 269cr, Huntstock.com 148bl, hxdbzxy 93cr, IKO 126bl, itsmejust, Ivonne Wierink 318bl, JanVlcek 301br, Jason Stitt 63tr, jcjgphotography, Josh Brown 97t, katatonia82 158bl, Kirill Kleykov 192br, Peter Kirillov, Kzenon 4tr, 127, 141cr, lenetstan 2bl, Lucky Business 142b, John Lumb 137br, Maridav 260br, mick20 194c, Monkey Business Images 159tr, 233, 297t, muzsy 114cl, 259c, naluwan 102bl, Natursports 71b, 158tl, Vanessa Nel 193tl, Nicole Weiss 7t, Oleq Zabielin 321b, Olga Besna 52bl, Ostill 179c, Pavel Shchegolev 168cl, Photo Stock 10 175c, picture5479 250bl, PT Images 212tl, Radu Razvan 180bc, Raphael Daniaud 108cr, Rob Marmion 128tl, Galushko Sergey 60cl, Dmitriy Shironosov 16tl, .shock 105b, 192cl, Smith&Smith 166bl, spflaum 265tc, sportgraphic 51cl, 80cl, 81b, 85tr, 116tl, Stefan Schurr 98cr, Stephen Mcsweeny 147t, StockLite 183tr, 291tr, 317tr, Supri Suharjoto 74bl, 213c, 280bl, Konstantin Sutyagin 140c, Suzanne Tucker 150tl, tan4ikk 298, thelefty 154b, Tim Hester Photography 100cl, Tomasz Trojanowski, Valua Vitaly 241tr, wavebreakmedia ltd 24tl, Wayne0216 283b, xc 49br, Yeko Photo Studio 3c; **Veer/Corbis:** Greg Epperson 267tr, lightpoet 12bl, warrengoldswain 266bl; **www.imagesource.com:** 300tl, 320tl, MOODBOARD 252tl, SCIENCE PHOTO LIBRARY 234tl

Cover images: *Front:* **Getty Images:** OJO Images / Paul Bradbury

All other images © Pearson Education

Picture Research by: Harriet Merry, Caitlin Swain

Every effort has been made to trace the copyright holders and we apologise in advance for any unintentional omissions. We would be pleased to insert the appropriate acknowledgement in any subsequent edition of this publication.

The author and publisher would like to thank the following individuals and organisations for permission to reproduce their materials:

p. 28 Aerobic endurance results table. Adapted, with permission, from Luc A. Léger, 1982, 'A Maximal Multistage Fitness Test to Predict VO$_2$ Max', European Journal of Applied Physiology and Occupational Physiology, 1-12

p. 31 Forestry non-adjusted aerobic fitness values for males table. Adapted, with permission, from B.J. Sharkey, 1984, Physiology of Fitness, 2nd ed. (Champaign, IL: Human Kinetics), 258

p. 32 Forestry non-adjusted aerobic fitness values for females table. Adapted, with permission, from B.J. Sharkey, 1984, Physiology of Fitness, 2nd ed. (Champaign, IL: Human Kinetics), 259

p. 32 Forestry age-adjusted aerobic fitness values table. Adapted, with permission, from B.J. Sharkey, 1984, Physiology of Fitness, 2nd ed. (Champaign, IL: Human Kinetics), 260-61

p. 33 Forestry aerobic fitness values table. Adapted, with permission, from B.J. Sharkey, 1984, Physiology of Fitness, 2nd ed. (Champaign, IL: Human Kinetics), 262

p. 35 Illinois agility run test results table. Adapted, with permission, from Ross Bull, Robert Davis, Jan Roscoe, Physical Education and the Study of Sport, 2nd ed., copyright Mosby (2000)

p. 35 Lewis Nomogram. Adapted. © Fox, Edward et al. The Psychological Basis of Physical Education and Athletics, 1988, McGraw-Hill. Material is reproduced with permission of the McGraw-Hill Companies.

p. 41 J-P Nomogram. Research Quarterly for Exercise and Sport (RQES), Vol. 52, 380–384

p. 82 Eysenck's Personality Dimensions. Figure is reproduced with permission from The H.J. Eysenck Memorial Fund

p. 83 Profile of Mood States graph. Adapted, with permission, from P. Klavora and J.V. Daniel, Coach, Athlete and the Sport Psychologist (1979)

p. 114 Bone density differences due to playing sport. Adapted, with permission, from the American Society for Bone and Mineral Research (ASBMR).

p.274 Health and Safety at Work (etc.)1974. Adapted, with permission, from the Health and Safety Executive. Contains public sector information published by the Health and Safety Executive and licensed under the Open Government Licence v1.0.

p.274 HSE and accident statistics. Quoted, with permission, from the Health and Safety Executive. Contains public sector information published by the Health and Safety Executive and licensed under the Open Government Licence v1.0.

p.274 Health and Safety (first aid) regulations 1981. Quoted, with permission, from the Health and Safety Executive. Contains public sector information published by the Health and Safety Executive and licensed under the Open Government Licence v1.0.

p.205 Sport and leisure activity industry statistics. Adapted, with permission, from State of the Industry report, 2012, SkillsActive.

p.298 Sport and leisure activity industry statistics. Adapted, with permission, from State of the Industry report, 2012, SkillsActive.

p.302 UK health club and leisure centre figures. Adapted, with permission, from State of the Industry report, 2012, SkillsActive.

About this book

This book is designed to help you through your BTEC First in Sport, and covers 17 units of the qualification.

About your BTEC First in Sport

Choosing to study for a BTEC First Sport qualification is a great decision to make for lots of reasons. More and more people are looking to improve their personal fitness, so there is a growing demand for personal trainers and fitness instructors. There is also an increased interest in professional sport due to the UK hosting the 2012 Olympic Games. The sport sector offers a wide variety of careers. Your BTEC will sharpen your skills for employment or further study.

About the authors

Mark Adams is head of Sport and PE at Loreto Sixth Form College, Manchester, and is also a consultant with the Premier League education learning team. He has been involved in the development of sport qualifications for 12 years.

Rob Armstrong is a department manager currently teaching BTEC qualifications at a Sixth Form College. He has taught BTEC Sport qualifications for 13 years across all levels and has been involved with qualification development for 8 years.

Adam Gledhill has 12 years' experience teaching in Further and Higher Education, and has been involved with qualification development for a number of years. Alongside teaching, Adam is currently working toward a PhD in Sport Psychology, while also providing Sport Science support to youth athletes in a range of sports.

Julie Haines has over 14 years of teaching experience. Julie started out as a PE teacher in secondary schools, then became a sports development officer and latterly a lecturer and Head of Department for Sport in a Further Education college. She has been involved with qualification development for a number of years.

Julie Hancock has taught for over 23 years, first as a PE teacher in secondary schools, then as a lecturer in Further Education. She now teaches in Higher Education. Julie has contributed to a range of educational resources and teacher training programmes. She has been involved in the development of sport qualifications for over 19 years.

Bob Harris has been in education for over 30 years and has delivered BTEC Sport courses at all levels. Bob is the author of best-selling student books and teacher resources.

Pam Phillippo has played a key role in the development of BTEC Sport qualifications and is an expert in psychophysiology. Formerly a lecturer in Further Education and Higher Education, and having worked with GB athletes, her specialist fields include fitness testing and training, exercise prescription, and experimental methods.

Alex Sergison specialises in outdoor education and has spent 14 years instructing and lecturing at all levels. He has provided management and advice for a number of outdoor activity centres. Alex is responsible for outdoor education course development for Weymouth College and has been involved in the development of outdoor qualifications at level 2 and 3.

How to use this book

This book is designed to help you use your skills and knowledge in work-related situations, and assist you in getting the most from your course.

These introductions give you a snapshot of what to expect from each unit – and what you should be aiming for by the time you finish it.

How this unit is assessed

Learning aims describe what you will be doing in the unit.

A learner shares how working through the unit has helped them.

Features of this book

There are lots of features in this book to help you learn about the topics in each unit, and to have fun along the way!

Topic references show which parts of the BTEC you are covering.

Get started with a short activity or discussion about the topic.

Key terms are important words or phrases that you will come across. Key terms appear in blue bold text and are defined within the topic or in a key terms box on the page. Also see the glossary.

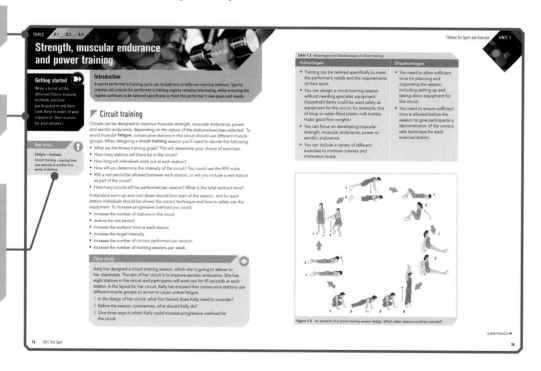

Activity 3.1   Assessing personality

Watch a selection of different sports, pick an athlete to watch in each, and then answer the following questions:

- Which traits and behaviours do they display while they are performing?
- What do these traits/behaviours suggest about their personality type?

Activities will help you learn about the topic. These can be completed in pairs or groups, or sometimes on your own.

Assessment practice 1.1

1 Which component of fitness can have kgm/s as its unit of measurement? Select the correct answer. [1]

A Anaerobic power

B Reaction time

C Speed

D Muscular strength

2 Give three reasons why speed is an important component of physical fitness for basketball players. [3]

A chance to practise answering the types of test questions that you may come across in the onscreen test. (For Unit 1 and Unit 7 only.)

Assessment activity 3.3   *English*   2C.P6 | 2C.P7 | 2C.M4 | 2C.D3

You have been asked to prepare a presentation for a group of young athletes to educate them on anxiety, the effects of arousal and the different ways of controlling anxiety. As part of your presentation, you need to include information about:

- different types of anxiety, using relevant examples of each
- the effects of arousal and anxiety on sports performance, using four theories
- imagery and relaxation techniques as methods of controlling arousal and anxiety, and improving sports performance.

Tips

- Give your views on which theories you believe accurately explain the relationship between arousal, anxiety and performance, which you think don't, and why.
- Consider each of the different methods to control arousal – which techniques would be most effective at controlling arousal, and why?

Activities that relate to the unit's assessment critera. These activities will help you prepare for your assignments and contain tips to help you achieve your best results. (For all units **except** Unit 1 and Unit 7.)

Just checking

1 What do the initials EPI stand for?

2 Which mood states does the POMS questionnaire measure?

3 What would you look for when conducting behavioural observations?

Use these to check your knowledge and understanding of the topic you have just covered.

Someone who works in the sport industry explains how this unit of the BTEC First applies to the day-to-day work they do as part of their job.

This section gives you the chance to think more about the role that this person does, and whether you would want to follow in their footsteps once you've completed your BTEC.

The Mind and Sports Performance   **UNIT 3**

WorkSpace

Samantha

19-year-old football coach

I really like my job. I get to coach football to all different age ranges and abilities, all of which present different challenges.

One of the biggest issues that I face is trying to get people to train outside when it is cold and wet. Trying to get them to concentrate on different areas for improvement is difficult when they just want to keep moving all the time if the weather is bad!

Another issue that I often come across is when players start to worry about the opposition, thinking that they might not be able to beat them because they might have lost to the same opposition before. It is really difficult for me as the coach if players go into a game already having lost in their minds.

One of the biggest benefits of understanding the mind and sports performance is knowing about different ways to motivate my players and different ways of helping them to cope with their performance-related worries.

Think about it

1   Why do you think it is important for sports coaches to have an understanding of the mind and sports performance?

2   How would the information on motivation benefit Samantha in her coaching role?

3   How would the information on arousal, anxiety and performance benefit Samantha in her coaching role?

4   Is this a job that you would be interested in, and if so, why?

101

BTEC Assessment Zone

You will be assessed in two different ways for your BTEC First in Sport qualification. For most units, your teacher/tutor will set assignments for you to complete. These may take the form of projects where you research, plan, prepare, and evaluate a piece of work or activity. The table in the BTEC Assessment Zone explains what you must do in order to achieve each of the assessment criteria. Each unit of this book contains a number of assessment activities to help you with these assessment criteria.

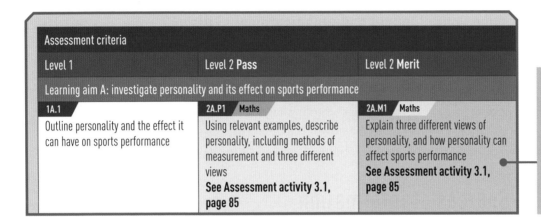

Assessment criteria		
Level 1	Level 2 **Pass**	Level 2 **Merit**
Learning aim A: investigate personality and its effect on sports performance		
1A.1	**2A.P1** Maths	**2A.M1** Maths
Outline personality and the effect it can have on sports performance	Using relevant examples, describe personality, including methods of measurement and three different views **See Assessment activity 3.1, page 85**	Explain three different views of personality, and how personality can affect sports performance **See Assessment activity 3.1, page 85**

The table in the BTEC Assessment Zone explains what you must do in order to achieve each of the assessment criteria, and signposts assessment activities in this book to help you to prepare for your assignments

For Unit 1 and Unit 7 of your BTEC, you will be assessed by an onscreen test. The BTEC Assessment Zone for these units helps you to prepare for your test by showing you some of the different types of questions you will need to answer.

A Questions where the answers are available and you have to choose the correct answer(s). *Tip: always read carefully to see how many answers are needed and how you can show the right answer.*

Examples:

Which **two** of the following are **not** components of skill-related fitness? Select the two correct answers. [2]

A Agility

B Coordination

C Body composition

D Aerobic endurance

E Balance

F Power

Answers: C and D

Sharon is 27 years old and has just started training at her local gym. Calculate Sharon's maximum heart rate (HRmax). Select the correct answer. [1]

A 193 bpm

B 173 bpm

C 183 bpm

D 203 bpm

Answer: A

You will find examples of the different types of questions you will need to answer, as well as sample answers and tips on how to prepare for the onscreen tests.

Study skills

Planning and getting organised

The first step in managing your time is to plan ahead and be well organised. Some people are naturally good at this. They think ahead, write down commitments in a diary or planner and store their notes and handouts neatly and carefully so they can find them quickly.

How good are your working habits?

Improving your planning and organisational skills

1 Use a diary to schedule working times into your weekdays and weekends.

2 Also use the diary to write down exactly what work you have to do. You could use this as a 'to do' list and tick off each task as you go.

3 Divide up long or complex tasks into manageable chunks and put each 'chunk' in your diary with a deadline of its own.

4 Always allow more time than you think you need for a task.

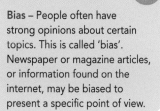

Take it further

If you become distracted by social networking sites or texts when you're working, set yourself a time limit of 10 minutes or so to indulge yourself. You could even use this as a reward for completing a certain amount of work.

Sources of information

You will need to use research to complete your BTEC First assignments, so it's important to know what sources of information are available to you. These are likely to include the following:

Key term

Bias – People often have strong opinions about certain topics. This is called 'bias'. Newspaper or magazine articles, or information found on the internet, may be biased to present a specific point of view.

Textbooks
These cover the units of your qualification and provide activities and ideas for further research.

Internet
A vast source of information, but not all sites are accurate and information and opinions can often be **biased** – you should always double-check facts you find online.

Sources of information

Newspapers and magazines
These often cover sport topics in either dedicated sport sections or through articles about sports performers and sports events.

People
People you know can be a great source of opinion and experience – particularly if you want feedback on an idea.

Television
Programmes such as *Soccer AM* and *Match of the Day* can give you an insight into the world of sport. The news also regularly reports on the world of sport.

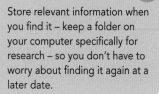

Remember!

Store relevant information when you find it – keep a folder on your computer specifically for research – so you don't have to worry about finding it again at a later date.

Organising and selecting information

Organising your information

Once you have used a range of sources of information for research, you will need to organise the information so it's easy to use.

- Make sure your written notes are neat and have a clear heading – it's often useful to date them, too.
- Always keep a note of where the information came from (the title of a book, the title and date of a newspaper or magazine and the web address of a website) and, if relevant, which pages.
- Work out the results of any questionnaires you've used.

Selecting your information

Once you have completed your research, re-read the assignment brief or instructions you were given to remind yourself of the exact wording of the question(s) and divide your information into three groups:

1 Information that is totally relevant.

2 Information that is not as good, but which could come in useful.

3 Information that doesn't match the questions or assignment brief very much, but that you kept because you couldn't find anything better!

Check that there are no obvious gaps in your information against the questions or assignment brief. If there are, make a note of them so that you know exactly what you still have to find.

Presenting your work

Before handing in any assignments, make sure:

- you have addressed each part of the question and that your work is as complete as possible
- all spelling and grammar is correct
- you have referenced all sources of information you used for your research
- all work is your own – otherwise you could be committing **plagiarism**
- you have saved a copy of your work.

Key term

Plagiarism – If you are including other people's views, comments or opinions, or copying a diagram or table from another publication, you must state the source by including the name of the author or publication, or the web address. Failure to do this (when you are really pretending other people's work is your own) is known as plagiarism. Check your school's policy on plagiarism and copying.

Introduction

All sports performers want to be the best they can be. To reach optimal levels requires dedication to training, taking into account all factors that contribute to sports performance.

To perform well, you need good levels of fitness achieved by maintaining good health and adopting the behaviours needed to lead your life to the highest quality. A training cycle can incorporate different fitness training methods, the choice of which will often depend on the performer's sport and their personal training needs.

Fitness testing can be incorporated into the training cycle to determine baseline fitness levels and identify areas needing improvement to help the performer reach their potential and perform better in their sport.

Fitness and exercise for sport is core to your programme of study. This unit links to, and underpins, all other units, and is particularly relevant if you would like to work in sports coaching, elite sport or personal training.

Assessment: You will be assessed using an onscreen test lasting one hour.

Learning aims

In this unit you will:

A know about the components of fitness and the principles of training

B explore different fitness training methods

C investigate fitness testing to determine fitness levels.

I have learned all sorts of things about fitness and exercise training in this unit. I've been able to apply this knowledge in my own training and sports performance, and it's helped to give me clearer training goals, which I know I will achieve.

Temi, *16-year-old gym enthusiast*

Fitness for Sport and Exercise

1

Components of fitness and their importance for sporting success

Introduction

In this section you will learn about physical fitness and skill-related fitness, and why these are important for success in different sports.

Components of physical fitness

There are six components of physical fitness:

1 **Aerobic endurance** – the ability of the cardiorespiratory system to work efficiently, supplying nutrients and oxygen to working muscles during sustained physical activity.

2 **Muscular endurance** – the ability of the muscular system to work efficiently, in which a muscle can repeatedly contract over a period of time against a light to moderate fixed-resistance load.

3 **Flexibility** – the ability to move all joints fluidly through their complete range of movement.

4 **Speed** – distance divided by the time taken, measured in metres per second (m/s). There are three basic types of speed: accelerative speed (sprints up to 30 metres), pure speed (sprints up to 60 metres) and speed endurance (sprints with a short recovery period in-between).

5 **Muscular strength** – the maximum force that a muscle or muscle group can produce. This is measured in kilograms (kg) or Newtons (N).

6 **Body composition** – the relative ratio of fat mass to fat-free mass (vital organs, muscle, bone) in the body.

Components of skill-related fitness

There are five components of skill-related fitness:

1 **Agility** – the ability to move quickly and precisely or change direction without losing balance or time.

2 **Balance** – the ability to maintain your centre of mass over a base of support. There are two types: **static balance** and **dynamic balance**. For instance, a gymnast would use static balance when performing a handstand on the balance beam and dynamic balance when tumbling during a floor routine.

3 **Coordination** – the ability of parts of the body to work together to move smoothly and accurately.

4 **Power** – the work done in a unit of time. It is calculated in the following way:

$$\text{Power} = \text{Force (kg)} \times \text{Distance (m)} / \text{time (min or s)}.$$

This is expressed as kilogram-metres per minute (kgm/min) or kilogram-metres per second (kgm/s).

5 **Reaction time** – the time taken for a sports performer to respond to a stimulus; for example, the time taken for a footballer to analyse a goal-scoring opportunity and decide to attempt a shot at goal by starting the kicking/heading action.

Which fitness components are important to a cricketer?

A gymnast uses static and dynamic balance. What other components of fitness are important for success?

Why fitness components are important for sporting success

In order to meet the demands of their sport and reach **optimal** levels of performance, a sports performer needs to train specific components of fitness. These will vary from sport to sport and position to position. For example, a basketball player needs aerobic endurance, speed, flexibility, power, muscular endurance and strength in order to move effectively around the court, intercept passes and score baskets. They also need to have great agility and footwork, so they can change direction quickly and respond rapidly to the positions of their opponents.

Key term

Optimal – the best, or most favourable.

Activity 1.1   Fitness for different sports

Work in pairs or small groups.

1 Think about the different sports activities you participate in.

2 Select four different sports and draw a spider diagram showing what components of fitness you think are important for success in each one. Depending on the sports selected, you may also need to consider differences between positions played and how this might impact on your choices.

3 Discuss the reasons for your answers and prepare a short presentation to feed back to the rest of your class.

Assessment practice 1.1

1 Which component of fitness can have kgm/s as its unit of measurement? Select the correct answer. [1]

A Anaerobic power

B Reaction time

C Speed

D Muscular strength

2 Give three reasons why speed is an important component of physical fitness for basketball players. [3]

Determining exercise intensity

Getting started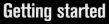

Exercising at the right intensity for you helps you get the most out of your workout. In pairs, discuss how often you work out. How hard do you work during these workouts? Do you think you over work sometimes, or could you push yourself further?

Remember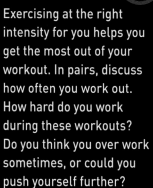

If the carotid pulse is to be used for measuring your pulse, take care not to apply too much pressure against the carotid artery. This may result in specialised receptors slowing down your heart rate, thereby leading to an invalid resting heart rate result.

Introduction

Exercise intensity is a term used to describe how hard an individual is training; for example the relative speed, rate or level of an individual's exertion. In this topic you will learn about two methods that can be used to determine exercise intensity: heart rate (HR) and Rating of Perceived Exertion (RPE).

Measuring heart rate

Heart rate is measured in beats per minute (bpm), and may indicate an individual's fitness level when taken at rest.

Measuring resting heart rate

At rest, heart rate should preferably be measured via the radial artery in the wrist (rather than the carotid pulse, which is found on either side of your neck).

Sitting down, locate your radial artery by placing your index and middle fingers together on the thumb-side of your opposite wrist; do not use your thumb because it has a light pulse of its own.

Once you find your pulse, ask a friend to start a stopwatch and then count the number of beats you feel for 60 seconds. This is your resting heart rate in beats per minute (bpm).

Measuring radial pulse. Can you measure your resting heart rate (HR)?

Activity 1.2   Measuring heart rate

You'll need a stopwatch for this activity.

1 Measure and record your resting HR.

2 Undertake 15 minutes of light to moderate physical activity. For example, jogging on a treadmill.

3 After 15 minutes of physical activity, sit down immediately and measure your pulse via the radial artery.

4 Record your HR results every minute, until you reach your resting HR.

5 Draw a graph: HR (bpm) against time (seconds or minutes). What do your results suggest about your fitness levels?

6 How long did it take you to reach your original resting HR? How do your results compare to those of your peers? Discuss in small groups.

Measuring exercise heart rate

Training or exercise heart rate can be monitored to ensure you do not push yourself too hard, and to check if you are progressing well with your training regime.

The easiest, most convenient and most accurate way to measure exercise heart rate is to use a heart rate monitor. These are used by professional and amateur sports performers and athletes alike. Athletes and sports performers calculate their **heart rate training zone** to check that they are exercising at the right level of intensity.

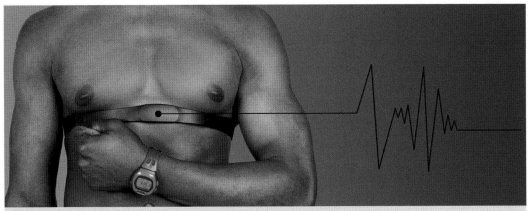

Why not train using a heart rate monitor: what will your results show?

Calculating heart rate training zones

To work out your heart rate training zone, first calculate your maximum heart rate (HRmax):

HRmax = 220 − age (years).

Next, work out 60% of your HRmax (0.6 × HRmax), which is the lower heart rate training zone. Finally, work out 85% of your HRmax (0.85 × HRmax), which is the upper heart rate training zone. The range between these two numbers is the recommended training zone for cardiovascular health and fitness. You'll need plenty of practice at measuring resting heart rate, exercise heart rate and calculating training zones.

Worked example

A healthy 20-year-old would work out their heart rate training zone using the following calculations:

- HRmax: 220 − 20 = 200 bpm
- lower heart rate training zone: 0.6 × 200 = 120 bpm

- upper heart rate training zone: 0.85 × 200 = 170 bpm.

Therefore, a healthy 20-year-old has a recommended exercise heart rate of between 120 bpm and 170 bpm.

Assessment practice 1.2

Malcolm is 30 years old and Vivienne is 48 years old.

1 Calculate their maximum heart rates. (4)	2 Calculate their lower and upper heart rate training zones for cardiovascular health and fitness. (4)

CONTINUED ▸▸

Using the RPE scale as a measure of exercise intensity

Another way of determining exercise intensity is to use the Rating of Perceived Exertion (RPE) scale, developed by Professor Gunnar Borg in 1970. The scale can be used to rate an individual's level of physical exertion during physical activity or exercise.

The scale starts at 6 and goes up to 20, where 6 means 'no exertion at all' (at rest) and 20 is 'maximal exertion' (for example, the feeling you have as you make an all out effort for the finish line of a sprint race). You will see in Figure 1.1 that some of the numbers are represented by verbal cues.

Plenty of practice is needed to learn how to use the scale properly. When giving a rating, the individual needs to take into account all sensations of physical stress, effort and fatigue that they are feeling. This will include strain and fatigue in exercising muscles, and feelings of breathlessness.

Rating of Perceived Exertion	Intensity
6	No exertion at all
7	Extremely light
8	
9	Very light
10	
11	
12	
13	Somewhat hard
14	
15	Hard (heavy)
16	
17	Very hard
18	
19	Extremely hard
20	Maximal exertion

Figure 1.1 The Borg (1970) 6–20 RPE scale

Relationship between RPE and HR

Instead of using a HR monitor, you can use the RPE scale to predict the exercise HR of an individual using the relationship:

$$RPE \times 10 = HR \text{ (bpm)}$$

Worked example

If an individual gives a rating of '15 Hard (heavy)', they can predict their exercise HR by using the following calculation:

- RPE × 10 = HR (bpm)
- 15 × 10 = 150 bpm

Therefore, the individual's exercise HR will be approximately 150 bpm.

Why not train using a treadmill? What RPE would you achieve?

Activity 1.3   Determining exercise intensity

Work in small groups.

1 Perform a short warm-up.

2 Set up a 30-minute circuit training session for aerobic endurance. One person in each group should be in charge of recording HR data. Everyone else in the group should wear a heart rate monitor and participate in the training session.

3 Work out your HRmax using the equation: 220 − age (years).

4 Next, calculate your HR training zone for cardiovascular health and fitness (60–85% HRmax).

5 Take part in the training circuit. Your HR and RPE will be recorded after you have exercised at each station.

6 On completion of the 30 minutes, analyse HR and RPE data collected. Answer the following questions:

- Did each participant reach their calculated training zone for cardiovascular health and fitness?
- According to their RPE, how difficult/tiring did participants find it training at this level?
- Did participants go above their training zone? If so, what were possible reasons for this?

7 Discuss your results as a group.

Assessment practice 1.3

1 **Frida is 33 years old and exercises in the gym. She records her RPE during the following activities:**

Exercise	RPE	Heart rate (bpm)
Exercise bike	13	
Free weights	15	
Treadmill	16	

a **Complete the table to show Frida's heart rate (bpm) for these three activities. (3)**

b **Frida wants to work at 70% HRmax. Using the table above, work out which type of exercise would give her this HR training zone? (1)**

2 **Describe how the Borg RPE Scale can be used to determine exercise intensity. (2)**

The principles of training

Getting started

In pairs, discuss the types of sport and leisure activity you do. How frequently do you partake in this sport or activity? How hard do you work while partaking? How long do you do this sport or leisure activity for and what types of exercise do you do, e.g. aerobic or strength training?

Introduction

When planning and undertaking training programmes you need to incorporate the basic principles of training.

The basic principles of training (FITT)

The **FITT principle** is:

- **Frequency** – the number of training sessions you complete over a period of time. Aim for three to five sessions per week.
- **Intensity** – how hard you train. Intensity can be prescribed using HR or RPE.
- **Time** – how long you train for. Aim for 15 to 60 minutes of activity, depending on the intensity. If you have low levels of fitness, then reduce intensity and increase time.
- **Type** – how you train. The appropriate method(s) of training should be selected according to your needs and goals. For example, to train for muscular strength, endurance and power, you could do circuit training, or use free weights in the gym.

Additional principles of training

Fitness training programmes are designed and based on the FITT principle and the following additional principles of training, which can be discussed and agreed between performer and coach:

- **Progressive overload** – in order to progress, training needs to be demanding enough to cause your body to adapt, improving performance. Increase your training workload gradually. This can be done by increasing frequency, intensity or time, or by reducing recovery times. But don't use all of these methods at once, as the increase in workload may lead to over training resulting in injury or illness.
- **Specificity** – training should be specific to your preferred sport, activity, or developing physical/skill-related fitness goals.
- **Individual differences/needs** – the programme should be designed to meet your training goals, needs, ability, level of fitness, skill level and exercise likes/dislikes.
- **Adaptation** – this occurs during the recovery period after the training session is complete. Adaptation is how your body increases its ability to cope with training loads.
- **Reversibility** – if you stop training, or the intensity of training is not sufficient to cause adaptation, training effects are reversed. Reversibility is also known as de-training.
- **Variation** – it is important to maintain interest; this helps an individual keep to their training schedule. Vary your training programme to avoid boredom and maintain enjoyment.
- **Rest and recovery** – these are essential to allow the body to repair and adapt, and for the renewal of body tissues. If your body doesn't get a chance to recover then the rate of progression can be reduced.

Training must be specific to the performer's needs. What are your training goals and needs?

WorkSpace

▶ Charlie McLaren

Personal trainer and life coach

I work for a private gym. I am responsible for:

- working with clients to agree training goals and needs
- assessing client fitness to determine baseline levels
- fitness training programme design
- monitoring client progress towards meeting training goals
- contributing to the gym's lifestyle and fitness activities programme.

I love my job, and in this line of work that's really important. It's my role to motivate clients, encourage personal belief and self-confidence, and give them the support needed to achieve their personal training goals.

My main role at the gym is fitness testing and assessment – clients need to know their baseline fitness levels so that clear goals can be agreed. I usually carry out a range of different fitness tests on clients, which cover the different components of fitness, such as skinfold testing for % body fat. Once I have talked clients through their results we can then discuss training goals and move forward with programme design.

Establishing a regular fitness training regime in everyday life can often mean people having to juggle their work and life commitments, but there's always a way to fit training in.

To be successful in this industry you need leadership and coaching skills and qualities, but personality is important too. Being enthusiastic, approachable, honest and confident are all important traits that clients look for in a personal trainer.

Think about it

1. What areas have you covered in this unit that provide you with knowledge and skills used by a personal trainer and lifestyle coach?

2. What further skills might you need to develop if you were to become a personal trainer?

3. Think about how you would measure clients' heart rates to aid training programme design.

Flexibility training

Key terms

Flexibility – having an adequate range of motion in all joints of the body.

Isometric – muscular action in which tension develops, but there is no change in muscle length and no joint movement. For example, when doing a side plank.

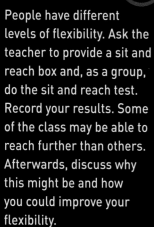

What type of stretch is this athlete performing?

Introduction

Flexibility is important for all sports performers, whether you are a 110 metres hurdler stretching to clear the hurdle, a footballer extending for the ball or a tennis player reaching to take a forehand. There are three types of flexibility fitness training methods: static stretching, ballistic stretching and the Proprioceptive Neuromuscular Facilitation (PNF) technique.

Static stretching

Static stretching involves slowly stretching a muscle to the limit of its range of movement and then holding the stretch still for 10 to 20 seconds. It is usually used as part of a standard warm-up routine, to help warm muscles and joints ready for exercise. There are two types of static flexibility training:

- **Active stretching** – stretches are performed by a sports performer on their own. The performer applies force to stretch and lengthen the muscles.
- **Passive stretching** – this is also known as assisted stretching and requires the help of another person or an object, such as a chair or wall. The other person (or object) applies an external force, causing the muscle to stretch.

Ballistic stretching

Ballistic stretching involves making fast, jerky movements, usually in the form of bouncing or bobbing through the full range of movement. This form of stretching can incorporate sport-specific movements that take a joint past its normal range of movement. Ballistic stretching must be performed with care, as incorrect technique can lead to muscle soreness and injury.

Proprioceptive Neuromuscular Facilitation (PNF) technique

This is an advanced form of passive stretching, which is often used in rehabilitation programmes. The PNF technique inhibits the stretch reflex, which occurs when a muscle is stretched to its full capability, so that an even greater range of movement can occur. When performing PNF, remember to listen to your body – pain signals will tell you if you have taken the stretch too far. PNF must be performed carefully with a partner. There are three phases:

1 Stretch the muscle to the upper limit of its range of movement.
2 With the help of your partner, contract the muscle **isometrically** for 6–10 seconds.
3 Relax the muscle, and then with the help of your partner perform a static (passive) stretch enabling an even greater stretch to be achieved.

Table 1.1 Advantages and disadvantages of the PNF technique

Advantages	Disadvantages
• Flexibility training can be made sport-specific • Little cost involved, no need for specialist equipment • Improved flexibility may help to reduce injuries	• Need to be experienced to perform PNF training safely • May require two individuals working together to perform the technique

Activity 1.4 — Limbering up

Work in small groups.

1 Look at Figure 1.2. For each labelled area of the body, each group member needs to practically demonstrate a different active stretch, which should be held for approximately 10 seconds.

2 Once you have demonstrated a stretch, the person next to you has to demonstrate your stretch and also select their own stretch for a different part of the body, and so on. Repeat in your group until all labelled parts of the body have been covered.

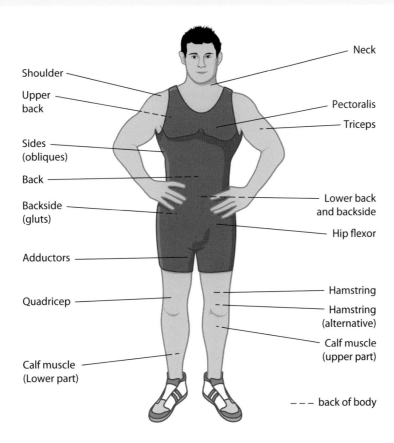

Figure 1.2 Major muscles of the body

13

Strength, muscular endurance and power training

Getting started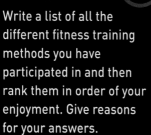

Write a list of all the different fitness training methods you have participated in and then rank them in order of your enjoyment. Give reasons for your answers.

Introduction

A sports performer's training cycle can include lots of different training methods. Sports coaches will ensure the performer's training regime remains interesting, while ensuring the regime continues to be tailored specifically to meet the performer's own goals and needs.

Key terms

Fatigue – tiredness.
Circuit training – moving from one exercise to another at a series of stations.

Link

This unit links to *Unit 7: Anatomy and Physiology for Sport and Performance* and *Unit 13: Profiling Sports Performance, Topic A.3.*

Circuit training

Circuits can be designed to improve muscular strength, muscular endurance, power and aerobic endurance, depending on the nature of the stations/exercises selected. To avoid muscular **fatigue**, consecutive stations in the circuit should use different muscle groups. When designing a **circuit training** session you'll need to decide the following:

- What are the fitness training goals? This will determine your choice of exercises.
- How many stations will there be in the circuit?
- How long will individuals work out at each station?
- How will you determine the intensity of the circuit? You could use the RPE scale.
- Will a rest period be allowed between each station, or will you include a rest station as part of the circuit?
- How many circuits will be performed per session? What is the total workout time?

A standard warm-up and cool down should form part of the session, and for each station individuals should be shown the correct technique and how to safely use the equipment. To increase progressive overload you could:

- increase the number of stations in the circuit
- reduce the rest period
- increase the workout time at each station
- increase the target intensity
- increase the number of circuits performed per session
- increase the number of training sessions per week.

Case study

Kelly has designed a circuit training session, which she is going to deliver to her classmates. The aim of her circuit is to improve aerobic endurance. She has eight stations in the circuit and participants will work out for 45 seconds at each station. In the layout for her circuit, Kelly has ensured that consecutive stations use different muscle groups so as not to cause undue fatigue.

1 In the design of her circuit, what four factors does Kelly need to consider?
2 Before the session commences, what should Kelly do?
3 Give three ways in which Kelly could increase progressive overload for the circuit.

Table 1.2 Advantages and disadvantages of circuit training

Advantages	Disadvantages
• Training can be tailored specifically to meet the performer's needs and the requirements of their sport. • You can design a circuit training session without needing specialist equipment. Household items could be used safely as equipment for the circuit; for example, tins of soup or water-filled plastic milk bottles make good free weights! • You can focus on developing muscular strength, muscular endurance, power or aerobic endurance. • You can include a variety of different exercises to maintain interest and motivation levels.	• You need to allow sufficient time for planning and organising the session, including setting up and taking down equipment for the circuit. • You need to ensure sufficient time is allowed before the session to give participants a demonstration of the correct, safe technique for each exercise/station.

Figure 1.3 An example of a circuit training session design. Which other stations could be included?

CONTINUED ▸▸

Individual using free weights

◤ Free weights

Barbells or dumb-bells are types of free weights and can be used to perform a range of **constant-resistance exercises**. Examples of exercises include: bicep curls, tricep extensions, upright rows, squats, bent-over rows, seated overhead presses, lateral raises, front raises and bench presses.

There is a greater chance of injury when using **free weights** as opposed to **fixed-resistance machines**, and care must be taken to ensure correct, safe technique and use of equipment. When using heavy weights, the use of a **spotter** is recommended. A standard warm-up and cool down should form part of the session.

Weight training tips

- **Warm-up** – a good warm-up and range of stretches before you start training will help prepare your joints for movement and help avoid injury.

- **Body alignment** – if standing, feet should be shoulder-width apart with knees slightly bent. As the weight is lifted, movement should be slow and controlled.

- **Breathing technique** – do not hold your breath as this can increase blood pressure and could cause a heart attack. Breathe out as the weight is lifted.

- **Intensity** – do not use weights that are so heavy that they can't be lifted at least six times. Heavy resistance can be damaging to skeletal and joint structures. Intensity can be determined by using the percentage of an individual's **repetition maximum** (% 1–RM).

- **Number of sets** – every set should consist of 8 to 12 repetitions (reps). As training progresses, overload can be achieved by increasing the number of repetitions in a set (up to 20), and then by increasing the weight and dropping the reps back to 8.

- **Training for maximum strength** – use low reps and heavier weights (90% 1–RM and 6 reps).

- **Training for strength endurance** – use high reps and lighter weights (50% to 60% 1–RM and 20 reps).

- **Training for elastic strength** – use medium reps and weights (75% 1–RM and 12 reps).

- **Number of exercises** – include one to two sets of six different exercises in each workout. Training should cover all the major muscle groups.

- **Order of exercises** – focus on core exercises before assistance exercises; alternate between upper and lower body and push and pull exercises.

- **After training** – perform a cool down and developmental stretching (where stretches are held for 15–20 seconds). This will help to reduce muscle soreness, prevent cramps and increase joint range of movement.

Table 1.3 Advantages and disadvantages of training with free weights

Advantages	Disadvantages
• Training can be sport-specific, targeting specific muscles and muscle groups • Effective method for strength and endurance gains	• Session needs careful organisation, ensuring use of correct, safe technique • May need access to a gym or leisure/ sports centre for full range of equipment • The equipment needed can be expensive • May need a spotter

Plyometrics

Plyometrics training develops sport-specific explosive power and strength and is used widely in sports such as track athletics, netball, basketball and volleyball.

Plyometrics training involves exercises in which muscles are quickly and repeatedly stretched/ lengthened and then contracted/shortened, thus producing great force.

Plyometrics drills, such as skipping, arm swings and jogging drills, performed at **submaximal** levels, are usually used as a warm-up. Low-stress activities are used for cool down, such as light jogging and walking. Plyometrics training must be undertaken with care and should take into account the experience of the person and the level of intensity of the exercises to be performed. This type of training can be physically stressful and cause muscle soreness.

The basic equipment needed to perform plyometrics exercises includes: boxes, benches, hurdles, cones and medicine balls.

Different types of exercises include standing jumps, **incline press-ups**, jumping, bounding, skipping, hopping and medicine ball exercises for core strength.

Plyometrics training is used to increase explosive power and strength.

Table 1.4 Advantages and disadvantages of plyometrics

Advantages	Disadvantages
• Training can be made sport-specific • Little cost involved; no need for specialist equipment	• Need to be experienced to perform this type of training safely

Aerobic endurance training

Getting started

Think about the different sports and physical activities you take part in over the course of a month. What different fitness training methods do you use? Write a list and compare in small groups.

Introduction

In this section you will explore the different fitness training methods that can be used to develop your aerobic endurance.

Continuous training

Continuous training – also known as long, slow, distance or steady-state training – is where performers train at a steady pace and moderate intensity for at least 30 minutes. Because the training intensity is relatively low, it is a useful training method for beginners who may have a lower level of fitness and also for sports performers who are recovering from injury. A standard warm-up and cool down should form part of the session.

Table 1.5 Advantages and disadvantages of continuous training

Advantages	Disadvantages
• No special equipment needed • Easy training method to organise and carry out • Training can be made sport-specific • Good for building an endurance base	• Training for long distances can be monotonous • Higher risk of injury if running on a hard surface • Only develops aerobic endurance, not anaerobic

Fartlek training

The term 'fartlek' refers to a Swedish training method meaning 'speed play'. A standard warm-up and cool down should form part of the session. Training is usually performed outdoors, and is continuous, with no rest. The performer varies the intensity of training by running at different speeds or over different terrains (such as cross-country running or training on a beach). Intensity of training may be increased using equipment, such as running with a harness or a weighted backpack.

Fartlek training uses a variety of terrains.

Table 1.6 Advantages and disadvantages of fartlek training

Advantages	Disadvantages
• Can be made sport-specific • No need for specialist equipment • The performer can control the intensity level • Adds variety and interest to training	• Need for careful control of training intensity • Performer needs good self-discipline and motivation to maintain work rates

Interval training

For this training method the individual alternates work periods with rest or recovery periods. By varying the intensity and length of work periods, training can improve anaerobic and aerobic endurance. Work intervals for aerobic endurance will be approximately 60% **VO₂ max**. Typical work time varies from 30 seconds to 5 minutes, and recovery can be jogging or walking or even a complete rest.

A standard warm-up and cool down should form part of the session. For aerobic endurance training, decrease the number of rest periods and decrease work intensity. When planning interval training you need to consider:

- the duration of the work interval
- the duration of the rest interval
- the intensity of the work interval
- the intensity of the rest interval
- the total number of intervals in the training session.

Rest and recovery periods can involve jogging, walking or even complete rest.

> **Key term**
>
> VO₂ max – the maximum amount of oxygen uptake, usually measured in ml of oxygen per kg of body mass per minute. It is a measure of cardiorespiratory endurance.

Table 1.7 Advantages and disadvantages of interval training

Advantages	Disadvantages
• Allows clear progressive overload to be built into training by increasing the number of intervals, increasing intensity of the work periods, increasing the intensity of the rest period, or decreasing the duration of the rest period • Can be tailored to specific sports • No special equipment required • Can be used for aerobic and anaerobic endurance • Distance, time and intensity can meet individual training need	• Performer may lose interest due to repetition • Needs careful planning

Assessment practice 1.4

Rudi has joined his local gym with the aim of improving his strength and muscular endurance.

1 **Which fitness training method should Rudi follow to help him achieve his aim? (1)**

2 **Explain why Rudi should increase progressive overload and give an example of how he could do this in circuit training. (2)**

3 **Rudi wants to train for maximum strength. What % 1–RM and reps should he be working at? (2)**

Speed training

Getting started ▶▶

Work individually or in pairs. Choose an elite sports performer: this could be your favourite sports person or perhaps someone who is a personal role model for you. What different fitness training methods do you think are important for your selected performer? Prepare a table listing each method and give your reasons.

Introduction

The following fitness training methods are designed to improve a performer's speed. Speed training can be made sport-specific and often takes the form of drills.

Hollow sprints

This technique involves completing a series of sprints separated by a 'hollow' period of jogging or walking. A standard warm-up and cool down should form part of the session. A typical session could be as follows:

1 Set out ten cones at 20-metre intervals.

2 Sprint for 20 metres, then jog for 20 metres, alternating between the two until you reach the final cone. This is one set.

3 Complete eight sets in total. If intensity is too great, replace 'hollow' jog period with a walk instead.

Table 1.8 Advantages and disadvantages of hollow sprints

Advantages	Disadvantages
• No special equipment needed • Easy training method to organise and carry out • Training can be made sport-specific	• Performer may lose interest due to repetition • Need to maintain focus and motivation throughout

Acceleration sprints

For this type of training the pace is gradually increased from a standing or rolling start to jogging, then to striding and a maximum sprint. A standard warm-up and cool down should be carried out. Different drills can be used, such as resistance drills and hill sprints. Rest intervals of jogging or walking are used in-between each repetition. For example, an acceleration hill workout involves:

1 25-metre hills (at 15-degree gradient) × 8 repetitions

2 Walk or jog back down the hill to the start

3 1.5 to 2.5 minute rest between each repetition.

Table 1.9 Advantages and disadvantages of acceleration sprints

Advantages	Disadvantages
• No special equipment needed • Easy training method to organise and carry out	• Performer may lose interest due to repetition • Need to maintain focus and motivation throughout

Interval training

Interval training involves the individual alternating work periods with rest and recovery periods. For speed training, the work intervals are shorter and more intense, where the individual will work at a high intensity, close to their maximum possible level of physical effort.

A standard warm-up and cool down should form part of the session.

When designing an interval training session to develop speed, increase the number of rest periods, decrease the work interval and increase the work intensity.

Performers undertaking sprint drills. What type of training session could you design?

Table 1.10 Advantages and disadvantages of interval training

Advantages	Disadvantages
• No special equipment required • Can be tailored to specific sports • Can be tailored specifically for speed and anaerobic endurance gains • Distance, time and intensity can meet individual training needs	• Performer may lose interest due to repetition • Needs careful planning

Activity 1.5   Designing a training programme

1 Plan and design your own six-week training programme specific to your own personal goals and needs.
  You'll need to show how you have:

  • incorporated the principles of training into your design
  • included details of why you have selected the particular training methods.

2 Maintain a training diary to show how you have:

  • applied exercise intensity and principles of training to your selected fitness training method(s)
  • applied fitness training method(s) to your own needs/goals/aims/objectives.

 Link

This activity could be carried out alongside *Unit 5: Training for Personal Fitness*, giving you the opportunity to implement the programme you have designed.

Fitness testing

Introduction

In this topic you will learn about the requirements for fitness test administration and the procedures that need to be carried out before testing begins.

Why are fitness tests important?

Fitness tests are important because they:

- Provide a coach with baseline data results, which they can compare to normative published data in order to draw conclusions about an individual's fitness level.
- Give a starting point on which to base training programme design. Once training commences, fitness tests can then be used during the training cycle to show the progress of a training regime and its success so far.
- Can give a sports performer or athlete clear goals and targets to aim for. Appropriate recommendations for fitness improvements can be made according to the individual's test results and specific training needs.

An athlete performing the press-up test. How will you perform?

Pre-test procedures

Gaining informed consent

Before administering or participating in fitness tests the participant should complete an informed consent form. This is documented evidence that shows that the participant has been provided with all the necessary information to undertake each fitness test. Informed consent forms cover the following key points, which confirm that the participant:

- is able to follow the test method
- knows exactly what is required of them during testing
- has fully consented to participation in the fitness tests
- knows that they are able to ask the tester/teacher/assessor any questions relating to the tests
- understands that they can withdraw their consent at any time.

Activity 1.6 — Designing informed consent forms

Work in pairs or small groups.

1 Design your own informed consent forms for the different fitness tests to be undertaken.

2 You may design one consent form to cover all fitness tests listed in the unit content, or you may design different consent forms with fitness tests grouped under the relevant component of fitness.

Calibration of equipment

Calibration of equipment is the process of checking (and if necessary adjusting) the accuracy of fitness testing equipment before it is used, by comparing it to a recognised standard.

Prior to testing, equipment should be checked carefully. If equipment isn't correctly calibrated it could lead to inaccurate (invalid) results.

INFORMED CONSENT FOR THE MULTISTAGE FITNESS TEST

1. The purpose of the test is to predict an individual's maximal oxygen uptake (aerobic endurance) (VO_2 max in ml/kg/min)
2. This will be determined using the Multistage fitness test. The test will be carried out in the school/college sports hall
3. The participant will carry out standard warming-up and cool down procedures for the test
4. The participant will be required to run between two cones placed 20 metres apart to the 'bleeps' dictated by the audiotape
5. The test is progressive and maximal i.e. the participant is required to continue running until maximal exhaustion or until they are no longer able to keep up with the bleeps
6. All participants will receive method details in full
7. The tester/tutor/assessor is available to answer any relevant queries which may arise concerning the test
8. The participant is free to withdraw consent and discontinue participation in the test at any time
9. Only the tester/tutor/assessor and participant will have access to data recorded from the test which will be stored securely. Participant confidentiality is assured.

I fully understand the scope of my involvement in this fitness test and have freely consented to my participation.

I _____(insert participant name),_____ , understand that my parents/guardian have given permission for me to take part in this fitness test, which will be supervised by _____(insert tutor/assessor name)_____ . I am participating in this fitness test because I want to, and I have been informed that I can discontinue participation without any issues arising.

Participant signature: _____ Date: _____

Tester/tutor/assessor signature: _____ Date: _____

Figure 1.4 Example of an informed consent form

CONTINUED ▶▶

Make sure to record all fitness test results as you get them, so you don't forget.

Accurate measurement and recording of test results

- Allow sufficient time to practise each fitness test method before you begin collecting data. This will increase the likelihood of your results being accurate and reliable.
- Use an appropriate data collection sheet to record your results.
- Record each result as you get it, so you don't forget.
- For reliable results, all fitness tests should be repeated. In a **submaximal fitness test** it may be repeated on the same day (i.e. half-day test–retest). For a **maximal fitness test**, a longer recovery period is required between trials, so a separate day test–retest would be appropriate.
- Use the correct units of measurement. Some fitness tests will require the use of tables or **nomograms** (special charts) to process data and obtain the correct units of measurement for interpretation of test results.
- You will need to use published **normative data tables** to interpret fitness test results.

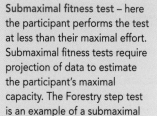

Key terms

Submaximal fitness test – here the participant performs the test at less than their maximal effort. Submaximal fitness tests require projection of data to estimate the participant's maximal capacity. The Forestry step test is an example of a submaximal fitness test.

Maximal fitness test – this requires the participant to make an 'all-out' maximal effort with results recorded at the all-out effort stage. The multistage fitness test is an example of a maximal test.

Reliability, validity and practicality of fitness test methods

By gaining direct experience through undertaking and administering different fitness tests, you will gain an understanding of factors which could affect test reliability and validity.

- **Reliability** is repeatability – the fitness test results obtained should be consistent. If you were to carry out the same fitness test method again, using exactly the same conditions and environment, you should expect the same results.
- **Validity** is the accuracy of the fitness test results, i.e. whether the results you have recorded are a true reflection of what you were actually trying to measure.
- **Practicality** is about how easy it is to carry out the test in terms of the costs involved, time available and equipment requirements. For example, can large groups be tested at once (good practicality) or do participants have to be tested individually because of a lack of resources (poor practicality)?

Advantages and disadvantages of fitness test methods

You'll need to be aware of the advantages and disadvantages of different fitness tests and how these might impact on test selection and administration. Therefore, try to gain first-hand experience by participating in the tests yourself.

Table 1.11 Advantages and disadvantages of fitness test methods

Fitness test	Advantages	Disadvantages
Sit and reach test	• Easy to complete – you can use a bench and ruler if a sit and reach box is unavailable • Quick to administer • Published tables of norms available • Modified tests exist which take into account the distance between the end of the fingers and the sit and reach box	• The test may not be valid for all populations. Research by Jackson and Baker (1986) found that the sit and reach test does not assess lower back flexibility in teenage girls • There are different, inconsistent test methods. For example, some methods include a warm-up, others do not
Multistage fitness test	• Minimal cost involved • Large numbers of participants can be tested at once • Gives good predictions of aerobic endurance provided that participants run until maximal exhaustion	• Reliability and validity of the test depends on the correct technique being used; participants need to run and turn in time with the bleeps. • Not suitable for certain populations, e.g. the elderly • Well-motivated participants needed – for results to be valid, participants must only drop out when they can no longer physically continue • Favours sports performers who make endurance demands of the leg muscle groups (e.g. cyclists and runners)
Illinois agility run test	• Minimal cost involved • Simple test method to administer; no specialist equipment required • Valid test for games players	• Different surfaces can affect times recorded • Risk of slipping depending on choice of surface • Inconsistencies with times recorded • Test cannot distinguish between left and right turning ability • Need to ensure standard layout is used for valid test interpretation against normative published data tables

Activity 1.7   Advantages and disadvantages of the step test

This activity is best completed after you have gained direct experience with the step test method. Work in small groups. In your group, discuss the step test you have participated in and produce a list of the advantages and disadvantages. Where appropriate, give reasons for your answers.

Link

See *Topic C1* for information on how to administer the forestry step test.

Assessment practice 1.5

1 Give two reasons why fitness testing is important. (2)

2 With reference to fitness testing, which term is defined as 'the consistency' of fitness test results? (1)

    A Practicality

    B Reliability

    C Validity

    D Responsibility

Fitness testing methods and results

Introduction

In this section you will learn 12 different fitness tests. You will need to know the standard test methods, equipment and resources required, the purpose of each test, and how to accurately measure and record test results. You will need to use **published normative data tables** to interpret fitness test results. We'll look at each test method in turn.

Sit and reach test (flexibility)

This test is used to measure trunk forward flexion, hamstring, hip and lower back range of motion. You will need a standard sit and reach box.

Method

1 Perform a short warm-up prior to this test. Remove your shoes.
2 Sit with your heels placed against the edge of the sit and reach box. Keep your legs flat on the floor, i.e. keep your knees down.
3 Place one hand on top of the other and reach forward slowly. Your fingertips should be in contact with the measuring portion of the sit and reach box. As you reach forward, drop your head between your arms and breathe out as you push forward. Don't use fast, jerky movements, as this may increase risk of injury.
4 The best of three trials should be recorded.

Interpreting results

Use Table 1.12 to interpret your results.

Table 1.12 Sit and reach test results

Rating	Males (cm)	Females (cm)
Excellent	25+	20+
Very good	17	17
Good	15	16
Average	14	15
Poor	13	14
Very poor	9	10

Figure 1.5 A participant performing the sit and reach test.

Grip dynamometer test (strength)

This test is used to measure static strength of the power grip-squeezing muscles, where the whole hand is used as a vice or clamp.

What you will need

Grip dynamometer – a grip dynamometer is a spring device. As force is applied, the spring is compressed and this moves the dynamometer needle, which indicates the result. Digital dynamometers are also available.

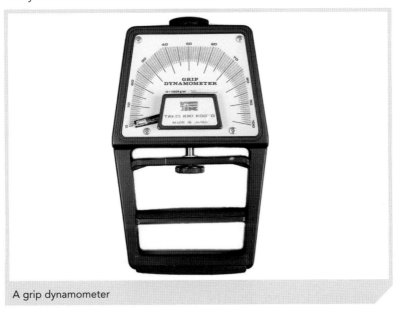

A grip dynamometer

Method

1 Adjust the handgrip size, so the dynamometer feels comfortable to hold.
2 Stand up, with your arms by the side of your body.
3 Hold the dynamometer parallel to the side of your body, with the dial/display facing away from you.
4 Squeeze as hard as possible for 5 seconds, without moving your arm.
5 Carry out three trials on each hand, with a 1 minute rest between trials.

Interpreting results

Use Table 1.13 to interpret your results.

Table 1.13 Grip strength results

Rating	Males aged 15–19 years (kgw)	Females aged 15–19 years (kgw)
Excellent	>52	>32
Good	47–51	28–31
Average	44–46	25–27
Below average	39–43	20–24
Poor	<39	<20

CONTINUED ▶▶

Multistage fitness test (aerobic endurance)

This test is used to predict maximum oxygen uptake (aerobic fitness) levels. The test should be conducted indoors, usually in a sports hall using two lines (or cones) placed 20m apart.

What you will need

- Access to an indoor sports hall
- Cones
- Test audiotape (pre-recording)

Method

1 Perform a short warm-up. Then line up on the start line and on hearing the triple bleep run to the other line, 20m away. You must reach the other line before or on the single bleep that determines each shuttle run.

2 Make sure you turn to run to the other line on the next bleep.

3 You will find that the bleeps get closer and closer together, so you'll need to continually increase your pace.

4 A spotter is used to check that you have reached each line in time with the bleep. If not, you will receive two verbal warnings before being asked to pull out of the test.

5 Continue running until you are physically exhausted, i.e. you have reached maximum exhaustion, at which point your level and shuttle reached are recorded.

Processing and interpreting results

Use Table 1.16 to predict your maximum oxygen consumption (ml/kg/min) and Tables 1.14 and 1.15 to compare your results.

> **Did you know?**
>
> VO_2 max, your maximum oxygen uptake, is predicted or measured in millilitres of oxygen per kilogram of body mass per minute (ml/kg/min).

Table 1.14 Aerobic endurance results

Rating	Males aged 15–19 years (ml/kg/min)	Females aged 15–19 years (ml/kg/min)
Excellent	>60	>54
Good	48–59	43–53
Average	39–47	35–42
Below average	30–38	28–34
Poor	<30	<28

Table 1.15 How do your aerobic endurance test results compare to those of elite performers?

Rating	Males aged 18–22 years (ml/kg/min)	Females aged 18–22 years (ml/kg/min)
World-class	>80	>70
Elite	70	63
Trained	57	53
Active	50	43
Untrained	45	39

Table 1.16 Predicted maximum oxygen uptake values (ml/kg/min)

Level	Shuttle	VO$_2$max	Level	Shuttle	VO$_2$max	Level	Shuttle	VO$_2$max	Level	Shuttle	VO$_2$max
4	2	26.8	10	2	47.4	15	2	64.6	19	6	79.2
4	4	27.6	10	4	48.0	15	4	65.1	19	8	79.7
4	6	28.3	10	6	48.7	15	6	65.6	19	10	80.2
4	9	29.5	10	8	49.3	15	8	66.2	19	12	80.6
5	2	30.2	10	11	50.2	15	10	66.7	19	15	81.3
5	4	31.0	11	2	50.8	15	13	67.5	20	2	81.8
5	6	31.8	11	4	51.4	16	2	68.0	20	4	82.2
5	9	32.9	11	6	51.9	16	4	68.5	20	6	82.6
6	2	33.6	11	8	52.5	16	6	69.0	20	8	83.0
6	4	34.3	11	10	53.1	16	8	69.5	20	10	83.5
6	6	35.0	11	12	53.7	16	10	69.9	20	12	83.9
6	8	35.7	12	2	54.3	16	12	70.5	20	14	84.3
6	10	36.4	12	4	54.8	16	14	70.9	20	16	84.8
7	2	37.1	12	6	55.4	17	2	71.4	21	2	85.2
7	4	37.8	12	8	56.0	17	4	71.9	21	4	85.6
7	6	38.5	12	10	56.5	17	6	72.4	21	6	86.1
7	8	39.2	12	12	57.1	17	8	72.9	21	8	86.5
7	10	39.9	13	2	57.6	17	10	73.4	21	10	86.9
8	2	40.5	13	4	58.2	17	12	73.9	21	12	87.4
8	4	41.1	13	6	58.7	17	14	74.4	21	14	87.8
8	6	41.8	13	8	59.3	18	2	74.8	21	16	88.2
8	8	42.4	13	10	59.8	18	4	75.3	–	–	–
8	11	43.3	13	13	60.6	18	6	75.8	–	–	–
9	2	43.9	14	2	61.1	18	8	76.2	–	–	–
9	4	44.5	14	4	61.7	18	10	76.7	–	–	–
9	6	45.2	14	6	62.2	18	12	77.2	–	–	–
9	8	45.8	14	8	62.7	18	15	77.9	–	–	–
9	11	46.8	14	10	63.2	19	2	78.3	–	–	–
			14	13	64.0	19	4	78.8	–	–	–

CONTINUED ▶▶

Figure 1.6 A participant performing the forestry step test.

33 cm

Forestry step test (aerobic endurance)

This test is used to predict maximum oxygen uptake (aerobic fitness) levels. The test was developed in 1977 by Brian Sharkey, and is a modified version of the Harvard step test. It is widely used in fitness selection procedures (e.g. for the police force).

A different bench height is used for males and females. For males, the height of the bench should be 40cm, for females, 33cm. The stepping rate of 22.5 steps per minute is the same for both males and females, which means the metronome should be set at a cadence of 90bpm.

What you will need

- Bench
- Metronome
- Stopwatch

Method

1 Stand directly facing the bench and start stepping in time with the beat of the metronome. As soon as you start stepping, the helper should start the stopwatch.

2 Keep to the beat of the metronome, putting one foot onto the bench, then your other foot, then lowering the first foot to the floor, then your other foot – i.e. up, up, down, down.

3 Straighten your legs when you fully step up onto the bench.

4 Keep stepping for 5 minutes, at which point your helper will stop the metronome and you will need to sit down immediately and locate your radial pulse.

5 After 5 minutes and 15 seconds (15 seconds after you have sat down) you will need to count your pulse for 15 seconds (stopping at 5 minutes and 30 seconds).

6 Record your 15-second pulse rate and perform a short cool down.

Processing and interpreting results

Use Tables 1.17a–d to obtain your non-adjusted aerobic fitness level.

- See Table 1.17a or 1.17b (depending on your gender): locate your 15-second pulse in the 'Pulse count' column and find the closest value to your body weight (kg). Where these two values intersect is your non-adjusted aerobic fitness level (ml/kg/min).

- See Table 1.17c: adjust your fitness level to take into account your age, which will provide a more accurate prediction of your aerobic endurance. Locate your closest age in years (left-hand column) and locate your non-adjusted aerobic fitness value (fitness score) along the top. Where these two values intersect is your age-adjusted fitness level (ml/kg/min).

- See Table 1.17d: interpret your aerobic fitness level.

Did you know?

Having a high VO_2 max means that your body has a fantastic ability to use oxygen, and is very efficient in extracting oxygen from the air and getting it quickly into the bloodstream and to your working muscles. A high VO_2 max means your muscles have a high capacity to work aerobically over extended periods of time, which is an advantage for endurance-based sports and activities.

Table 1.17a Forestry non-adjusted aerobic fitness values (ml/kg/min) for males

Pulse count	Maximal oxygen consumption (VO$_2$ max)												
45	33	33	33	33	33	32	32	32	32	32	32	32	32
44	34	34	34	34	33	33	33	33	33	33	33	33	33
43	35	35	35	34	34	34	34	34	34	34	34	34	34
42	36	35	35	35	35	35	35	35	35	35	35	34	34
41	36	36	36	36	36	36	36	36	36	36	36	35	35
40	37	37	37	37	37	37	37	37	35	35	35	35	35
39	38	38	38	38	38	38	38	38	38	38	38	37	37
38	39	39	39	39	39	39	39	39	39	39	39	38	38
37	41	40	40	40	40	40	40	40	40	40	40	39	39
36	42	42	41	41	41	41	41	41	41	41	41	40	40
35	43	43	42	42	42	42	42	42	42	42	42	42	41
34	44	44	43	43	43	43	43	43	43	43	43	43	43
33	46	45	45	45	45	45	44	44	44	44	44	44	44
32	47	47	46	46	46	46	46	46	46	46	46	46	46
31	48	48	48	47	47	47	47	47	47	47	47	47	47
30	50	49	49	49	48	48	48	48	48	48	48	48	48
29	52	51	51	51	50	50	50	50	50	50	50	50	50
28	53	53	53	53	52	52	52	52	51	51	51	51	51
27	55	55	55	54	54	54	54	54	54	53	53	53	52
26	57	57	56	56	56	56	56	56	56	55	55	54	54
25	59	59	58	58	58	58	58	58	58	56	56	55	55
24	60	60	60	60	60	60	60	59	59	58	58	57	
23	62	62	61	61	61	61	61	60	60	60	59		
22	64	64	63	63	63	63	62	62	61	61			
21	66	66	65	65	65	64	64	64	62				
20	68	68	67	67	67	67	66	66	65				
Weight (kg)	54.5	59.1	63.6	68.2	72.7	77.3	81.8	86.4	91	95.4	100	104.5	109

CONTINUED ▶▶

Table 1.17b Forestry non-adjusted aerobic fitness values (ml/kg/min) for females

Pulse count	Maximal oxygen consumption (VO$_2$ max)											
45										29	29	29
44								30	30	30	30	30
43							31	31	31	31	31	31
42			32	32	32	32	32	32	32	32	32	32
41			33	33	33	33	33	33	33	33	33	33
40			34	34	34	34	34	34	34	34	34	34
39			35	35	35	35	35	35	35	35	35	35
38			36	36	36	36	36	36	36	36	36	36
37			37	37	37	37	37	37	37	37	37	37
36		37	38	38	38	38	38	38	38	38	38	38
35	38	38	39	39	39	39	39	39	39	39	39	39
34	39	39	40	40	40	40	40	40	40	40	40	40
33	40	40	41	41	41	41	41	41	41	41	41	41
32	41	41	42	42	42	42	42	42	42	42	42	42
31	42	42	43	43	43	43	43	43	43	43	43	43
30	43	43	44	44	44	44	44	44	44	44	44	44
29	44	44	45	45	45	45	45	45	45	45	45	45
28	45	45	46	46	46	47	47	47	47	47	47	47
27	46	46	47	48	48	49	49	49	49	49		
26	47	48	49	50	50	51	51	51	51			
25	49	50	51	52	52	53	53					
24	51	52	53	54	54	55						
23	53	54	55	56	56	57						
Weight (kg)	**36.4**	**40.9**	**45.4**	**50.0**	**54.5**	**59.1**	**63.6**	**68.2**	**72.7**	**77.3**	**81.8**	**86.4**

Table 1.17c Age-adjusted fitness levels

Fitness score		30	31	32	33	34	35	36	37	38	39	40	41	42	43	44	45	46	47	48	49	50
Nearest age	15	32	33	34	35	36	37	38	39	40	41	42	43	44	45	46	47	48	49	50	51	53
	20	31	32	33	34	35	36	37	38	39	40	41	42	43	44	45	46	47	48	49	50	51

(cont.)

Fitness score		51	52	53	54	55	56	57	58	59	60	61	62	63	64	65	66	67	68	69	70	71	72
Nearest age	15	54	55	56	57	58	59	60	61	62	63	64	65	66	67	68	69	70	71	72	74	75	76
	20	52	53	54	55	56	57	58	59	60	61	62	63	64	65	66	67	68	69	70	71	72	73

Table 1.17d Aerobic fitness levels

Age and gender	Fitness category						
	Superior	Excellent	Very good	Good	Fair	Poor	Very poor
	Maximum oxygen consumption (ml/kg/min)						
15-year-old male	57+	56–52	51–47	46–42	41–37	36–32	<32
15-year-old female	54+	53–49	48–44	43–39	38–34	33–29	<29
20-year-old male	56+	55–51	50–46	45–41	40–36	35–31	<31
20-year-old female	53+	52–48	47–43	42–38	37–33	32–28	<28

35-metre sprint test (speed)

This test is used to measure and interpret an individual's speed.

What you will need

- Access to an indoor sports hall
- Stopwatch

Method

1. The test is best performed on an indoor athletics track, or an outdoor track on a day when weather conditions will not affect test results.
2. Perform a warm-up.
3. Three people should time the sprint, using stopwatches capable of measuring to one-tenth of a second.
4. Line up on the start line, in a standing start position.
5. As soon as you start sprinting, the timers will start their stopwatches.
6. Sprint as fast as you can, crossing the 35m line.
7. When you cross the 35m line, the timers should stop their stopwatches.
8. Record your time for the sprint to the closest tenth of a second. Take an average result from the three timers.
9. No more than two to three trials can be performed in one day. Allow at least 3 minutes of recovery time between trials. A third trial should only be performed if the difference in times between your first and second trial is greater than 0.20 seconds.
10. Record the best time from your trials as your 35m sprint result.
11. To prevent muscle soreness, perform a cool down followed by static stretching.

Interpreting results

Use Table 1.18 to interpret your results.

Figure 1.7 A participant performing the 35-metre sprint test.

Table 1.18 35m sprint results

Rating	Males (s)	Females (s)
Excellent	<4.80	<5.30
Good	4.80–5.09	5.30–5.59
Average	5.10–5.29	5.60–5.89
Fair	5.30–5.60	5.90–6.20
Poor	>5.60	>6.20

CONTINUED ▸▸

Illinois agility run test (speed and agility)

This test is used to measure an individual's speed and agility, i.e. the ability to move precisely and quickly and change direction without losing balance or time.

The test is performed indoors on a flat non-slip surface, with cones to mark the layout. The length of the course is 10 metres and the width (between start and finishing points) is 5 metres. Four cones mark the start, finish and the two turning points. Four more cones are placed down the centre of the course, 3.3m apart.

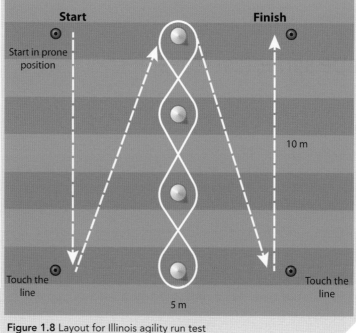

Figure 1.8 Layout for Illinois agility run test

What you will need

- Access to an indoor sports hall
- Cones
- Stopwatch

Method

1 Perform a short warm-up.

2 The starting position for this test is to lie face down, with your elbows flexed and hands placed by the sides of your chest, palms flat on the floor. Your head should be in line with the starting line.

3 On the starter's 'go' command, the stopwatch is started and you must stand up and sprint around the course in the direction indicated, without knocking any of the cones over.

4 Sprint through the finish line; the timing will stop when your chest passes over the finish line.

5 If part of your foot does not touch or go beyond the turning lines or you knock over any cones while navigating the course, you will need to discontinue the test and start again.

6 Complete two trials and interpret your best result (in seconds) using Table 1.19.

Interpreting results

Use Table 1.19 to interpret your results.

Table 1.19 Illinois agility run test results

Results (seconds)					
Gender	Excellent	Above average	Average	Below average	Poor
Male	<15.2	15.2–16.1	16.2–18.1	18.2–19.3	>19.3
Female	<17.0	17.0–17.9	18.0–21.7	21.8–23.0	>23.0

Did you know?

The world record for the Illinois agility run test is held by Australian-rules footballer, Daniel Kerr, who set a time of 11.29 seconds in Melbourne in 2010.

Key term

Dominant side – an individual may have a dominant/preferred side of the body: i.e. a right-handed individual stands with the right side against the vertical jump board and reaches up with the right hand.

Vertical jump test (anaerobic power)

This test is used to predict the anaerobic power of the quadriceps muscle group.

What you will need

- A vertical jump board
- Gymnasts' chalk (if board is not digital)

Method

1. Perform a short warm-up prior to the test.
2. Stand with your **dominant side** against the board, feet together, and reach up as high as you can to record your standing reach height.
3. Only one dip of the arms and knees is permitted. Make the jump and touch the vertical jump board at the peak of your jump.
4. Perform three trials. No rest is required; the time taken to observe and record the height of the jump is all that is needed for recovery between consecutive trials.

Processing and interpreting results

A nomogram is a special chart/diagram that can be used to obtain fitness test results. Use the Lewis nomogram (Figure 1.9) to predict the power of your quadriceps in kgm/s.

- Plot the difference (D) between your standing reach height and your best jump height (cm) on the nomogram line (D).
- Plot your weight in kilograms on the nomogram line (Wt).
- Using a sharpened pencil and ruler, join up the points; the line will cross over the power line (P) to give a prediction of the anaerobic power of your quadriceps muscles (in kgm/s).

Table 1.20 Vertical jump test results

Rating	Males (kgm/s)	Females (kgm/s)
Above average	>105	>90
Average	95	80
Below average	<85	<70

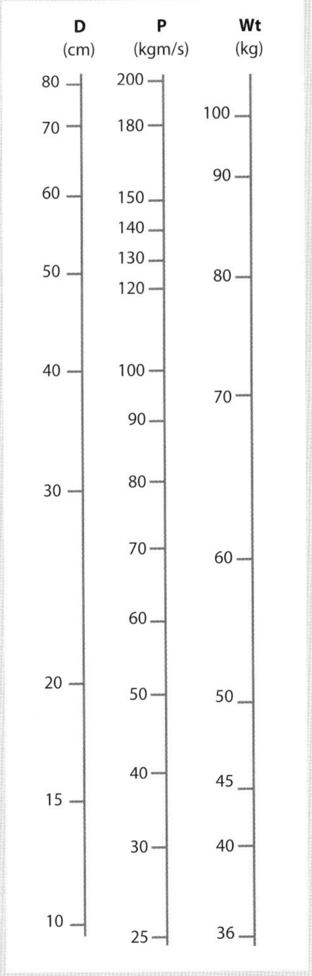

Figure 1.9 Lewis nomogram

CONTINUED ▸▸

One-minute press-up test (muscular endurance)

This test is used to assess the endurance of the muscles of your upper body.

What you will need

- Access to an indoor sports hall
- Exercise mat
- Stopwatch

Method

1 Position yourself on a mat, with your hands shoulder-width apart and arms fully extended.

2 Next, lower your body until your elbows are at 90 degrees.

3 Return to the starting position, with your arms fully extended.

4 Make sure your push-up action is continuous, with no rests in between.

5 Record the total number of press-ups for 1 minute.

6 Due to reduced upper body strength, females may choose to use a modified press-up technique, where in the starting position a bent knee position is assumed.

Interpreting results

Use Table 1.21 or 1.22 to interpret your results.

Table 1.21 One-minute press-up test results (full-body press-ups)

Rating	Males (no. of reps)	Females (no. of reps)
Excellent	>45	>34
Good	35–44	17–33
Average	20–34	6–16
Poor	<19	<5

Table 1.22 One-minute press-up test results (modified press-ups)

Rating	No. of reps
Excellent	>39
Good	34–38
Average	17–33
Fair	6–16
Poor	<6

Activity 1.8   Interpreting fitness test results

Participate in each different fitness test featured in this unit. Then process and interpret your test results:

- Compare your results to normative published data tables. What do your results show?
- Compare your results to those of your peers. How do your results compare?
- Analyse and evaluate your test results. Prepare charts or graphs to show the main results and trends. What conclusions can you draw?
- Using one test result for each component of fitness, suggest appropriate recommendations you could make to your own fitness levels.
- Suggest three different training methods you could use to help achieve your fitness goals, and give reasons for your choice.

One-minute sit-up test (muscular endurance)

This test is used to assess the endurance and development of your abdominal muscles.

What you will need

- Access to an indoor sports hall
- Exercise mat
- Stopwatch

Method

1 Lie on a mat with your knees bent and feet flat on the floor, with your arms folded across your body.
2 Raise yourself up to a 90-degree position, then return to the floor.
3 Your feet may be held by a partner if you wish.
4 Record the total number of sit-ups for one minute.

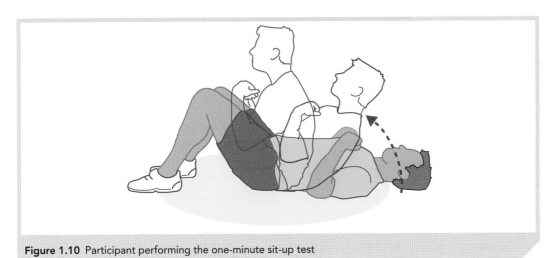

Figure 1.10 Participant performing the one-minute sit-up test

Interpreting results

Use Table 1.23 to interpret your results.

Table 1.23 One-minute sit-up test results

Rating	Males (no. of reps)	Females (no. of reps)
Excellent	49–59	42–54
Good	43–48	36–41
Above average	39–42	32–35
Average	35–38	28–31
Below average	31–34	24–27
Poor	25–30	18–23
Very poor	11–24	3–17

CONTINUED ▶▶

◤ Body Mass Index (BMI) (body composition)

This test is used to give a simple measure of body fat and is used to check whether a person is overweight.

The test can determine if a person is at increased risk of developing coronary heart disease (CHD) and other cardiovascular diseases.

BMI is widely used for the general population to determine the degree of overweight.

However, the test isn't always valid for elite sports performers and athletes, because it doesn't take into account frame size or muscle mass.

If a body builder had their BMI measured, they would be classed as obese; their large frame size and high muscle mass would give an invalid test result.

What you will need

- **Height stadiometer**
- Weighing scales

Method

1 Measure your body weight in kilograms (kg).

2 Measure your height in metres (m).

3 Carry out this calculation to determine your BMI (kg/m²):

$$BMI = \frac{\text{Body weight (kg)}}{\text{Height (m)} \times \text{Height (m)}}$$

4 Interpreting results:

Use Table 1.24 to interpret your results.

Table 1.24 BMI: interpreting results

Rating	BMI (kg/m²)
Desirable	20–25
Overweight	26–30
Obese and increased risk of CHD	31+

Bioelectrical Impedance Analysis (BIA) (body composition)

This test is used to predict % body fat.

A BIA machine is required to conduct the test (such as Bodystat 1500). The method is based on the fact that fat-free mass in the body (muscle, bone, connective tissues) conducts electricity, whereas fat mass does not. Therefore, the higher the resistance to a weak electrical current (bioelectrical impedance) the higher the % body fat of the individual.

Hydration levels can affect validity of test results. To ensure the test is valid, the subject should not:

- exercise for 12 hours prior to the test
- drink or eat within 4 hours of the test
- drink caffeine prior to the test.

What you will need

- A **bioelectrical impedance analysis (BIA)** machine

Method

1 The participant should urinate 30 minutes prior to conducting the test.
2 The participant should lie down and remove their right sock and shoe.
3 Place the BIA electrodes on the right wrist, right hand, right ankle and right foot.
4 Attach the cable leads (crocodile clips) to the exposed tabs on the electrodes.
5 Enter data into the BIA machine (e.g. participant's age, gender, height, weight, activity level).
6 The participant should lie still as the weak electrical current is passed through their body. The test only takes a few seconds.
7 The % body fat test result will be shown on the LCD display of the BIA machine.

Interpreting results

Use Table 1.25 to interpret the results.

Key term

Bioelectrical impedance analysis (BIA) – method used for measuring body composition.

Table 1.25 Interpreting % body fat test results

Rating	Males % body fat (16–29 years)	Females % body fat (16–29 years)
Very low fat	<7	<13
Slim	7–12	13–20
Ideal	13–17	21–25
Overweight	18–28	26–32
Obese	>28	>32

CONTINUED ▸▸

Anterior auxiliary line – the crease at which the top of your arm, when hanging down, meets the chest.

Umbilicus – belly button.

Acromion process – the outer end of the scapula, forming the highest point of the shoulder.

Olecranon process – bony projection at the elbow.

◣ Skinfold testing (body composition)

In this section you will be using the Jackson–Pollock nomogram method to predict % body fat. Following a standard method will help to ensure your results are valid.

Work in pairs or small groups for skinfold testing. Measurements should be taken on dry skin on the right side of the body. Exceptions to this would be if the participant has a tattoo or deformity on the site location, in which case the left side of the body would need to be used.

What you will need

- Skinfold calipers (such as Harpenden or SlimGuide)
- Tape measure
- A pen to mark the sites

Method

1 The participant should keep their muscles relaxed during the test.
2 Mark each skinfold site with a pen and use a tape measure to find the midpoints.
3 Grasp the skinfold firmly between your thumb and index finger, about 1cm away from the site marked, and gently pull away from the body.
4 Place the skinfold calipers perpendicular to the fold, on the site marked, with the dial facing upwards.
5 Maintaining your grasp, place the calipers midway between the base and tip of the skinfold and allow the calipers to be fully released so that full tension is placed on the skinfold.
6 Read the dial of the skinfold calipers to the nearest 0.5mm, 2 seconds after you have released the calipers. Make sure you continue to grasp the skinfold throughout testing.
7 Take a minimum of two measurements at each site. If repeated tests vary by more than 1mm, repeat the measurement. If consecutive measurements become smaller, this means that the fat is being compressed, and will result in inaccurate results. If this happens, go to another site and return to the first site later.
8 Make sure you record each measurement as it is taken.
9 The final value is the average of the two readings (mm).

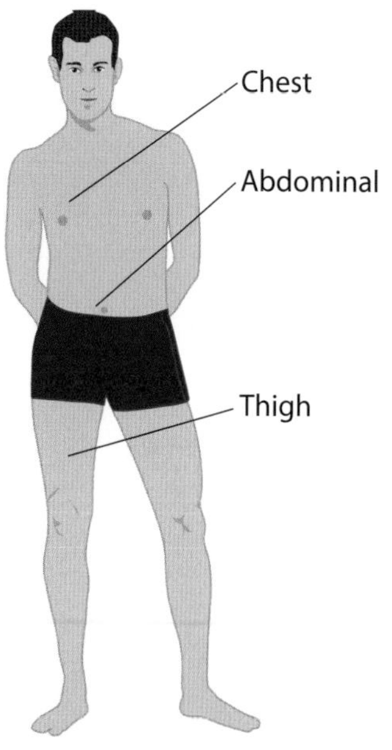

Males: skinfold site selection

Male participants will need to gain skinfold results (mm) for the following three sites:

- **Chest** – a diagonal fold, half the distance between the **anterior auxiliary line** and the nipple.
- **Abdomen** – a vertical fold, 2cm to the right side of the **umbilicus**.
- **Thigh** – a vertical fold on the front of the thigh, halfway between the hip joint and the middle of the kneecap. The leg needs to be straight and relaxed.

Figure 1.11 Site locations for males

Females: skinfold site selection

Female participants will need to gain skinfold results (mm) for the following three sites:

- **Triceps** – a vertical fold on the back midline of the upper arm, over the triceps muscle, halfway between the **acromion process** and **olecranon process**. The arm should be held freely by the side of the body.
- **Suprailiac** – a diagonal fold just above the hip bone and 2–3cm forward.
- **Thigh** – a vertical fold, on the front of the thigh, halfway between the hip joint and the middle of the kneecap. The leg needs to be straight and relaxed.

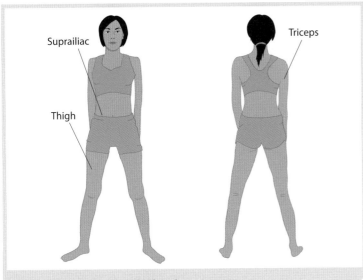

Figure 1.12 Site locations for females

Processing and interpreting results

1 Add up the sum of your three skinfolds (mm).
2 Obtain the % body fat result by plotting your age in years and the sum of the three skinfolds (mm) on the nomogram.
3 Use a ruler and sharpened pencil to join up the two points, which will cross over the % body fat (wavy) vertical lines.
4 Read your % body fat result to the nearest 0.5% according to your gender.
5 Use Table 1.25 to interpret the % body fat result obtained.

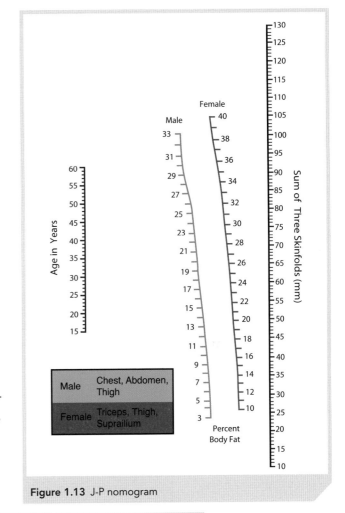

Figure 1.13 J-P nomogram

Assessment practice 1.6

1 Rob is 18 years old. He reached Level 12 Shuttle 12 in the multistage fitness test. Use Table 1.16 on page 29 to predict Rob's VO_2 max. Then use Tables 1.14 and 1.15 on page 28 to interpret Rob's aerobic endurance test result. (2)

2 Ana has just completed the Forestry step test. Her 15 second pulse count is 33. Ana is 15 years old and weighs 59kg. Use Tables 1.17b–d on pages 32–33 to work out and interpret Ana's VO_2 max (ml/kg/min). (2)

3 Pablo weighs 84kg and is 1.84m tall. Calculate and interpret Pablo's BMI (kg/m²) using Table 1.24 on page 38. (2)

This section has been written to help you to do your best when you take the onscreen test. Read through it carefully and ask your teacher if there is anything you are still not sure about.

How you will be assessed

You will take an onscreen assessment, using a computer. This will be set over 15-20 screens and have a maximum of 50 marks. The number of marks for each question will be shown in brackets e.g. [1]. The test will last for one hour.

There will be different types of question in the test:

A Questions where the answers are available and you have to choose the correct answer(s). *Tip: always read carefully to see how many answers are needed and how you can show the right answer.*

Examples:

> Which **two** of the following are components of skill-related fitness? Select the two correct answers. [2]
>
> | **A** | Agility |
> | **B** | Flexibility |
> | **C** | Body composition |
> | **D** | Aerobic endurance |
> | **E** | Balance |
>
> **Answers:** A and E

> Sharon is 27 years old and has just started training at her local gym. Calculate Sharon's maximum heart rate (HRmax). Select the correct answer. [1]
>
> | **A** | 193 bpm |
> | **B** | 173 bpm |
> | **C** | 183 bpm |
> | **D** | 203 bpm |
>
> **Answer:** A

B Questions where you are asked to provide a short answer worth 1–2 marks. *Tip: Look carefully at how the question is set out to see how many points need to be included in your answer.*

Examples:

> Louise reports an RPE of 17. What will her approximate heart rate be? [1]
>
> **Answer:** 170 bpm

> Name **two** types of static stretching. [2]
>
> **Answers:** Active stretching and passive stretching

Disclaimer: these practice questions and sample answers are not actual exam questions and have been provided as a practice aid only. They should be used as practice material only and should not be assumed to reflect the format or coverage of the real external test.

C **Questions where you are asked to provide a longer answer – these can be worth up to 8 marks.** *Tip: Plan your answer, making sure that you include the correct level of detail indicated by the amount of marks allocated. Check through your answer – you may need to use the scroll bar to move back to the top.*

Example:

> Agility is an important component of fitness for a footballer. Explain how two other components of fitness can contribute to success in football. [4]
>
> **Answer:** Aerobic endurance is needed so the player can 'keep-up' with the pace of the game, so they can run efficiently for the full duration of a match, creating opportunities on the pitch for his/her team mates.
>
> Strength is needed so the footballer can perform effective tackles/blocks, allowing them to maintain position without being nudged off the ball.

Many questions will have images. Sometimes you will be asked to click to play a video or animation. You can do this as many times as you want within the time allowed for the test.

Sometimes you may be asked to do a calculation – you can use the calculator provided in the onscreen test system if you need to.

Hints and tips

- **Use the pre-test time** – make sure you have read the instructions, tested the function buttons, adjusted your seat and that you can see the screen clearly.
- **Watch the time** – the screen shows you how much time you have left. You should aim to take about 1 minute per mark. Some early questions will take less time than this and some later questions will take you longer.
- **Plan your longer answers** - read the question carefully and think about the key points you will make. You can use paper or the onscreen note function to jot down ideas.
- **Check answers at the end** – you should keep moving through the questions and not let yourself get stuck on one. If you are really unsure of answer or cannot give an answer, then you can use the onscreen system to flag that you need to come back to that question at the end.
- **Read back your longer answers** – make sure you view the whole answer if you are checking back. There is no spell check facility.
- **Do you find it harder to read onscreen?** – talk to your teacher/tutor in advance of your test about how the system can be adjusted to meet your needs. During the test, tools within the test player will allow you to apply colour filters, change the font size and colour, as well as allowing you to zoom in on the images and text.

How to improve your answer

Read the two student answers below, together with the feedback. Try to use what you learn here when you answer questions in your test.

Question

Patrick and David are 20 years old. They are both keen amateur basketball players and would like to begin training with a new coach.

a) The new coach has identified two fitness tests which could be used to determine Patrick's and David's baseline levels of fitness. Explain why the coach would have chosen each of these tests:

- Vertical jump test [2]
- Illinois agility test [2]

b) Describe how one method of training could be used to develop and improve their performance in basketball. [2]

Student 1's answer

a) The vertical jump test can be used to determine a player's anaerobic power. The Illinois agility run test could be used because this test can be used to determine a player's speed and agility.

b) They could use plyometric training.

Feedback:

a) *For each test, an attempt has been made at justifying its selection in relation to fitness components. However, the learner has not strengthened their justifications by linking these fitness tests and components of fitness to their importance for a basketball player, so only 1 mark is awarded for each explanation rather than 2 marks. For part a) the student would achieve 2 marks.*

b) *The student has correctly identified that plyometric training could be used by the basketball players, but has not provided any further details on how it could actually improve their performance. For part b) the student would achieve 1 mark.*

Student 2's answer

a) The vertical jump test could be used because it can determine a player's anaerobic power, which is important for their jumping ability when dunking or intercepting a pass. The Illinois agility run test could be used, because this test can determine a player's speed and agility, which are important so they can run a fast-break, stop, start or change directions quickly to avoid an opponent, moving quickly and efficiently around the basketball court.

b) Plyometric training would be a great way for Patrick and David to develop their basketball skills and overall performance on the court. They could use bounding, hopping and jumping drills to develop explosive power and strength, helping improve their jumping ability to score baskets and their sprinting ability to drive to the basket before opponents catch up.

Feedback:

a) *The learner has justified the choice of the two fitness tests by linking these tests to the components of fitness (1 mark) and also their importance for success in basketball (1 mark). For part a) the student will achieve 2 marks for each test, totalling 4 marks.*

b) *The student has correctly stated that plyometric training could be used by the basketball players (1 mark). They have described what this training method could involve (1 mark), with further details on how this training method could actually improve performance (1 mark). For part b) the student will achieve 3 marks.*

Assess yourself

Question 1

Body fat can be predicted using the Jackson-Pollock (J-P) Nomogram method. This method uses three skinfold sites for females.

Select the **three** correct skinfold sites for **females** from the list below [3].

Suprailiac

Chest

Thigh

Triceps

Subcapular

Question 3

Describe how a greater range of movement is achieved using the PNF technique. [2]

Question 2

Fitness testing can play an important part in an athlete's training cycle.

a) Name the piece of fitness testing equipment shown in the photograph [1].

b) State the component of fitness this piece of equipment is used to test [1].

c) State the units of measurement [1].

For further practice, see the Assessment Practice questions on pages 5, 7, 9, 19, 25 and 41.

Answers can be found on page 339.

Introduction

Participation in sport is growing, as people become more aware of the benefits of physical activity. This unit focuses on developing and improving your own practical sports performance. You will be given the opportunity to participate in selected sports and carry out skills, techniques and tactics in different situations within those sports.

Through your participation you will develop knowledge of the rules, regulations and scoring systems associated with these sports and how to apply them, and you will be introduced to the roles and responsibilities of sporting officials.

High-achieving sports performers reflect on their own performance to identify what they are good at (their strengths) and also assess the areas of their performance they need to develop (areas for improvement). As you progress through this unit you will develop an understanding of the processes for reviewing your own performance and finding ways to improve your skills.

Assessment: You will be assessed by a series of assignments set by your teacher/tutor.

Learning aims

In this unit you will:

A understand the rules, regulations and scoring systems for selected sports

B practically demonstrate skills, techniques and tactics in selected sports

C be able to review sports performance.

I had rarely played hockey before and never thought I would be good enough to play for a team. It was only when I was given the opportunity to play practice matches and develop a further understanding of the sport as part of my BTEC Sport course at school that I was asked to join a local club.

Ben, *16-year-old club hockey player*

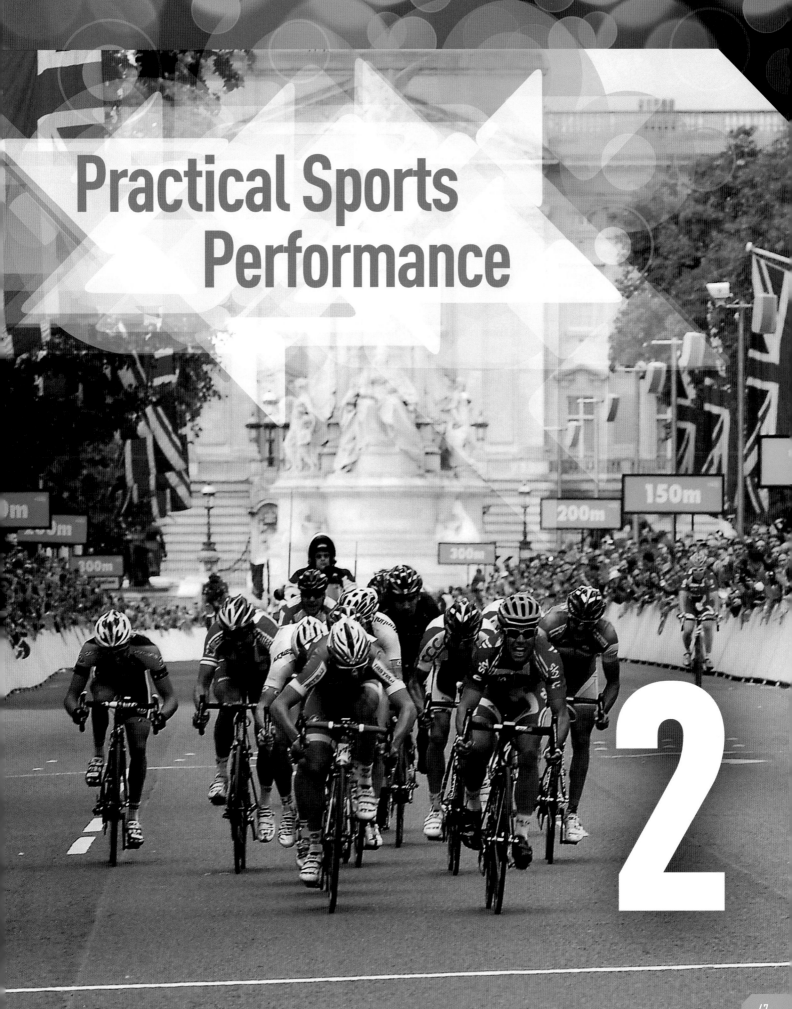

Practical Sports
Performance

2

47

BTEC
Assessment zone

This table shows you what you must do in order to achieve a **Pass**, **Merit** or **Distinction** grade, and where you can find activities to help you.

Assessment criteria			
Level 1	**Level 2 Pass**	**Level 2 Merit**	**Level 2 Distinction**
Learning aim A: understand the rules, regulations and scoring systems for selected sports			
1A.1 English Describe the rules, regulations and scoring systems of a selected sport	**2A.P1** English Describe the rules, regulations and scoring systems of two selected sports **See Assessment activity 2.1, page 57**	**2A.M1** English For each of two selected sports, explain the roles and responsibilities of officials and the application of rules, regulations and scoring systems **See Assessment activity 2.1, page 57**	**2A.D1** English Compare and contrast the roles and responsibilities of officials from two selected sports, suggesting valid recommendations for improvement to the application of rules, regulations and scoring systems for each sport **See Assessment activity 2.1, page 57**
1A.2 Apply the rules of a selected sport in two given specific situations	**2A.P2** Apply the rules of a selected sport in four specific situations **See Assessment activity 2.1, page 57**		
1A.3 Describe the roles of officials from a selected sport	**2A.P3** Describe the roles and responsibilities of officials from two selected sports **See Assessment activity 2.1, page 57**		
Learning aim B: practically demonstrate skills, techniques and tactics in selected sports			
1B.4 Describe the technical demands of two selected sports	**2B.P4** Describe the technical and tactical demands of two selected sports **See Assessment activity 2.2, page 69**		
1B.5 Use relevant skills and techniques effectively, in two selected sports, in isolated practices	**2B.P5** Use relevant skills, techniques and tactics effectively, in two selected sports, in conditioned practices **See Assessment activity 2.2, page 69**	**2B.M2** Use relevant skills, techniques and tactics effectively, in two selected sports, in competitive situations **See Assessment activity 2.2, page 69**	

Assessment criteria			
Level 1	**Level 2 Pass**	**Level 2 Merit**	**Level 2 Distinction**
Learning aim C: be able to review sports performance			
1C.6 English Produce, with guidance, an observation checklist that can be used effectively to review own performance in two selected sports	**2C.P6** English Independently produce an observation checklist that can be used effectively to review own performance in two selected sports **See Assessment activity 2.3, page 73**		
1C.7 Review own performance, in two selected sports, identifying strengths and areas for improvement	**2C.P7** Review own performance, in two selected sports, describing strengths and areas for improvement **See Assessment activity 2.3, page 73**	**2C.M3** Explain strengths and areas for improvement in two selected sports, recommending activities to improve own performance **See Assessment activity 2.3, page 73**	**2C.D2** Analyse strengths and areas for improvement in two selected sports, justifying recommended activities to improve own performance **See Assessment activity 2.3, page 73**

English	Opportunity to practise English skills

How you will be assessed

Your knowledge and understanding of this unit will be checked through a series of assignments set by your teacher/tutor. You will be expected to show that you understand the rules, regulations and scoring systems for selected sports, and how to apply these in given situations. You will also be required to demonstrate knowledge of the roles and responsibilities of officials. You will then be observed and assessed for your ability to use skills, techniques and tactics while playing sports, and will need to show that you know how to review your own performance to identify your strengths and weaknesses.

Your assessment could be in the form of:

- practical demonstrations
- verbal/written work to show understanding of rules, regulations and roles of officials
- observation checklists.

Rules (or laws) in sport

Key terms

Sport – an activity such as athletics, hockey, netball or swimming that involves physical exertion, skill, competition and rules.

National Governing Body (NGB) – an organisation responsible for the promotion and development of a particular sport at a national level.

International Governing Body (IGB) – an organisation responsible for the promotion and development of a particular sport at an international level. For example, FIFA.

Introduction

All **sports** have set rules or laws. It is these rules that determine the format of the game and provide structure and discipline.

Rules are determined by the International Governing Body for each sport. It is the role of **National Governing Bodies (NGBs)** in the UK to work closely with these **International Governing Bodies (IGBs)** to ensure that rules are observed by officials, clubs and performers during organised competitions.

In the past ten years a number of sports have announced some changes to the rules to make events more entertaining for the spectators. For example, in 2011 the International Association of Athletics Federations (IAAF) adapted the rules for false starts, changing the original rule from giving all athletes a warning if there was a false start in a race to having no warning procedure; in the event of a false start, the athlete who commits it is instantly disqualified. This rule change came under a high level of scrutiny in the World Athletics Championships in Daegu in 2011 when in the 100 metres final Usain Bolt was disqualified for committing a false start in the race. In most sports rules are updated regularly, and it is the responsibility of everybody involved in a sport to have a thorough knowledge of these changes.

Due to the high number of participants in certain sports, some NGBs require Regional Governing Bodies to support the coordination and organisation of sport at regional level. For example, in football each county in England has its own Football Association. In East Yorkshire the East Riding County FA (ERCFA) organise all leagues and competitions that are played within that region. It is the role of ERCFA to administer all football played within the county in line with the Football Association's guidance and support.

Table 2.1 Different sports have different National Governing Bodies (NGBs)

Sport	NGB	Website
Football	The Football Association	www.thefa.com
Rugby union	The Rugby Football Union	www.rfu.com
Rugby league	The Rugby Football League	www.therfl.co.uk
Athletics	UK Athletics	www.uka.org.uk
Orienteering	British Orienteering	www.britishorienteering.org.uk
Skiing	Snow Sport England	www.snowsportengland.org.uk

Every sport must have an NGB. If your preferred sport is not listed in the table above, research it and add details of its NGB to a table like Table 2.1.

```
                          FIFA:
                        Fédération
                      Internationale
                       de Football
                        Association
```

AFC:	CAF:	CONCACAF:	CONMEBOL:	OFC:	UEFA:
Asian Football Confederation (Asia)	Confédération Africaine de Football (Africa)	Confederation of North, Central America and Caribbean Association Football	Confederación Sudamericana de Fútbol (South America)	Oceania Football Confederation	Union of Europe Football Associations

Other European national associations

FA: The Football Association (England)

Figure 2.1 Chart showing the organisation of football across the world

Activity 2.1 — Finding out about Governing Bodies

1 Research the Regional Football Association closest to your school. Provide an address and telephone number for the Regional Office.
2 Identify the National Governing Bodies for three other sports and identify whether or not there are any regional governing bodies within your local area.

Unwritten rules

As well as sports having written rules there are also some underpinning values that are associated with all sports. These values, known as the unwritten rules, contribute towards fair play. The concept of fair play includes:

- respect towards other sports performers
- respect towards coaches and spectators
- respect towards officials
- playing within the rules of the sport
- equality for all sports performers.

In football, the handshake is a common way of showing respect for another player.

Applying fair play in sport, and promoting the concept of fair play at all levels, can help to reduce some of the negative elements of sport such as violence, verbal abuse, physical abuse and gamesmanship, whereby players cheat to gain an advantage; for example, by doping.

Just checking

1 Summarise five major rules that you are required to know and understand in order to play your chosen sport.
2 What is the role of a National Governing Body?
3 What is the NGB in the United Kingdom for athletics?

Regulations in sport

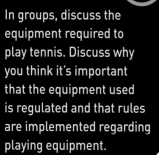

Getting started

In groups, discuss the equipment required to play tennis. Discuss why you think it's important that the equipment used is regulated and that rules are implemented regarding playing equipment.

Link

See *Topic A.1* for more information on governing bodies.

Key term

Regulations – rules in sport that are controlled by an authority (a National Governing Body).

Tennis is played at the highest level on a variety of surfaces (grass, clay and hard courts).

Introduction

Regulations are the rules or principles that are applied consistently in a sport. These differ across all sports, which is why each sport requires a regulator, or Governing Body.

Players and participants

Different sports have different numbers of players participating in competitive situations. Sports such as golf, tennis, gymnastics and athletics are usually considered individual sports (with some exceptions – e.g. doubles in tennis, relays in athletics). Other sports such as rugby union, hockey, basketball and American football, are team sports. These sports have restrictions on the numbers of players allowed in a competitive situation at any one time.

Playing surfaces

Some NGBs and IGBs dictate the surface types on which a sport can be played. For example, in the sport of rugby league the International Governing Body, until very recently, ruled that competitive games must be played on grass pitches. It was only in the 2012 season that Widnes Vikings were allowed to introduce the first artificial pitch into the European Super League. However, some sports can be played both inside and outside, and the requirements for the types of surfaces may differ. For example, after many years of research and more than two decades of preventing the use of artificial surfaces in football, in 2005 the Union of European Football Associations (UEFA) approved the use of a new artificial surface, known as the third generation pitch (3G), to be used within all their competitions.

Equipment

In one form or another all sports require equipment. It may be the specific protective equipment which the performers are required to wear to reduce or prevent injury. For example, in the sport of track cycling all participants must wear helmets when competing. Or it may be the equipment which is required to play the sport, such as the goalposts in a football game or a rugby game, the racket in tennis, the high jump bar, starter blocks and track in athletics, or the bicycle in mountain biking.

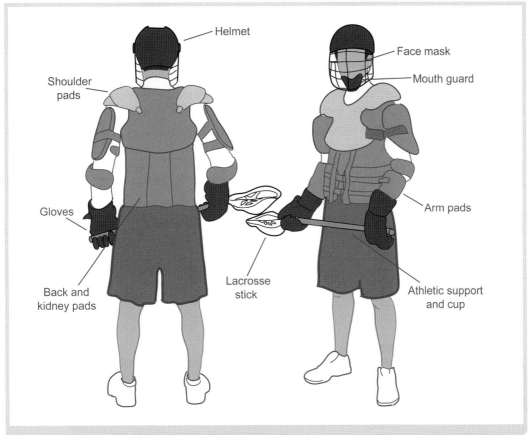

Figure 2.2 Lacrosse player with all the equipment required

1 Provide the list of equipment which may be required for a cricket player, in order to ensure that the player is both safe and playing the game in line with the rules of the sport.

2 For your own sport provide a list of the equipment which is required in line with the rules of the sport and the equipment that players wear in order to protect themselves from injury.

Health and safety

Many rules and regulations within sports have evolved to prevent the risk of injuries to sports performers. This continues to be the case in all sports. For example, in June 2008 the FA brought out further regulations with regards to goalpost safety, which applied to all football clubs. See the FA website for more details, please go to Pearson Hotlinks (www.pearsonhotlinks.co.uk) and search for this BTEC Sport title.

CONTINUED ▶▶

◤ Facilities

One of the key regulations in sport involves the court, pool, course, track, ring or pitch layout. It is up to the governing bodies to agree on the dimensions of the playing area in order for a competition to take place. Some sports are more flexible when it comes to the size of the playing area and its surface, whereas other sports are very strict regarding these dimensions. For example, FINA (International Swimming Federation) state that all international competitions use a 50 metre Olympic-style pool, whereas FIFA (International Football Federation) state that football can be played on slightly different-sized pitches as long as they are between 90 metres and 120 metres long and 45 metres and 90 metres wide, although the goals must be of a standard size.

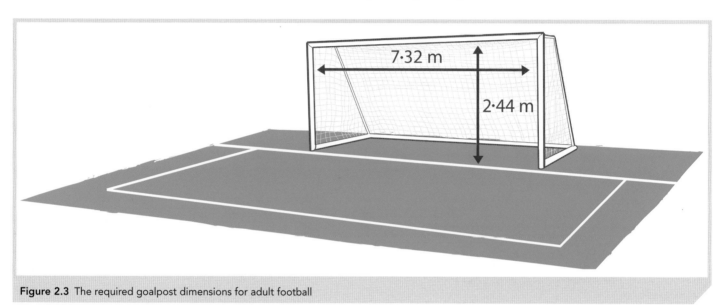

Figure 2.3 The required goalpost dimensions for adult football

◤ Time

Most team sports have a restriction on the duration of matches or competitions. This time is often divided into equal periods. For example, England Basketball have determined that all games competed within the England Basketball league are played in four quarters of 10 minutes each. This gives teams sufficient time to attempt to outscore the opposing team. In sports such as basketball, there is also an option to stop the clock and discuss tactics and make alterations (a 'time out'). In other sports, e.g. football, the only time tactical instructions can be made to the whole team is during the allocated breaks. In football, this break is called 'half-time'.

In some sports competitions, when the scores are even at the end of 'normal' time, 'extra' time is played to determine a winner. If there is no clear winner after extra time, some sports have a final method of concluding the match. An example of this is the use of sudden-death extra time in rugby league knock-out cup competitions such as the Challenge Cup. Play is ended when either team scores a point (drop goal, penalty conversion or try) to finally win the game outright.

For other sports, a winner can be confirmed before the allocated time has run out. A test match in cricket is allocated five full days; however, each side is only allocated two innings each. So if one team scores 500 runs in one innings after one day and on the second day the other team is bowled out for 50 and instructed to follow on and is bowled out again for 150 on the same day, the match is over – the team first in to bat has won the fixture.

Officials

Officials have clear roles and responsibilities regarding the application of the rules and regulations for a sport as stated by the Governing Body.

Scoring systems

Every sport has a different method of scoring. In most games the performer or team who scores the most points within a designated time period, or who reaches a certain number of points, is the winner. The main exception to this is golf, where the winner is the player who hits the lowest number of shots.

However, some sports require a different method of scoring, such as athletics where a performer is measured on times, distances and heights, depending on the discipline. Gymnastics events are scored using a subjective scoring method, where performances are assessed against the perfect model through the eyes of judges.

Every sport has clear rules that determine victory. It is important that as a performer in a sport you are aware of the requirements of winning.

Activity 2.3 Scoring systems

Select two sports.

1 For each sport highlight the scoring systems that are applied.
2 Identify any different methods of scoring that may be applied to alternative competitions (e.g. doubles in tennis).
3 Can you think of any methods of developing the scoring systems within each sport to make the sport more entertaining?

Link

See *Topic A.6 Roles of officials* for further information.

Discussion point

In your sport, what happens if the scores are tied at the end of normal time – how is the contest decided? Is this method of extra time applied in all competitive matches or just in specific competitions?

Figure 2.4 Baseball scoreboard

Just checking

1 What size of pool must be used for international swimming competitions?
2 Make a list of the different playing surfaces that tennis can be played upon competitively.
3 List three officials required in your own selected sport.

TOPIC A.4

Application of the rules/laws of sports

Getting started

Look at the image of a rugby referee applying the rules of rugby. It is important to follow the rules, laws and regulations of sport and apply the appropriate sanctions. In this instance the player is receiving a yellow card for spear-tackling an opponent. Discuss rules in your sport that can result in dismissal or a warning from the referee.

Introduction

As well as understanding the rules, laws and regulations of your selected sport, you need to develop knowledge of how to apply these within specific situations. This will require you to take the role of the official within a competitive situation and demonstrate how to apply the rules, laws and regulations.

When applying rules and regulations in a specific situation you will need to ensure that you use the correct method of communication to stop the game and take the correct action against the performer or team. It is important that you justify the reasons behind your decision within each situation.

For example, when a player breaks a rule in basketball the referee communicates that a rule has been broken by using a whistle to stop play. The official then uses a hand signal to communicate to all players, spectators and coaches which rule has been broken. Finally, the official verbally communicates the sanction to the player involved.

Officials have other methods of communicating with players, spectators and coaches in other sports. An assistant referee in football will wave a flag in a certain way to demonstrate that a rule has been broken or to stop play.

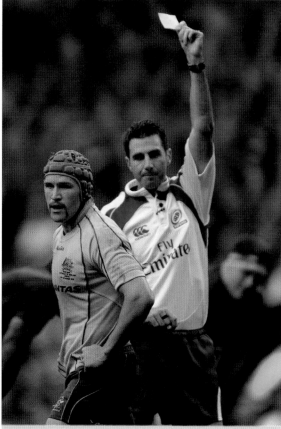

A rugby referee awarding a yellow card to a player during a rugby match

A badminton line judge will shout to communicate with players and spectators. They will also produce a hand signal to communicate their decision with the players, spectators and coaches who are observing. In sports where there is the use of an off-field umpire the decision may be communicated using technology. For example, in rugby league when the video referee makes a decision the result of the decision is displayed on a television screen for the on-field officials, players, coaches and spectators to see all at the same time.

In football an assistant referee will use their flag to demonstrate that a rule has been broken.

Table 2.2 gives examples of situations in which officials would need to take action.

Table 2.2 Situations in which rules would need to be applied in certain sports

Sport	Situation
Football	A goal is scored when a player is in an offside position
Cricket	The ball hitting the batsman's legs directly in front of the wickets before hitting the bat
Basketball	Charging in lead-up to scoring
Rugby league/ union	Forward pass resulting in a try
Hockey	The ball running behind the end line after touching a defender
Tennis	The ball landing in the court boundaries after hitting the net post during a rally

---

Assessment activity 2.1   *English*   2A.P1 | 2A.P2 | 2A.P3 | 2A.M1 | 2A.D1

The PE coordinator from a local primary school has asked you to help the Year 6 students with their understanding of the rules and scoring systems for two sports.

1 Develop a short video that gives information about the following for two sports of your choice:
  - the rules, regulations and scoring systems
  - the roles and responsibilities of the officials.

2 Are there similarities and differences between the roles and responsibilities of the officials? Can you recommend ways to improve the application of the rules, regulations and scoring systems?

3 For the next part of the video, select one of these sports and take the role of a referee. You should demonstrate how the rules are applied correctly in four situations.

Tips
- Provide examples to show how each official applies the rules effectively within competitive situations.
- Give your ideas for how the rules of each sport could be developed to make the sport more entertaining – consider methods of scoring and other rules which could be adapted to make the game more exciting.
- You will need to demonstrate the methods of communication used to apply these rules in each of the situations.

Roles of officials

Introduction

Different sports require different types of **official**, each with their own **roles** and responsibilities. Some sports require more officials than there are players, such as tennis, in which there are up to eleven people officiating during a competitive match. In other sports there may be very few officials.

Umpires

An example of a sport that uses umpires is cricket. Traditionally there will be two umpires per match and they are in charge of all decisions made on the pitch. For example, the umpire makes the decisions regarding whether or not a batsman is out, or whether a shot has been hit for four or six runs. The umpires ensure that the match is played in accordance with the laws of the game.

Key terms

Official – a representative of a National Governing Body who applies the rules of a specific sport in competitive situations.

Role – the actions and activities assigned to or required or expected of a person.

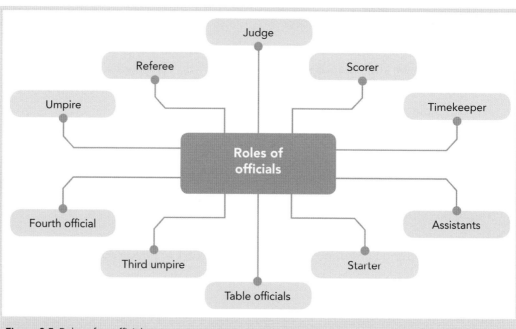

Figure 2.5 Roles of an official

Figure 2.6 Examples of hand signals that a cricket umpire uses.

Referees

The role of the referee is to ensure that all of the rules (or laws) of the game are followed by performers. The referee can apply the rules on the field of play, although a referee can also manage the game from off-field.

An example of a referee who is on the field of play and constantly making decisions that affect the end result is a lacrosse referee. An example of a referee who is off the field of play is a volleyball referee.

Judges

Sports such as gymnastics and boxing use judges to **officiate**. In gymnastics, the judge observes the performance of the athlete and assesses the demonstration of the skill or technique against a set of **criteria**. These are based on a perfect model of the skill or technique. A boxing judge will observe the performance of a boxer competing in a ring and will award points for every clean punch connected, or at the end of each round award victory to one of the boxers. Rounds can also be drawn if the judge deems that there is no clear winner. In each case, the judge makes a decision based on observations.

Which rules of tennis does a line judge apply during a competitive game of tennis?

Timekeepers

Some sports have a restriction on the amount of time allocated to a match or competitive situation. In basketball there are official timekeepers to record the duration of the game and to start and stop the clock at specific stages of the game. For some sports it is a requirement that every time the ball is out of play or play stops, time is stopped and not started again until play resumes. The timekeeper has the sole responsibility to stop and start the clock.

Starters

In sports such as swimming and athletics the starter plays a vital role. It is the starter who informs the participants in a race when to start. The starter is also in charge of monitoring false starts and sanctioning performers appropriately when the starting rules are broken. In many sports the starter also has the responsibility to verbally communicate with the performers and prepare them for the start of the race.

Activity 2.4   List of officials

For your sport, provide a list of the officials who are involved in applying the rules of the sport and also include a summary of the rules that each official applies during a competitive situation. You could present your findings in a table.

Responsibilities of officials

Getting started ▶▶

Select an official from your own sport. Complete a 10 point guide of what makes them an effective official in your selected sport – look at how many responsibilities you have covered within your 10 point guide.

Introduction

Officials in each sport have a defined set of responsibilities.

Appearance

For most sports it is a requirement that officials wear a specific uniform. This uniform differentiates them from the performers and reinforces their importance. The uniform worn by the officials must not clash with the colours of the sports performers.

Equipment

If specific equipment is required to support the application of the rules and regulations of the sport, it is each official's responsibility to bring the appropriate kit to every competition or game. For example, a netball umpire will need to arrive at a game equipped with a whistle, a scorecard, a stopwatch, a coin and a pen.

Equipment required by a football referee. Can you think of any other equipment that a football referee may require?

Did you know?

In most sports, the more qualifications you obtain as a referee/umpire the higher the level you can officiate in the selected sport.

Qualifications

For some sports, the official must hold a recognised officiating qualification. All National Governing Bodies provide training and qualifications to educate and develop existing officials. Properly trained officials help to ensure that the game is played within the laws stated and takes place in a safe and appropriate environment.

Activity 2.5 — Find out about officiating courses

For one team sport and one individual sport of your choice, visit the NGB website and carry out some research into officiating courses for each (this will often be found under 'Education'). Make a list of the different courses and underline the one that you feel would be most appropriate for you.

Fitness

For some sports it is a requirement for officials to be on the field of play and keep up with the play to ensure that they are close at hand to make decisions and **sanction** performers as necessary. This requires a high level of fitness, as play can be very fast, and the official may even do more running than some of the players on the pitch.

Interpretation and application of the rules

One of the major responsibilities of an official in any sport is the ability to apply the rules and regulations. It is a requirement of all officials to observe the state of play carefully. If they spot that the rules of the sport have been broken, officials must take appropriate action and apply sanctions as stated within the laws of the sport.

It is important that the official is in the best position possible to make the correct decision. Officials have to be confident in the decisions that they make, as once a decision is made they should stand by it.

Control of players

An official will demonstrate control of the sports performers and ensure that they are safe during the competitive situation by applying regulations correctly and confidently. In some sports, if the laws are broken because of serious foul play the officials have the power to discipline the players by sending them off the field of play. Control can also be applied through effective communication.

Effective communication

In some sports there are numerous officials involved in competitive situations. It is important for them to communicate clearly, and listen carefully to each other. This is also necessary when officials are enforcing the rules or laws of a sport – the official should clearly inform the players about each decision made. An official who communicates effectively and confidently will gain respect from performers. In some sports a referee is also provided with a whistle as a tool for controlling the performers and applying the rules. In some instances specific sanctions may require specific whistle usage.

Activity 2.6	The importance of the whistle

Referee a game of five-a-side football, basketball or hockey. For the first 5 minutes use a whistle and then for the next 5 minutes do not use a whistle. After the activity discuss the following points with the rest of your group.

1 Did you use the whistle effectively?

2 What was the response of the participants when you blew the whistle?

3 How did you communicate with the performers when the whistle was removed?

4 What was the most effective form of communication while officiating?

5 How could you develop your ability to officiate effectively?

CONTINUED ▸▸

Accountability to spectators

Spectators who observe sports often come to watch a specific individual or specific team. Therefore, it is important that the official demonstrates an unbiased opinion at all times.

An official should apply the rules and laws of sport equally to all competitors, using clear methods of communication to display which laws and rules have been broken.

Hawk-eye is now used in tennis if a player wants to challenge the umpire's decision.

Health and safety

A major responsibility of officials in sport is to ensure that every event is carried out safely, in order to protect players, spectators, coaches and officials.

Officials should carry out safety checks before, during and after a sports event.

These should include checks of:

- **Equipment** – to ensure that equipment is suitable, in good condition, and has no chance of causing injury to the sports performers.
- **Facilities** – the area in which the competition is going to take place must be safe for spectators. Playing surfaces must not pose a risk of injury to sports performers.
- **Players** – if an official feels at any time during a competitive situation that sports performers are under threat of injury or illness they have the responsibility to stop play and resolve the health and safety hazards.

Fair play

Officials should promote fair play at all times through respecting the sports performers that they are officiating, respecting the coaches and spectators observing the sport, and applying the rules fairly and consistently to both teams.

Use of technology

As technology has developed, more sports have moved towards using it to apply laws consistently.

For some sports the introduction of technology is still under debate. However, other sports have embraced the use of technology to support the officials who are on the field of play and may require a second opinion.

Cricket has introduced the **third umpire**, and rugby league and rugby union have introduced a **video referee**.

Key terms

Third umpire – an off-field umpire who makes the final decision in questions referred to him by the two on-field umpires. Television replays are available to the third umpire to assist him in making a decision.

Video referee – some sports allow referees to consult replay footage before making or revising a decision about unclear or dubious play. In rugby league and rugby union this person is called the video referee.

Discussion point

In your group discuss the advantages and disadvantages of goal-line technology.

WorkSpace

▶ Denise Robinson

Basketball Level 1 referee (apprentice)

I have been a basketball official for my local basketball team for over two years now. As a basketball official I have the responsibility of keeping the score, updating the scoreboard and recording individual and team fouls. I have played basketball for a number of years and as I developed my own knowledge of the rules I became more confident.

When I was asked by my club if I was interested in helping out as a basketball official I was nervous initially, but over time my confidence has developed. The club also decided that I was good enough to officiate in some of the national league matches, but prior to doing this I had to attain the appropriate basketball official's qualification. It took me over a year to achieve both my Level 1 and Level 2 basketball official awards.

As a basketball official I have learned a lot more about the application of the rules of basketball through watching the floor officials apply the rules. It was observing the referees in charge of the game that actually made me want to become a referee. I have recently completed my Level 1 (apprentice) referee qualification with the NGB. Since gaining this award I have been able to officiate at school matches within my club.

I have found refereeing basketball very enjoyable and I hope to continue with this for the rest of my life. I see this as an opportunity to put something back into a sport which I truly love.

Think about it

1   When officiating, why is confidence so important?

2   In your sport can you identify the officials required in a competitive situation? Can you identify the rules and regulations that each of these officials have to apply during a competitive situation?

3   What courses would you need to undertake to become an official in your sport?

Technical demands of sport

Getting started

Select one skill from your sport and show your partner/rest of the group how to apply the skill effectively and successfully.

Key term

Skill – something that we learn how to do.

Introduction

Every sport requires specific **skills**; mastering the application of these skills supports the development of a sports performer. The skills you require will depend on the sport you play and in some sports these skills will be different. A skill is learned, and is not something we can do without coaching, training or observation of others. When we are first introduced to a skill it is often very difficult to master and takes a lot of physical and mental effort.

Figure 2.7 shows examples of some skills and techniques used in sports. For your own sport think about which of these are appropriate, and add any others as you see fit.

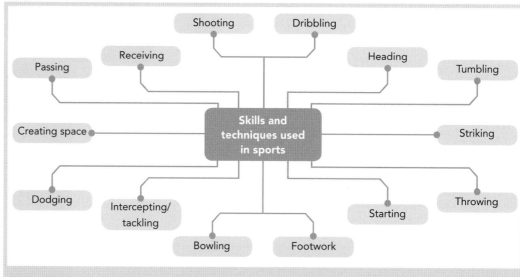

Figure 2.7 Skills and techniques used in sports

In sport we often use the word 'skilful' to identify a quality that a performer displays. This can sometimes be confused with performance. A hockey player who can demonstrate a variety of tricks while dribbling can be seen as skilful, but these skills are not a measurement of the ability to play hockey in a competitive scenario. A skilful player is someone who makes skills look easy, using very little effort, and who always applies skills successfully.

Skills in sport can be categorised as follows:

- **Continuous skills** are those that have no obvious beginning or end; they could be continued for as long as the performer wishes. For example, running.
- A **discrete skill** has a clear beginning and end. The skill can be repeated, but the performer will start the full action again in a controlled and timely manner. For example, a golf putt.
- A **serial skill** is a series of discrete skills that together produce an organised movement. The order of the movement is often very important but the requirements of each part of the skill will require specific development. For example, a gymnastic tumble.

Sailors must become skilful at handling the ropes.

Activity 2.7   Listing skill requirements

Cricket is a game where different skills are required within different components of the game.

1 List the skills and techniques required for the following roles:
   - batsman
   - bowler
   - fielder.

2 For your own sport (or another sport) complete the same activity, listing all the different positions (if appropriate) and the skills, techniques and abilities required for each.

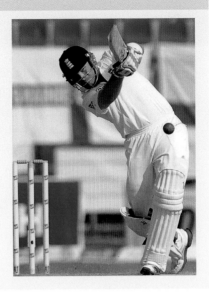

Movement

The ability to move efficiently and effectively around the designated area of play is very important in some sports (for example, tennis and volleyball). The more efficiently a sports performer can move around the court or pitch, the more time they have to apply the appropriate skills within a competitive situation.

Use of equipment

In sports there is an additional requirement for performers to master the use of equipment to compete in the sport effectively. For example, when mountain biking the rider of the bike has to develop the skill to use the bike effectively to maximise their performance during a race. The level of technique can often determine the performer's ability level.

Communication and interaction

The ability to communicate with other people when competing in sport as part of a team is a very important skill. Sports performers use various methods of **interaction** in a competitive situation to get the best result for the team.

In rugby union the forwards will rehearse the line-outs during their training sessions. The team might apply code words or non-verbal signs to indicate to their players where the ball will be directed to in the line-out. The ability to master this effectively is a skill.

Other demands

In some sports there are other demands to consider. These may not be a physical requirement but rather a mental challenge. For example, in orienteering, prior to completing the planned course, the competitors need to plan their route. Such meticulous forward planning can provide the edge over other competitors completing the same course.

Discussion point

In your group, make a list of sports that require performers to use equipment. Also in your group look at a sport that the majority of the group has played and discuss the issues around learning how to use the equipment – was this an easy skill to learn or did it take time to master?

Key term

Interaction – when sports performers communicate effectively with the aim of attaining a joint goal.

Tactical demands of sport

Introduction

Tactics are required in all sports. The desired goal in sport is for the sports performer to win. When you think about tactics you will often think about team sports and set plays. However, tactics can be applied to individual sports as well. Whenever you have to make a decision in sport, you are applying a tactic. It is very important that sports performers make the correct decisions at the crucial points within their performance. This could be the difference between a gold medal and a silver in some instances.

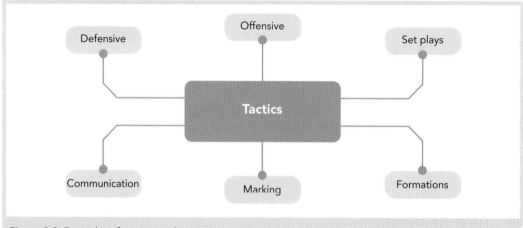

Figure 2.8 Examples of tactics used in sport

Decision making

After skills have been developed it is important that sports performers apply these skills correctly and strategically in competitive situations.

When competing in any sport it is important that a performer makes the correct decisions throughout the game, match or competition. The more you participate within your selected sport the more effective you should be at making correct decisions. For example, a netball player must choose the right player to pass to so that the team maintain possession of the ball.

Decisions within a competitive situation can often mean the difference between winning and losing.

Defending and attacking

Within all sports there are a great many strategies and tactics which are applied to defending and attacking. Particularly within **invasion games** like lacrosse and handball, strategies are applied to gain an advantage over the opposing team.

Choice and use of shots or strokes

It is important that sports performers make the correct decisions to give themselves every opportunity to succeed.

Variation

In most sports it is important that the performers vary the strategies, tactics and skills that are applied within competitive situations, to avoid becoming predictable.

If a tennis player always plays a drop shot in the third shot of every rally, their opponent will start to predict the shot and react more effectively, thereby gaining an advantage.

Conditions

It may be relevant to apply different strategies within different situations in an attempt to gain an advantage over opponents.

In football, if a team is losing by one goal with only minutes to go and they win an attacking corner, they may make a decision to send the goalkeeper into the attacking penalty box in an attempt to increase their chances of scoring a goal.

Use of space

In many sports, the ability to create and find space provides a performer or team with a tactical advantage over their opponents.

In rugby if a team can pass the ball quickly out to the wing and create an overlap, space will be created for a winger (one of the quicker, more agile players on the team) to exploit and either gain yards or score a try.

A golfer must select the correct clubs to ensure that the next shot gets as close to the hole as possible.

Activity 2.8	Thinking about tactics

Tactics can take many different forms. For each of the following situations describe the strategies and tactics you would use in an attempt to gain an advantage over your opponents within your sport:

- attacking
- defending
- when it looks as if you are going to lose but have a chance of victory
- when you feel as if you have no chance of winning at all.

Safe and appropriate participation

Getting started

Discuss in small groups the difference between isolated practices, conditioned games and competitive situations. Can you think of times when you have been involved in each situation?

Key terms

Isolated practices – training drills and skill-specific exercises.

Component – a part of something.

Link

This unit links to *Unit 13: Profiling Sports Performance, Topic A.3* for more information on technical and tactical requirements.

Introduction

When developing skills, techniques and tactics within sports it is important that this is done in a safe and appropriate manner, controlled and delivered at a pace which will support learning. By practising skills, techniques and tactics in a safe and controlled environment in isolated practices, technical errors can be highlighted and corrected by coaches before participants are required to apply these skills, techniques and tactics within competitive situations.

Relevant skills and techniques

Each sport has specific skills and techniques that are required for effective participation within that sport. In some instances, skills appropriate for one player's role in a sport are not the same as those for another player. For example, in order to be an effective batter in rounders the skills required are different from those required to be an effective fielder.

Relevant tactics

It is important that a sports performer or team apply relevant and appropriate tactics when participating in their sport, given any particular settings or situations. Tactics may depend upon a variety of factors, including:

- the weather
- the score/position the performer is in
- the time/distance left
- the opponent's weaknesses
- the performer's weaknesses
- injuries, if a substitute is replacing original opponents
- the opponent's tactics.

Effective use of skills and techniques, and the correct application of each

When using any skill it is important that this is done in a technically correct way, to ensure efficiency and effectiveness.

In order to consider the correct application of a skill the sports performer must consider the position that each part of the body should be in during each stage of the skill.

Through detailed analysis, elite sports performers have developed every **component** of each specific skill, which has resulted in improvements to their overall performance.

Activity 2.9   Sport-specific skills

Look at Figure 2.9.

- Think of a skill from your own sport.
- Explain the correct technical application of each component for that particular skill.

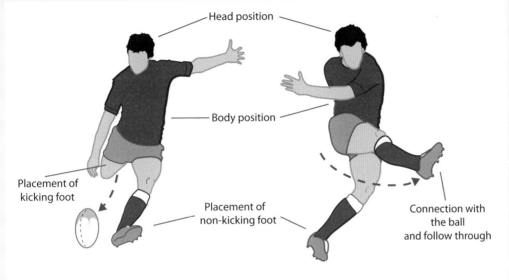

Figure 2.9 The components associated with taking a rugby conversion

Effective use of skills, techniques and tactics

Similar to the applications of skills and techniques, tactics also need to be applied correctly and at the appropriate time when you participate in **conditioned practices** and **competitive situations**. This ensures that they have the utmost effect on the outcome of the overall performance. For example, if marathon runners decide to break away from other athletes in a race too fast or too early, this may be at the cost of their own performance – they may become fatigued, resulting in them losing the race because of this poor application of tactics.

 Key terms

Conditioned practices – practices with special rules or restrictions that support the development of a skill, technique or tactic in a natural, game-like scenario.

Competitive situations – events or contests where more than one sports performer competes to achieve a set goal, following rules regulated by officials.

Assessment activity 2.2   2B.P4 | 2B.P5 | 2B.M2

You have been asked to produce a blog with video clips to support the promotion of sport within your local community. Select two sports of your choice.

- Produce written information for the blog about the technical and tactical demands of these two sports.
- Produce video clips to demonstrate the skills, techniques and tactics of the two sports in conditioned practices and competitive situations.

Tips

- You will need to give information about all of the skills and techniques required in each sport.
- Produce a voiceover for the video clips to discuss the skills, techniques and tactics that are being demonstrated.
- Remember your audience – you are promoting sport in your local community. Use your blog to give information about the skills involved in both sports, and how these skills can be developed for those who are new to the sports and are looking to find out more.

Observation checklist

Getting started

In groups, discuss methods of effectively assessing a skill. Select a skill from a selected sport and observe a sports performer applying the skill, using a variety of methods of measuring success. Agree as a group on the most effective method of measuring success.

Link

This unit links to *Unit 13: Profiling Sports Performance*, *Topic A.1 and A.2* for more information on performance analysis.

Introduction

An observation checklist is used by many sports coaches and sports performers to generate a picture of a performer's or team's overall performance. It is a tool to help a sports performer to assess their own strengths and weaknesses. The information obtained from the checklist can then be used to develop an action plan for development. It is important that before making decisions regarding such action plans sports performers discuss their findings with a coach or mentor.

Observation checklists should be used to prioritise the performance components for the future development of training programmes for performers, and they can also be used to monitor progress towards goals and targets.

The first requirement before completing an observation checklist is to identify the demands of a selected sport; often these can be divided into three areas of performance:

- **physical demands** (e.g. coordination, speed)
- **technical demands** (e.g. passing, serving)
- **tactical demands** (e.g. defending, attacking).

It is important that the performer has a clear understanding of the requirements for each component being observed and assessed within the checklist.

Table 2.3 An example of the components required for each area of performance for a netball player

Physical demands	Technical demands	Tactical demands
Aerobic endurance	Passing	Attacking
Speed	Receiving	Defending
Flexibility	Dodging	Creating space
Agility	Shooting	Positioning
Coordination	Blocking	
Reaction time	Intercepting	
	Rebounding	

Activity 2.10   Physical, technical and tactical demands

For your own sport, make a list of the required attributes to perform effectively under the following headings:

- physical components
- skills and technical components
- tactical components.

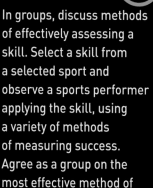
Shooting is one of the required skillls for netball.

Observing the full competition and then making an overall judgement for each component of performance after the event for the player/team is called performance profiling. When using this method, it is important to have a clear scale to indicate the levels of performance being measured. For example, if a 10-point scale is used, 1 on the scale may be unsuccessful application of the skill, technique or tactic, while 10 is faultless application of the skill, technique or tactic. Therefore if a performer scores 5, his application of the skill in question would be judged as having been average. Table 2.4 shows an example of a performance profile for a sprint start.

Table 2.4 Performance profile for sprint start

Performance Profile: Athletics Sprint Start	1	2	3	4	5	6	7	8	9	10
Athlete A										X

Alternatively, a tally chart can be completed for the full duration of the competition, identifying successful application of each component, and then drawing conclusions from the results obtained. Table 2.5 shows a performance profile completed in this way.

Table 2.5 A tally chart observation for a rugby match

Tally Chart – Rugby – Core Skill – TACKLING	
Number of successful tackles	卌 |||
Number of missed tackles	卌 卌 卌 卌

What are the physical, technical and tactical demands of rugby?

Reviewing performance

Introduction

Gathering information and making evaluations is the next process after the observation. The information collated by the observer must be interpreted to make judgements on the performer's **strengths** and **areas for improvement**.

Sport-specific strengths and areas for improvement

Skills and techniques

Through assessing performance, either by watching a live performance or through **video analysis**, an observer may notice that a sports performer is much better at applying some skills and techniques than others within specific situations. The observer should complete a summary of the performer's strengths and areas for improvement, providing possible reasons for each.

Tactics and effective decision-making

It is important that the observer examines the sports performer's application of tactics within a variety of situations, and analyses the performer's ability to make decisions under pressure. Feedback should be provided to the sports performer regarding their application of the tactics and strategies within conditioned practices and competitive situations as appropriate.

Activity 2.11   Team selection

When an international manager selects a team for a game, they have to consider the following factors:

- strengths and weaknesses of the opposing team
- strengths and weaknesses of the available squad
- having a balance of players

Work in groups to complete the following tasks:

1 Decide on a selection of players to play in the starting team of the next international match for a team sport of your choice. For each player, justify their selection.

2 Select the positions where each player will play. Justify your formation.

3 Decide on the specific tactics you would ask the team to apply, for both attacking and defending.

Non-sport-specific strengths and areas for improvement

Other areas for development may be highlighted which may not be specific to the sport, such as the components of fitness.

Activities to improve performance

After review, long- and short-term goals for technical and tactical development should be produced.

- **Short-term goals** are set over a short period of time, such as between matches or within a season.
- **Long-term goals** are set with the bigger picture in mind. Some long-term goals aim towards the next major competition, e.g. the next Olympics. These goals are often based around a training cycle or season.

Training programmes

Performance reviews should be used to create a training programme targeted to maintain strengths and improve areas for development. It is important to have clear goals in order to design a programme that is realistic and achievable.

Use of technology

Technology can be used to further assess performance, such as **dartfish technology** and **candlestick technology**. It is often used by elite sports performers to develop the finer details of technical application of skills.

Attending courses

In some instances it may be appropriate for performers to attend courses that support their own technical and tactical development. These courses could range from skills development sessions with coaches to coaching courses delivered by National Governing Bodies.

Where to seek help and advice

All of these performance development objectives should be negotiated with your coach/teacher, but be specific to you.

> ### Key terms
>
> **Dartfish technology** – video software which shows a sports performance in slow motion, used by coaches to identify technical deficiencies.
>
> **Candlestick technology** – video software which shows a sports performance in slow motion, used by coaches to identify technical deficiencies.

Assessment activity 2.3 | *English* | 2C.P6 | 2C.P7 | 2C.M3 | 2C.D2

A coach from a local sports club has asked for your support. His club members are reluctant to take part in any form of self-analysis and rely heavily on the coaches within the club. The coach is a strong believer in self-analysis and would like to show the club members how this can be done.

1 Produce an observation checklist that could be used by sports performers to review their own performance. Do this for two sports of your choice.

2 The coach would then like you to show the club members how this checklist can be used:

- Review your own performance in each sport using the checklist.
- On completion of the review you should consider your strengths and areas where you can improve. Think of activities that will help you to improve your performance in the two sports.
- Prepare a presentation for the club to summarise your findings and how you went about this review.

Tips

- Before preparing an observation checklist, it is useful to first make a list of all the skills, techniques and tactics required to participate in that sport.
- If you have chosen the same sports as those you looked at in Assessment activity 2.2, you could carry out the analysis using the videos you made demonstrating skills, techniques and tactics for these sports.

Introduction

Have you ever thought about why some people seem larger than life when they play sport, but are really quiet and shy in everyday life? Or why some people stay focused and cope really well with pressure, but others crumble in high-pressure situations?

It is important for sports performers to develop ways of meeting mental demands in order to achieve sporting success, which involves training the mind as well as the body.

Those who work with sports performers, including sports coaches and sports psychologists, will need to understand factors that affect performance such as motivation, self-confidence and personality. No two athletes are the same so it is important to have a breadth of knowledge, understanding and skills.

This unit will help you to understand the different factors that can influence the mind in sporting situations and some of the ways you can improve your own preparation and performance, and that of others.

Assessment: You will be assessed by a series of assignments set by your teacher/tutor.

Learning aims

In this unit you will:

A investigate personality and its effect on sports performance

B explore the influence that motivation and self-confidence have on sports performance

C know about arousal and anxiety, and the effects they have on sports performance.

This unit has really helped with my performance as a footballer. I understand now some of the reasons why I act the way I do when I play football and have been able to develop as a player as a result.

Halima, *16-year-old female football player*

The Mind and Sports Performance

3

BTEC
Assessment Zone

This table shows what you must do in order to achieve a **Pass**, **Merit** or **Distinction** grade, and where you can find activities to help you.

Assessment criteria			
Level 1	**Level 2 Pass**	**Level 2 Merit**	**Level 2 Distinction**
Learning aim A: investigate personality and its effect on sports performance			
1A.1 Maths Outline personality and the effect it can have on sports performance	**2A.P1** Maths Using relevant examples, describe personality, including methods of measurement and three different views **See Assessment activity 3.1, page 85**	**2A.M1** Maths Explain three different views of personality, and how personality can affect sports performance **See Assessment activity 3.1, page 85**	**2A.D1** Maths Analyse three different views of personality, and how personality can affect sports performance **See Assessment activity 3.1, page 85**
Learning aim B: explore the influence that motivation and self-confidence have on sports performance			
1B.2 Describe types of motivation and the benefits motivation and self-confidence have on sports performance	**2B.P2** Describe types and views of motivation and the benefits motivation and self-confidence have on sports performance **See Assessment activity 3.2, page 97**	**2B.M2** Discuss the benefits motivation and self-confidence have on sports performance **See Assessment activity 3.2, page 97**	**2B.D2** Analyse the benefits motivation and self-confidence have on sports performance **See Assessment activity 3.2, page 97**
1B.3 Outline appropriate methods to increase self-confidence in sport	**2B.P3** Summarise, with relevant examples, methods to increase self-confidence in sport **See Assessment activity 3.2, page 97**		
1B.4 Outline factors that influence self-efficacy in sport	**2B.P4** Describe, using relevant examples, factors that influence self-efficacy in sport **See Assessment activity 3.2, page 97**		
1B.5 Outline goal setting, different types of goals that can be set and how these can influence sports performance	**2B.P5** Describe goal setting, different types of goals that can be set, and how these can influence sports performance and motivation **See Assessment activity 3.2, page 97**	**2B.M3** Discuss how goal setting can influence motivation and the roles of the different types of goals that can be set **See Assessment activity 3.2, page 97**	

Assessment criteria			
Level 1	Level 2 **Pass**	Level 2 **Merit**	Level 2 **Distinction**
Learning aim C: know about arousal and anxiety, and the effects they have on sports performance			
1C.6 Outline different types of anxiety	**2C.P6** Describe, using relevant examples, different types of anxiety **See Assessment activity 3.3, page 100**	**2C.M4** English Assess, using four theories, the effect arousal and anxiety have on sports performance and their control **See Assessment activity 3.3, page 100**	**2C.D3** English Evaluate imagery and relaxation techniques as methods of controlling arousal and anxiety, and in improving sports performance **See Assessment activity 3.3, page 100**
1C.7 English Describe, using two theories, the effect arousal and anxiety have on sports performance and their control	**2C.P7** English Describe, using four theories, the effect arousal and anxiety have on sports performance and their control **See Assessment activity 3.3, page 100**		

English Opportunity to practise English skills

Maths Opportunity to practise mathematical skills

How you will be assessed

This unit will be assessed though a series of assignments set by your teacher/tutor. You will be expected to show an understanding of personality and its effects on sports performance; of motivation and self-confidence and their influence on sports performance; and of the relationship between arousal, anxiety and performance. The tasks will be based on scenarios involving working in a sports setting. For example, you might be asked to imagine you are assisting a sports psychologist and have been asked to produce information to benefit different athletes.

Your assessment could take the form of:

- presentations
- leaflets
- posters.

Definition and structure of personality

Getting started

Think about famous sportspeople that you have watched. Do you think they act the same in their normal life as they do while playing sport? Why do you think there may be some differences?

Introduction

Have you ever sat down and thought about what your personality actually is? If you have, you will probably have described yourself using terms like 'bubbly', 'happy' or 'outgoing'. These are all terms that can be used to describe what makes up somebody's personality. You might also have found yourself thinking about how personality may differ from person to person, or in different situations. To be able to understand these things, you need to be able to define personality and understand the structure of personality.

Key terms

Personality – the sum of characteristics that make a person unique.

Discussion point

Discuss with a friend and try to come up with a list of words that you think best describe your personality. You may also want to start thinking about any differences that occur when you are taking part in sport, when you are hanging around with friends, or when you are spending time with your close family.

Mark Cavendish won Sports Personality of the Year 2011. What aspects of his personality helped him to achieve sporting success?

Definition of personality

Personality is the sum of the characteristics that make a person unique. People working within sport have long been interested in trying to find out just how much personality can influence sports performance. One way to start trying to answer this question is by looking at the structure of personality.

Structure of personality

Personality is a complex thing that is made up of lots of different levels. One way of understanding personality is by looking at it as three levels that are related to each other (see Figure 3.1):

- **Role-related behaviours** – this relates to changes in behaviour based on how you perceive the situation that you are in and your understanding that different situations require different roles. This is the most changeable part of your personality, because it is the one that is most closely linked to different environments. For example, a young rugby player may demonstrate more leadership qualities when captaining his rugby team than when he is sitting in a classroom doing his maths.

- **Typical responses** – this is the way that you usually respond in certain situations, for example, when somebody deliberately fouls you in a game. It is usually a good indicator of your psychological core.

- **Psychological core** – this represents the 'real you', rather than who you want people to believe you are. It contains your attitudes, your values, your interests and your beliefs. The psychological core is the most stable part of your personality and the most difficult part for people to get to know.

Remember

Role-related behaviours and typical responses don't always truly reflect a person's psychological core because of how much they can be affected by different social situations.

Key terms

Role-related behaviours – the least stable part of the personality, which is influenced by the environment.

Typical responses – the way that we usually respond to different situations.

Psychological core – the most stable and innermost, 'real' part of the personality.

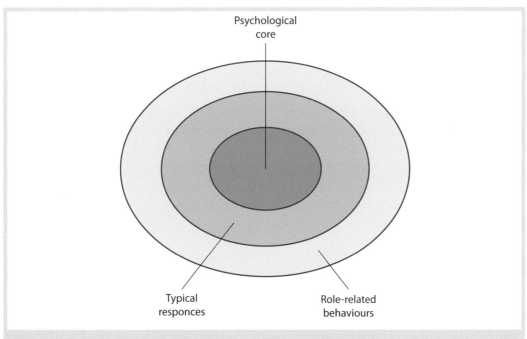

Figure 3.1 What does this diagram say about the structure of our personality?

Just checking

1 What is personality?

2 What is the structure of personality?

Personality types

Getting started

Do you think there is such a thing as a sporting or an athletic personality? Discuss your ideas with other people in your group.

Introduction

Have you ever heard athletes described as being aggressive, calm or a 'good leader', and ever wondered how those things may affect their sports performance? When people discuss these things, they are talking about personality type; the influence of the different personality types on sports performance has long been of interest to sports psychologists and coaches. In this section, you will learn about the different personality types, the differences between athletes and non-athletes and the difference between team and individual sport athletes.

Personality types

There are four key personality types that you need to know about: **introvert**, **extrovert**, **type A** and **type B**.

Introvert

Introvert personality types tend not to actively seek excitement and prefer calm environments. Introverts also tend to prefer tasks that require lots of concentration.

Extrovert

Extrovert personality types can become bored with tasks quite quickly if the task requires lots of concentration and they have a tendency to seek change and excitement. Extroverts also tend to be able to cope with change better than introverts, and can cope with distractions like large crowds and lots of noise. Finally, extroverts also tend to be able to cope with pain better than introverts.

Type A

Type A personalities tend to work at a very fast pace and always need to be in control of situations. Unfortunately, this can lead to high levels of stress and can make them more susceptible to different cardiovascular diseases associated with stress.

Type B

Type B personalities tend to be less competitive and less concerned about things being done straight away. Type B personalities are also prepared to delegate jobs, are more tolerant and tend to experience lower levels of stress than type A personalities.

Other personality types

There are two other personality types that are important to know about – **stable** and **unstable**.

Individual sport athletes, such as long-distance runners, tend to be more introverted.

Key terms

Stable – people who have a relatively unchangeable mood and are not easily affected by their emotions.

Unstable – people who have a relatively changeable mood and are easily affected by their emotions.

Effects of personality on sports performance

One of the things that a lot of people have tried to find out is the effect of personality on sports performance. To try to answer this, people have looked at the difference between athletes and non-athletes, and the difference between team and individual athletes.

Athletes and non-athletes

Some athletes have been found to have higher levels of independence, self-confidence and competitiveness, while also being more outgoing. Athletes also tend to suffer less anxiety (see Topic C.1) than non-athletes. However, the general conclusion is that there isn't a particular personality profile that will distinguish an athlete from a non-athlete.

Team versus individual sports

There are also some differences observed between athletes in different types of sports. For example, individual sport athletes, such as long-distance runners, tend to be more introverted, whereas team players, such as footballers, tend to be more extroverted.

To be able to understand the background to personality, you need to know the different methods of measuring personality (see Topic A.4).

Discussion point

Why could a personality type that makes you more tolerant to pain be a dangerous thing in competitive sport?

Remember

Some personality differences have been suggested between athletes and non-athletes but these differences are not well understood.

What personality type do you think Mo Farah has?

Measuring personality

Introduction

So far, you have learned about the structure of personality and the different personality types. It is also important to understand how personality is measured. There are two main ways in which personality is measured: by using questionnaires and by conducting behavioural observations.

Questionnaires

Sometimes personality is measured by asking athletes to fill in questionnaires. Two popular questionnaires are Eysenck's Personality Inventory (EPI) and the Profile of Mood States (POMS).

Eysenck's Personality Inventory (EPI)

In Topic A.3, you learned about introvert, extrovert, stable and unstable personality types. The EPI is a questionnaire that helps you decide which of these personality types you fall into and measures your personality in two dimensions: introvert–extrovert and stable–unstable (see Figure 3.2). As these dimensions are independent of each other, you will get a personality result that combines both (e.g. unstable extrovert). It asks you to answer questions that require yes or no answers. Your score is calculated based on these answers and your personality type is suggested based on that score. Most people tend to score somewhere near the middle of the EPI.

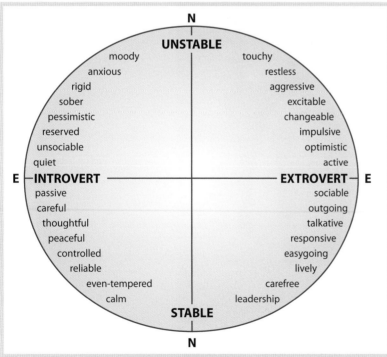

Figure 3.2 Look at the personality dimensions above. Which personality type do you think you would be if you completed the EPI?

Profile of Mood States (POMS)

The POMS questionnaire contains 65 questions and measures the following mood states: tension, depression, anger, vigour, fatigue and confusion. You are given a score for each mood state based on your responses to different statements (see Figure 3.3 for an example of the graph that is drawn from your results). For each statement, you say how you feel at that moment, or how you felt recently by choosing one of the following responses: 'not at all', 'a little', 'moderately', 'quite a lot' or 'extremely'.

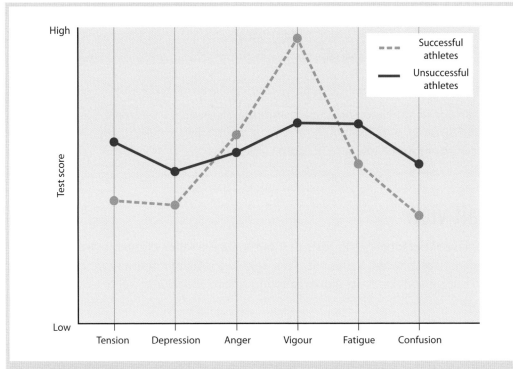

Figure 3.3 How does this POMS results graph show that mood state differs between successful and unsuccessful athletes?

Link

This unit links to *Unit 11: Running a Sports Event, Topic D.3* for more information on SMARTER targets.

Observations

Another way to measure personality is by **observing** people. When you observe people, you are looking for them to display particular **traits** or behaviours that will give you an insight into their personality. For example, when watching a football match, you may see the team captain regularly shouting out instructions, talking and listening to teammates and then always being the first person to do the television interviews after the games. From this, you might assume that the captain has high levels of leadership qualities, is quite outgoing and is quite talkative – all of which would suggest a stable extrovert (see Figure 3.2).

Key terms

Observing – watching people to see which traits or behaviours they display.

Traits – personality characteristics that can be used to predict or understand behaviours in different settings.

Activity 3.1 Assessing personality

Watch a selection of different sports, pick an athlete to watch in each, and then answer the following questions:

- Which traits and behaviours do they display while they are performing?
- What do these traits/behaviours suggest about their personality type?

Just checking

1 What do the initials EPI stand for?
2 Which mood states does the POMS questionnaire measure?
3 What would you look for when conducting behavioural observations?

Views of personality

Getting started

Why do you think it is important for sports psychologists to understand the different views of personality?

Key terms

Views of personality – the explanations that have been given to help us understand why we behave in particular ways.

Trait view – the explanation that suggests our behaviour is based on personality traits.

Situational view – the explanation that suggests behaviour is shaped by our social environment.

Interactional view – the explanation that suggests behaviour is shaped by a combination of traits and the social environment.

Trigger – something that starts off a particular behaviour.

Introduction

The methods of studying and understanding personality in sport are known as the different **views of personality**. Three of the main views of personality are the **trait view**, the **situational view** and the **interactional view**.

Trait view

The trait view of personality suggests that our traits are relatively stable and consistent across a variety of different situations. This view suggests that the way we behave is based on our personality traits alone, ignoring effects that our social environment may have on us.

Not accepting the role of our social environment is a problem with this theory. For example, a boxer will get very aggressive in an important fight, but perhaps not in other settings. This suggests that the environment in which we find ourselves may influence the way that we behave.

How does Usain Bolt's personality differ on and off the track?

Situational view

The situational view of personality suggests that our behaviour is determined mainly by the environment in which we find ourselves and helps us to understand how a particular situation may **trigger** different behaviours.

This view explains behaviour using observational learning (seeing a behaviour such as a hard tackle in football) and reinforcement (seeing a significant other such as a coach or parent cheer on that hard tackle, even if it was a foul) to explain the influence of a situation.

A problem with this view is that different people will not react to the same situation in the same way, so their personality traits must have played a role in making them react differently.

Interactional view

The interactional view considers both your traits and the situation that you find yourself in when trying to explain behaviour.

A person with high levels of anger may not always display these in calm situations (for example, if their favourite rugby team is winning in an important game). However, if that same person's rugby team starts losing and an opposing fan starts to make offensive comments, then they could become angry and aggressive quite quickly.

What different views might there be on why a football player chooses to foul another player?

| **Assessment activity 3.1** | *Maths* | 2A.P1 | 2A.M1 | 2A.D1 |

You have applied for a work placement as an assistant to a sports psychologist who is working with a sports club. As part of the application process, you need to prepare a presentation to demonstrate your understanding of personality and how it can affect sports performance. You should use examples to support the points you are making.

Tips

- Make sure that you include a clear definition of personality and the different personality types.
- Remember to give information about the methods of measuring personality and a description of the views of personality.
- Explain how the different views of personality describe behaviour in sporting environments?
- Analyse the three different views of personality. Which view best explains behaviour in sporting environments? You will need to give your reasons.

Influence of motivation on sports performance

Getting started

Why do you think that some people seem more motivated than others at different times? What do you think are the different factors that can influence motivation?

Introduction

Have you ever been frustrated by teammates who don't seem to be trying as hard as you? Their poor effort could be due to a lack of motivation. Understanding motivation can often be the key factor in being able to work well with clients as a sports coach or fitness instructor – it is an important part of getting the best out of people.

Key terms

Motivation – the internal mechanisms and external stimuli that arouse and direct behaviour.

Intrinsic motivation – internal factors that influence motivation, such as enjoyment.

Extrinsic motivation – external factors that influence motivation, such as trophies.

 Definition of motivation

Motivation is the term we use to describe the internal mechanisms and external stimuli that arouse and direct our behaviour. This definition suggests that motivation is dependent on two sets of factors:

- factors from within us that influence our motivation.
- factors from outside of us, such as external pressures or rewards, that influence our motivation.

Our motivation will influence how hard we work towards a set task.

 Types of motivation

There are two key types of motivation:

Intrinsic motivation

Intrinsic motivation comes from within you and has three key features:

- it comes from fun and enjoyment of the task itself
- it comes from personal satisfaction
- there is no external reward or pressure.

Extrinsic motivation

Extrinsic motivation comes from external sources and has the following features:

- it can come from rewards such as money, grades or trophies
- it can come from the threat of punishment
- it can come from the desire to win and beat others.

Discussion point

Can you think of different internal and external factors that could influence your motivation?

Activity 3.2   Understanding motivation

1 Working in a small group, discuss all of the reasons that you take part in your favourite sport or exercise activity.

2 Produce a spider diagram of all of the reasons that you come up with and say whether you think you are more extrinsically or intrinsically motivated.

Views of motivation

As with personality, there are different views of motivation that help us understand it. These views are the **trait-centred view**, the **situation-centred view** and the **interactional view**.

Trait-centred view

The trait-centred view suggests that motivation is created by our personality traits, our needs and our goals. When a coach refers to an athlete as a 'born winner', they are supporting the trait-centred view of motivation. A problem with this view is that it does not take into account the situational factors that can influence motivation.

Situation-centred view

The situation-centred view suggests that it is the situation that you are in and not your personality traits that will determine your motivation. A problem with this view is that it doesn't accept that your personality plays a role in shaping motivation, so this view struggles to explain how you stay motivated in situations that you don't like. For example, you may have played your favourite sport for a coach that you didn't like because you were determined not to give up.

Interactional view

The interactional view combines both the trait- and the situation-centred views to say that it is your personality and the situation that you find yourself in that will determine your motivation levels (see Figure 3.4). This view says that we have to think about how these two groups of factors interact if we are to best understand motivation.

Remember

A person who plays a sport purely for fun is intrinsically motivated whereas a person who plays a sport solely for money and trophies is extrinsically motivated.

Key terms

Trait-centred view – the view that motivation is determined by our personality, needs and goals.

Situation-centred view – the view that motivation is determined by the situation we find ourselves in.

Interactional view – the view that to understand motivation we must think about the interaction of personality and the situation.

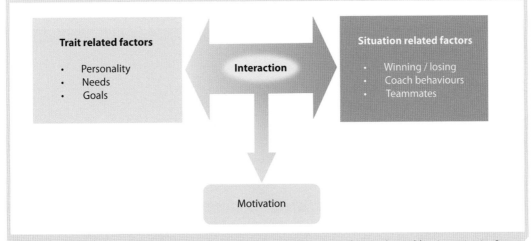

Figure 3.4 How does the interactional view of motivation help us to understand an athlete's motivation?

CONTINUED ▶▶

▶▶ CONTINUED

Key terms

Achievement motivation – an individual's efforts to master a task, achieve excellence, overcome obstacles and perform better than others.

Motive to achieve – the part of achievement motivation that means that you will eagerly accept challenges and strive for success.

Motive to avoid failure – the part of achievement motivation that means you will worry about failing and avoid taking on challenges that may result in failure.

Discussion point

Why do you think understanding achievement motivation is important for sports coaches, teachers and fitness instructors?

Achievement motivation

Think about two football players. It is the last penalty in the UEFA Champions League final, the score is 4–4 and the opposition have just missed their last penalty. Which of the two players would take the penalty? The answer comes partly from a third type of motivation, known as **achievement motivation**.

Achievement motivation has two main components: the **motive to achieve** and the **motive to avoid failure**. In the penalty shoot-out example, the player who decides to take the penalty is determined to score and so has a high motive to achieve; whereas the player who thinks they will miss and decides against taking the penalty has a high motive to avoid failure.

Benefits of motivation on sports performance

So far you have learned about motivation, the different types of motivation and different views of where motivation comes from. Another important part of understanding motivation is knowing how it benefits sports performance. There are four key benefits of motivation on sports performance: choice of activity, effort to pursue goals, intensity of effort and persistence in adversity.

Choice of activity

Your motivation can determine who you choose to play against. For example, will you choose to play against people as good as you because they provide more of a challenge or will you prefer to play against people that you know you can beat because there is no risk of failure?

What types of motivation do you think are at work when an athlete makes an all-out effort for the line?

Effort to pursue goals

Motivation can increase your effort to pursue goals. This means that you are more likely to spend more time practising so that you can achieve your goals and become a better sports performer.

Intensity of effort

Your motivation can also affect the **intensity** of your effort. A more motivated person may train longer and harder in order to try to achieve a goal. If you are prepared to put more effort into practice, you are more likely to become a better athlete.

Persistence in adversity

When faced with **adversity**, people who have higher levels of motivation are more likely to keep trying so that they can experience success. For example, a basketball player with high levels of motivation is more likely to keep trying to play well even if their team is losing badly.

Discussion point

Do you think it is possible to have too much motivation? How could this be a problem for athletes?

Key terms

Intensity – how hard you are working.

Adversity – an unfavourable or negative experience that can happen during sport.

Why do you think that intensity of effort and persistence in the face of adversity are important to achieve goals?

Just checking

1 What is motivation?
2 What is intrinsic motivation?
3 What is extrinsic motivation?

Influence of goal setting on motivation and sports performance

Getting started

What do you think might be a problem with setting goals that are just general statements of intent? Do you think that they would have any positive influence on motivation?

Introduction

Have you ever set yourself the target of 'doing well' but then wondered what that actually means? Or have you ever had a target set for you and not known how you should try to achieve it? These problems are quite common and it is important to set effective goals so that you can get the greatest benefit from them. Understanding appropriate goal setting is important in lots of jobs, including sports coaching and fitness instructing.

Key terms

Goal – something that you want to achieve.

Barrier – something that could potentially stop you from achieving your goal if you do not work around it.

Link

This topic links to *Unit 5: Training for Personal Fitness* and *Unit 13: Profiling Sports Performance, Topic A.1, A.2* and *A.3* for more information on psychological profiles

Principles of goal setting to increase and direct motivation

To set effective **goals**, you should remember the acronym 'SMARTER'. This stands for:

- **S**pecific – the goal must be clearly related to something you want to achieve, so rather than just saying, 'I want to get fit', you should say, 'I want to improve my speed.'
- **M**easurable – your goal must be produced so that you can monitor your progress towards it. For example, you could expand the specific statement by saying, 'I want to improve my speed by 0.3 seconds over 30m.'
- **A**chievable – it must be possible for you to achieve the goal.
- **R**ealistic – this links in with 'achievable', and takes into account any **barriers** that may prevent you from achieving your goal. For example, if you were injured, this would be a barrier to you achieving the speed-related goal mentioned before.
- **T**ime-related – there should be a timescale in which you will achieve your goal. For example, you could expand the goal by saying, 'I want to improve my speed by 0.3 seconds within 3 months of starting my training programme.' This provides you with a way to measure the goal.
- **E**xciting – the goal that you set should be challenging enough to motivate you to want to achieve it. So, for example, a sprinter who was told that they would be selected for a national squad if they could improve their sprint time by 0.3 seconds would be more likely to work towards the goal.
- **R**ecorded – have you ever heard the saying 'out of sight, out of mind'? The goal should be recorded in an appropriate way for the athlete and be kept somewhere visible. Progress towards the goal should also be recorded and placed on view.

Almost all athletes use formal goal setting as part of their training to improve performance.

Why do you think effective goal setting would be important for somebody like Wayne Rooney?

Remember

There is a relationship between motivation and sports performance. In order to perform well, athletes need to be motivated. As athletes improve their performance, they become more motivated to carry on improving.

Activity 3.3   Setting goals for yourself

For the sport that you play, set yourself three goals. Make sure that you apply the SMARTER principle so that your goals are effective.

CONTINUED ▶▶

▸▸ CONTINUED

Key terms

Outcome goals – these focus on the outcome of an event, such as winning a race.

Performance goals – these focus on the athlete developing their own performance, and allow the athlete to make comparisons with their own performance.

Process goals – these focus on what needs to be done to improve performance.

Goals

There are three main types of goals set in sport: **outcome goals**, **performance goals** and **process goals**.

Outcome goals

Outcome goals can benefit motivation when you are away from competition in the short term but can also decrease motivation in the long term if too much emphasis is placed on the outcome of an event.

Achieving this type of goal is partly dependent on your opponents. For example, if you are a 200m runner who has just started competing, you may run a personal best time every race, but are likely to lose if you are competing against more experienced runners. If your coach only focuses on the outcome of an event, you may get fed up because your personal improvement isn't being recognised.

How would you feel if you'd run your best time ever but came last against your opponents?

Performance goals

To attain performance goals, you compare yourself to your previous performances. These type of goals are normally more flexible than outcome goals. An example would be you saying that you wanted to improve your 200m personal best time by 0.5 seconds.

Process goals

Taking the 200m performance goal example, a coach may identify that the reason the personal best time is a little slower than expected is because the sprinter has got a slow push-off from the starting blocks. Therefore, the process goal might be to increase the speed and strength of push-off.

Influence of goal setting on sports performance

There are lots of different ways that goal setting can benefit sports performance. The four main ways are:

- **Directing attention to certain aspects of performance**: for example, a basketball player may set a goal to make sure they release the ball at the peak of a jump shot.
- **Mobilising effort**: for example, if a rugby player has put on weight during a period of injury, they may set a goal of losing 4kg prior to returning to competition. Once the goal is set, the player is likely to start to work towards achieving it.
- **Prolonging persistence**: for example, if the same rugby player is struggling with their weight loss programme because it sounds quite difficult, you can help to prolong their persistence by making the goal appear more manageable. The goal might be losing 0.5kg per week over 8 weeks rather than losing 4kg in one go.
- **Developing new strategies**: for example, the free-kick taker in football may find that they have increased their shooting accuracy, but to improve further (score more goals), they learn how to direct different types of free kick to different parts of the goal.

What types of goals might a participant in your sport set themselves?

Influence of goal setting on motivation

There is a relationship between improved performance and improved motivation. When a goal is set, the athlete's behaviour will be focused on achieving that goal. By monitoring and adjusting the goals, the athlete is likely to maintain focus on the task in hand, which can result in an increased performance. When an athlete improves their performance, they are likely to become more motivated as they wish to carry on improving.

Activity 3.4   Setting goals for yourself

Looking at the goals you developed for Activity 3.3, make sure that they focus on a combination of outcome, performance and process goals.

Remember

The most effective way to use outcome, performance and process goals is to use a combination of them at the right times. For example, you may set a target of trying to win a 200m race (outcome goal) by improving your personal best time by 0.5 seconds (performance goal). To do this, you would need to improve the speed and strength at push-off from the blocks (process goal).

Self-confidence and self-efficacy

 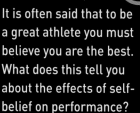
Introduction

Have you ever heard athletes talk about having a strong belief in their capabilities, or believing in their teammates? Or how about walking into a competition, like a race or a game, taking one look at the opponents and thinking 'I've lost already'? These are factors that can be explained by understanding self-confidence and self-efficacy.

Definition of self-confidence

Self-confidence is the belief that a desired behaviour can be performed. It is one of the most important factors that separates highly successful athletes from less successful ones. The desired behaviour could be anything from taking a free throw in basketball to potting the black in snooker – the key part is your belief that you can do it.

Benefits of self-confidence

Athletes think self-confidence is important because it has lots of different benefits for performance. The main benefits are that it can produce positive emotions, improve performance, concentration and effort, and help you develop positive game plans.

Producing positive emotions

When you are more self-confident, you are more likely to remain calm and relaxed. You are also more likely to view symptoms of anxiety in a positive way and see them as beneficial for performance (see Topic C.3).

Improving concentration and effort

Self-confidence increases concentration because you are able to focus on the task in hand, rather than worrying about the negative parts of your performance. Also, when people believe that they are able to do something, they are likely to put more effort into achieving that goal.

Development of positive game plans

Athletes with high levels of self-confidence are likely to compete with the 'play to win' mentality.

Self-confidence often helps to focus sports performers before a competitive situation.

They are happy to make positive contributions and take responsibility, for example taking an important penalty in football. Athletes who have less self-confidence tend not to adopt this approach because they are worried about making mistakes.

Improving performance

There is a positive relationship between self-confidence and performance, but it is not completely clear why. Factors such as positive emotions, improved concentration and effort, and producing positive game plans have all been linked to explaining how self-confidence can improve performance. Every person has an optimal level of self-confidence but they can also sometimes become over-confident or lacking in confidence, both of which can negatively affect performance.

Methods to increase self-confidence

An important skill for people working with athletes is to help them build self-confidence. Two ways that this can be done are through **self-talk** and **imagery**.

Self-talk

Self-talk is a method of improving self-confidence. It works by athletes talking to themselves in a positive way, telling themselves that they will be successful. Positive statements like 'keep calm, keep focused and I can beat them' can help improve self-confidence as they help to remove negative thoughts. Simple positive statements that focus on an athlete's strengths tend to be most effective. You could try using the following types of statements:

- **emotional**: positive statements that can produce excitement
- **technical**: positive statements that focus on successfully performing a skill
- **memory**: positive statements that remind you of when you have done something successfully in the past.

Imagery

Imagery can help to improve self-confidence by providing you with an opportunity to picture yourself doing things that you have not previously been able to do or find difficult to do. It can also help you re-create a time when you have been successful and confident, and remind you of the fact that you are able to perform a particular task. For example, if you are a centre in netball and have suffered a badly injured ankle, as part of your injury rehabilitation you could picture yourself successfully pivoting on your injured ankle to increase your self-confidence in your ability to move, twist and change direction quickly.

Activity 3.5	Inspirational quotes

1 Research different inspirational quotes from famous athletes such as Michael Jordan, Bradley Wiggins and Tiger Woods.

2 Make a poster that shows a variety of quotations and explain what these athletes thought about the importance of self-confidence based on what they said in their quotation.

Key terms

Self-talk – a technique used to improve self-confidence by telling yourself that you will be successful.

Imagery – a technique used to enhance self-confidence by picturing yourself being successful.

Discussion point

Using the descriptions of the different types of self-talk statements, try to produce one example of each type of statement that you could use in competition and/or training.

CONTINUED ▶▶

Definition of self-efficacy

Self-efficacy is self-confidence in a specific situation, and is related to being able to perform a task with a specific goal in mind. For example, self-efficacy not only means stepping up and attempting a penalty in football, but also firmly believing that you will score.

Factors affecting self-efficacy

There are four key factors that can affect your self-efficacy, and ultimately your performance: **performance accomplishments**, **vicarious experiences**, **verbal persuasion** and **imaginal experiences**.

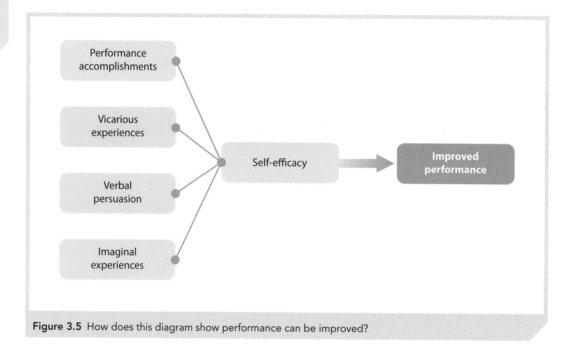

Figure 3.5 How does this diagram show performance can be improved?

Performance accomplishments

Performance accomplishments are one of the strongest factors that can affect self-efficacy. If you have a lot of accomplishments, your self-efficacy is likely to improve, but if you have experienced failure regularly, your self-efficacy is likely to be reduced.

Imaginal experiences

Have you ever sat and pictured yourself scoring the perfect goal, running the perfect race or hitting the perfect serve? Picturing this type of performance is known as imaginal experience and has been shown to increase self-efficacy.

Vicarious experiences

Have you ever watched a friend playing sport and thought 'If they can do it, so can I'? Vicarious experiences use modelling and demonstration to enhance self-efficacy. Seeing someone else perform well (particularly somebody of a similar level to you) will help to enhance your own self-efficacy, which can lead to improved performance.

Verbal persuasion

Has a coach or teacher ever said to you, 'I know you can do this, so just keep going'? This is a technique known as verbal persuasion and is important for developing self-efficacy. By knowing that other people have confidence in your ability to do something and be successful at it, you are more likely to start believing it yourself.

Discussion point

In groups, discuss the factors affecting self-efficacy that you have come across in your experience. Which did you find most useful for increasing your self-confidence and motivation?

The best coaches are able to use verbal persuasion to inspire and motivate those they are coaching.

Assessment activity 3.2   2B.P2 | 2B.P3 | 2B.P4 | 2B.P5 | 2B.M2 | 2B.M3 | 2B.D2

You have successfully made it through the first stage of the application process for a work placement as an assistant to a sports psychologist who is working with a sports club. You have now been asked to produce an information leaflet about motivation and self-confidence for young athletes as part of the second stage. This should include the following information:

- the types and views of motivation
- the benefits that motivation and self-confidence have in relation to sports performance
- factors that influence self-efficacy in sport
- the different types of goals that sports performers can set for themselves, and how these can influence performance and motivation.

Tips

- You will need to include sport-based examples to demonstrate your points.
- Make sure that you include all of the self-confidence and motivational factors that can enhance sports performance and say how they can improve performance.
- Consider how goal setting and outcome, performance and process goals can be used both together and separately to enhance motivation.
- Draw all of these points together by looking at the benefits motivation and self-confidence have on sports performance.

Know about the effects of anxiety and arousal on sports performance

 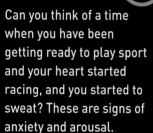
Introduction

Understanding anxiety and arousal, their relationship with sports performance and the different ways they can be controlled is essential to the work of sports coaches and sports psychologists when trying to improve an athlete's performance.

Definition of anxiety

Anxiety is the level of worry or nervousness an individual experiences.

Types of anxiety

There are four main types of anxiety:

State anxiety

State anxiety is a constantly changing mood state. It is the anxiety that happens when you find yourself in different situations. This type of anxiety is temporary and involves feelings of tension and apprehension due to the nervous system becoming activated.

Trait anxiety

Trait anxiety is a personality characteristic. It involves stable, consistent feelings of tension and apprehension across many different situations due to the nervous system being continually activated.

What types of anxiety might runners in the starting blocks experience?

Somatic anxiety

Somatic anxiety relates to the physical effects of anxiety. Some examples of this type of anxiety are butterflies in the stomach, increased muscle tension, increased heart rate and increased breathing rate.

Cognitive anxiety

Cognitive anxiety refers to the mental effects of anxiety. Examples of this type of anxiety are an increased feeling of worry, being unable to concentrate and being quick-tempered.

How arousal and anxiety affect sports performance

Drive theory

The drive theory says that as your arousal levels go up, so will your performance levels. A problem with this theory is that there are lots of athletes who report playing badly when they felt too anxious or over-aroused.

Inverted-U hypothesis

The inverted-U hypothesis tells us that arousal will benefit performance up to an optimal point, but before or after that point, performance will be lower. Most people can relate to this theory, but a problem is that it assumes everybody has the same optimal point of arousal and that everybody's performance will gradually get worse after this optimal point. This is a problem because different people have different optimal levels of arousal and sometimes performance won't decrease steadily – it will get worse really quickly.

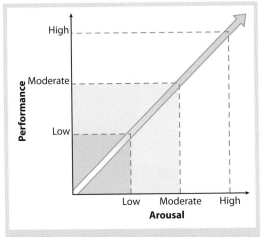

Figure 3.6 How does the drive theory explain the relationship between arousal and performance?

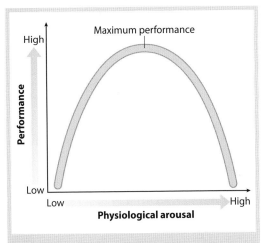

Figure 3.7 How does the inverted-U theory explain the relationship between arousal and performance?

Catastrophe theory

The catastrophe theory is a more recent development of the inverted-U hypothesis that says performance won't necessarily decrease steadily after the optimal point of arousal and that any further increases in arousal will lead to a dramatic decline in performance. This theory tells us that this dramatic decline in performance will occur if high arousal levels are accompanied by high levels of cognitive anxiety.

Reversal theory

The reversal theory says that it is the individual's interpretation of arousal that can influence performance. If an athlete interprets their arousal as pleasant excitement rather than unpleasant anxiety, they are more likely to perform well.

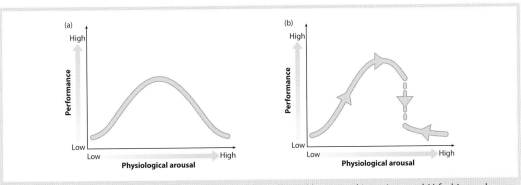

Figure 3.8 Catastrophe theory says that performance is affected by arousal in an inverted-U fashion only when an individual has low levels of anxiety.

▶▶ CONTINUED

Why do you think creating images in your mind, such as this one, helps people to relax?

How anxiety and arousal can be controlled

There are two main ways that arousal and anxiety can be controlled: through imagery and through relaxation techniques.

Imagery

Imagery can be used to increase and decrease arousal levels. You can decrease arousal levels by imagining a relaxing experience (such as walking on a beach) or rehearsing a successful performance (such as scoring a basket).

Relaxation techniques

Relaxation techniques such as progressive muscular relaxation (PMR) and breathing techniques can be used to control arousal levels. PMR can reduce arousal levels by enabling you to detect levels of tension in your muscles and then relax those muscles. Breathing control helps to reduce muscle tension, which benefits performance by improving coordination and skill execution.

What techniques might Jonny Wilkinson use to control his anxiety before a penalty kick?

Assessment activity 3.3 *English* | 2C.P6 | 2C.P7 | 2C.M4 | 2C.D3

You have been asked to prepare a presentation for a group of young athletes to educate them on anxiety, the effects of arousal and the different ways of controlling anxiety. As part of your presentation, you need to include information about:

- different types of anxiety, using relevant examples of each
- the effects of arousal and anxiety on sports performance, using four theories
- imagery and relaxation techniques as methods of controlling arousal and anxiety, and improving sports performance.

Tips

- Give your views on which theories you believe accurately explain the relationship between arousal, anxiety and performance, which you think don't, and why.
- Consider each of the different methods to control arousal – which techniques would be most effective at controlling arousal, and why?

WorkSpace

Samantha

19-year-old football coach

I really like my job. I get to coach football to all different age ranges and abilities, all of which present different challenges.

One of the biggest issues that I face is trying to get people to train outside when it is cold and wet. Trying to get them to concentrate on different areas for improvement is difficult when they just want to keep moving all the time if the weather is bad!

Another issue that I often come across is when players start to worry about the opposition, thinking that they might not be able to beat them because they might have lost to the same opposition before. It is really difficult for me as the coach if players go into a game already having lost in their minds.

One of the biggest benefits of understanding the mind and sports performance is knowing about different ways to motivate my players and different ways of helping them to cope with their performance-related worries.

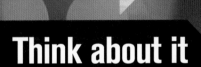

Think about it

1 Why do you think it is important for sports coaches to have an understanding of the mind and sports performance?

2 How would the information on motivation benefit Samantha in her coaching role?

3 How would the information on arousal, anxiety and performance benefit Samantha in her coaching role?

4 Is this a job that you would be interested in, and if so, why?

Introduction

Have you ever thought about what happens to your body when you exercise? How does your body get to a point where it can run faster or longer or lift heavier weights?

As soon as you start to take part in any form of activity, such as walking to the shops, playing football or lifting weights, your body starts to respond so that you can perform that activity well. These responses will vary based on the activity and it is important that anybody advising individuals about the types of activities they are doing should be aware of these different responses. After taking part in regular activity, these responses will become long-term adaptations, and your body will change permanently if regular activity is maintained – for example, your muscles may get bigger or your heart stronger.

This unit will help you to understand how these different responses and adaptations occur in the body and prepare you for careers including fitness instructing and sports coaching.

Assessment: You will be assessed by a series of assignments set by your teacher/tutor.

Learning aims

In this unit you will:

A know about the short-term responses and long-term adaptations of the body systems to exercise

B know about the different energy systems used during sports performance.

When I went on work placement to a gym, this unit was really helpful because I could inform members about the benefits of different exercises. This made me feel more useful and they really appreciated my help.

Jamie, *16-year-old aspiring personal trainer*

The Sports Performer in Action

BTEC
Assessment Zone

This table shows you what you must do in order to achieve a **Pass**, **Merit** or **Distinction** grade, and where you can find activities to help you.

Assessment criteria			
Level 1	**Level 2 Pass**	**Level 2 Merit**	**Level 2 Distinction**
Learning aim A: know about the short-term responses and long-term adaptations of the body systems to exercise			
1A.1 Outline two ways in which the musculoskeletal system responds to short-term exercise	**2A.P1** Describe ways in which the musculoskeletal system responds to short-term exercise **See Assessment activity 4.1, page 121**	**2A.M1** Explain responses of the musculoskeletal system to short-term exercise **See Assessment activity 4.1, page 121**	**2A.D1** Maths Using three different sports activities, compare and contrast how the musculoskeletal and cardiorespiratory systems respond and adapt to exercise **See Assessment activity 4.1, page 121**
1A.2 Maths Outline ways in which the cardiorespiratory system responds to short-term exercise	**2A.P2** Maths Describe ways in which the cardiorespiratory system responds to short-term exercise **See Assessment activity 4.1, page 121**	**2A.M2** Maths Explain responses of the cardiorespiratory system to short-term exercise **See Assessment activity 4.1, page 121**	
1A.3 Summarise two long-term adaptations of the musculoskeletal system resulting from exercise	**2A.P3** Summarise, using relevant examples, long-term adaptations of the musculoskeletal system to exercise **See Assessment activity 4.1, page 121**	**2A.M3** Explain long-term adaptations of the musculoskeletal system to exercise **See Assessment activity 4.1, page 121**	
1A.4 Maths Summarise two long-term adaptations of the cardiorespiratory system resulting from exercise	**2A.P4** Maths Summarise, using relevant examples, long-term adaptations of the cardiorespiratory system to exercise **See Assessment activity 4.1, page 121**	**2A.M4** Maths Explain long-term adaptations of the cardiorespiratory system to exercise **See Assessment activity 4.1, page 121**	
Learning aim B: know about the different energy systems used during sports performance			
1B.5 Describe the two main energy systems, including examples of sports that use each system	**2B.P5** Describe the function of the three energy systems in the production and release of energy for sports performance **See Assessment activity 4.2, page 125**	**2B.M5** Using two selected sports, explain how the body uses both the anaerobic and aerobic energy systems **See Assessment activity 4.2, page 125**	**2B.D2** Compare and contrast how the energy systems are used in sports with different demands **See Assessment activity 4.2, page 125**

Maths Opportunity to practise mathematical skills

How you will be assessed

This unit will be assessed through a series of assignments set by your teacher/tutor. You will be expected to show an understanding of short-term responses and long-term adaptations of the body systems to exercise, and the different energy systems that are used during sports performance. The tasks will be based on scenarios involving work or activity in a sports setting. For example, you might be asked to imagine you are working in a leisure centre as an assistant fitness instructor and have been asked to produce posters to make customers more aware of the different benefits of exercise.

Your assessment could be in the form of:

- informative materials such as posters or leaflets
- presentations
- practical investigations.

Short-term effects of exercise on the musculoskeletal system

Getting started

Think about the last time you played your sport. What happened to your muscles while you were playing, straight after playing and then over the next couple of days?

Key terms

Musculoskeletal system – a combination of the muscular and skeletal systems.

Synovial fluid – a fluid that lubricates and nourishes a joint.

Cartilage – a tissue that protects the ends of bones.

Pliable – a muscle being able to stretch and change shape more easily without breaking.

Micro-tears – tiny tears in muscles that are necessary 'damage' for a muscle to get bigger and stronger.

Remember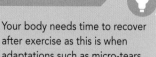

Your body needs time to recover after exercise as this is when adaptations such as micro-tears in muscles being repaired take place. If you didn't rest, your micro-tears would not repair and may get bigger, which would eventually result in injury.

Introduction

The **musculoskeletal system** is made up of your muscular system and your skeletal system. We use this term when describing how our muscles and bones work together when we are active. In this topic, you will learn about how the musculoskeletal system responds to exercise, including learning about **synovial fluid** production, increased range of movement, how muscles get bigger, how new bone is formed and increased metabolic activity.

Increased production of synovial fluid

Before we take part in exercise, we should always warm up. This prepares our body for exercise and means we are less likely to get injured. This is partly because as we mobilise our joints as part of a warm-up, more synovial fluid is released into the joint. As we exercise more, the synovial fluid warms and becomes thinner, easing joint movement.

Synovial joints also contain a layer of **cartilage** surrounding the bones which helps to protect the joint. Cartilage does not have a good blood supply, so cannot be nourished by the blood. When you exercise, your joint cartilage absorbs nourishment from the synovial fluid, helping provide the joint with extra protection.

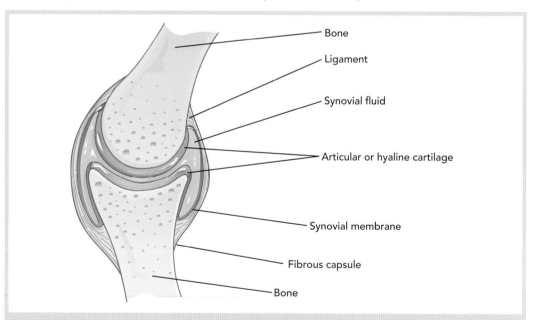

Figure 4.1 As we warm up, more synovial fluid is released into the joint to ease movement.

Increased range of movement in the joints

During exercise, our blood flow and muscle temperature start to increase. Our muscles get warmer because blood is being pumped to them at a faster rate. As the muscles warm, they become more **pliable**. This, combined with the increased level of synovial fluid in the joints means an increased range of movement.

Micro-tears in muscle fibres

When you take part in resistance exercise, such as free weight training in a gym, this type of activity is designed to cause **micro-tears**, which are necessary breaks in the muscle that stimulate your body to rebuild the muscle bigger and stronger.

New bone formation

New bone is formed after it has been placed under stress. After a load, such as the additional weight experienced during a squat exercise, has been applied to the bone, bone cells travel to the stressed area and start to lay down new bone. The bone cells then produce and release proteins, mainly **collagen**, which is dropped in between the bone cells to increase bone strength in that area. Generally, people who take part in high-impact activity will form more new bone and it will be thicker and stronger.

Weight-bearing activities encourage the formation of new, stronger bone, which helps to decrease the risk of osteoporosis.

Key terms

Collagen – a protein that is important for bone formation.

Osteoporosis – a condition where you have brittle bones.

Metabolic activity – the body's way of releasing energy so that it can be used for exercise.

Enzymes – the catalyst for chemical reactions that release energy for exercise.

Take it further

Using the internet, research a disease called **osteoporosis**. How do you think that exercise can benefit osteoporosis sufferers?

Increased metabolic activity

Have you ever noticed that when you have trained for a long time you start to get hungrier? This is because exercise requires energy and your body needs to meet that energy demand, through **metabolic activity**. In order to maintain exercise, our body starts to produce and use more energy by using **enzymes** to start off chemical reactions that turn the food and drink that we consume into a useable form of energy. As well as providing energy, this process also produces a lot of heat, which can be useful when we exercise in cold conditions.

Short-term effects of exercise on the cardiorespiratory system

Introduction

The **cardiorespiratory system** is made up of the cardiovascular system and the respiratory system. You will often use this term when explaining how the body transports blood, provides oxygen to working muscles and removes waste products. Throughout this section, you will learn about important factors such as increased **heart rate**, increased breathing rate, how blood flow changes during exercise and how our body deals with increased build-up of carbon dioxide.

Increased heart rate and blood flow

Before you start to exercise, your body experiences an **anticipatory rise**. This is because your body knows that you are about to start exercising and releases **adrenaline**, which increases heart rate to prepare you for exercise. As you start to exercise, your body releases more adrenaline to increase your heart rate further.

The blood is used to transport oxygen and nutrients, and remove waste products. Your increased heart rate is an important short-term response because the heart has to work harder during exercise to be able to supply enough blood to meet the demands of the exercise. Your body needs to be supplied with more nutrients and oxygen, as well as having waste products removed during exercise.

During exercise your heart and breathing rates increase so that more oxygen can be supplied to the muscles.

Activity 4.1   Effects of exercise on heart rate

1 Find a pulse point on your wrist; or if you have one, put on a heart rate monitor.

2 Sit in a relaxed state for 5 minutes and record your resting heart rate.

3 You are now going to take part in a stepping activity for 3 minutes. Before you begin, think about that activity for 1 minute. It may help if you are looking at the piece of equipment that you will be stepping on. Record your heart rate at the end of the minute.

4 Now complete your stepping activity at a fast, but not unsafe, pace. Record your heart rate after every minute of exercise.

5 Draw a graph of your heart rate from resting through to the final minute of exercise. What has happened to your heart rate at each stage and why?

Increased breathing rate

As well as increasing heart rate, your body also increases its breathing rate during exercise. This is so that more oxygen can be supplied to the working muscles and carbon dioxide can be removed.

Sweat production and skin reddening

Body temperature increases during exercise because of increased heat caused by metabolic activity (see Topic A.1) and other exercise-related factors, so your body needs to cool down.

As your body temperature rises during exercise, your sweat production increases. When sweat reaches the surface of your skin, it changes from a liquid to vapour and results in heat loss, which cools the body down. This process is known as **evaporation**.

Your skin goes red during exercise because the blood vessels in the skin dilate (known as **vasolidation**) allowing heat to escape from the blood to the skin's surface to cool the body down.

Redistribution of blood flow

During exercise, the body reduces the amount of blood to places where it is not required and sends it to other places that need more blood (see Table 4.1). This process happens when the arterioles that supply the less-active parts of the body, such as the liver and kidneys, narrow (a process known as **vasoconstriction**), while the arterioles that supply more active parts of your body, such as your muscles, vasodilate.

Table 4.1 Percentage blood flow in different areas of the body

Area of the body	Percentage blood flow at rest (approximate)	Percentage blood flow during exercise (approximate)
Skeletal muscles	15–20	80–88
Coronary vessels	5	4
Skin	10	2.5
Liver, kidneys, stomach, intestines	45–55	2.5
Brain	10–15	2.5–5

CONTINUED ▶▶

Lactic acid in the blood

Think about when you have been training or competing really hard, such as doing a heavy weights session or running a 400m sprint really fast. Remember that burning sensation in your arms or legs? That is caused by a build-up of **lactic acid**.

Lactic acid forms in your blood during **anaerobic exercise**. When you are low on oxygen or performing intense exercise and can't produce energy using oxygen, your body uses carbohydrates as a fuel source.

As carbohydrates are broken down into energy, lactic acid is produced in the muscles as a protective mechanism, causing your body to reduce your performance, by slowing you down when you are running, for instance. This allows you to recover and rebuild your oxygen stores.

After exercise, you should cool down so that excess lactic acid is removed. A cool down helps with this because it keeps blood vessels dilated, which means that lactic acid can be removed quickly. Having a sports massage after exercise can also help to remove lactic acid.

Cardiac output

An important short-term response to exercise is an increase in **cardiac output**.

Cardiac output is the amount of blood pumped per minute by the heart, and is important because it helps the body cope with the increased demands of exercise by transporting more oxygen and nutrients to the working muscles.

Cardiac output is the product of your heart rate and your **stroke volume**.

During exercise, there can be an increase of up to eight times resting cardiac output.

Your cardiac output can change depending on the types and levels of activity, gender and age.

Why do you think people might experience a high lactic acid build-up during intense work-outs?

Blood pressure

During exercise, your body has to work hard to deliver more oxygen and nutrients such as glucose to help you continue to exercise.

Blood pressure is the product of your cardiac output and the resistance to blood flow within the blood vessel. Therefore during exercise when cardiac output increases, so too does blood pressure.

Blood pressure has two parts; **systolic pressure** (when the heart pumps blood) and **diastolic pressure** (when the heart is relaxing and filling with blood).

Blood pressure is measured in millimetres of mercury (mmHg) and a healthy blood pressure value is 120/80mmHg. The first number relates to systolic pressure and the second number to diastolic pressure.

When taking part in aerobic activities such as marathon running that involve large muscle groups, your systolic blood pressure will increase because of the increased cardiac output, whereas your diastolic blood pressure will remain unchanged.

In contrast, during high-intensity anaerobic exercise such as weightlifting, both systolic and diastolic pressure will increase because your large muscle groups press against your blood vessels. The resistance to the flow of blood is increased, which increases total blood pressure.

Key terms
Blood pressure – the force exerted by blood against the walls of the blood vessels; the product of cardiac output and the resistance to blood flow.
Systolic pressure – pressure that results when the heart contracts.
Diastolic pressure – pressure that results when the heart relaxes and fills with blood.

What are the signs that this bodybuilder's blood pressure has increased?

CONTINUED ▶▶

Key term

Key term

Tidal volume (TV) – the amount of air inhaled and exhaled with each breath.

Discussion point

Why do you think the various cardiorespiratory responses to exercise differ between sports?

Increased tidal volume

Think about what happens to your breathing rate when you start exercising – why do you think it increases as exercise gets harder? It is because we need to increase the amount of air breathed in and out with each breath.

Tidal volume (TV) is the amount of air inhaled and exhaled during normal breathing. At rest, the average TV is about 500ml of air but this volume increases with exercise.

During exercise, there is an increase in muscular activity, which results in an increased amount of carbon dioxide in the muscles. When your body realises the amount of carbon dioxide is getting too high, your brain tells the muscles responsible for breathing to work harder so that you can remove the unwanted carbon dioxide quickly.

Tidal volume is easily measured with a spirometer.

Just checking

1   Why does the majority of blood flow to the muscles during exercise?
2   What is cardiac output and how does it change during exercise?
3   What do the terms 'systolic pressure' and 'diastolic pressure' mean?
4   What is tidal volume and why does it increase during exercise?

WorkSpace

▶ Emma

19-year-old fitness instructor

I work in a fitness centre that allows me to work with a range of clients – from older people and females who suffer from osteoporosis, to office workers who are sitting down all day so have terrible posture. I love the variety this brings me.

I get a different issue every day, which can be challenging at times and it is important that I know my stuff and can think on my feet. I also get to build a relationship with some of my long-term clients, which makes the job really fulfilling. I particularly like it when clients start to notice the benefits of their exercise, so that I can start talking to them about how much further they could progress if they keep going.

A typical day involves holding one-to-one sessions with clients, group-based sessions or sometimes team training sessions. It is really important for me to know not only what I am going to do with my clients during their session, but also to know why I am doing it by understanding the short-term responses and the long-term adaptations that result from exercise.

Think about it

1   How would the information on the short-term effects of exercise benefit Emma in her job role?

2   Why do you think it is important for Emma to know about each of the body systems when she is working with clients?

3   How do you think Emma would be able to tell if the fitness sessions she is doing with her clients are working? What adaptations would she look for?

4   Is this a job that you would be interested in, and if so, why?

Long-term adaptations of the musculoskeletal system

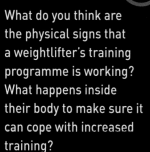

Introduction

When we talk about long-term adaptations to exercise, we mean changes that happen in your body after about 6–8 weeks of training. These happen because your body realises that exercise is harder than normal day-to-day activities, so it needs to make sure that it can cope with the increased demands. In this topic, you will learn about how your muscles, bones and joints change so your body can maintain participation in sport and exercise, as well as some of the general health-related benefits.

Long-term benefits for bones

Exercise has two main benefits for bones: increased **bone density** and a decreased risk of osteoporosis.

Bone density

As a result of long-term training, you will start to get an increase in bone density. This benefits the body because it means our bones get stronger, making it less likely that we will get injured if we fall over or take a bad tackle in football. Our bones get stronger due to increased **calcium** content. Table 4.2 shows some data relating to bone density in different types of athletes. Why do you think that the different groups of athletes have such different bone densities in the four different areas?

Why do you think volleyball players have a high hip bone density?

Discussion point

Look at Table 4.2.

- Why do you think that bone density is much higher in areas that are important for that particular sport?

- Why do you think that athletes who take part in non-weight-bearing sports such as cycling and kayaking have similar bone density levels to non-athletes in their legs, hips and spine?

Key terms

Bone density – the amount of minerals (such as calcium) in your bone, sometimes referred to as bone mineral density.

Calcium – a mineral that is important for maintaining bone health.

Table 4.2 Bone density differences due to playing sport

Sport	Bone density differences when compared to normal populations (percentage increase by body location)			
	Spine	Hip	Arm	Leg
Football	7	20	14	16
Weightlifting	12	6	20	11
Volleyball	12	17	6	12
Skating	5	4	5	5
Swimming	3	3	1	3
Gymnastics	12	24	7	10
Cycling	0	2	1	1
Running	0	10	0	10
Kayaking	0	0	10	0

Decreased risk of osteoporosis

Long-term exercise can reduce the risk of osteoporosis because it increases bone density, making the bones stronger and reducing the risk of fractures. Performing resistance, load-bearing exercise three to five times per week can reduce the risk of osteoporosis.

The University of Arizona has a useful acronym – **LIVE** – for remembering how to use exercise to benefit osteoporosis:

- **L**oad- or weight-bearing exercises make a difference to your bones.
- **I**ntensity builds stronger bones.
- **V**ary the types of exercise and your routine to keep interested.
- **E**njoy your exercises. Make exercise fun so you will continue into the future!

Link

This topic links to *Unit 5: Training for Personal Fitness.*

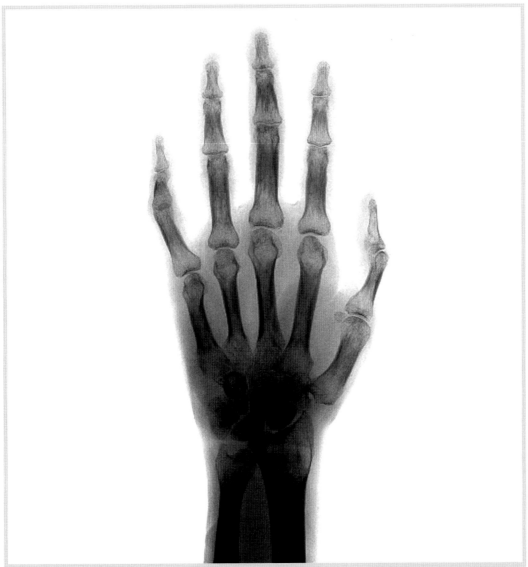

Standard x-rays do not detect osteoporosis until about a quarter of bone mass is already lost.

CONTINUED ▶▶

A triple-jumper will benefit from increased joint protection and stability.

Long-term benefits for joints

These benefits include stronger connective tissues, increased cartilage thickness and increased stability of joints.

Connective tissues

Tendons and ligaments are made up of connective tissue. Exercise increases ligament and tendon strength because it causes them to stretch further than normal. This increases the number of collagen fibres in the connective tissues. This change means that you will be more resistant to injury for two reasons:

- you will have stronger connections between bones due to stronger ligaments
- you will have stronger connections between muscles and bones due to increased tendon strength.

Cartilage

Hyaline cartilage absorbs synovial fluid during exercise. Over time, by absorbing the nutrients from the synovial fluid, your cartilage becomes thicker and is able to protect the joints better.

Increased joint stability

Joint stability is how much your joints can withstand changes in body position without getting injured, and is an important part of all sports. For example, rugby players need to be able to change direction quickly without twisting or dislocating their ankles. Your joints become more stable because of the increased strength of tendons, ligaments and cartilage.

Take it further

Using the internet, research injuries in sports such as football, gymnastics and tennis and find out which types of injuries are most common. How do you think factors such as connective tissues, cartilage and increased joint stability can influence these common injuries?

Some websites that may help include:

- Physio Room
- Gymnastics Rescue

You can access these by going to Pearson Hotlinks (www.pearsonhotlinks.co.uk) and search for this BTEC Sport title.

Key terms

Hypertrophy – an increase in the size of skeletal muscle.

Mitochondria – the part of the muscle that produces energy aerobically.

Remember

Maintaining the correct diet and ensuring you have enough recovery time between training sessions are essential for hypertrophy to happen.

Long-term benefits for muscles

Long-term exercise has a number of benefits for muscles that can help you perform better in a range of sports. These benefits include muscle **hypertrophy**, increased number of **mitochondria**, the ability to use more oxygen, and improved posture.

Hypertrophy

Earlier in the unit, you learned about how exercise can result in micro-tears to the muscle and the body recognising this as a need to change (see Topic A.1). During your recovery periods, your body not only repairs the muscle fibres but also makes them bigger and stronger than before. This process is known as hypertrophy.

Regular endurance training will cause hypertrophy of slow-twitch muscle fibres, which will benefit performance in aerobic activities such as marathon running. Training that is more anaerobic, such as speed training or high-intensity resistance training, will cause hypertrophy of fast-twitch muscle fibres, which will increase performance in sports such as 100m sprint.

Mitochondria

Long-term endurance training can increase the size and number of mitochondria in a muscle. The size of the mitochondria can increase by up to 40%, while the number of mitochondria can increase by up to 100%. As mitochondria are responsible for aerobic energy production, this increase will benefit performance in sports such as marathon running, but will have little effect on sprinters or high jumpers.

Improved posture

Posture is affected over time by things such as slouching or leaning forwards over desks when working. These change the ways your **core muscles** work. The strength of these muscles plays a key role in the support and position of your spine. When these muscles are strengthened by long-term training, they support your spine and provide a more stable centre of gravity. These are essential for all sports techniques and can prevent some injuries.

Key terms

Posture – a position that the body can assume.

Core muscles – muscles, such as abdominals, that are responsible for maintaining good posture.

Did you know?

As a result of long-term training, muscles are more able to use oxygen; the muscles and their capillaries become more efficient and so you can exercise for longer periods of time.

Exercises that work your core muscles include bridges, planks, sit-ups and crunches.

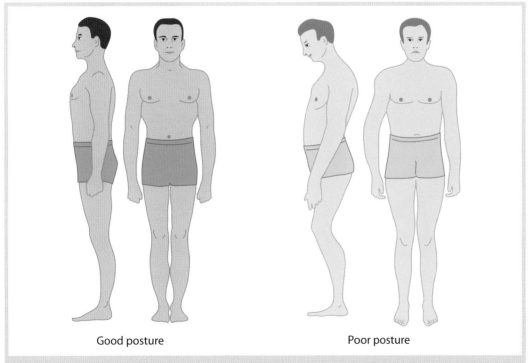

Good posture   Poor posture

Figure 4.2 How do you think exercising the core muscles can help maintain good posture?

Long-term adaptations of the cardiorespiratory system

Getting started

Think about when you have been training. Remember how it used to be quite difficult for you to run long distances, but now it is a lot easier? What has happened inside your body to allow you to improve performance?

Introduction

In this topic, you will learn about how long-term exercise can benefit your cardiorespiratory system. There are lots of benefits that increase health and sports performance, including changes to your heart, a decreased risk of hypertension, an increased vital capacity, increased maximum oxygen uptake and increased lung efficiency and **gaseous exchange**.

Key terms

Gaseous exchange – the exchange of oxygen and carbon dioxide between the lungs and blood.

Cardiac hypertrophy – increasing size and strength of the heart muscle.

Bradycardia – a decreased resting heart rate.

Changes to your heart

As a result of long-term training, your heart increases in size and strength. This increase in size and strength of the muscles in the wall of the heart is known as **cardiac hypertrophy** (see Figure 4.3). Increasing the size and strength of the heart means that more blood can be pumped per beat, which results in an increased resting stroke volume and decreased resting heart rate. When your resting heart rate decreases to 60 beats per minute or less it is known as **bradycardia** and happens because the heart has become more efficient and does not need to beat as quickly for the body to be supplied with blood.

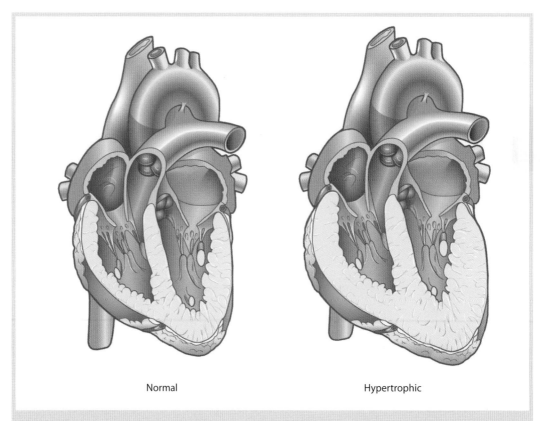

Normal   Hypertrophic

Figure 4.3 Why does cardiac hypertrophy lead to increased stroke volume?

Decreased risk of hypertension

A key health-related benefit of long-term training is a decreased risk of **hypertension**. This occurs partly because of the increased ability of blood vessels to vasoconstrict and vasodilate, but it is also partly because of an increase in **blood plasma** content. The increased ability to vasoconstrict and vasodilate means that blood vessels transport blood more efficiently, and the increased blood plasma volume makes the blood thinner. These two factors together mean that there is less resistance to blood flow, which decreases blood pressure.

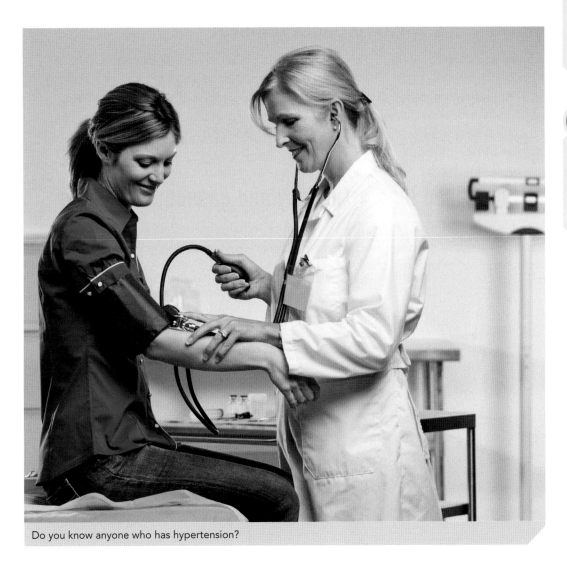

Do you know anyone who has hypertension?

Increased vital capacity

Vital capacity (VC) is the amount of air that you can forcibly expel from the lungs, and it increases as a result of long-term exercise. This increase is mainly due to the muscles that control your breathing becoming stronger, which means that your lungs can inflate and deflate more forcefully. This process helps the cardiovascular system to function more efficiently during sport.

CONTINUED ▶▶

Increased maximal oxygen uptake (VO_2 max)

Your **VO_2 max** is your maximum ability to take in and use oxygen while exercising and increases as a result of long-term training. This is particularly important for sports such as marathon running, long-distance cycling and cross-country skiing. Two key factors that influence your VO_2 max values are the efficiency of delivering oxygen to the working muscles and the efficiency of gaseous exchange.

Increased efficiency of oxygen delivery and waste product removal

A key factor in determining your VO_2 max is the ability to deliver oxygen to the working muscles. Because of increased cardiac output, vasoconstriction, vasodilation and **capillarisation**, blood is more efficiently transported to the working muscles, which means there is more oxygen available for the muscles to use. This improved blood movement also means that it is easier for your body to remove waste products such as carbon dioxide.

Increased lung efficiency and gaseous exchange

Your lungs become more efficient after long-term exercise because activities such as endurance training cause an increase in the amount of alveoli in your lungs and increased capillarisation.

Alveoli and capillaries are key parts of the cardiorespiratory system because they extract oxygen from the air, transfer it to your blood and on to working muscles.

Alveoli and capillaries also remove carbon dioxide from blood and send it back out into the atmosphere. This process of 'swapping' the oxygen in air for the unwanted carbon dioxide in your body is known as gaseous exchange.

Figure 4.4 shows the process of gaseous exchange.

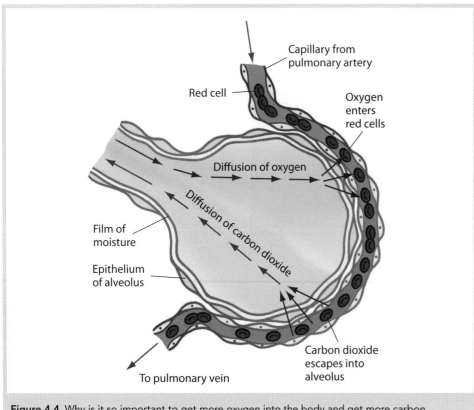

Figure 4.4 Why is it so important to get more oxygen into the body and get more carbon dioxide out?

A long-distance swimmer will benefit from an increased maximal oxygen uptake (VO_2 max).

Assessment activity 4.1   *Maths*   2A.P1 | 2A.P2 | 2A.P3 | 2A.P4 | 2A.M1 | 2A.M2 | 2A.M3 | 2A.M4 | 2A.D1

You have a part-time job at a leisure centre as an assistant fitness instructor. You have been asked to produce some educational materials that will make customers more aware of the different benefits of exercise. Produce posters that can be put up around the centre so the customers can read them at their leisure while using different facilities in the centre.

The posters should give information about responses of the musculoskeletal and cardiorespiratory systems to exercise, including:

- short-term responses
- long-term adaptations
- similarities and differences between the responses of these two systems, using three different sports activities as examples to demonstrate your points.

Tips

- Use results from practical activities to show the different ways these two systems respond.
- You will need to use relevant examples to describe the changes. For example 'In weightlifting, systolic blood pressure increases because …'
- Give information about how the short-term responses and long-term adaptations occur. For example 'Mitochondria increases by … this benefits performance because …'
- When deciding which three sports activities to focus on, consider those which are widely contrasting. This will help you to make these clear comparisons. For example, 'In marathon running … whereas, in sprinting … sprinting is similar to weightlifting because …'

Energy systems used during sports performance

Getting started

Why do you think that a 100m sprinter would struggle to be able to complete a marathon? What do you think might be some of the signs that you are running out of energy?

Key terms

Anaerobic – producing energy without being dependent on oxygen.

Aerobic – using oxygen to produce energy.

Adenosine triphosphate (ATP) – a molecule that is the only useable form of energy in your body.

Creatine phosphate (CP) – a molecule that can quickly be converted to ATP for energy.

Energy system – method of converting nutrients to energy.

Glycolysis – the process of converting glycogen/glucose to ATP for energy.

Glycogen – a form of carbohydrate stored in the liver and muscles.

Introduction

In these topics you will learn about how the body releases energy through **anaerobic** and **aerobic** systems to be able to take part in different types of activities. Understanding these different energy systems can be the key to structuring training programmes correctly or realising why you may get tired easily in different sports.

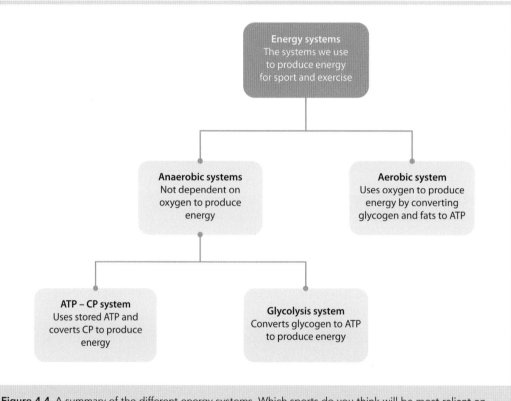

Figure 4.4 A summary of the different energy systems. Which sports do you think will be most reliant on each system?

The anaerobic energy system

This energy system is not dependent upon oxygen to produce energy and is used in sports that are high-intensity and of short duration. It is most commonly used for short bursts of activity lasting only a few seconds, such as sprinting, a shot put or the high jump.

Within the anaerobic energy systems there are two different pathways; the ATP–CP/alactic acid anaerobic system, and the glycolysis/lactic acid anaerobic system.

ATP–CP/alactic acid anaerobic system

This system has a reliance on stored **adenosine triphosphate (ATP)** to produce energy. The body has enough stored ATP to be able to sustain activity for approximately 4 seconds.

When stores of ATP run out, another molecule, **creatine phosphate (CP)**, is used to restore ATP levels. This is used because it can be quickly converted to ATP to provide the energy needed for short-duration, high-intensity exercise. The CP in your body is restored aerobically. There is enough ATP and CP combined in your body to produce energy for up to 20 seconds of activity, but often the stores will have run out after about 10 seconds. Therefore, this system is mainly used in sporting events such the long jump, 100m sprint or weightlifting. When the stores of ATP–CP have run out, the body uses a process of **glycolysis** to produce energy.

The Glycolysis/lactic acid anaerobic system is used in sporting events such as the 400m, 800m and 1500m sprint.

Glycolysis/lactic acid anaerobic energy system

Energy is produced using this system when the ATP–CP system cannot produce energy any more. This system uses glucose stored in the liver and muscles to produce energy. Your body gets this glucose from food and drink that are high in carbohydrates.

In this system, energy is supplied by a combination of stored ATP, CP and muscle **glycogen** from 20–45 seconds. After this time, energy is supplied by muscle glycogen alone for up to 240 seconds of activity, although this system does tend to reach its peak from 60–90 seconds. As energy is produced for this period of time and at a fast rate, sports that use this system mainly include the 400m, 800m or 1500m. Alongside glycolysis, there will be a large lactic acid build-up, which explains the burning sensation you will feel. This build-up stops any more glycogen from being broken down, so you then start to produce energy aerobically.

Discussion point

Can you think of any other sports that this energy system would be important for?

Remember

Think of ATP as the only currency that your body can spend. Whenever you eat or drink anything, your body has to convert those things to ATP before it can use them for energy, just as when you go on holiday to Spain, you have to change your pounds to euros before you can buy anything.

Take it further

Find out why carbohydrates are useful for many athletes. Think about the following two questions:

1 Where can you find the main sources of carbohydrates in your daily diet?
2 Why are sports drinks thought to be better for athletes than water?

CONTINUED ▸▸

The aerobic energy system

The aerobic energy system uses oxygen to keep producing ATP over a long period of time. This is important for providing energy for sustained activity in events such as marathon running, long-distance swimming and long-distance cycling.

As the glycolysis pathway only uses 5% of the available energy from glycogen, the aerobic pathway produces ATP from the other 95%. As well as energy being supplied by glycogen, this system also uses **fatty acids** to produce energy for 240–600 seconds of activity. The aerobic energy system uses oxygen to **re-synthesise** ATP and is the most important energy system for activities that are low to moderate intensity and last longer than 90 seconds.

The three energy systems do not just work on their own; during rest and all activities you will be using all of the energy systems (Figure 4.5 shows this in a graph), even if it is a tiny percentage (say 0.1%) of each. For example, during a marathon run, you would use the energy systems in the following way:

- ATP–CP system used to set off and run for the first couple of seconds up to about 10 seconds
- glycolysis used from approximately 10 seconds to approximately 3 minutes
- aerobic energy system used for the bulk of the race when you are running at a steady pace
- for the sprint finish, you will start producing energy anaerobically again because energy is needed at a faster rate than the aerobic system can manage.

Key terms

Fatty acids – produced from the breakdown of fat. Fatty acids are converted to ATP for energy.

Re-synthesise – to reproduce ATP.

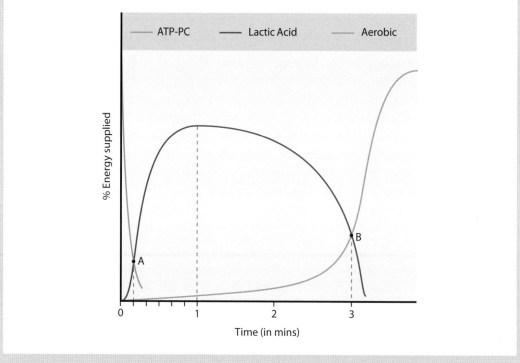

Figure 4.5 How does this graph suggest that the energy systems work together?

The aerobic system is important for providing energy during longer events such as long-distance cycling.

Assessment activity 4.2

2B.P5 | 2B.M5 | 2B.D2

While working at the leisure centre as an assistant fitness instructor, your manager asks you to deliver a presentation to some of the community-based athletes (three young sprinters and three young long-distance swimmers) about the different energy systems that are used during sports performance. Use sprinting and long-distance swimming as your example sports.

Tips

- When describing the different energy systems, you should include factors such as whether they use oxygen to produce energy, the length of time that they work for and how they produce ATP.
- What are the differences between these systems?

Just checking

1 Answer true or false to each of the following statements:
   a The anaerobic energy systems use oxygen to re-synthesise ATP.
   b The aerobic energy system uses oxygen to re-synthesise ATP.
   c We only use one energy system per sport.
   d The ATP–CP system uses creatine phosphate to restore ATP.
   e The glycolysis system uses fatty acids to restore ATP.
   f The aerobic system uses glycogen and CP to restore ATP.
   g The ATP–CP system is used in activities lasting longer than 90 seconds.
   h The glycolysis system peaks at about 20 seconds.
2 For any statements where you answered 'false', amend the statement using the correct answer.

Introduction

Have you ever wanted to start a training programme but didn't know where to begin? How do you train your body to the point where it can run faster, lift heavier weights or run for longer?

When you first start out training, you may find it a little bit daunting, but everybody starts somewhere. You will need to make sure that any training programme you design is specific to your needs and will allow you to improve different components of fitness to meet your goals. You will also need to make sure you are using training methods that you enjoy.

Whether you are training to become a high-level athlete or just want to be able to walk upstairs without getting out of breath, this unit is about understanding how to gather background information to help you design appropriate training programmes. It will also enable you to identify different barriers to training and how to overcome them before taking part in and reviewing a personal training programme.

Assessment: You will be assessed by a series of assignments set by your teacher/tutor.

Learning aims

In this unit you will:

A design a personal fitness training programme

B know about exercise adherence factors and strategies for continued training success

C implement a self-designed personal fitness training programme to achieve own goals and objectives

D review a personal fitness training programme.

"I'm a competitive rugby player who plays for a Super League youth team, so getting a better understanding of training methods that can be used to benefit my sport was really useful for me.

Sam, *16-year-old aspiring rugby league player*

Training for Personal Fitness

5

BTEC
Assessment Zone

This table shows you what you must do in order to achieve a **Pass**, **Merit** or **Distinction** grade, and where you can find activities to help you.

Assessment criteria			
Level 1	**Level 2 Pass**	**Level 2 Merit**	**Level 2 Distinction**
Learning aim A: design a personal fitness training programme			
1A.1 English Outline personal information for designing a fitness training programme	**2A.P1** English Summarise personal information for designing a fitness training programme **See Assessment activity 5.1, page 143**	**2A.M1** English Assess personal information for fitness training programme design **See Assessment activity 5.1, page 143**	
1A.2 English Design a safe four-week personal fitness training programme, with guidance	**2A.P2** English Independently design a safe six-week personal fitness training programme **See Assessment activity 5.1, page 143**	**2A.M2** English Design a safe six-week personal fitness training programme, showing creativity in the design **See Assessment activity 5.1, page 143**	**2A.D1** English Justify the training programme design, explaining links to personal information **See Assessment activity 5.1, page 143**
1A.3 Outline the importance of warm-up, cool down and FITT	**2A.P3** Maths Describe the principles of training and their application to the personal fitness training programme design **See Assessment activity 5.1, page 143**		
Learning aim B: know about exercise adherence factors and strategies for continued training success			
1B.4 Describe two personal exercise adherence factors and two strategies for training success	**2B.P4** Describe four personal exercise adherence factors and four strategies for training success **See Assessment activity 5.1, page 143**		
Learning aim C: implement a self-designed personal fitness training programme to achieve own goals and objectives			
1C.5 Maths English Safely implement, with guidance, a four-week personal fitness training programme, maintaining a training diary	**2C.P5** Maths English Safely implement a six-week personal fitness training programme, maintaining a training diary **See Assessment activity 5.2, page 147**	**2C.M3** Maths English Safely implement a successful six-week personal fitness training programme, maintaining a training diary summarising outcomes for each session **See Assessment activity 5.2, page 147**	**2C.D2** Maths English Safely implement a successful six-week personal fitness training programme, maintaining a training diary to evaluate performance and progress **See Assessment activity 5.2, page 147**

Assessment criteria			
Level 1	Level 2 **Pass**	Level 2 **Merit**	Level 2 **Distinction**
Learning aim D: review a personal fitness training programme			
1D.6 Review the four-week personal fitness training programme, identifying strengths and areas for improvement	**2D.P6** Review the six-week personal fitness training programme, describing strengths and areas for improvement **See Assessment activity 5.2, page 147**	**2D.M4** Explain strengths of the training programme and areas for improvement, providing recommendations for future training and performance **See Assessment activity 5.2, page 147**	**2D.D3** Justify recommendations for future training and performance **See Assessment activity 5.2, page 147**

English Opportunity to practise English skills   **Maths** Opportunity to practise mathematical skills

How you will be assessed

This unit will be assessed through a series of assignments set by your teacher/tutor. You will be expected to show an understanding of training programme design and factors affecting exercise adherence, as well as being able to take part in and review a training programme. The tasks will be based on scenarios involving work or activity in a sports setting. For example, you might be asked to think about the barriers that could stop you from taking part in exercise and then come up with strategies to remove these barriers.

Your assessment could be in the form of:

- training programme plans
- practical observations of training
- training diaries.

Personal information to aid training programme design

Introduction

When planning training programmes, you need to gather lots of personal information to ensure your training programme is effective; for example, there is no point including lots of long-distance running in a training programme if you want to improve speed and power.

Personal goals

Personal goals should be '**SMARTER**', which stands for specific, measureable, achievable, realistic, time-related, exciting and recorded. It is not enough to say, 'I want to get fitter', you need to make your goals much more focused. An example of a SMARTER goal could be 'I want to improve my leg strength by 20kg within 6 weeks.'

Goals can also be set over different timescales. These are known as:

- **short-term (ST) goals**: between 1 day and 1 month
- **medium-term (MT) goals**: to give progressive support towards achievement of long-term goals
- **long-term (LT) goals**: what you want to achieve in the long term.

Aims and objectives

The **aims** of your training programme are details of what you would like to achieve by the end of the programme. Your aims will be based on the goals you have set.

The **objectives** of your training programme are how you plan to achieve your aims.

Activity 5.1   Training aims

Think about the sport that you play or exercise activities that you take part in, and write down your training aims in relation to this sport or activity.

Lifestyle and physical activity history

When designing a training programme, you need to know about different lifestyle factors such as current physical activity levels (including physical activity, exercise and sport), alcohol intake, diet, free time, occupation, family and financial situation; all of these will influence how you design your training programme.

Medical history questionnaire

As well as understanding lifestyle and physical activity, medical history can also influence training programme design. You should complete a Physical Activity Readiness Questionnaire (PAR-Q) prior to training. This is a questionnaire that asks questions about medical factors such as joint pain, chest pains and dizziness.

As well as the questions on the PAR-Q, you may also need to give information about any medication that you are using. For example, if you have asthma, you need to make sure that you have your medication with you when you train.

Attitudes to training and personal motivation

Have you ever been getting ready to go to the gym and just thought to yourself 'I really can't be bothered'? This is a sign of a poor **attitude** towards training and a lack of motivation. Attitude and motivation are two factors that can affect your **intention** to train. This can in turn affect whether you decide to go training or not, and if you do, how hard you will try during your training session.

Key terms

Attitude – how positive or negative you generally feel about something.

Intention – planning to do something.

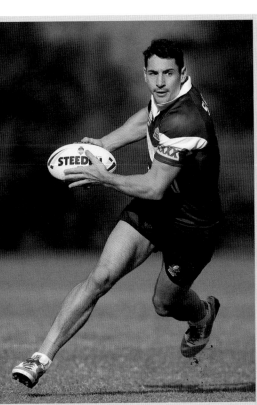

All sports performers must be motivated to train hard, play well and win sporting events.

Just checking

1 What do the terms 'aims' and 'objectives' mean?
2 Which lifestyle factors could you ask about when conducting a physical activity and lifestyle questionnaire?

The basic principles of training (FITT)

Introduction

The basic **principles of training** are those that you need to consider as a minimum when planning training sessions and programmes. These principles can be remembered using the acronym 'FITT', which stands for: Frequency, Intensity, Time, Type.

▶ Frequency

The frequency of training refers to the number of training sessions per week that you will train. Novice trainers will usually start off training about three times per week, whereas experienced trainers or high-level athletes will train five or six times per week, and sometimes even twice in one day.

▶ Intensity

The intensity of training refers to how hard your training will be. This is usually stated in terms of percentage **heart rate** or Rating of Perceived Exertion.

▶ Time

The time spent training refers to how long you may spend exercising or how long training sessions will last for. You should make sure that you always think about the time of your training alongside the intensity of your training as they influence each other.

If you are doing some aerobic training at a moderate intensity, you would probably work for about 20–30 minutes continuously, but imagine what would happen if you tried to sprint as fast as you could for that long!

▶ Type

The type of training refers to the method(s) (sometimes called modes) of training that you will use as part of the training programme.

If a sprinter was trying to increase the power in their legs in order to improve their sprint start, there would be little point in doing lots of long distance continuous running; they would be better suited to completing a plyometric training programme.

Can you think of specific types of training that would be useful when training for your favourite sport?

What principles of training do you use?

WorkSpace

► Ritchie

19-year-old rugby coach

I have always wanted to be involved in sport in some way. When I was younger I thought I would be a professional rugby player but I got seriously injured in the first year of my contract and had to quit, so I then set my sights on becoming a coach.

To start myself off I enrolled on a BTEC First course at my local college and worked towards that qualification alongside doing my rugby coaching qualifications. I really enjoyed the course, particularly the units on fitness testing and training. These units gave me a much greater understanding of the importance of the fitness side of sports coaching, which has helped me to give more advice to the young players I work with. The course was particularly useful as I got to experience the whole process of planning, taking part in and reviewing my own fitness training programme.

Think about it

1 Which parts of this unit do you think would be useful for a sports coach?

2 How would completing this unit benefit young athletes who are developing in their sport?

3 Are there any other jobs that you think would benefit from the content of this unit?

Further principles of training and how they are applied to training methods

Link

This topic links to *Unit 1: Fitness for Sport and Exercise*.

Introduction

As well as the FITT principles, there are more advanced principles of training that you need to understand to be able to design training programmes effectively, to make sure that you are working at the correct level and will help prevent injuries.

Intensity

There are two main ways that you can monitor the intensity of your training programme: **heart rate** and **Rating of Perceived Exertion**.

Heart rate

When training, you can use target zones and training thresholds to select the correct intensity. This involves you calculating and applying your maximum heart rate (HRmax) to training. You calculate your HRmax by using the following equation: 220 − age. When training for cardiovascular health and fitness, 60% to 85% of your HRmax is the recommended training zone.

Rate of Perceived Exertion	Intensity
6	No exertion at all
7	Extremely light
8	
9	Very light
10	
11	
12	
13	Somewhat hard
14	
15	Hard (heavy)
16	
17	Very hard
18	
19	Extremely hard
20	Maximal exertion

Figure 5.1 The Borg (1970) Rating of Perceived Exertion (RPE) scale

Activity 5.2 Calculating HRmax

Using the equation 220 − age, calculate your HRmax. After you have done this, calculate your training zone for cardiovascular training by working out 60% to 85% of your HRmax.

Rating of Perceived Exertion

The Borg (1970) Rating of Perceived Exertion (RPE) scale is a measure of exercise intensity that runs from 6 to 20 (see Figure 5.1). It is designed to show people how hard they think they are working while exercising so that the intensity can be changed if necessary.

Relationship between HR and RPE

There is a relationship between RPE and HR, where RPE × 10 = HR (bpm).

Progressive overload

For your body to develop, the training needs to be demanding enough to cause it to adapt, helping to improve sports performance or overall health. You can overload the body by increasing the frequency, intensity or time of activity, or by reducing the recovery time. You should not alter all of these factors at once if you are a novice trainer because you will risk injury or developing a poor technique.

Specificity

When planning your training around the needs of your particular sport or activity, you should take into account the muscle groups used, the duration of the activity, the movement patterns and the energy systems used. You should set goals that are specific to the activity and components of fitness.

Individual differences/needs

Any training programme that you design should be specific to your needs. Everyone has different ability levels, goals, physical attributes, medical history and training activity preferences.

Variation

You should include a range of training methods to avoid boredom and maintain enjoyment. By doing this, you are more likely to stay motivated and adhere to your training programme.

Adaptation

An adaptation is where one or more of your physiological systems change as a result of long-term training. Your body notices that you need it to work harder when you are training and competing, so it reacts to the demands of the training and changes so that it can allow you to continue with training and competition in future.

Rest and recovery

Recovery time is essential in any training programme so that the body can recover from training and to allow adaptations to occur. Without this recovery time, the rate of progression will reduce and the risk of injury will increase.

Reversibility

If training stops or the intensity of training is too low to cause adaptation, the training effects are reversed.

Link

This topic links to *Unit 4: The Sports Performer in Action*. Refer to Unit 4 when you are learning about how the different physiological systems adapt to training.

Discussion point

Research the terms 'overuse injuries' and 'over training', and give an example of one. Discuss with friends how you think the correct use of the basic and further principles of training could prevent an overuse injury.

Just checking

Answer 'true' or 'false' to each of the following statements:

1 Specificity is making sure that you have enough recovery time in your training programme.
2 Variation helps to avoid boredom in training programmes by including a range of activities.
3 An adaptation is where the body reacts to a training load and changes to make sure that it can cope with training.
4 Progressive overload means that you gradually make things harder so that your body keeps adapting.
5 Rest and recovery is wasted time that could be spent training.

Programme design

Getting started

Why do you think it is important for fitness instructors and personal trainers to have a detailed knowledge of lots of different training methods?

Link

This topic links to *Unit 1: Fitness for Sport and Exercise.*

Introduction

There are lots of factors that you need to take into account when you are designing your training programme, including the selection of appropriate methods, safety in design, warm-up, cool down and maintaining adherence.

Selection of appropriate training methods

Speed and power training

Many sports require **speed** and **power** if you are to compete successfully. Although these are two different components of fitness, they do affect each other: for example, your power will determine how quickly you can accelerate to top speed. It is because of this that speed and power training are often combined.

Three common training methods to develop speed and power are **resisted sprints**, **plyometric training** and **speed ladder training**.

If you are planning to use speed and power training within a training session, it should take place after a warm-up or a low-intensity training method.

Resisted sprints are when you use equipment to make a sprint harder. By doing this, you make your muscles get used to sprinting against resistance so that when you stop using the equipment, you will be able to sprint faster because the extra weight is not there. These methods will often use distances of 10–200m depending on the sport. Examples of this type of training include parachute sprints and sled sprints.

Activity 5.3	Speed and power training

Using the internet, search for film clips of the different methods of speed and power training that are suited to your particular sport or activity.

Then use these along with information from the websites to plan a plyometric training session.

You may want to visit the following websites by going to Pearson Hotlinks (www.pearsonhotlinks.co.uk) and search for this BTEC Sport title.

- Live Strong
- Newitts
- Sports Fitness Advisor
- Strength Coach
- Youtube.

Speed ladder training involves people sprinting through the rungs of plastic ladders that are placed on the floor. It increases speed by forcing the feet to adapt to fast footwork patterns through repetition. You should begin with slow, controlled movements and progress to more advanced movements so that your muscle system can get used to the movement patterns.

How does plyometric training improve Andy Murray's power?

Plyometric training is regularly used to increase power in sports. Try to think of a muscle as an elastic band – the elastic band will fly further if you stretch it more before letting go. Plyometric training takes a muscle through an eccentric muscle action that lengthens and stretches it before a powerful concentric action. Over time, this makes for a faster rate of muscle contraction, which will improve power and speed.

Why is speed ladder training popular in sports such as football, rugby and basketball?

CONTINUED ▶▶

Flexibility training

Flexibility training works by stretching the muscles beyond their usual limits. As flexibility is affected by temperature, it is best to do this type of training after you have warmed the muscles up. There are three main types of flexibility training: **static stretching**, **dynamic stretching** and **Proprioceptive Neuromuscular Facilitation (PNF)**.

Static stretching uses slow, controlled movements to stretch a muscle and joint to its limit (see Figure 5.2 for examples of different static stretches). You can do this type of stretching on your own (active stretching) or you may be assisted by a partner, who stretches the area for you (passive stretching). This type of stretch can be held for up to 60 seconds.

Standing calf stretch   Pectoralis stretch   Quadriceps stretch

Standing hamstring stretch   Hip flexor stretch   Double knee to chest

Figure 5.2 Examples of different static stretches

Dynamic stretching involves performing activities that are similar to the sporting movements that will be needed during a game or event. For example, before games, you will see football players performing kicking movements without actually kicking the ball. This is a form of dynamic stretching.

PNF stretching is an effective form of passive stretching that involves three stages:

1 Stretch the targeted muscle group as far as it can go.

2 While in that position, **isometrically** contract the muscle group against a partner for 6 seconds.

3 Relax the muscle group and allow your partner to stretch it again. It should go further now.

Using the information on flexibility training, design a flexibility training session that you could use as part of a training programme.

Muscular strength and endurance training

To improve muscular strength and endurance you will usually use the same training methods but will alter the **repetitions**, **sets** or frequency to suit either strength development or endurance development (see Table 5.1). The most common methods of improving muscular strength and endurance are:

- resistance machines
- free weights
- medicine ball training
- circuit training
- core stability training.

Key terms

Repetitions – the number of times you perform a single exercise such as a biceps curl; often abbreviated to 'reps'.

Sets – a group of repetitions; for example, an experienced strength trainer may complete three sets of six reps.

1-RM – the maximum amount of weight that you can lift in a single repetition. This is a measure often used to decide on the intensity of strength training programmes.

Table 5.1 Guidelines for strength and endurance training

Strength/ endurance	Intensity	Reps	Sets	Frequency	Length of programme
Inexperienced strength trainers	70–80% 1-RM or 8–12-RM	8–12	≥1	3	≥6 weeks
Experienced strength trainers	85–100% 1-RM or 1–6-RM	1–6	≥3	5–6	≥12 weeks
Muscle endurance	≤60% 1-RM or 15–20-RM	15–20	≥1	3	≥6 weeks

Circuit training is also a way of improving muscular strength and endurance. Circuit training uses a number of different stations that have exercises on them. The circuit can be designed so that exercises that use either body weight as resistance (for example, press-ups), or that use additional weight such as dumb-bells (for example, triceps extensions) can be included. You will usually exercise for about 1 minute per station and have a rest period in between stations. You can make your circuit easier or harder by changing the following:

- length of rest periods
- number of stations
- number of circuits
- time spent at each station.

Using the information on muscular strength and endurance training, design two training sessions – one for muscular endurance training and one for muscular strength training.

Remember

When designing circuit training sessions, you should make sure that you do not work the same muscle group on consecutive stations to prevent fatigue.

CONTINUED ▶▶

Aerobic endurance training

The three main methods of training **aerobic endurance** are **continuous training**, **fartlek training** and **interval training**.

Continuous training is also known as steady-state or long, slow, distance training. It involves the athlete training at a moderate intensity over a long distance and time, usually by running, swimming or cycling. Due to the lower level of intensity, an athlete can train for longer. It can also be useful for beginners who are starting structured exercise, athletes recovering from injury and 'specific population' individuals such as children or elderly people. Some problems with this training method include a higher risk of injury when running long distances on hard surfaces; it can get boring and it is not always sport-specific.

Fartlek training is based on running outdoors, and varies the intensity of work according to the athlete's requirements. The simplest way of varying intensity is by alternating between walking, jogging, running and sprinting; the intensity can also be varied by running on different surfaces such as hills, soft grassland or woodland. Fartlek training can be more useful than continuous training because it can be made sport-specific. The variation it provides can also be used to make training more interesting.

Would you enjoy fartlek training more than continuous training or interval training?

In **interval training**, athletes perform a work period, followed by a rest or recovery period, before completing another work period. When designing interval training sessions, you should think about:

- the number of intervals (rest and work periods)
- the intensity of the work interval
- the duration of the work interval
- the duration of the rest interval
- the intensity of the rest interval.

An example of an interval training prescription for aerobic endurance could be one set of three repetitions of 5-minute runs alternated with 2 minutes and 30 seconds of rest.

Activity 5.6   Identifying training methods

Match the training method to the component of fitness:

Training method	Component of fitness
Plyometric training	Flexibility
PNF	Muscular strength/muscular endurance
Resisted sprints	Aerobic endurance
Continuous training	Speed and power
Free weight training	Aerobic endurance
Fartlek training	Speed and power

Safe design

In order to make sure that your training programme is safe, you should select appropriate training methods or an appropriate combination of training methods. These methods should allow you to meet your personal training needs, goals, aims and objectives.

Selection of appropriate activities for warm-up

When warming up, you should make sure that you use light, continuous physical activity to prepare the body for exercise. This will help prepare the body by increasing heart rate, increasing breathing rate and increasing muscle temperature. It could include activities like jogging, running in different directions and completing different sporting actions such as passing a rugby ball between teammates.

When you design a training programme you must think about your goals, aims and objectives.

Selection of appropriate activities for cool down

In the same way that you need to warm up, you need to use similar activities to cool down. These activities will help you to reduce heart rate at a steady pace, which will help to remove lactic acid and prevent **blood pooling**. It could include activities like jogging or cycling.

Creative design

To creatively design your training programme, you need to think about how you can prevent **barriers** (see Topics B.1 and B.2) to ensure that **exercise adherence** is maintained and the programme is enjoyable. You could make the programme interesting by including a range of activities. This will help to maintain motivation and commitment as well as prevent boredom.

Key terms

Blood pooling – the process whereby, when exercise is suddenly stopped, blood is no longer forced to return to the heart and so stays in the legs, which potentially causes pain and swelling.

Exercise adherence – how well you stick to your exercise programme.

Just checking

1 Name three ways of improving flexibility.

2 What are the three stages of PNF?

3 What do the terms 'repetitions' and 'sets' mean?

4 Name three methods of aerobic endurance training.

5 What factors can you change to make circuit training either easier or harder?

6 How does a warm-up prepare the body for exercise?

7 What are the benefits of cooling down?

Exercise adherence factors and strategies to overcome barriers

Getting started

What do you think would be the main barriers to exercise that people would report?

Introduction

There are lots of factors that can determine whether people will adhere to a training programme or not. It is important that you know about them so you can come up with strategies to overcome them.

Factors affecting exercise adherence

There are lots of reasons why people don't take part in enough exercise:

Link

This unit links to *Unit 11: Running a Sports Event, Topic A.1 and A.2* for information training programmes.

- **Access to facilities**: if people think they don't have access to facilities such as gyms and fitness centres, they are less likely to exercise.
- **Time**: quite often people who don't exercise will say that they don't have time to fit it into their daily routine.
- **Commitment**: sometimes people will think that they are likely to give up exercising so don't bother to start a training programme or drop out soon after starting.
- **Lack of interest**: some people just don't like the idea of exercise so choose not to take part.
- **Personal injury**: if people have been injured they may be scared of repeat injury.
- **Emotional**: some people can feel quite embarrassed when exercising, worrying about how they look and feeling that they cannot do it.
- **Cost**: people sometimes think that exercise comes with a lot of costs for things such as gym memberships and kit.

Discussion point

Can you think of any other factors that could be classed as barriers to exercise? How do you think the different barriers to exercise vary across genders, ages and different levels of sporting ability?

Would you feel confident training with these people?

Strategies to overcome barriers

There are many ways to overcome barriers to exercise.

SMARTER targets

By setting SMARTER targets and using rewards for achieving goals, you can help to improve commitment and motivation.

Implementing enjoyable activities

If you use activities that you enjoy as part of your training programme, it will become less of a chore and you will stay interested.

Training with others

Training with others can often provide the necessary support to motivate you to keep training. Reinforcement from friends that your training is having a positive impact will also help to motive you.

Knowing the benefits of training programmes

If you know the benefits of training programmes you are more likely to take part. For example, if you have been injured, understanding the benefits of training and the potential for rehabilitation could make you more confident.

Link

See *Topic A.1* for more information on SMARTER targets.

Remember

Rewards are good but don't rely on them; they should not be the only reason to take part in exercise.

Assessment activity 5.1   *Maths English*   2A.P1 | 2A.P2 | 2A.P3 | 2B.P4 | 2A.M1 | 2A.M2 | 2A.D1

1 You are playing for a local sports team and are looking to improve your fitness levels so that you can be more competitive in your sport. You have decided to design a safe and creative six-week training programme to improve your performance. You should:
   - outline your personal goals, aims and objectives
   - outline other relevant personal information
   - outline two personal exercise adherence factors and two success strategies
   - use this information to design a programme (including warm-up and cool down) that appropriately applies the principles of training.

2 To make sure your programme is appropriate for your needs, justify to your coach why you have designed your programme in the way you have.

Tips

- Remember to use SMARTER goals.
- Consider how realistic your aims and objectives are.
- Include your lifestyle and physical activity history, highlighting any strengths and areas for improvement.
- Include a completed medical history questionnaire and a description of any medical factors that could influence training programme design (such as recent injuries or asthma).
- Consider your attitudes and personal motivation to train, highlighting the positive and negative aspects of both.
- You will need to show that your programme is safe by showing that you are using the right equipment, following correct training techniques and taking into account your fitness and medical history.
- You will need to show that your programme is creative.

Implement a self-designed personal fitness training programme

Getting started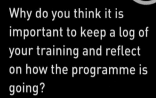

Why do you think it is important to keep a log of your training and reflect on how the programme is going?

Link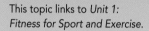

This topic links to *Unit 1: Fitness for Sport and Exercise.*

Introduction

Safety is an important part of your training programme. You need to take into account the different safety factors when taking part in any sporting activity. You should also keep a training diary so that you can reflect on how the programme is progressing. This can help maintain your safety and ensure that the training programme is effective.

Safely implement a personal fitness training programme

To implement your personal fitness training programme safely, you should:

Undertake appropriate training methods and complete planned sessions. You should use the descriptions of the different training methods in Unit 1: Fitness for Sport and Exercise, and in Topic A.4 to help you complete the training methods appropriately.

Use the correct technique through the different training methods and follow the manufacturer's instructions when using equipment. These two factors will mean that your training will be most effective with reduced risk of injury.

Always perform to the best of your ability to get the best out of your training sessions and lower the risk of injury.

Make sure you have the agreement of your teacher or coach if you plan to miss any training sessions.

Stay committed throughout the training programme. Think about the principle of reversibility – by missing sessions you are likely to start losing the gains made by training.

Wear correct kit.

Be aware of wider safety issues. For example, if exercising outdoors make sure that people know where you are training, that they have a way of contacting you and that the surface you will be training on does not pose hazards.

Take full responsibility for recording details for each training session. This will help you to see if your training programme is working.

Using a training diary to record each session

When keeping a training diary, you should record the following details:

- date, time and location
- aims and objectives for each session
- session duration
- type of training undertaken – selected methods/activities
- programme details (FITT)
- log of personal performance and achievements
- resources required, e.g. equipment
- the principles of progressive overload and details of how progressive overload has been achieved over the course of the programme
- programme intensity using percentage HRmax and RPE.

Measures for success

In your training diary, you should also describe the different measures for success. These include your motivation to train, how your programme has been adapted, achieving aims and overcoming barriers.

Motivation for training

When describing this part, include details in the diary of your feelings before, during and after each training session. For example, did you want to train, or did you feel that you had to train but couldn't really be bothered.

How the programme has been adapted

As your programme progresses, you will probably change it to ensure continued commitment to training; for example, using a new variety of activities/training methods. You should record in your diary when, how and why you adapted your training programme.

Achievement

Achievement against personal aims, goals or objectives should also be recorded in the training diary; for example, if you were able to lift your target weight in the gym or achieve your target time on a run.

Overcoming barriers

In this section of your training diary, describe how you overcame your barriers to training and issues/problems that you faced while training.

Reflect

If you highlighted poor motivation to train as a barrier as part of Assessment activity 5.1, how did you overcome this barrier before and during your training?

Just checking

1 What details should you include in your training diary for each session?
2 What factors should you consider when thinking about measures for success?

Review your programme

Getting started

Which factors might you consider to be strengths or areas for improvement after a training programme? How could you use this information to suggest future training recommendations?

Introduction

At the end of a training programme it is important to review its strengths and areas for improvement so that you can suggest and justify future training recommendations.

Review programme

It is important that you review your training programme before and after each training programme. Your reviews should show **strengths** and **areas for improvement**, as well as providing evidence of where you have modified the training programme to achieve personal goals.

Key terms

Strengths – areas of the training programme where personal aims and objectives have been achieved.

Areas for improvement – areas where training outcomes did not meet planned goals; for example, you planned to improve muscular strength but did not improve over the 6 weeks specified.

Training that uses more than one activity can provide welcome variety.

Future recommendations

When thinking about future recommendations, you should consider the areas for improvement first as these will still be your future training priorities. By thinking about the areas for improvement, you will be able to decide on your personal training needs and will be able to think about the use of different training methods where appropriate. For example, it may be that you have not improved your aerobic endurance as much as you would have liked because you didn't really enjoy the continuous running programme that you had set, so in future you would want to consider using a range of aerobic training methods (e.g. Fartlek training and interval training) and activities (e.g. alternating between running, swimming and cycling in different training sessions) to maintain your motivation and enjoyment.

How could you improve your training programme for the future?

| Assessment activity 5.2 | *Maths English* | 2C.P5 | 2D.P6 | 2C.M3 | 2D.M4 | 2C.D2 | 2D.D3 |

You now need to safely implement your six-week training programme.

1 You should maintain a training diary to summarise outcomes and appraise your performance and progress throughout.

2 At the end of the six weeks, consider your strengths and areas for improvement, providing recommendations for future training.

Tips

- Record the main points about the outcomes of your training sessions.
- Keep a record of your strengths and areas for improvement throughout the training programme.
- When preparing recommendations for your future training, say how and why they would improve your performance.

Introduction

Behind every great sports performer and sports team is a great leader. Sports leaders are often the unsung heroes, the people who spot weaknesses and develop them, turning athletes into winning Olympians and teams into league or cup champions. It is the sports leader who plans physical activity sessions and steers the development of a performer's skills and techniques to meet aims and objectives. They often make key decisions at important times which change the fortunes of individuals and teams. It's a lot of responsibility, so a sports leader must be appropriately prepared and have had adequate experiences within their sport. At grass roots level sports leaders are vital in ensuring that young people remain interested and enthused.

In this unit you will be introduced to the basics of sports leadership and will be required to plan and deliver sports activity sessions. You will then evaluate your own effectiveness to determine if there are areas where you can further develop your abilities.

Assessment: You will be assessed by a series of assignments set by your teacher/tutor.

Learning aims

In this unit you will:

A know the attributes associated with successful sports leadership

B undertake the planning and leading of sports activities

C review the planning and leading of sports activities.

I have always wanted to be a swimming coach. My own coach was such an inspiration to me and I hope to share my own experiences with younger swimmers at my club. After completing this unit I know which attributes I need to develop in order to fulfil this ambition.

Megan, *17-year-old aspiring swimming coach*

Leading Sports Activities

Assessment Zone

This table shows you what you must do in order to achieve a **Pass**, **Merit** or **Distinction** grade, and where you can find activities to help you.

Assessment criteria			
Level 1	Level 2 **Pass**	Level 2 **Merit**	Level 2 **Distinction**
Learning aim A: know the attributes associated with successful sports leadership			
1A.1 Outline the attributes required for, and responsibilities of, sports leadership	**2A.P1** Describe, using relevant examples, the attributes required for, and responsibilities of, sports leadership **See Assessment activity 6.1, page 163**	**2A.M1** Explain the attributes required for, and responsibilities of, sports leadership **See Assessment activity 6.1, page 163**	
1A.2 Describe the attributes of a selected successful sports leader	**2A.P2** Describe the attributes of two selected successful sports leaders **See Assessment activity 6.1, page 163**	**2A.M2** Evaluate the attributes of two successful sports leaders **See Assessment activity 6.1, page 163**	**2A.D1** Compare and contrast the attributes of two successful sports leaders **See Assessment activity 6.1, page 163**
Learning aim B: undertake the planning and leading of sports activities			
1B.3 Plan a given sports activity	**2B.P3** Plan two selected sports activities **See Assessment activity 6.2, page 173**	**2B.M3** Justify the choice of activities within the sports activity plan **See Assessment activity 6.2, page 173**	
1B.4 English Lead a component of a sports activity session, with guidance and/or support	**2B.P4** English Independently lead a sports activity session **See Assessment activity 6.2, page 173**	**2B.M4** English Lead a successful sports activity session **See Assessment activity 6.2, page 173**	
Learning aim C: review the planning and leading of sports activities			
1C.5 Maths Review the planning and leading of the warm-up, main component or cool down, describing strengths and areas for improvement	**2C.P5** Maths Review the planning and leading of the sports activity session, describing strengths and areas for improvement, and targets for future development as a sports leader **See Assessment activity 6.2, page 173**	**2C.M5** Explain targets for future development as a sports leader, including a personal development plan **See Assessment activity 6.2, page 173**	**2C.D2** Justify targets for future development as a sports leader and activities within the personal development plan **See Assessment activity 6.2, page 173**

English / Opportunity to practise English skills

Maths / Opportunity to practise mathematical skills

How you will be assessed

This unit will be through a series of assignments set by your teacher/tutor. You will be expected to show that you understand the attributes required for successful sports leadership using examples of successful sports leaders. You will also be required to plan two sports activity sessions, and then deliver one of these. On completion of the session you will be required to review your effectiveness as a leader by commenting on your strengths and areas for improvement.

Your assessment could be in the form of:

- a written report
- session plans with detailed justification of selected activities
- observation of you leading a session (or a component of a session)
- visual evidence of you leading a session (video/photographs)
- report of the outcomes of the session and review of session including a development plan.

Sports leaders and their attributes

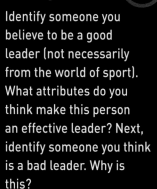
Introduction

In this section, you will learn about the different types of leaders in sports and the attributes that sports leaders need in order to be successful.

Sports leaders

There are many types of leadership role in sport. Examples of sports leaders include sports coaches, fitness instructors, school/college coaches, and local and national club coaches. A sports leader's main aim is to encourage participation in sport and ensure that sports sessions are safe and well organised.

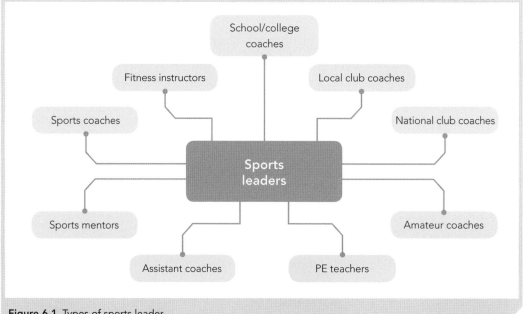

Figure 6.1 Types of sports leader

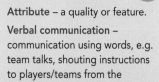
Attributes

Skills

Sports leaders need to develop certain skills if they are to be effective in leading sport and physical activity sessions.

Communication

Sports leaders use a variety of methods when communicating to participants in their sports sessions:

- **verbal communication** – e.g. giving technical instructions to sports performers
- **non-verbal communication** – e.g. facial expressions and bodily gestures
- **listening** – e.g. after asking a sports performer a question and requesting a response.

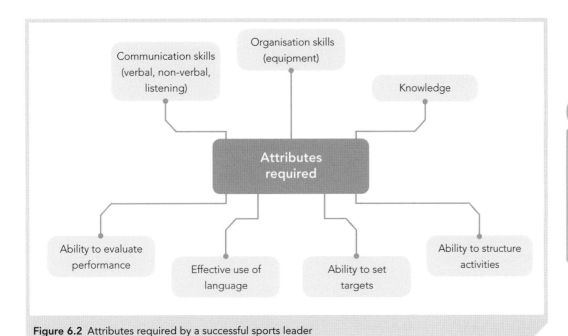

Figure 6.2 Attributes required by a successful sports leader

Research

1 For two sports, research the qualifications required to coach and lead different age groups and abilities. You may find this information under 'Education' on the website for the National Governing Body for each sport.

2 Present the information you find to the rest of your group.

The more effective your methods of communication the easier it is to get a variety of messages across to players, spectators, other coaches and officials when appropriate.

Non-verbal communication often helps sports performers read the mood of the sports leader.

Communication between the leader and performer should be a two-way process, supporting the development of knowledge for both.

Organisation of equipment

As a sports leader, you must have a clear understanding of the equipment you are going to need to deliver each sports or physical activity session or event. Prior to the session, you should make sure you have all the equipment prepared, check that it is in full working order and make sure that you are aware of how to use it in a safe and effective way.

Knowledge

Sports leaders should have a wealth of knowledge about the sport they are delivering, including:

- the technical and tactical demands of the sport
- the specific fitness requirements of the sport
- laws, rules and regulations of the sport
- the treatment of basic sports injuries and first-aid techniques.

As sports leaders develop, their knowledge will increase. It is a requirement in many sports that people involved in the organisation and planning of sports activity sessions attain sport-specific leadership and coaching qualifications.

An example of non-verbal communication. What do you think are effective and ineffective methods of communication?

CONTINUED ▶▶

▶▶ CONTINUED

Link

This unit links to *Unit 11: Running a Sports Event*. For more information regarding activity structure and the components of a sports leadership session refer to *Topic B.2*.

Key terms

Aims – what you want to achieve in your session.

Objectives – how you are going to achieve your aims in the session.

▼ Advanced skills

Activity structure

When delivering a sports session, it is important that you follow the correct format:

1 **warm-up**
2 **main component**
3 **cool down**
4 **feedback/debrief**.

You should ensure that each component of the session is safe, as well as effective in developing technical ability and/or tactical knowledge.

Target setting

When planning a session a sports leader will set out specific goals or targets. These are called the **aims** and **objectives**.

The leader will further develop these throughout a series of sessions, as his or her knowledge of the individual development needs of the performers increases.

Sports leaders should set short-term targets that need to be achieved by the end of the session. They should also set medium- or long-term targets to be achieved by the end of a series of sessions, by the end of a season, or over a longer period of time.

What skills will a coach use when talking one-on-one with a sports performer?

Use of language

Successful sports leaders have a clear voice and use language that is appropriate for the performers they are working with. Through effective use of language you will develop:

- a rapport with and between the performers
- a high level of sport-specific knowledge (including technical and tactical knowledge and rules and regulations of the sport) between performers
- a sense of respect between performers
- the sports performance of individuals and teams.

When working with beginners you will need to use basic language to explain each activity. Language for elite performers will be much more technical. A good leader will increase performers' knowledge by explaining techniques, tactics, rules and regulations in a clear and concise way.

At all times, a good sports leader will think before speaking, to demonstrate respect for all people involved in the session or sports event.

Evaluation

Sports leaders should provide participants with feedback on their strengths and areas for improvement relating to their performance. However, they should also reflect on their own performance as a sports leader. The key to effective self-evaluation is honesty. It can be easy to identify what you have done well, but more difficult to comment on the things you haven't done well. Try to seek support from experienced sports leaders and coaches and learn from them. This will enable you to develop your weaknesses and enhance your effectiveness in leading sports activity sessions.

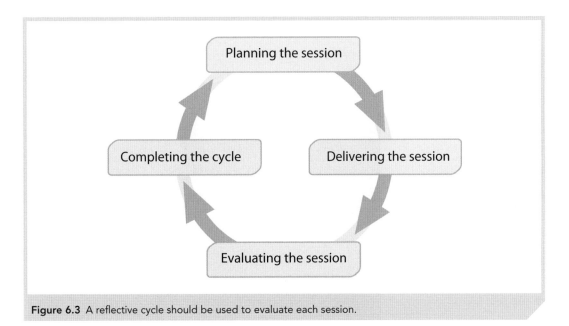

Figure 6.3 A reflective cycle should be used to evaluate each session.

CONTINUED ▶▶

Sir Alex Ferguson is famous for his leadership style. Can you think of positive leadership qualities he has?

Qualities

It is important that good sports leaders demonstrate a number of positive qualities. These will shape the relationships they develop with participants in the sessions they are leading.

Appearance

Sports leaders should take care of their appearance and dress appropriately for each session. As a sports leader, you are a role model – this involves wearing the right kit and behaving appropriately in each session, and ensuring that performers follow your lead by doing the same.

Enthusiasm

Good leaders must be able to combine innovative ways of delivering sports and physical activity sessions with:

- knowledge of the sport or activity
- effective communication
- leadership skills
- high levels of enthusiasm.

An enthusiastic and knowledgeable sports leader can leave a lasting impression on sports performers. When a sports leader is smiling and happy, this feeling often rubs off on the performers in the session.

Confidence

A sports leader should have the confidence to stand in front of performers and direct them towards achieving a target or goal. Confidence will develop as you increase your own experience and knowledge. This is a key quality for a sports leader.

Activity 6.1 / Thinking about qualities for sports leadership

Look at the image of Hope Powell (CBE), one of the most successful England football coaches.

1 Using the image, identify the leadership qualities she is showing.

2 Select your favourite sports leader who has led you in a sports or physical activity session. Comment on each of the following qualities:
  - appearance
  - enthusiasm
  - confidence.

3 Feed back your findings to the rest of the group.

4 Select three famous sports leaders from three different sports and describe how they demonstrate effective qualities when leading sports performers.

Hope Powell (CBE)

Additional qualities

Leadership style

There are three identifiable sports leadership styles, which are outlined in Table 6.1.

Table 6.1 Characteristics, advantages and disadvantages of leadership styles

Leadership style	Characteristics	Advantages	Disadvantages
Autocratic	• Leader makes all decisions, and tells sports performers what to do and how to do it.	• Good for beginners when delivering basic skills and techniques.	• Only works on single skills in isolation. • Difficult to assess prior knowledge of performers.
Democratic	• Leader involves sports performers in the decision-making process, but makes the final decision on what is to be delivered in the session.	• Develops close relationships between leader and sports performers. • Develops communication and confidence of sports performers.	• Time-consuming. • May be problematic in large groups if there are many differing opinions.
Laissez-faire	• Performers make the decisions. • Sports leader is used as a mentor and helps the performers when appropriate.	• Helps develop self-confidence and decision-making skills of sports performers. • Can increase motivation of sports performers.	• May be a lack of structure to the sessions. • May take a long time to meet goals. • If leader does not intervene when necessary, performers could learn incorrect techniques.

In order to be a successful sports leader, you will be required to use all of these effectively. Different types of leadership suit different types of performers and different activities. The style you choose will depend on a number of factors, including the aim of the session (what is to be achieved), the performers within the session (how they work together) and how the performers react to different leadership styles (this may depend on their level). It is important to consider how every individual is going to be enhanced by the session.

Motivation

Our level of motivation can determine what we do (and possibly what we don't do). As a sports leader it is important to understand what motivates performers to participate in sports to ensure that they remain focused and achieve their goals.

There are two forms of motivation:

- **intrinsic motivation** – when a sports performer participates in an activity or sport for its own sake. They are motivated by the pleasure of the activity and the satisfaction or sense of accomplishment they feel from playing or participating.
- **extrinsic motivation** – this concerns the influence of things outside the athlete or activity, such as external rewards. An extrinsically motivated sports performer is motivated by external factors rather than the sport or activity. They play the sport with a desire to achieve something, such as a medal or prize.

CONTINUED ▶▶

José Mourinho is often seen as an extrovert. Do you agree?

Link

For more information on personality types see *Unit 3: The Mind and Sports Performance*.

Fabio Capello is often seen as an introvert. Do you agree?

Humour

It is important for sports leaders to have a sense of humour; this enables them to relate to the performers. Obviously it is important that laughter is only used at appropriate times. Performers' enjoyment is increased when they know their sports leader can share a joke with them.

Personality

Personality can be defined as the characteristics that make each individual unique. All sports leaders have their own individual characteristics and methods. It is important that sports leaders are confident and have the ability to plan and lead sport and physical activity sessions. Personalities fall into two categories: **introvert** and **extrovert**.

- **Introverts** are individuals who do not actively seek excitement and would rather be in calm or quiet places. In the world of sport introverts tend to prefer sports that require low levels of excitement but require high concentration levels and accuracy in their delivery.

- **Extroverts** are inclined to get bored quickly and are often poor at tasks that require a great deal of concentration. They constantly seek stimulation and excitement.

Activity 6.2   Introvert or extrovert?

Make a list of ten famous sports performers. Place each one into a category: introvert or extrovert. Write the performer's sport in brackets after their name.

Introvert	Extrovert
Roger Federer (Tennis)	Usain Bolt (Athletics)

Make a list of your friends and complete the exercise again. Think about the characteristics of your friends and discuss with the group what makes them introverted or extroverted.

Just checking

1. What are the different methods of communication that should be used by sports leaders?
2. What is an aim?
3. Provide an example of an aim for any sports leadership session.
4. What is an objective?
5. What structure should a sports session follow?
6. Identify each stage of the reflective cycle.

WorkSpace

Luke Damas

Football coach

I have recently attained my Level 1 Award in Coaching Football and have been helping out with the under-11s at my own football club, alongside my old team coach, Hannah.

It first started when I went to watch my younger brother training – I wanted to play, as I always do when I see anyone playing football. However, Hannah would not let me play; I am more than five years older than my brother and much bigger.

Hannah did ask if I wanted to help her out with the team and I agreed. At first I really struggled with not playing and joining in, but Hannah taught me to constantly watch over the players in order to ensure they don't make mistakes or do anything silly. Similarly, Hannah has developed my ability to spot hazards and deal with potentially dangerous situations.

During a recent game one of the players was injured. As Hannah's assistant, I ran onto the pitch and spotted that the injury was much more serious than a normal kick to the shin. I panicked and shouted for Hannah to come over. She was very calm, and calmed me down as well as the player who was injured. She dealt with the incident appropriately and effectively – she ensured that the correct action was taken and that the player (I later found out he had broken his leg) was taken to hospital with a parent to support him. The rest of the players were kept away from the incident to ensure they were not distressed by the injury.

Think about it

1   When leading sports activity sessions, why is health and safety so important?

2   Can you think of a plan that you should follow when serious injuries take place on a football field, or within a competitive situation in your own sport?

3   What courses would you need to undertake to become a qualified first aider?

Responsibilities of sports leaders

Getting started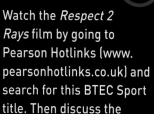

Watch the *Respect 2 Rays* film by going to Pearson Hotlinks (www. pearsonhotlinks.co.uk) and search for this BTEC Sport title. Then discuss the conduct of the coach (Dad) who is leading the young children's football team.

Introduction

Sports leaders must fulfil a number of core and additional responsibilities. Every sports leader represents the sport they are delivering, so it is important that they do so with appropriate care and attention to all of the required areas of legislation. It is not always the sports performer who judges a sports leader, but possibly the club that the sports leader works for or the parents of children in the care of the leader.

Core responsibilities

Professional conduct

It is important that performers see their sports leaders conduct themselves in an appropriate manner. The expectations about leaders' behaviour come from the performers and spectators of the sport, as well as the people who have appointed the leader.

Sports leaders should promote participation in physical activity by providing participants with positive values, including playing within the rules of the sport.

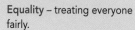

Key terms

Equality – treating everyone fairly.

Inequality – social disparity, e.g. inequality between the rich and the poor.

Prejudice – intolerance of or dislike for people based on, for example, race, religion, sexual orientation, age or disability.

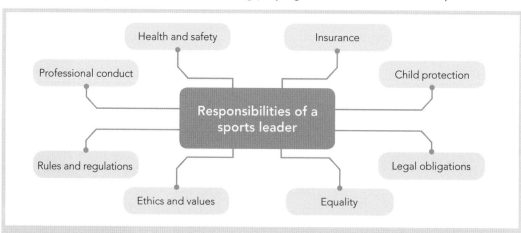

Figure 6.4 Responsibilities of a sports leader

Equality

As a sports leader you will deliver sports and physical activity sessions to a range of performers with different abilities. Whatever their differences, you must provide all sports performers with the same opportunities to develop and improve their performance – this is what **equality** is about. Sports leaders should lead sport and physical activity sessions without any **inequality** or **prejudice** and must ensure all participants are treated equally and included in all of their sessions.

Activity 6.3 Code of conduct

Develop a code of conduct for all sports leaders to follow when leading sport and physical activity sessions.

Sports leaders are responsible for the health, safety and well-being of sports performers during the period of time in which they are under their supervision.

Health and safety

Sport is a physical activity and carries an element of challenge for all who participate. Achieving the challenges and targets set will demand a mixture of skill, fitness and coordination. The risk of accidents is always there, so the skill of identifying hazards that could cause accidents, and minimising the risk, is a key requirement when planning and leading sport and physical activity sessions.

Sports leaders have responsibility for sport performers during the period of time in which they are under their supervision; this includes the health, well-being and safety of participants. It is therefore important that a sports leader not only checks on the performers throughout the session to ensure they are safe and healthy at all times, but also makes sure they are always aware of risks and hazards that could cause injury.

Case study

As a sports leader at an athletics club you are shocked to be informed that during the previous week's training session an athlete was injured after being hit by a discus. After investigation, it seems that this happened because an athlete ran across the throwing area during the end of the training session in an attempt to get to the changing rooms before his friends. The club have taken this minor injury very seriously and would like to devise a strategy to ensure that incidents like this do not happen in the future.

1 Complete a five-point plan to be followed by every sports leader prior to the start of every session.

2 Develop a code of conduct for sports performers and sports leaders at the club with regards to health and safety.

3 Identify five hazards that could cause injury and the types of injuries that each hazard could cause.

4 Identify for each of the hazards the measures that could be put in place to reduce the risk of injury to participants and sports leaders who may be affected.

CONTINUED ▶▶

Did you know?

You must gain a recognised qualification if you want to be insured for planning and leading sports activities independently. Without a recognised and appropriate qualification you are only allowed to support a qualified sports leader/coach.

Wider responsibilities

Insurance

Sports leaders must have appropriate insurance cover to participate in physical activity, and lead sports or physical activity sessions. They are responsible for the safety of all performers under their supervision. If a sports performer were to get injured the sports leader would be held responsible for the accident and might be considered negligent.

Child protection

Child protection has become a concern in sport and physical activity. When children are introduced to new people in new settings it is vital that a sports club keeps children safe and adheres to their statutory duties set out in legislation such as the Children Act (1989 and 2004). It is the duty of sports clubs to fulfil this responsibility.

Many sports clubs now complete police checks and ensure that sports leaders undertake child protection training via workshops on a regular basis.

Take it further

To find out more about child protection and sports leadership visit the NSPCC Child Protection in Sport Unit website. You can access this by going to Pearson Hotlinks (www.pearsonhotlinks.co.uk) and search for this BTEC Sport title.

Legal obligations

There are a number of legal requirements that can affect the work of a sports leader. It is your responsibility to know and understand the relevant legislation and all that you should be doing to follow it. Laws are passed by the government to support the safety of people who wish to undertake physical activity. The following Acts have been implemented by the government and are relevant to sports leaders at the time of publication:

- **Disability Discrimination Act 1995**: this act makes it illegal for anyone providing a service to discriminate against disabled people. This includes accessibility and provision in sport and physical activity.

- **Activity Centres (Young Persons' Safety Act) 1995**: this act requires that all centres offering adventure activities for children under the age of 18 are registered and licensed to HM Government's Adventure Activities Licensing Service. The requirements are that all staff possess specific qualifications, and follow specific operation and emergency procedures in their centre. It is also a requirement that the centre has the correct ratio of staff to children participating in any activity.

Rules and regulations

Link

See *Unit 2: Practical Sports Performance* for more information on the rules and regulations in sport.

When leading sessions it is important to promote the rules and regulations of the sport. As well as developing an individual's technical ability the session should also develop their knowledge of the game. Sports leaders should ensure that participants learn how to follow the rules and respect officials.

Sports leaders should promote friendship and respect for others.

Ethics and values

Ethical practice can be described as honest, fair and responsible conduct and actions. Values are ideas to which we attach worth or importance. Effective sports leaders should promote ethics and values within their sports sessions. The following principles should be encouraged:

- friendship
- respect for others
- playing with the right spirit
- equal opportunities
- fair play.

Assessment activity 6.1   2A.P1   2A.P2   2A.M1   2A.M2   2A.D1

You have been approached by Sport Makers, an initiative within your local council that supports the development of leadership skills in sport in your local area. They have asked you to develop a leaflet for all potential sports leaders about the attributes required to be an effective sports leader.

1 Consider the skills, qualities and responsibilities that leaders must adopt and use to be effective when leading sports sessions.

2 Select two sports leaders of your choice and compare the attributes they have that make them so successful as leaders.

Tips

- For each sports leader, describe the attributes they are demonstrating when they are successfully leading a sports activity session.
- Identify the strengths of your chosen sports leaders, and also the areas where they might have weaknesses they would benefit from developing. Give evidence for each of your statements.
- Consider the attributes the leaders share, as well as those that are different.
- 'Evaluate' means bringing together your information and reviewing it to reach a conclusion. Do this by identifying the strengths of your chosen sports leaders, and also the areas where they might have weaknesses that they would benefit from developing. Give evidence for each of your statements.

Sports activity sessions and their components

 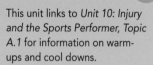
Link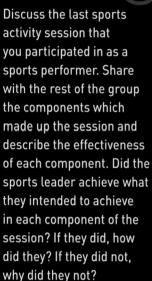

This unit links to *Unit 10: Injury and the Sports Performer, Topic A.1* for information on warm-ups and cool downs.

Key term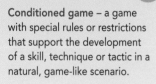

Conditioned game – a game with special rules or restrictions that support the development of a skill, technique or tactic in a natural, game-like scenario.

Introduction

Sports activities can take many different forms; for instance, they can involve individual or team sports, or fitness activities such as circuit training. In this unit you will be required to deliver all, or a component of, a sports activity session to a specific group of performers and demonstrate your ability to plan and lead it effectively.

Components of sports activity

Warm-up

Every sports session should start with a warm-up to prepare the sports performers both physically and mentally.

The warm-up should last for at least 10 minutes. It should take a methodological approach which:

- initially increases body heat and the respiratory and metabolic rates
- stretches the muscles and mobilises the joints that will be used in the session
- includes rehearsal and practice of some of the activities that are required in the sport.

Main components of the session

The session could include a variety of activities depending on the aims and objectives. If these are to introduce or develop a specific skill, the sports leader will need to include technical drills and skill practices, depending on the sport and skill being covered in the session. If the aims and objectives are to develop a specific aspect of fitness, the session will have to include appropriate fitness activities.

The main body of the session often includes a competitive element. Some sports leaders will use this to develop the skill or component of fitness covered earlier in the session. To do this a sports coach may choose to use a **conditioned game**. For example, if the aim of the session is to develop short passing in football, the coach may choose to condition a competitive game at the end where a team can score a goal for completing ten or more consecutive passes.

Cool down

At the end of the session a sports leader should ensure that all participants spend an appropriate amount of time cooling down. The aim of this is to bring the body gradually back to the pre-exercise condition. If performed correctly, a cool down should prevent muscle stiffness and injury and improve flexibility, provided stretches are performed correctly and controlled effectively by the coach.

Discussion point

Look at the image of a sports performer stretching. Stretching should be an integral part of all sports leaders' sessions.

1 Select a sport that you enjoy participating in.

2 For that sport, identify all of the muscles required for effective participation.

3 As a group, for each muscle select a stretch that can be used in a warm-up to prepare the muscle for physical activity and in a cool down to help return the muscle to its pre-activity state.

Just checking

1 What should the main components of a warm-up be?

2 Provide an example of a skill development drill.

3 What is a conditioned game/practice?

4 Provide an example of an effective cool down for a volleyball session, which is fun and appropriate for young children.

Planning sports activities

Introduction

In order to ensure that sports participants develop in every session, it is important that a sports leader plans each session thoroughly. Such plans should be both inclusive and flexible.

Participants

Prior to planning your sport or physical activity session you should collect information about your group. This should include:

- group size
- age
- ability of performers
- gender mix

- interests and previous experience
- medical information
- specific needs of participants.

The session plan that you design will have to be realistic for the needs and aspirations of the performers you will be delivering your session to. Sports leaders will deliver sessions to a range of participants, including children, young adults, the elderly and disabled performers.

Resources

When planning any sports or physical activity session, the equipment is often essential in meeting the aims and objectives of your session. Prior to sports or physical activity sessions the sports leader should check the availability of the equipment and facilities and ensure that these are safe and appropriate for the session.

When planning a sports activity, a sports leader must check the availability and suitability of the facilities they want to use.

When using a new venue it is important that the sports leader is aware of the **environment** in which they are delivering their session, including emergency procedures and the location of the changing rooms and toilets.

Another important resource to consider when planning a sports or physical activity session is time. The amount of time which you have to deliver the session is very important and can determine the activities that are included.

Aims and objectives

All sports sessions should have aims, which should be clearly stated on your session plan and agreed with participants at the start of the session. Each aim should be an expected **outcome**, which will be achieved by all or some of the sports performers within the session. For example, 'I want everyone in this session to be able to throw a ball by the end of it.' You may aim towards different outcomes for different sports performers within the session.

To achieve your aim, you will need to set some objectives. These should be written clearly on your session plan and should express how you will meet each of your aims.

Health and safety

Health and safety is the most important responsibility of a sports leader.

It is important that risk assessments and all appropriate checks are carried out before you complete your session or event to ensure that it runs as smoothly as possible without risk of injury to any of the sports performers or other leaders involved. Safety checks should be carried out throughout the session.

When planning an event where there may be large numbers of participants, every possible occurrence should be considered. Sports leaders must have knowledge of basic first aid and understand what action to take if serious injuries occur during the session. It is your responsibility to ensure that someone who has a relevant first aid certificate is available during the delivery of your event and that they have appropriate equipment and resources to carry out this role.

> ### Link
>
> *Unit 10: Injury and the Sports Performer* explores the importance of health and safety in greater detail.

> **Activity 6.4**   Health and safety planning
>
> Put together a 10-point safety checklist that you will use before any sport or physical activity session.

Risk assessment

A risk assessment is a careful examination of the various hazards within the environment in which your session is taking place, including the equipment you are using to deliver the session. It should identify the level of risk posed to the sports performers, the spectators and you as the sports leader. Within the risk assessment you should ensure that you identify all the hazards and clearly plan what actions will be taken to minimise the risks.

Informed consent

Before running any sports session, the sports leader should ensure that all sports performers who are participating in the session have completed a **consent form** to confirm that they:

- are able to participate in the session
- know what is required from them within the session
- have consented to their participation if old enough (if below the age of 18 this will need to be done by a parent/carer); this is indicated by a signature on the form
- have provided you with any details of medical issues that may prevent them from participating, and any injuries or underlying health issues.

> ### Key term
>
> **Consent form** – used to obtain permission to participate in a physical activity session (this must be completed by a parent/carer for all sports performers under the age of 18).

Leading a session, and measuring success

Link

For more information on each of the attributes required to lead a sports activity session successfully, refer back to *Topic A.2.*

A sports leader should be able to clearly communicate tactics to sports performers.

Link

For more information on how to apply each of the responsibilities and wider responsibilities within a sports activity session successfully, refer back to *Topic A.3.*

Introduction

When leading a sports or physical activity session, it is important to stick to the session plan and use a variety of methods to measure the success of the session.

Demonstration of attributes

When leading an activity session or sports event a sports leader will demonstrate skills, qualities and responsibilities that have already been covered in this unit. The leader should ensure that the session flows and provide a variety of activities for the sports performers, and most importantly ensure that performers are safe at all times. This should be measured through effective planning and preparation, pre-activity checks and through the sports leader monitoring the performance of the athletes during the session.

The sports leader should set out the aims and objectives of the session at the start and for each activity, and clearly state the rules and regulations. When possible the sports leader should relate these to the rules and regulations of the sport being coached to reinforce knowledge and develop the participants' understanding.

An important skill that sports leaders have to master is communication. Sports leaders will have to be able to communicate effectively to ensure that their group understands the instructions provided and can follow them to support their own development.

Completion of core and wider responsibilities

When leading a sports activity session you should ensure that all of the core responsibilities and wider responsibilities required to be a successful sports leader are appropriately applied.

A sports activity session should be delivered using methods that are as visual as possible. Sports leaders should demonstrate to learners what they want them to do. The sports leader should have sufficient knowledge of the technical requirements of the skills to demonstrate the correct methods to the learners. A sports leader who is unable to carry out the demonstration because of injury or any other reason should still carry out a demonstration but using another member of the group, or another coach or sports leader who is available. A sports leader who is unable to carry out the demonstration should describe each key factor of the technique and discuss its importance in the application of the skill.

The sports leader should ensure that the session is aimed at the correct level and that the language used is appropriate to the participants. The session must be exciting and enjoyable for the performers but should also develop them, by providing them with appropriate guidance and feedback throughout the session. The leader should ensure that all participants are monitored throughout the session and that positive feedback is used to encourage performers.

Look at the image of a sports leader assisting with the demonstration of a skill to a group of children. Select four skills from a selected sport and discuss with your group the correct technical method of demonstration of each skill to a group of sports performers.

Measures of success

It is important as sports leaders that we measure the success of the sessions that we deliver. The methods we use to measure success can take many different forms.

Figure 6.5 Measures of success by sports leaders

Within your session plan it is important that you clearly state which measures of success you will be using.

1 What are:

   a The skills required to lead a successful sports activity session?

   b The advanced skills required to lead a successful sports activity session?

2 What are:

   a The qualities required to lead a successful sports activity session?

   b The additional qualities required to lead a successful sports activity session?

3 What are:

   a The core responsibilities when leading a successful sports activity session?

   b The wider responsibilities required to lead a successful sports activity session?

Reviewing the planning and leading of sports activities

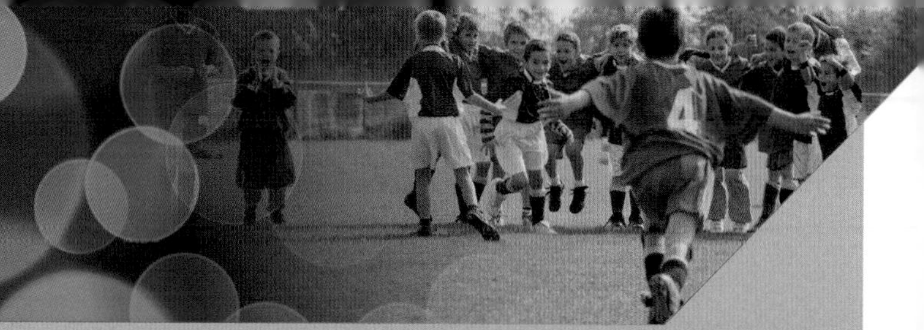

Introduction

After the completion of a session or event a sports leader should invite participants to give **feedback**. This feedback can then be used by the sports leader to identify components of the session that went well and components of the session that may require development in future.

Key term

Feedback – the information you obtain from yourself and others which reflects on your performance. In this instance the feedback you obtain will be the opinions of others about your performance as a sports leader.

It is key for your development as a sports leader that you obtain feedback from others, including your teachers/supervisors and any observers of the session who may be able to provide you with guidance and support. The feedback you obtain from experienced sports leaders/coaches can be used to improve and develop your performance.

It is important that, on completion of the session, you also complete a self-analysis. This is where you give your own comments on the session. The questions you should ask yourself when completing a self-analysis are as follows:

1. Did I meet the aims, targets and objectives of the sessions as listed within the session plan?
2. Did the participants enjoy the session?
3. Was the session risk-free and did I ensure that nobody got injured?
4. Did I demonstrate all of the attributes required to lead a sports leadership session successfully?

Methods

A range of methods can be used to generate feedback. These could include:

- questionnaires
- comment cards
- observation records
- direct verbal feedback.

The method you use to collect feedback from participants in the session will be different from the method you use to collect feedback from the observers.

You could ask the performers how they felt the session went (direct verbal feedback), but this method may not always generate honest feedback; the use of a questionnaire may generate more genuine opinions.

Please tick your answers

Did you enjoy the session?
☺ ☐ 😐 ☐ ☹ ☐

Did you enjoy the warm-up?
☺ ☐ 😐 ☐ ☹ ☐

Did you enjoy the drills in the session, e.g. dribbling between cones, shooting into the hockey net?
☺ ☐ 😐 ☐ ☹ ☐

Did the sports leader communicate clearly?
☺ ☐ 😐 ☐ ☹ ☐

Did the sports leader demonstrate clearly what you had to do in the session?
☺ ☐ 😐 ☐ ☹ ☐

Did you feel that your performance improved in the session?
☺ ☐ 😐 ☐ ☹ ☐

What extra activities would you like to have done in the session?

....

....

....

....

....

Figure 6.6 After a sports event you could obtain feedback from performers using a questionnaire.

Within your group, complete four different warm-ups.

To assess the effectiveness of each warm up, obtain feedback from each of the participants.

Prior to the session, you should develop a variety of methods to obtain feedback from the participants after each of the warm-ups.

Ensure you use a different method of feedback for each of the sessions.

Once all of the feedback has been collected, discuss which methods collected the most honest and useful responses.

Strengths and areas for improvement

After receiving feedback from participants and observers you should then conclude what you felt were the strengths of your session/event and what parts you would like to develop and improve on.

Once you have gathered all of the feedback from the session you should consider the following components and complete your review of the session.

- What sort of feedback did you get about your successful demonstration of attributes when leading the session?
- With reference to the feedback, how do you think you managed each of the responsibilities required to lead a sports activity session successfully?
- How effective was the planning for the sports activity session?
- What was the content of the sessions like – what did different people like, and why do you think they liked some parts but not others?
- How organised did people think the session was? Did you ensure that everyone was safe at all times?
- What did you achieve within the session, and what did the performers achieve within the session?

When developing areas for improvement it is important to ask yourself a number of questions:

- What went well in the session?
- What went wrong in the session?
- Why does a particular component of the session need developing?
- What did other people say (feedback) about this part of the session?
- What can I do to develop this part of the session?

CONTINUED ▶▶

◤ Targets for development

After you have considered what your strengths and areas for improvement are when leading sports sessions, you should then set a series of targets to support your own development as a sports leader.

SMARTER targets

When setting yourself targets you should use the SMARTER model:

- **Specific** – make the target as precise and detailed as possible.
- **Measurable** – consider the methods used to measure your performance against the targets.
- **Achievable** – goals should be attainable and should be relevant to the sports performer.
- **Realistic** – appropriate targets that can be met within the timescales set.
- **Timed** – ensure you set yourself a deadline to have achieved your targets by.
- **Exciting** – the targets that are set should motivate and challenge the individual or team.
- **Recorded** – progress towards the attainment of each target should be recorded.

Development plan

A development plan is a formal way of planning methods to enhance your ability as a leader. By making a record of activities, you will be able to measure the progress you are making over time.

A development plan should have clear aims and objectives – these can be short-, medium- and long-term goals, but importantly should all be attainable. You should consider using the SMARTER method to plan your aims.

Link

For more information on targets see *Unit 3: The Mind and Sports Performance* and *Unit 13: Profiling Sports Performance*.

Key term

Barriers – obstacles that may prevent someone from participating in a sport or physical activity. For example, money – if a young child does not have enough money for golf clubs they will be unable to play golf.

Within your development plan, list and justify all the activities and opportunities you feel would develop you as a sports leader. These may include specific training courses or qualifications to develop your skills. They may even include observing and supporting other, more experienced, sports leaders at other sports clubs.

Within your development plan it is also important that you include a summary of the potential **barriers** that may prevent you from achieving your aims, objectives and goals. These might include lack of time, lack of money, lack of transport or lack of availability of courses, for example.

Sports leaders should always be setting targets for their development.

Assessment activity 6.2 *English Maths* | 2B.P3 | 2B.P4 | 2B.M3 | 2B.M4 | 2C.P5 | 2C.M5 | 2C.D2

You have been asked to help out with your school's Year 6 Taster Day, where pupils from local primary schools come in to see what different subjects are like at your school. The Head of PE has asked you to plan and support some of the PE taster sessions.

1 Prepare a session plan for:

- a circuit session
- an activity session for any team game.

You should give reasons for your choice of activities.

2 The Head of PE was particularly impressed with your circuit session plan and would like you to lead this session. Carry out the session with a group of pupils.

3 Review your planning and leading of the circuit session. What were your strengths? Are there areas where you could improve? Set some targets for your future development as a sports leader using a personal development plan, and give reasons for these.

Tips

For Task 1, ensure your plans include:

- information about the participants' age, ability, gender and specific needs; aims and objectives; resources; and health and safety considerations
- a warm-up, main activity/components of activity, and cool down
- a risk assessment
- an informed consent form for each participant
- different methods to collect feedback from the performers in the sessions to help you evaluate your performance as a leader and the success of the session.

For Task 2:

- lead the activity confidently, knowing the requirements of each component of your session
- demonstrate a variety of attributes and responsibilities throughout the session and lead independently
- on completion of the session, obtain feedback from all participants.

For Task 3:

- remember to refer to the feedback you obtained from your teacher and participants in your session.
- present your areas for improvement as aims and objectives
- produce a development plan which highlights your goals and the SMARTER targets you are going to follow in order to develop as a sports leader
- include opportunities and activities which could develop your leadership attributes and responsibilities, justifying how each opportunity or activity will develop your skills.

Introduction

Sports students need a good understanding of how the human body is built and how it works. Without this, how can fitness levels in an individual be improved? How can a coach help improve an athlete's skills and abilities for a given sport? And, importantly, how can the risk of injury be minimised during sports participation if you do not know what the body can and cannot do?

To perform any sports activity, it is essential that we understand how the body is structured. This is called anatomy.

We must also be able to understand how the body functions. This is called physiology.

These two things help us to understand how the body can adapt to improve certain functions and therefore enable us to perform at a better level. The human body has many systems contained within it. This chapter will consider some of those vital to sports performance.

Assessment: You will be assessed using an onscreen test lasting one hour.

Learning aims

In this unit you will:

A know about the structure and function of the musculoskeletal system

B know about the structure and function of the cardiorespiratory system.

> Knowing how the skeleton works together with the muscular system helped me design an aerobics sequence for my aerobics instructing qualification. I was able to come up with lots of different movements that made my sessions more fun for everyone in the group.
>
> Imogen, *18-year-old aerobics instructor*

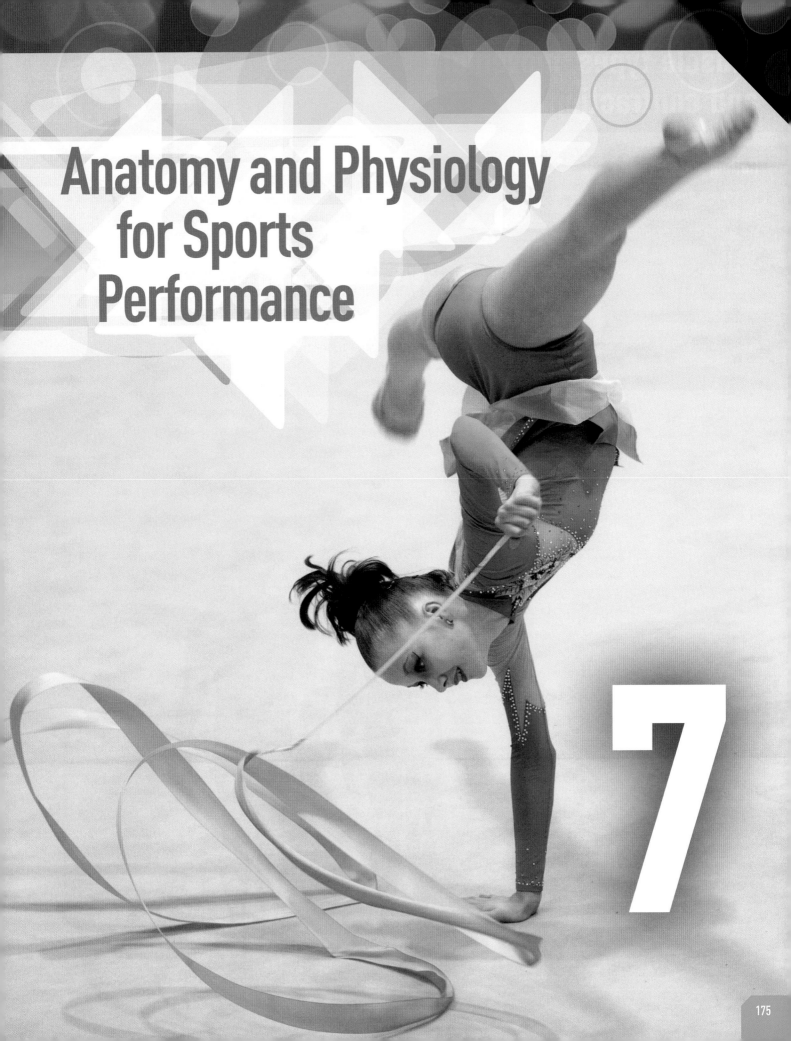

Anatomy and Physiology for Sports Performance

7

Muscle types, movement and contraction

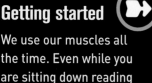

Key term

Muscle – a tissue made up of fibres that are capable of contracting to produce movement.

Introduction

The human body is like a machine or a car. There are different components that together make it work. Bones give the body its shape and muscles help the body to move. In a car the engine helps create motion, in the human body, muscles do this job!

It would be impossible for you to do anything without your **muscles**. Absolutely everything that you think of with your brain is expressed as muscular motion. For example, the only ways for you to express an idea are with the muscles of your mouth and tongue (spoken words), with the muscles of your fingers (written words or 'talking with your hands') or with the skeletal muscles (body language, dancing, running, playing sport and so on).

Because muscles are so crucial to any movement you produce, they have to be really sophisticated. They have to be efficient at turning energy into motion, they have to be long-lasting and self-healing, and they have to be able to become stronger with practice.

When most people think of 'muscles', they think about the muscles that they can see. Figure 7.1 shows all of the major muscles of the human body.

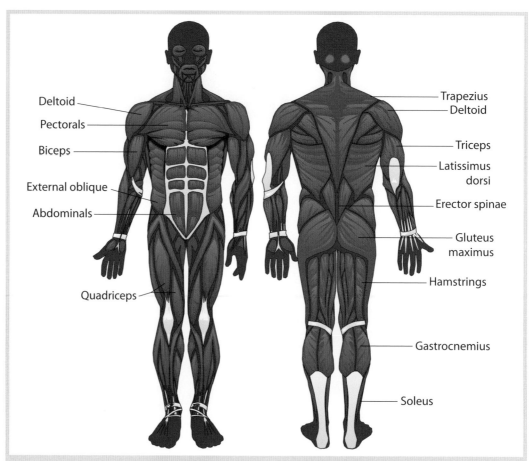

Figure 7.1 How many of these muscles are you familiar with already?

Types of muscles

There are three types of muscle in the human body.

- **Skeletal or voluntary muscle** – used primarily for movement of the skeleton, for example the biceps or hamstrings. They produce rapid and powerful contractions brought about by a conscious thought process.

- **Smooth or involuntary muscle** – found in the stomach and intestines, this has several functions, including forcing food through the digestive system (by peristalsis) and squeezing blood throughout the circulatory system. It comprises about 40% of the body mass in the human body. This muscle type produces a slow and rhythmic contraction that is controlled unconsciously by the nervous system.

- **Cardiac or heart muscle** – found only in the heart and used to force blood into the circulatory vessels. This type of muscle has a fairly rapid and sustained contraction and is controlled unconsciously by the heart's pacemaker.

Voluntary muscle movements

Most major movements rely on a number of voluntary muscles working together. In order for a coordinated movement to be produced, the muscles must work as a group or team, with several muscles working at any one time.

Antagonistic muscles

Some muscles work in pairs in order to produce a movement and its opposite movement. These are called **antagonistic muscles**.

An example of this can be seen in the arm. The muscle responsible for **flexion** of the arm at the elbow (bending of the arm) is the biceps. The muscle is called the **agonist** or **prime mover** because it produces the desired joint movement.

In order for the biceps muscle to shorten when contracting, the triceps muscle must lengthen. The triceps is known as the **antagonist** in this instance; its action is opposite to that of the agonist.

The two muscles must work together to produce the required movement.

Did you know?

It takes the interaction of 72 different muscles to produce human speech.

Key terms

Antagonistic muscles – a pair of muscles working together to produce movement; one muscle works and the other opposes the action.

Flexion – the bending of a limb at a joint.

Agonist or prime mover – the muscle that is directly involved in the initial contraction to produce a movement.

Antagonist – a muscle that opposes the agonist muscle during a movement.

CONTINUED ▶▶

Activity 7.2   Agonist/antagonist

Fill in the missing words, stating which muscle is the agonist and which one is the antagonist:

1 The biceps is the _____ and the triceps is the _____ when bending the elbow.
2 The hamstrings are the _____ and the quadriceps are the _____ when straightening the leg.
3 The rectus abdominus is the _____ and the erector spinae is the _____ when sitting up doing a sit-up.
4 The trapezius is the _____ and the pectoralis major is the _____ when bringing the arms together using a pec deck (fixed weight machine).

Types of contraction

There are three main types of muscle contraction:

1 concentric
2 eccentric
3 isometric.

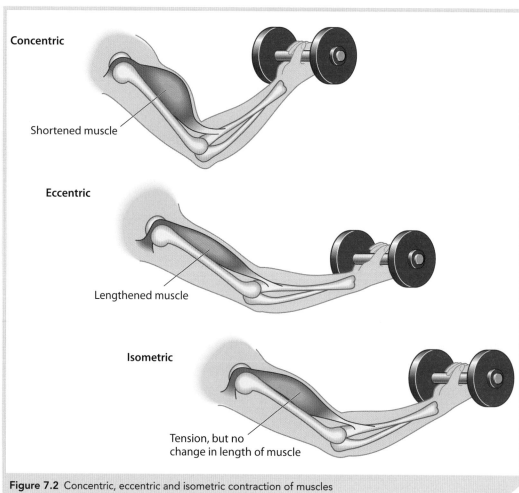

Concentric

Shortened muscle

Eccentric

Lengthened muscle

Isometric

Tension, but no change in length of muscle

Figure 7.2 Concentric, eccentric and isometric contraction of muscles

Concentric

A **concentric contraction** happens when a muscle shortens as it contracts. An example of concentric contraction can be seen when you contract the biceps to bring about flexion of the arm at the elbow.

Eccentric

Eccentric contraction is the opposite of concentric; the muscle lengthens as it gains tension: for example, when lowering weights, the biceps must contract in this way to help control the downwards movement.

Isometric

An **isometric contraction** happens when there is tension on the muscle but no movement is made, causing the length of the muscle to remain the same: for example, the muscles of the legs in holding a position such as a plank.

Can you feel the muscles working if you try a plank?

Activity 7.3   Exercising specific muscles

Identify at least two more exercises for each of the three different types of muscle contraction described. Explain clearly how to perform each exercise and use simple diagrams to support your explanation.

Assessment practice 7.1

1 Which of the following descriptions best describes antagonistic muscles? [1]

A When muscles are painful after exercise.

B Muscles that work together to produce a movement and its opposite movement.

C When muscles are not strong enough and may need assistance to perform a task.

D Muscles that shorten as they contract.

2 Name the two types of muscle found in the human body. [2]

Muscle movements and sports performance

Getting started

It is essential in sport that our muscles are ready to work without being damaged as soon as we start to take part.

How might you prepare your muscles in readiness for taking part in your chosen sport? Can you describe which muscles you need to get ready to take part – and more importantly, why preparation is important?

Introduction

You have already looked at how muscles work in pairs, identifying the agonist and antagonist in each pair, and considered three different types of muscle contraction. But how does this knowledge help you when you participate in sport?

Agonist and antagonist muscles in relation to sports performance

Analysis of movement is complex and generally relies on very sophisticated equipment, but basic analysis of movement can easily be done by carefully watching someone perform a movement.

Try the activity below just using the photographs.

Activity 7.4   Which muscles?

1 Which leg muscles are working to bend the knee so the footballer can kick the ball?

2 In this picture, which muscle is the agonist and which is the antagonist?

3 Explain what type of muscle contraction is taking place.

4 Which stomach and back muscles are working to help keep the gymnast in this handstand position?

5 Explain what type of muscle contraction is taking place.

6 Which muscles are working to allow this person to perform sit-ups?

7 In this picture, the person is going back down after performing a sit-up – which muscle is the agonist and which is the antagonist?

8 Explain the types of muscle contraction taking place.

Types of muscle fibre

Skeletal (or voluntary) **muscle** is made up of individual cells or fibres embedded in a matrix of **collagen**. At either end of the muscle, this matrix becomes the **tendon** that connects the muscle to bone. Tendons are composed of **fibrous tissue**. They are strong and flexible in order to allow movement to occur.

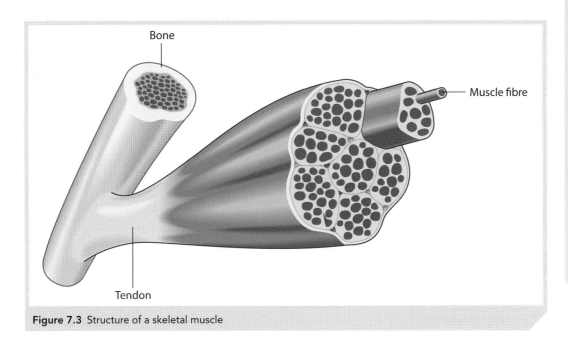

Bone

Muscle fibre

Tendon

Figure 7.3 Structure of a skeletal muscle

Skeletal muscle fibres contain many **myofibrils**. Each myofibril has strands of proteins (actin and myosin) that make muscle movement possible by shortening the muscle and causing **muscle contraction**. See Figure 7.4.

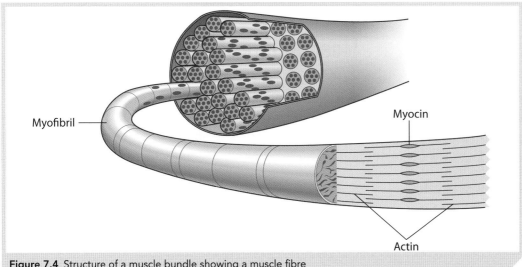

Myofibril

Myocin

Actin

Figure 7.4 Structure of a muscle bundle showing a muscle fibre

There are three muscle fibre types, each with very different characteristics. These are shown in Table 7.1.

Table 7.1 Muscle fibre types and their characteristics

Type	Speed of contraction	Force produced	Resistance to fatigue	Activities used for	Aerobic capacity
Type I – slow-twitch oxidative	Slow	Low	High	Endurance events, e.g. long-distance running	High aerobic capacity
Type IIa – fast-twitch oxidative (sometimes called intermediate fast-twitch)	Fast	Medium	Fair	Moderate intensity events, e.g. middle-distance running	Can use **aerobic** and **anaerobic** metabolism almost equally to create energy. In this way, they are a combination of type I and type II muscle fibres.
Type IIb – fast-twitch glycolytic	Fast	High	Low, due to build-up of **lactic acid**	Short, high-intensity events, e.g. sprinting	Strong anaerobic capacity

Key terms

Aerobic – with oxygen.

Anaerobic – without oxygen.

Lactic acid – a waste product, that builds up in the body during intense bouts of physical activity.

Assessment practice 7.2

1 **Slow twitch oxidative fibres are relied on for which type of exercise? [1]**

   A Moderate intensity events such as middle-distance running.

   B High intensity events such as power lifting.

   C Low intensity events such as long-distance swimming.

   D High intensity events such as sprinting.

2 **What are the single cells or fibres found in muscle embedded in? [1]**

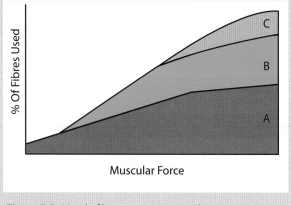

Figure 7.5 Muscle fibre recruitment graph

Muscle fibre recruitment

How many muscle fibres are needed to contract depends on the activity. If you are picking up a piece of paper, only a few muscle fibres in the necessary muscles will contract, but if you want to push a wall over, many muscle fibres will contract. The more fibres, the more force. Light force requires only slow-twitch fibres, whereas heavy loads need both fast- and slow-twitch fibres.

Section A of the graph shows that only a minimal amount of muscle contraction is taking place while sections B and C show an increased amount of muscle fibres being recruited in order to produce a greater contraction.

So section A might represent someone walking, section B someone running, section C someone sprinting. More muscle fibres are recruited to produce the greater output needed to perform a movement.

WorkSpace

Stevie Rodgers

Community sports coach

As a community sports coach, I work with local authorities, sports governing bodies, schools, sports clubs and leisure centres. My job is to ensure that I deliver safe and appropriate sports coaching and physical activities for young people who are 6–16 years of age.

In my role, I try to encourage young people to take part in more sport and physical activity with the aim of getting them to enjoy sport participation at a level that is right for them. I also help to identify talented individuals who need support to progress them in their particular sport.

My role requires many skills including:

- knowledge of how the body works
- awareness of how different sports require and work different muscle groups and energy systems
- a good understanding of training methods and activities, and how these can be used to improve sporting performance
- creativity for ensuring variation in activities.

My job is exciting because no two days are the same. Some days I work in schools helping with general activity sessions and on other days, I coach a specific sport at a sports centre.

All of my activities have to be appropriate for the individual's level of fitness and delivered in a safe manner so as not to risk injury. To reduce this risk, I use carefully designed session plans to ensure participants are appropriately warmed up and cooled down.

Understanding how the body functions and responds during exercise is important as it reduces the risks of injury and helps an individual improve their performance.

Constantly updating my skills and sports qualifications to make sure that I am fully aware of new training methods and activities is essential to my job. I also have to be enthusiastic and approachable as well as being patient and a good time manager!

Think about it

1   What areas have you covered in this unit that would help you if you were a community sports coach?

2   Stevie mentions some skills required to be a community sports coach. What other skills might you need?

3   Can you give two sports-specific examples to explain why understanding how the body is structured and how it works both normally and when taking part in physical activity is vital to a community sports coach?

Bones of the skeleton and their functions

Getting started

What happens to the 94 bones that we lose during the process of growing up? Where do they go?

Did you know?

A quarter of your body's bones are found in your feet; of the 200 or so bones in the body, the feet contain 52 of them.

Introduction

The human skeleton consists of 206 bones. When we are born, we actually have around 300 bones in our bodies, but as we grow up, many fuse together. The human skeleton is held together by a range of different connective tissues – some of which we have already mentioned, such as muscle and tendon.

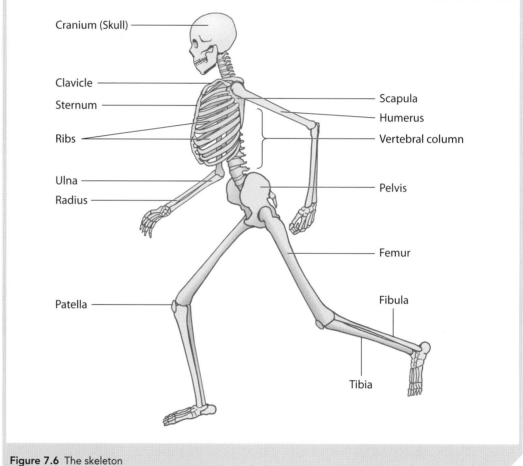

Figure 7.6 The skeleton

The largest bone is the pelvis, or hip bone. In fact, it is made of six bones joined firmly together.

The longest bone is the femur, in the thigh. It makes up almost one-quarter of the body's total height.

The smallest bone is the stirrup, deep in the ear. It is hardly larger than a grain of rice.

The ear itself and end of the nose do not have bones inside them. Their inner supports are **cartilage** or gristle, which is lighter and more flexible than bone. This is why the nose and ears can be bent.

Different types of bone

There are five main categories of bone that form the human skeleton.

Long bones

These are the bones connected with large movements. They are long and cylindrical with growth heads – **epiphyses** – at either end. The epiphysis is covered by **articular cartilage** (also known as **hyaline cartilage**). The outer layer of the bone is hard, and is called compact bone. The inside of the bone is spongy, and is called **cancellous bone**. Examples of long bones include the femur (thigh bone), the humerus (upper bone in the arm) and the phalanges (fingers and toes).

Short bones

These bones are almost cube-shaped and are associated with smaller, more complex movements. Examples of short bones include the carpals (small bones in the base of the hand) and tarsals (in the feet).

Flat bones

These bones protect the internal organs and include the skull (cranium), ribs, scapula (shoulder blade), sternum (breastbone) and the pelvic girdle.

Irregular bones

These bones are irregular in shape and include the vertebrae forming the vertebral column and some facial bones.

Sesamoid bones

These are small bones held within tendons and include the patella (knee cap).

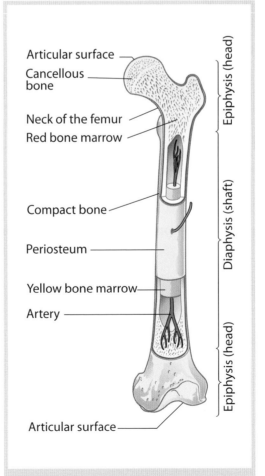

Articular surface
Cancellous bone
Neck of the femur
Red bone marrow
Compact bone
Periosteum
Yellow bone marrow
Artery
Articular surface
Epiphysis (head)
Diaphysis (shaft)
Epiphysis (head)

Figure 7.7 Diagram of a long bone

Key terms

Cartilage – a type of connective tissue that gives structure and support to other tissues.

Compact bone – hard, rigid connective tissue forming the shaft of the bone.

Marrow – the soft, vascular tissue that fills most bone cavities and is the source of red blood cells and many white blood cells.

Epiphyses – growth plates at the end of bones.

Articular cartilage or **hyaline cartilage** – a shiny, firm type of cartilage that is flexible and elastic. It is found on the articulating surfaces of bones that form joints and also in the trachea.

Cancellous bone – Spongy connective tissue forming the ends of bone.

Remember

Remember these different bone types and their examples for later in the chapter when you will look at how movement occurs.

CONTINUED ▶▶

Axial skeleton – consists of the skull, sternum (manubrium, body, xiphoid process), vertebral column, and ribcage.

Appendicular skeleton – consists of the pectoral (shoulder) girdles, upper extremities (arms), pelvic girdle and lower extremities (legs).

The axial and the appendicular skeleton

The human skeleton can be divided into two main parts.

- The **axial skeleton** includes the cranium (skull) including the jawbone, sternum (manubrium, body, xiphoid process), ribcage and vertebral column.
- The **appendicular skeleton** is made up of the shoulder (or pectoral) girdle, the pelvic girdle and the bones of the arms and legs.

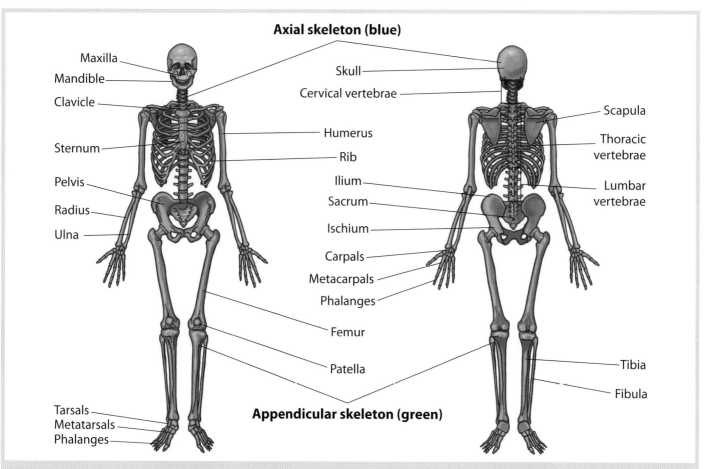

Figure 7.8 The axial and appendicular skeleton

Assessment practice 7.3

1 Where are flat bones found in the body? (1)

A In the arms and legs.

B Protecting vital organs.

C In the spine.

D In the cranium.

The ribcage and the vertebral column

Many features of the skeleton have specialised structures to help them function – for example, the ribcage and the vertebral column.

Structure of the ribcage

The main purpose of the ribcage is to protect the heart and lungs. It also serves as a chamber in which lungs can expand for breathing. Muscles between the ribs lift the ribcage during inhalation and move down to squeeze air out during exhalation.

All of the ribs are attached to the vertebrae at the back, but only some of the ribs are connected to the sternum at the front:

- **true ribs** (seven pairs) – attached to the vertebrae at the back, and to the sternum at the front
- **false ribs** (three pairs) – attached to the vertebrae at the back, and to the rib above at the front (via **costal cartilage**)
- **floating ribs** (two pairs) – attached to the vertebrae at the back only.

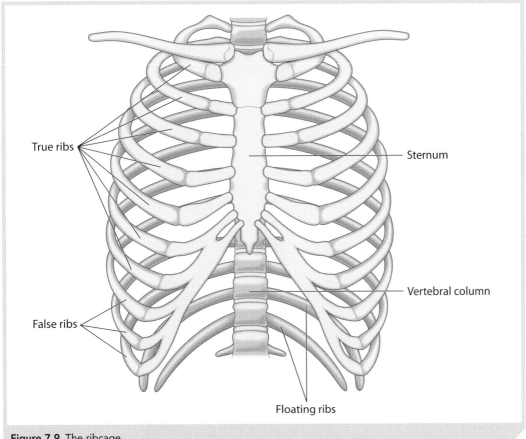

Figure 7.9 The ribcage

Key terms

Sternum – the large, flat bone in the centre and at the front of the cage.

True ribs – top seven (1–7) pairs of ribs that attach at the back to the thoracic vertebrae and at the front to the sternum.

False ribs – the next three (8–10) pairs of ribs which connect at the back to the thoracic vertebrae but only connect at the front by costal cartilage to the rib above.

Costal cartilage – layers of cartilage between each pair of ribs.

Floating ribs – last two (11–12) pairs of ribs that do not attach to anything at the front of the ribcage but attach to the thoracic vertebrae.

Vertebral column – also known as backbone or spine, consists of 33 vertebrae.

Spinal cord – protected by the vertebral column, is a long, thin bundle of nervous tissue transmitting nervous impulses/messages from the brain to the rest of the body.

CONTINUED ▶▶

Structure of the vertebral column

The vertebral column, also called the spine or the spinal column, consists of 33 bones: 24 bones are individual and unfused, while the remaining nine are fused together.

While the amount of movement between each vertebra is only small, when all 33 bones work together a vast range of movement is possible.

There are five main areas to the vertebral column.

- The **cervical vertebrae** (seven unfused bones) – these support the weight of the head by enabling muscle attachment through each of the vertebrae. The top two vertebrae, the atlas and the axis, enable the head to move up and down and from side to side respectively.
- The **thoracic vertebrae** (12 unfused bones) – these allow for the attachment of the ribs. These bones, together with the ribs, form the ribcage, which protects the heart and lungs.
- The **lumbar vertebrae** (five unfused bones) – these are the largest of all the individual vertebrae. They offer a great deal of weight-bearing capacity, and secure the attachment of a number of muscles. This, together with the intervertebral discs of cartilage, enables flexion of the trunk.

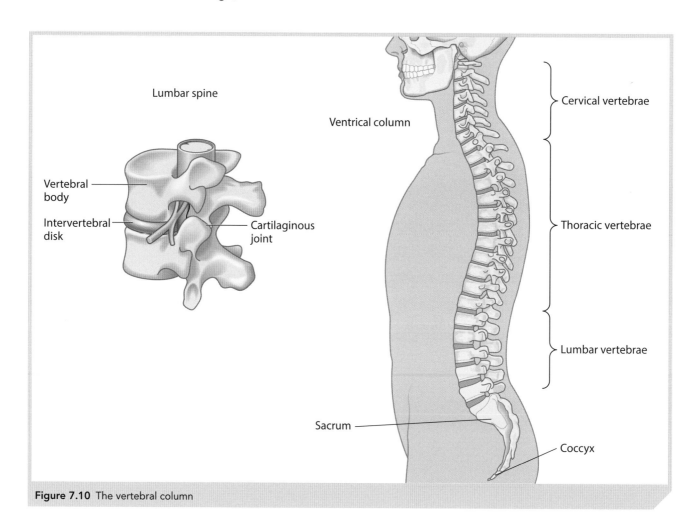

Figure 7.10 The vertebral column

- **The sacral vertebrae** (five fused bones) – these form the sacrum, which fuses to the pelvis. The sacrum and the pelvis bear and distribute the weight of the upper body.
- **The coccyx** (four fused bones) – this forms the very base of the vertebral column, and acts as a base for muscle attachment.

Activity 7.6 Back pain and injury

Although the lumbar vertebrae are large in size, this area of the vertebral column is the one most attributed to back pain and injury. Look at Figure 7.10 to see if you can explain why this might be.

Functions of the skeletal system

The skeleton has six important functions.

- Protection – for example, the brain is protected by the skull and the heart is protected by the ribcage.
- Movement and muscle attachment – working with skeletal muscles, tendons, ligaments and joints, the bones form the moving machinery of human body. Bones act as levers, which make use of the forces generated by skeletal muscles.
- Support – provides a framework for muscle attachment to support the body.
- Shape – bones provide a framework around which the body is built; they are responsible for the shape and form of the human body.
- Blood production – the bones themselves cannot do this, but long bones house the specific bone marrow which produces blood cells.
- Mineral storage – bones store minerals such as calcium, sodium, potassium and phosphorus.

Assessment practice 7.4

1 **Name two of the main types of bone. [2]**

2 **The vertebral column provides structural support and balance to maintain an upright posture and enable flexible motion. Identify one other function of the vertebral column. [1]**

Classification of joints, types of cartilage and joint structure

Introduction

So far we have considered two of the main body systems: the skeletal and the muscular. However, it is important that we also recognise how these two systems can work together.

Classification of joints

The purpose of most joints is to allow some movement, although the bones of the skull, for example, are joined so tightly that there is no movement at all. One way of classifying joints is by the quantity of movement permitted.

Joints can be:

- **fixed** or **immoveable**, e.g. fused joints of the skull and sacrum that provide no movement
- **slightly moveable** or **cartilaginous**, e.g. between each vertebra where a small range of movement occurs
- **freely moveable** or **synovial**, e.g. at the knee – a hinge joint – where a large amount of movement occurs. Many other freely moveable joints occur within the body, including in the hip and shoulder which contain ball and socket joints, and within the carpo-metacarpal joint of the thumb which contains a saddle joint.

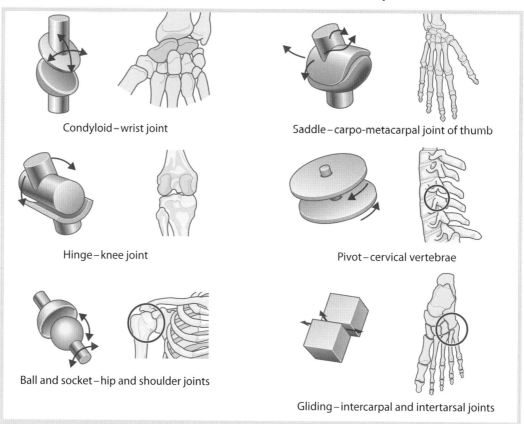

Condyloid – wrist joint

Saddle – carpo-metacarpal joint of thumb

Hinge – knee joint

Pivot – cervical vertebrae

Ball and socket – hip and shoulder joints

Gliding – intercarpal and intertarsal joints

Figure 7.11 The six types of synovial joints and where they are found in the body

Types of cartilage

Cartilage is a soft, slightly elastic tissue. It does not possess a blood supply. In fact, as human embryos develop, they begin by forming cartilage which then turns into bone.

There are three types of cartilage found in the body.

- **Fibrocartilage** is a dense, white tissue. It is found in tendons, the knee joint and, intervertebral discs of the spinal column. This type of cartilage is very tough, and its shock absorption properties mean that it is found in areas of the body under high stress. For example, the knee joint resists the huge amount of stress incurred as a result of performing activities such as the triple jump.
- Hyaline or articular cartilage is a fairly **resilient** tissue and is found on the articulating surfaces of bones that form joints. The cartilage protects the bone tissue from wear and reduces friction between articulating bones. Hyaline cartilage is also found in the trachea and the bronchi.
- **Elastic cartilage** is a much more **pliant** tissue that gives support and also flexibility. The external ear is an example of this.

Synovial joint structure

Synovial joints are the most evolved of the joints and therefore they are the most mobile. Synovial joints are surrounded by a **joint capsule**, which is made up of various fibrous connective tissues. Also called the articular capsule, this structure binds the bone ends together and is responsible for directing the movement allowed at that joint.

The joint capsule is lined by the **synovial membrane**. This membrane secretes synovial fluid into the joint cavity as a lubricant. Joints with tendons crossing the capsule have additional **synovial fluid** between the joint and tendon. This is called a **bursa**, and it acts to reduce friction between the tissues during movement.

Synovial joints permit varying degrees of movement. For a synovial joint to function fully it also needs to utilise two other structures: tendons and ligaments.

- Tendons are white fibrous cords of connective tissue that help to attach muscle to bone. They are very tough as they are made from collagen.
- Ligaments, while also tough connective tissues, are composed of lots of elastic fibres which join bone to bone and help form stability at a joint.

The function of both tendons and ligaments is to reduce friction and to protect the ends of the bones during movement. The ligaments cross the joint to hold the bones in place, whereas tendons cross the joint to help transfer energy from the contracting muscles.

Key terms

Fixed or immoveable – joints where there is no movement.

Slightly moveable or cartilaginous – joints that have a small degree of movement.

Freely moveable or synovial – joints that have a large degree of movement.

Fibrocartilage – highly fibrous cartilage found in places where shock absorption is key.

Resilient – able to return to original state after stress such as stretching or being compressed.

Elastic cartilage – gives support with some degree of flexibility.

Pliant – can be easily bent.

Joint capsule – fibrous tissue that encapsulates a synovial joint.

Synovial membrane – soft tissue that protects joints from wear and tear.

Synovial fluid – a lubricating fluid which helps to reduce friction. It has a similar consistency to raw egg.

Bursa – fluid-filled sac that helps reduce friction at a synovial joint.

Assessment practice 7.5

1 **What is the other name for the hyaline cartilage? [1]**

A Articular   C Elastic

B Fibro   D Synovial

2 **State the role synovial fluid plays within the synovial joint. [1]**

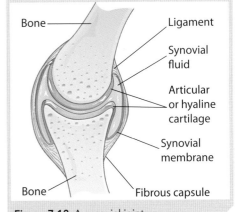

Bone — Ligament — Synovial fluid — Articular or hyaline cartilage — Synovial membrane — Bone — Fibrous capsule

Figure 7.12 A synovial joint

Joint movement

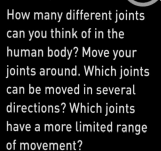

Getting started

How many different joints can you think of in the human body? Move your joints around. Which joints can be moved in several directions? Which joints have a more limited range of movement?

Introduction

Movement can occur in the human body because it has joints and because muscles, which contract, run across these joints. The range of movement that is possible depends on how a joint is constructed.

There are many types of joint movement.

Flexion – bending a joint, such as when the angle at a joint is decreased when preparing to kick a ball.

The footballer's knee is in flexion as he gets ready to kick.

Extension – straightening the joint, such as when the angle at a joint is increased, when shooting in basketball.

The elbow joint is in extension as the player goes to block the shot.

Adduction – movement towards the body, such as when the arms are pulled back together during breaststroke in swimming (adduction at the shoulder joint).

The swimmer's arms are in adduction as they pull back during breaststroke.

Abduction – movement away from the midline of the body such as when the legs go out during a star jump (abduction at the hip joint).

The limbs are in abduction when they are mid-air, with all four limbs extended away from the body.

Rotation – a circular movement of part of a girdle or a limb outwards or inwards, such as when the hip moves towards the body during a drive shot in golf.

The golfer's hip is in rotation during a drive shot in golf.

Circumduction – movement in which flexion, abduction, extension and adduction movements are combined in sequence, for example in the shoulder joint during an over-arm bowling action in cricket.

The cricketer's shoulder is in circumduction when they bowl over-arm.

Plantarflexion – moving the foot downwards, away from the tibia, such as pointing the toes in a gymnastic move.

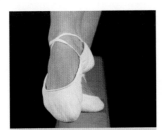

The gymnast's pointed toes show plantarflexion.

Dorsiflexion – moving the foot upwards, towards the tibia, such as when preparing to land in long jump.

An athlete preparing to land in the long jump, flat-footed with toes pointed towards the body.

Elevation – movement of a part of the body upwards, for example, when serving in tennis or raising the shoulder blade when lifting weights.

The athlete raises their arm up in elevation.

Depression – movement of a part of the body downwards, such as lowering the shoulder blade when pulling down on a pulley-system weights machine.

Lowering of the shoulder blade when using a pulley weights system demonstrates depression.

Activity 7.7

Types of movement

Can you think of another sporting example for each of the types of movement given? List the movement and then the sporting example. Have a go yourself to check – are you producing the movement by doing the action? Check with your teacher to see if you are right.

CONTINUED ▶▶

Joint movement related to sports performance

In reality you never actually produce just one movement at one joint; you are always producing a series of continuous movements in order to complete a sporting action outcome. Here are some more specific examples of types of movements used in sport.

- **Flexion** – part of the movement of running means that the hamstrings contract and therefore the angle at the knee decreases, which is seen by the knee bending. This is flexion at the knee joint. However, flexion can take place at the hip joint in the part of the movement just after a person has kicked a ball when the leg follows the direction of the ball. This movement is produced by the action of the quadriceps. The body becomes closer to the upper leg thereby reducing the angle at the hip joint and so flexion occurs at the hip joint between the hip and the femur.

Flexion occurs in runners when their hamstrings contract to bend the knee.

- **Extension** – can occur in running when the leg is straightened out at the knee and just before flexion occurs again. This could also be shown at the shoulder joint when a netball player either releases a shot, or at the elbow when chest-passing to someone.
- **Adduction** – normally this means bringing a limb back towards the body, so this could occur at the shoulder when bringing the arms back in from a star jump, and when they go out this would demonstrate abduction – movement away from the body.
- **Rotation** – this occurs at the hip as a javelin thrower looks to utilise all of the energy and momentum of a run-up prior to releasing a throw or when a tennis player tosses the ball to serve overhead.

In addition to the above four movements there is one other movement that can be produced by using all four together, called circumduction. For example, the shoulder joint will go through all of these movements when a swimmer is performing the front crawl.

Front crawl uses a variety of movements and demonstrates.

Just checking

1 When performing a biceps curl from start to finish, what two movements occur at the elbow joint?

2 What other muscle, besides the biceps, is responsible for producing this range of movement?

3 What is the difference between abduction and adduction?

4 What is circumduction?

Table 7.2 Joint movement and muscle group contractions related to sports performance

Muscle	Joints crossed	Action when contracting concentrically
Triceps	Elbow	• Elbow extension
Biceps	Elbow	• Elbow flexion
Quadriceps	Knee Hip	• Knee extension • Hip flexion
Hamstrings	Knee Hip	• Knee flexion • Hip extension
Deltoids	Shoulder	• Shoulder abduction • Shoulder flexion • Shoulder extension
Gluteus maximus	Hip	• Hip extension
Gastrocnemius	Ankle Knee	• Plantarflexion of ankle • Assists knee flexion
Abdominals	Spine	• Flexion of spine • Lateral flexion • Rotation of spine
Obliques	Intervertebral joints of the spine (lumbar and thoracic vertebrae) Hip	• Lateral flexion and rotation of spine • Compression of abdomen
Pectorals	Shoulder	• Adduction of arm • Horizontal flexion of arm
Trapezius	Shoulder girdle	• Neck extension • Shoulder elevation
Latissimus dorsi	Shoulder	• Shoulder adduction
Soleus	Ankle	• Plantar flexion of ankle with knee bent
Erector spinae	Spine	• Extension of spine

Structure of the cardiovascular system

Getting started

Using your index finger and your middle finger, locate your pulse, either on your wrist or in your neck. How many times does your heart beat in 30 seconds? Now jump up and down for 30 seconds, then stop and immediately take your pulse again in the same place. Has the amount of beats in 30 seconds increased or decreased? What is the difference? Can you explain why there is a difference?

Introduction

The cardiovascular system – sometimes called the circulatory system – consists of the heart, blood vessels and blood.

The heart

In order to function, the heart muscle, like any other muscle, requires a supply of blood. The coronary arteries are responsible for supplying the heart muscle with oxygenated blood, they cover the surface of the heart. The heart is located in the cavity between the sternum and the lungs. It is made up of four chambers: two upper and two lower. The two upper chambers are called **atria** and the two lower are called **ventricles**. The atria receive blood into the heart and the ventricles pump blood out of the heart. The right and left sides of the heart are divided by a muscular wall called the **septum**.

The heart is actually two separate pumps, making a double circulation system:

- the ventricle on the right side of the heart sends blood to the lungs to collect oxygen (**pulmonary**)
- the ventricle on the left side of the heart sends blood to the rest of the body (**systemic**).

Key terms

Ventricles – are the two lower chambers of the heart – they receive blood from the atria.

Atria – are the two upper chambers of the heart – they pump blood to the ventricles which pump blood out of the heart.

Septum – is muscular tissue which separats the two sides of the heart or the ventricles.

Valves – heart valves ensure blood flows in the correct direction through the heart, preventing back-flow.

Pulmonary – relating to the lungs.

Systemic – the non-pulmonary part of the circulatory system.

Sino-atrial node – located in the right atrium – is the heart's pacemaker.

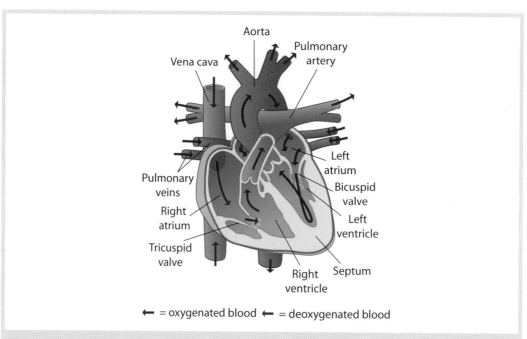

Figure 7.13 Did you know that the heart is actually two separate pumps?

Blood flows through the heart and around the body in one direction only. This direction is maintained by special **valves** in the heart. The tricuspid and bicuspid valves prevent blood flowing back in to the atria from the ventricles and the semi-lunar valves prevent blood falling back in to the ventricles once blood has left the heart via the pulmonary artery or aorta. The veins also have valves, which help control the flow of blood.

A pacemaker called the **sino-atrial node** is in the wall of right atrium, and this regulates the heartbeat.

Types of blood vessels

Blood circulates continuously via the heart through different types of blood vessels: arteries, arterioles, capillaries, veins and venules.

Arteries

Arteries have thick muscular and elastic walls and are used to carry blood away from the heart and around the body under high pressure. An exception to this is the pulmonary artery which carries de-oxygenated blood from the heart to the lungs.

Arteries branch repeatedly into smaller and smaller vessels. The smallest of these are **arterioles**, which have thinner walls than arteries.

Veins

Veins have thinner walls than arteries and carry blood to the heart. The smallest veins are called **venules**. Veins carry deoxygenated blood from the body towards the heart under low pressure. They have semi-lunar valves to maintain the direction of the blood flow (they prevent the blood from flowing backwards). The exception is the pulmonary vein, which carries oxygenated blood from the lungs back to the left atrium of the heart.

Capillaries

Capillaries have walls made up of only a single layer of cells. These walls are permeable to allow the exchange of oxygen, carbon dioxide, nutrients and waste products through them. These are the smallest blood vessels and they transport blood from the arteries to the veins by uniting the arterioles and venules.

Key terms
Arteries – thick muscular-walled vessels that carry blood away from the heart.
Veins – non-muscular vessels with valves that carry blood towards the heart.
Arterioles – these branch from arteries and are smaller in diameter. The arterioles branch and lead to even smaller blood vessels called capillaries – they allow for the passage of oxygenated blood.
Venules – these branch from veins and are smaller in diameter. They lead to even smaller braches called capillaries – they allow for the passage of de-oxygenated blood.
Capillaries – very thin vessels that allow oxygen and carbon dioxide exchange.

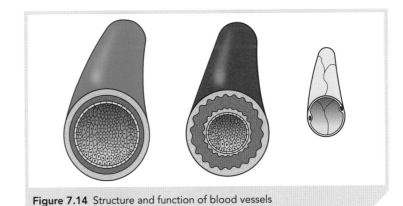

Figure 7.14 Structure and function of blood vessels

Assessment practice 7.6

1 Which of the following definitions best describes the septum? (1)

A It separates the right and left side of the heart.

B It pumps blood around the body.

C It regulates the heartbeat.

D It allows oxygen and carbon dioxide to be exchanged.

2 Complete this sentence. Blood vessels with single cell walls are known as... (1)

A veins

B capillaries

C arteries

D valves

Functions of the cardiovascular system

Introduction

The function of the cardiovascular system is to ensure that there is sufficient blood flow through the heart, body and lungs.

How does the cardiovascular system work?

Oxygen enters the body when you breathe in air through your mouth and nose. The oxygen is absorbed into the bloodstream from your lungs. Your heart then pumps the oxygen-rich (oxygenated) blood around the body through the arteries, to tissues including organs, muscles and nerves.

When blood reaches your tissues, it releases the oxygen, which is used by the cells to produce energy. In exchange, the cells release waste products – including carbon dioxide and water – that are absorbed and carried away by blood.

This 'used', or deoxygenated, blood then travels along veins back towards your heart. Your heart pumps this blood back to your lungs where carbon dioxide is breathed out and where, as you breathe in, the blood picks up fresh oxygen, and starts the cycle once again.

This continuous cycle of events allows the cardiovascular system to:

- circulate oxygen and remove carbon dioxide
- provide cells with nutrients
- protect the body against disease and infection
- stop bleeding after injury by clotting
- remove waste products
- transport hormones to cells and organs.

Each day the heart beats about 100,000 times and pumps about 7570 litres of blood. This network exists in conjunction with the **pulmonary network** – it is the lungs that supply the oxygen to the heart and eliminate the carbon dioxide waste.

Thermoregulation

Thermoregulation is the process used by the human body to keep a constant temperature of 37°C. Body temperature can alter because of the weather, the environment, through illness or by participating in sport. If the body becomes too hot or cold, this can affect its ability to function normally. This is why its temperature must be kept relatively constant.

■ = deoxygenated blood
■ = oxygenated blood

Blood is transported through the body by veins and arteries.

Cooling down

In order to help the body cool down if it becomes too warm, the blood vessels (arterioles) under the skin 'open up' or **dilate**, this is called **vasodilation**. This process helps promote heat loss through **radiation**. Your skin colour will be enhanced because of the blood flow close to the surface of your skin.

Your sweat glands may also start to produce sweat. This will evaporate from the skin and this helps to cool the body.

Warming up

If the body becomes too cold, three things help it to warm up.

- The blood vessels (arterioles) under the skin 'close down' or **constrict**, this is called **vasoconstriction**. This process helps conserve heat loss by decreasing the flow of warm blood at the body's surface – so very little heat is lost through radiation – and redirecting this flow to the body's core.
- The skin and subcutaneous fat help to **insulate** the body.
- You may start to shiver, which is your body's way of generating heat.

Activity 7.8   Assess the effects of temperature

See how temperature affects you. Watch your body respond using its own thermoregulation mechanism.

Make a note of your breathing rate, the colour and temperature of your skin and so on.

Undertake some aerobic exercise, such as an aerobics/keep-fit class or a netball or football match. Afterwards, look again at the things you noticed before, such as your breathing rate (is it quicker or slower?), your skin colour (more or less colour?) and your skin temperature (are you colder or hotter?). Then look at how your body has tried to get your breathing rate back to what it was, and how it has tried to remove the increased heat. Are you sweating? Have you gone red?

Assessment practice 7.7

1 **The body is exceptionally good at regulating its temperature. What temperature is the norm for the human body? (1)**

A 31°

B 34°

C 37°

D 38°

Structure of the respiratory system

Getting started

Try closing your mouth and holding/pinching your nose. See how quickly you want to open your mouth. Your body tells you very quickly it needs oxygen and you automatically open your mouth.

Key terms

Bronchioles – these branch from the bronchi and link to the alveoli. They are responsible for controlling air distribution and airflow resistance in the lungs.

Introduction

The respiratory system includes the nose and mouth, the **epiglottis**, the **trachea**, the **lungs** (the **bronchi** and **bronchioles** and the **alveoli**), the diaphragm and the intercostal muscles.

The respiratory system is complex in structure yet it works very efficiently. If one part of it is not working properly, we notice it very quickly. Just think – the last time you had a cold, your nose was blocked up and so you started to breath more through your mouth to keep your oxygen intake 'normal'.

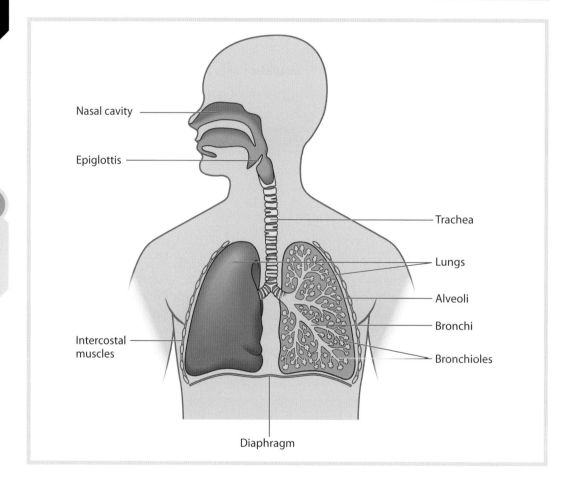

- Nasal passages – air entering from the nostrils is led to the nasal passages. The **nasal cavity** located behind the nose comprises the nasal passages and forms a very important part of the respiratory system in human beings. It is responsible for conditioning the air received by the nose. The process of conditioning involves warming or cooling the air received by the nose, removing dust particles from it using the fine structures called **cilia** and also moistening it with **mucus**, before it enters the pharynx.

- Epiglottis – food and liquids are blocked from entering the opening of the larynx by the epiglottis to prevent people from choking during swallowing.
- Trachea – also known as the windpipe and refers to the airway through which respiratory air travels. The rings of hyaline cartilage within its walls keep the trachea open. The trachea is a tube approximately 12 cm in length and 2.5 cm wide.
- Bronchi – the trachea divide into two main bronchi, which extend into the lungs and spread in a tree-like manner as bronchial tubes. These subdivide and with each subdivision, their walls get thinner. This dividing of the bronchi into thin-walled tubes results in the formation of bronchioles. The bronchioles terminate in small air chambers, each of which contains cavities known as alveoli. Alveoli have thin walls (about one cell thick), which form the respiratory surface. The exchange of gases between the blood and the air takes place through these walls.
- Lungs – these form the most vital component of the human respiratory system. They are responsible for transporting oxygen from the atmosphere into the blood and releasing carbon dioxide from the blood into the atmosphere.
- Pleural membrane – this is thin, moist, slippery and has two layers. The outer membrane lines the inside of the ribcage and the diaphragm while the inner layer covers the lungs. Between the two layers is the intrapleural space, which normally contains pleural fluid secreted by the membranes. This allows the two layers to slide easily over one another as the lungs inflate and deflate during respiration. It is difficult to compress or expand liquids so the two layers of pleura normally remain tightly adhered to one another. This enables the lungs, which do not contain any skeletal muscle, to be expanded and relaxed by movements of the chest wall.

Key terms

Epiglottis – a flap of cartilage that covers the windpipe when swallowing (to prevent food and liquid entering).

Nasal cavity – is a large air-filled space above and behind the nose in the middle of the face.

Cilia – microscopic hair-like structures that vibrate to trap particles from the air.

Mucus – a slippery secretion produced by, and covering, mucous membranes.

Trachea – often called 'the windpipe', and has a primary function of bringing air to your lungs. It contains strong rings of hyaline cartilage that prevent the passage from the collapsing.

Bronchi – the trachea divides into two bronchi that allows air to pass in to the lungs.

Lungs – main respiratory organ where gas exchange takes place.

Alveoli – air sacs that allow gas exchange within the lungs.

Assessment practice 7.8

1 Describe the function of the cilia and where they are found. [2]

2 What helps to keep the trachea open? [1]
   - A Alveoli
   - B Bronchi
   - C Hyaline cartilage
   - D Cilia

Functions of the respiratory system

Getting started

Breathing is something we do quite unconsciously all of the time. Occasionally, however, our breathing rate alters and that can cause a series of events to occur within our body. For instance, what happens to our breathing rate when we start to exercise hard? What effect does that have on our body and its related systems?

Introduction

The respiratory system allows air to be filtered through the respiratory tract and into the lungs where gas exchange can take place ensuring our body receives oxygen and carbon dioxide is removed.

Mechanics of breathing

Inspiration

Breathing in, or **inspiration**, happens when the external **intercostal muscles** contract, moving the ribcage up and out. The diaphragm moves down at the same time, creating negative pressure, meaning it acts as a vacuum and sucks air in. The lungs expand outwards as well. The diaphragm also contracts at the same time, flattening, creating negative pressure within the lungs, and so air rushes in.

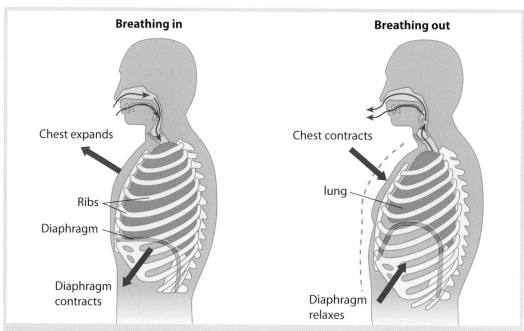

Figure 7.16 The movement of the ribcage when breathing in and out

Expiration

Breathing out, or **expiration**, is when the diaphragm and the external intercostal muscles relax and return to their normal dome position while the internal intercostal muscles contract, helping to lift and compress the ribcage so that inspiration and expiration can take place. The **thorax** gets smaller, increasing the air pressure in the lungs and forcing air out.

However, when deep breathing takes place – for example, during exercise – forceful contractions of the muscles produce larger changes in the volume of the thoracic cavity during both inspiration and expiration.

Working with a partner, one of you takes the role of the participant and the other that of observer.

- Participant – Sit still for 1 minute
- Observer – Count how many times the participant breathes in and out – that is when the chest rises and falls back to normal position = one. Record the number of breaths
- Participant – Run on the spot or around the sports hall/field for 2 minutes and then return immediately to sitting
- Observer – Count how many times the participant breathes in and out. Record the number of breaths

What is the difference in the number of breaths taken at rest and after activity? Can you explain what is happening?

Gaseous exchange

Gaseous exchange is the process by which oxygen and carbon dioxide move in opposite directions across the respiratory membranes, between the air (the external environment) and the body fluids (our internal environment).

Oxygen is needed by cells to extract energy from organic molecules, such as sugars, fatty acids and amino acids.

The oxygen is breathed in and enters the lungs. It is here that oxygen passes (by **diffusion**) through the membrane of the alveoli into the blood. It continues its journey around the body in the bloodstream.

Carbon dioxide is produced in the process and must be disposed of. It is carried back to the lungs via the bloodstream and diffuses through the membrane of the alveoli to be breathed out.

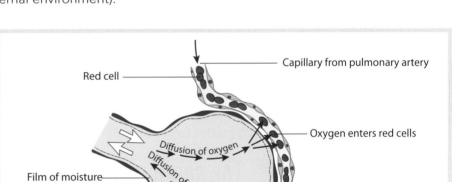

Figure 7.17 Gaseous exchange in the alveoli

1 Describe what we mean by gaseous exchange. [1]

2 What is the waste product of gaseous exchange? [1]

  A Helium   C Oxygen

  B Carbon dioxide   D Carbon monoxide

Functions of the cardiorespiratory system

Introduction

We have looked at the cardiovascular and the respiratory system as individual systems, but now we will consider how they work together to make the cardiorespiratory system.

The heart

The heart and its muscular power drive approximate 5.5 litres of blood around the entire cardiovascular system. The heart works with the lungs to ensure that blood can be transported to and from the heart via the lungs so that the exchange of oxygen and carbon dioxide can take place.

The lungs

The respiratory system is designed to deliver oxygen-rich air to the lungs. It is essential that the lungs and the airways are clear and fully functional, as the body has no means of compensating for a defective respiratory system; athletic performance will suffer, as without proper supplies of oxygen the body's energy stores cannot be used.

Impaired function

There are some typical conditions that impair respiratory function in athletes, such as **asthma**. If an athlete has a common cold or chest infection the bronchial tubes can restrict the passage of air into the lungs. Smoking and other forms of pollution will also inhibit proper lung function.

The cardiorespiratory system

The respiratory system begins where the air is inhaled into the body, through the nose or mouth (breathing in). All air passes through the throat and into the trachea (windpipe). The air then passes into the bronchial tubes (bronchi), which lead into each lung. Tubes known as bronchioles flow from the bronchi, tapering into ends composed of air sacs. The air sacs are groupings of tiny, round organic structures called alveoli. Each alveolus is encircled with capillaries, the tiny blood vessels by which oxygen is passed from the alveolus into the body and through which waste carbon dioxide is passed out.

From the capillaries, which are the cardiovascular point of contact with the respiratory system, the blood is directed into the circulatory system, and ultimately passes through the pulmonary artery.

The act of inhaling and exhaling air occurs due to the function of the diaphragm, located below the lungs, which have no muscle structure of their own. One function of athletic activity is a strengthening of the diaphragm.

Taking up oxygen to produce energy

In any sport where athletic endurance is a key component, training that will increase the amount of oxygen available to the athlete is essential. Improvement of performance will be limited if the body cells cannot obtain enough oxygen to assist in energy production with available glycogen or glucose stores.

The training effect

This is when exercise places demands on the body for an increase in energy to fuel muscle activity. The heart rate increases in response to the demands for oxygen-transporting red blood cells to metabolise glucose stores. The respiratory rate increases to obtain more oxygen and to take away greater amounts of waste carbon dioxide. Intense regular exercise will increase the amount of red blood cells and corresponding oxygen uptake.

Increased physical training will improve the ability of the lungs to inhale and exhale air due to the strengthening of the diaphragm, the muscle that powers the respiratory portion of the cardiorespiratory system.

The training effect is not permanent, and it is reversible through reducing or stopping physical activity.

> **Link**
>
> This topic links to *Unit 1: Fitness for Sport and Exercise.*

Activity 7.10   Training regime

Using the information gained from this unit and other units such as *Unit 1: Fitness for Sport and Exercise*, *Unit 4: The Sports Performer in Action* and *Unit 5: Training for Personal Fitness*, devise a training regime that within six weeks would start to improve the cardiorespiratory function of a sedentary person. Justify, using anatomical and/or physiological reasons, your choice of activities.

Ensure you identify the correct technique for each activity so that muscles and joints are working efficiently and effectively. The benefits of the duration of exercise will impact on the aerobic and anaerobic capabilities of an individual; this should be explained in detail to show full understanding of the physiological responses to exercise.

Assessment practice 7.10

1 **What system are the heart and lungs otherwise known as? (1)**

   A The energy system.

   B The muscular system.

   C The cardiorespiratory system.

   D The respiratory system.

2 **During exercise, explain how the body responds to the need to remove a greater amount of carbon dioxide from the red blood cells. (2)**

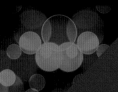 

Assessment Zone

This section has been written to help you to do your best when you take the onscreen test. Read through it carefully and ask your teacher if there is anything you are still not sure about.

How you will be assessed

You will take an onscreen assessment, using a computer. This will be set over 15–20 screens and have a maximum of 50 marks. The number of marks for each question will be shown in brackets e.g. [1]. The test will last for one hour.

There will be different types of question in the test.

A **Questions where the answers are available and you have to choose the correct answer(s).** *Tip. Always read carefully to see how many answers are needed and how you can show the right answers.*

Examples:

Which two of the following are types of muscular contraction used in movement?

A Eccentric

B Circumduction

C Voluntary

D Rotational

E Isometric

Answers: A and E.

Which of the following muscle pairs is an antagonistic pair?

A Hamstring and trapezius

B Quadricep and deltoid

C Bicep and tricep

D Gastrocnemius and abdominals

Answer: C.

B **Questions where you are asked to provide a short answer worth 1–2 marks.** *Tip: Look carefully at how the question is set out to see how many points need to be included in your answer.*

Examples:

Name two types of blood vessel. [2]

Answer: Vein, artery (Alternative answer: capillary.)

State why flat bones are important. [1]

Answer: Because they protect the body's vital organs.

C **Questions where you are asked to provide a longer answer – these can be worth up to 8 marks.** *Tip: Plan your answer, making sure that you include the correct level of detail indicated by the amount of marks allocated. Check through your answers – you may need to use the scroll bar to move back to the top.*

Example:

> Describe the journey of air from our surroundings, into our body until oxygen is passed into the capillaries around the alveolus. [2]
>
> **Answer:** The air is inhaled into the body, through the nose or mouth. Air passes through the throat and into the trachea. The air then passes into the bronchial tubes, which lead into each lung. Tubes flow from the bronchi, into ends composed of air sacs. The air sacs are groupings of tiny, round organic structures called alveoli.

Many questions will have images. Sometimes you will be asked to click to play a video or animation. You can do this as many times as you want within the time allowed for the test.

Sometimes you may be asked to do a calculation. You can use the calculator provided in the onscreen test system if you need to.

Hints and tips

- **Use the pre-test time** – make sure that you have read the instructions, tested the function buttons, adjusted your seat and that you can see the screen clearly.

- **Watch the time** – the screen shows how much time you have left. You should aim to take about 1 minute per mark. Some early questions will take less time than this and some later ones will take you longer.

- **Plan your longer answers** – read questions carefully and think about the key points you will make. You can use the onscreen note function to jot down ideas.

- **Check answers at the end** – you should keep moving through the questions and not let yourself get stuck on one. If you are really unsure of an answer or can not give an answer then you can use the onscreen system to flag that you need to come back to that question at the end.

- **Read back your longer answers** – make sure you view the whole answer if you are checking back. There is no spell check facility.

- **Do you find it harder to read onscreen?** – talk to your teacher/tutor in advance of your test about how the system can be adjusted to meet your needs. During the test, tools within the test player will allow you to apply colour filters, change the font size and colour, as well as allowing you to zoom in on the images and text.

How to improve your answers

Read the two student answers below, together with the feedback. Try to use what you learn here when you answer questions in your test.

Question

The cardiorespiratory system enables the process of transporting oxygen from the air around us into our body.

a) Describe the process of inspiration. [2]

b) Identify the primary waste product transported away from our muscles via the bloodstream. [1]

Student 1's answer

a) Muscles make the ribs rise causing the lungs to open up and air to rush in.

b) Gases.

Feedback:

a) *It has been correctly stated that the ribs rise however there is no mention of intercostal muscles or the diaphragm flattening. Although the learner has clearly said air rushes in they have not explained that the lung's volume increase and the pressure decreases. For this question the learner would receive 1 mark.*

b) *The learner's use of the term gases is very vague. For part B the learner would achieve 0 marks. The correct answer should include the identification of carbon dioxide.*

Student 2's answer

a) During inspiration our intercostal muscles contract raising our ribs and flattening our diaphragm. The volume of the lungs increases and the pressure decreases causing air to rush in.

b) The main waste product is carbon dioxide.

Feedback:

a) *The learner has clearly described the process and mentioned all elements vital to the process. For this question they would achieve 2 marks.*

b) *The learner has clearly identified carbon dioxide. For part B the learner would achieve 1 mark.*

Assess yourself

Question 1

There are three different classifications of joints in the human skeleton.

a) Which of the following would be classified as a slightly moveable joint? [1]

Between vertebrae

Carpo-metacarpal joint of thumb

Intercarpal and intertarsal joints

Cervical vertebrae

b) When we are born our skull is made up of smaller sections of bone. Over time these fuse together to form one. Which joint classification can be applied to this new bone formation. [1]

Question 2

a) Identify two muscles found in the upper arm. [2]

b) Which joint do these muscles cross? [1]

Question 3

The heart is found in a cavity between the sternum and lungs. It consists of atria, ventricles and the septum.

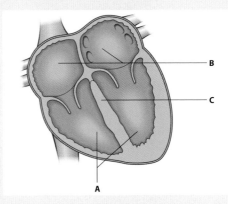

Identify the parts of the heart labelled A, B and C. [3]

Question 4

Describe two differences between arteries and veins. [4]

For further practice, see the Assessment Practice questions on pages 179, 182, 186, 189, 191, 197, 199, 201, 203, 205.

Answer can be found on page 339.

Introduction

Why do you wear a particular brand of sports shoe or clothing? Why do you follow a particular football team or sports performer? How can sport be used to help improve health, social integration and other social issues in this country? A simple answer to these questions is promotion. If you look around you, you will see many examples of how this is done. For example you will have seen the promotion of exciting sports products that improve our sporting performance; and examples of healthy living campaigns, emphasising the importance of sports in a healthy lifestyle.

Sponsorship logos and adverts in sport are all around us – in sports-related advertisements featured in the media and on billboards in sports arenas, to sports sponsor's logos being placed on athletes' clothing and equipment. Names of stadiums are even used to promote products, for instance, the Emirates stadium, home of Arsenal Football Club, carries the name of a major international airline. But how do sport teams and individuals gain sponsorship? How is it used? And why is it important?

This unit will explore these topics and show how the promotion of sport and the sponsorship of sports stars, teams and events is now vital to their success. It also covers where sponsorship comes from and the issues that have arisen and continue to arise, both good and bad, from the increase in both sports promotion and sponsorship in recent years. You can use this knowledge and understanding to plan the promotion of a sports event or scenario of your own.

Assessment: You will be assessed by a series of assignments set by your teacher/tutor.

Learning aims

In this unit you will:

A investigate issues involved in promoting sport

B explore sponsorship in sports promotion

C plan the promotion of a sports event or scenario.

This unit helped me to understand what sponsorship is, where it comes from and what sponsors expect in return. By completing this unit, I was able to identify different sources of sponsorship and how to obtain a range of sponsorship to help me improve as a tennis player.

Hayley, *17-year-old tennis player*

Promotion and Sponsorship in Sport

8

This table shows what you must do in order to achieve a **Pass**, **Merit** or **Distinction** grade, and where you can find activities in this book to help you.

Assessment Zone

Assessment criteria			
Level 1	Level 2 Pass	Level 2 Merit	Level 2 Distinction
Learning aim A: investigate issues involved in promoting sport			
1A.1 Describe two different reasons for the promotion of sport	**2A.P1** Describe four different reasons for the promotion of sport **See Assessment activity 8.1, page 220**	**2A.M1** Assess the role of the media in the promotion of two selected sporting events **See Assessment activity 8.1, page 220**	
1A.2 Describe the role of the media in the promotion of sport	**2A.P2** Explain the role of the media in the promotion of sport **See Assessment activity 8.1, page 220**		
1A.3 Describe the effects the promotion of a selected sporting event has on spectators	**2A.P3** Explain the effects the promotion of a selected sporting event has on participants and spectators **See Assessment activity 8.1, page 220**		
Learning aim B: explore sponsorship in sports promotion			
1B.4 Outline public, private, regional and national sources of sponsorship	**2B.P4** Describe public, private, regional, national, international and global sources of sponsorship available, including procedures involved in securing sponsorship **See Assessment activity 8.2, page 229**	**2B.M2** For two selected sports individuals, teams or events, summarise information on their sponsorship **See Assessment activity 8.2, page 229**	**2B.D1** Compare and contrast the impact of sponsorship on two selected sports individuals, teams or events **See Assessment activity 8.2, page 229**
1B.5 Outline three different ethical issues which can arise from sponsorship of a given sports individual, team or event	**2B.P5** Describe the range of different ethical issues which can arise from sponsorship of a selected sports individual, team or event **See Assessment activity 8.2, page 229**	**2B.M3** Explain ethical issues which can arise from sponsorship of a selected sports individual, team or event **See Assessment activity 8.2, page 229**	
Learning aim C: plan the promotion of a sports event or scenario			
1C.6 English Create, with guidance, a plan to promote a given sports event or scenario	**2C.P6** English Independently create a plan to promote a selected sports event or scenario, describing strengths and areas for improvement **See Assessment activity 8.3, page 231**	**2C.M4** Explain strengths of the plan and areas for improvement, providing recommendations for future promotion **See Assessment activity 8.3, page 231**	**2D.D2** Justify recommendations for future promotion of a selected sports event or scenario **See Assessment activity 8.3, page 231**

English Opportunity to practise English skills

How you will be assessed

This unit will be assessed through a series of assignments set by your teacher/tutor. You will be expected to show an understanding of the promotion of sport, including why it is needed, the role of the media and the effects promotion has on participators and spectators.

You will also need to show an understanding of sports sponsorship and ethical considerations that can arise from this. You will need to apply the knowledge you have gained from this unit to plan the promotion of a sports event or scenario, reviewing your plan, explaining its strengths and justifying your recommendations for future promotion.

Your assessment could be in the form of:

* written reports
* video reports, such as a TV-style documentary
* presentations
* discussions, observed by your teacher
* portfolio of evidence showing your plans for the promotion of an event.

Reasons for the promotion of sport

Introduction

Sport is promoted due to its many benefits both for individuals and for the community. Benefits of sport include:

- health benefits
- higher quality of life
- economic benefits
- social inclusion
- reduction in crime and antisocial behaviour
- fostering a sense of pride and achievement.

Sport in the community

For many people, playing or being involved in sport is an important part of their lives. This involvement might include being a coach or leader, helping to organise and run a local club or team, or raising funds to develop the clubs facilities. People give up time to act as a volunteer in the majority of cases. There are many benefits to people and communities who 'get involved' in sport including:

- improving the health, both physical and mental, of local people
- developing a community spirit among local people
- improving the quality of life of local people through providing greater opportunities to participate and learn new skills
- developing sports facilities, which leads to economic benefits within the community.

Healthy living

There is increasing concern that modern living is creating a lifestyle that is less active than it should be. Labour-saving devices, computer games and easily accessible food is creating a nation of unfit, overweight people, especially children. As a result, a number of organisations are involved in promoting and running campaigns to get more people more active. For instance, the NHS has promoted 'Change 4 life snack in a box' designed to promote a healthier lifestyle for young children by getting the contents of children's school lunchboxes to be healthier.

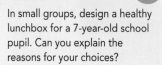

Social inclusion

Sport has the power to bring people together, regardless of their differences in culture, religion or ethnicity, and has many other social benefits. Think of how many countries were represented at the 2012 Olympics. Sport can provide employment for people, and earns money for the nation. It can reduce antisocial behaviour by giving a more positive outlook on life to people who might otherwise be drawn into activities such as vandalism and other forms of crime.

Activity 8.1

Visit Manchester City Football Club community scheme by going to Pearson Hotlinks (www.pearsonhotlinks.co.uk) and clicking on this BTEC Sport title.

What are the benefits of this scheme? How do you think it works for reducing crime and antisocial behaviour? How might it develop feelings of citizenship? What other positive effects could it have on the local community and its residents?

Have you seen for yourself how sport brings different people together?

Creating local and national identity

Success in sport reflects on the nation. For example, in 2010, the England cricket team was ranked number one in the world – the best! British track cycling also leads the world, with many British gold medallists and world champions having won over many years. Think about a number of different sports teams in your area. How successful have they been in the last year? What does this level of success say about the team and the town or city they are in? In 2011/2012, where did England finish in the European Football Championships? How many gold medals did British women win at the London Olympics? Which nation produced the most drivers in the Formula 1 World Championship? What does this say about our nation? Are we good at sport?

Discussion point

- How do you feel when a local sports team performs well, and perhaps wins a trophy? Why do you think you feel this way?

- How successful was Great Britain in the 2012 Olympics and Paralympics? How did the Games reflect on our nation?

Role of the media in the promotion of sport

Getting started

Collect the sports sections from a range of different newspapers and magazines. Then gather examples of sports stories from the internet. Collect some examples of adverts for sport, again, from a range of sources. In small groups, compare your examples. Can you see any similarities and differences? Discuss and record your findings, then discuss as a class.

Introduction

The media has a huge impact on all aspects of our lives, including sport. It influences how we perceive sports, sporting events and those that play sport. It can dictate the timing of sporting events and even make or break sports performers.

Communication

The media has many forms, including:

- newspapers and magazines
- television and radio
- the internet
- social media sites such as Facebook and Twitter.

From these media outlets, people today obtain huge amounts of information, not all of it always correct and factual. The media has two main features.

- Broadcasting – transmitting a programme or information such as the news or showing a sports event.
- Advertising – making readers and viewers aware of a particular product or service such as new running trainers or a dedicated sports channel. The two have very different aims and thus are carried out in very different ways.

Activity 8.2   Different angles

1 Collect sports pages from a range of newspapers covering the same story – it might be a report of a match or another event, or to do with the behaviour of a sports performer. Try to find the same story on the internet on a news channel and a social network site (if you are allowed).

2 Now look at how differently the information is presented. Do any of the reports give a different view of the incident or match? Why do you think this might be?

Creating a specific image

Imagery is the use of descriptive language and words to create a specific picture or feeling for the reader. By using words and images, sports promoters can help develop an image in our minds about a product or service. For instance, a particular golf club might create the image of being the best club by using a top golfer to promote it in adverts. For the Commonwealth Games, also referred to as 'The Friendly Games', specific words such as 'unite' are used by sports promoters to create the image of friendship for spectators, However, for the Olympics and Paralympics Games, also referred to as 'The Greatest show on Earth', although sportsmanship is an important part of the Olympic image, the concept of competition is encouraged through slogans such as 'Going for Gold' and the media attention to the medals tables supports the competitive imagery.

Read the report of a premiership football game or other sporting event. How do the *words* used create an image in your mind about the event?

Discussion point

What is your favourite training shoe brand? Why? What 'image' does it have?

◤ Presentation

The way a product or person is presented will depend on who the **target audience** is.

Consider adverts for mobile phones. Who do you think they are aimed at, based on the presentation of the adverts? Look at the covers of fashion or health magazines for men and women. Again, think about how they are presented and who this might appeal to. Why do you think they are presented in this way?

Sports events are presented using different forms of media depending on the target audience for a particular event. Generally, social networking sites such as Facebook are more relevant to a younger generation, whereas the older generation are more likely to use the radio or newspapers. Radio channels appeal to different age groups – BBC Radio 1 is targeted at young people, while older people are more likely to listen to BBC Radio 4. Sports events are presented in a number of different ways to appeal to, and attract, a wider audience. For instance, the annual Wimbledon tennis championships can be followed on the radio, television, in newspapers and via the internet allowing for everyone to follow the event using their preferred media form.

Key term

Target audience – the people a product or service is aimed at.

Just checking

1 Can you name four different media formats?
2 Explain the difference between broadcasting and advertising?
3 Why do sports promoters use a range of media types to present events?

Effects of promotion of sport on spectators and participants

Introduction

Sports promotion is designed to affect us in some way, whether it makes people more aware of an event, sport or individual, or whether it develops a desire in the viewer to have a particular item or take part in an activity. These effects are often psychological in that certain words and images are used to create a picture in our minds about a product of service for instance.

Effects of sports promotion on spectators

The way that sports events are promoted can have many effects on the **spectator**.

- **Cost** – the more popular the event, and the heavier the promotion, the more expensive tickets become. This is because the more people there are who want to see an event or show, the higher the price that can be charged for tickets. For example, a season ticket for Manchester United for 2011/2012 cost between £532 and £950. Tickets for the opening ceremony at the London Olympics cost up to £2,012. Spectators also pay for travel to the event, and will often buy merchandise, food, drink and a programme while they are there. All of these will be more expensive at high-profile events than at events held by smaller sports clubs.

- **Availability** – if an event has been promoted successfully, spectators will know when it is taking place, including the date, season and time of day. A one-off event that has been highly publicised will be more popular than one that happens frequently and receives little media coverage. These factors can influence ticket availability.

- **Accessibility** – this refers to how easy an event is to get to (location), the facilities on the day (seating, food outlets, information outlets, toilets) and the number of people who are permitted in the venue (capacity). A popular and highly promoted event is likely to be held at a larger venue in a central location with better facilities so that more people can attend.

- **Under-represented groups** – sometimes, these target audiences exclude under-represented groups of individuals, for example: families, specific social demographics, women or people with disabilities. To encourage participation amongst these under-represented groups, events targeting these individuals have become more popular, for example, the Race for Life events which are designed to raise awareness and funds for women's cancer. Race for Life started in 1994, and six million women have raised more than £493 million for Cancer Research making it the UK's largest women-only fundraising event.

Psychological effects of sports promotion on spectators

During the promotion of an event there will be advertising campaigns that affect people's views, feelings and behaviours.

Case study

Sometimes, before a boxing match, promoters will often 'hype' up the dislike between the two fighters to raise awareness and interest in the bout and increase ticket sales. Sometimes this animosity is made up but sometimes it is real. Research Muhammed Ali versus Joe Frazier. How did this personal animosity help to raise the profile of the fights that took place? Why did Ali encourage this bad feeling to become well known to the public? Can you think of examples in other sports? For instance, the rivalry between Manchester United and Liverpool or West Bromwich Albion and Wolverhampton Wanderers in football.

? Did you know?

There have been some surprising results when great rivalries in sport have competed against one another. For instance, in football, Celtic versus Rangers is 'THE' game in Scottish football. The first game was in 1891 and since then Rangers have won 159 times, Celtic 144 times with 96 games drawn! Find out about one of the following great sporting rivalries.

1 In Formula 1 motor racing, Alain Prost v Aryton Senna
2 In cricket, India v Pakistan
3 In tennis, Bjorn Borg v John McEnroe

Role models are used in a range of ways to promote sport and sports events. Tanni Grey-Thompson is one of Great Britain's most successful disabled athletes and has helped to raise the public's awareness of disability sport. Sir Steve Redgrave is the most successful Olympian ever, with five gold medals won over 20 years of Olympic competition, and is one of this country's 'senior statesmen' in sport – a person whose opinion is regarded as very important and worth listening to. Wayne Rooney is used to promote football computer games because he is an important role model to young people, who are the biggest users of computer games. However, this can work both ways. Tiger Woods has experienced a number of scandals in his private life and this has resulted in much negative publicity for Woods. As a result, a number of his sponsors have withdrawn their sponsorship because of concerns that this bad publicity will reflect negatively on their company or the products or services they offer.

Take it further

1 Who sponsors the following?
   * Manchester City FC?
   * The Premier League?
   * Test Match Cricket?
   * Rugby Union Premiership?
2 Research the details of one of these sponsorship deals.

CONTINUED ▶▶

Discussion point

The London Marathon is the world's biggest marathon with 36,748 runners finishing in 2012. In 2009 a total of 746,635 runners had finished the race since it started in 1981.

What reasons can you think of for such a large number of people wanting to run the London Marathon? Think about promotion, sponsorship, accessibility, etc.

Effects of sports promotion on participants

We have already looked at factors that affect spectators. We will now look at factors that affect the participants in sporting events:

- Availability – events that are well promoted make people more aware and are likely to attract more participants. If the event is not well promoted, it might fail because there is little awareness surrounding it and therefore people may not enter.

- Accessibility – a greater range of events and activities will help increase the range of activities available to people to choose from. This may help people access better facilities and coaching.

- Under-represented groups – promotion of specific events such as minority sports and activities for specific groups of people increases the range of media coverage and helps to raise awareness among others. This, in turn, may well help to increase participation in the future and raise the importance of events such as the Paralymics.

- Perceived status – the more often an activity is seen or heard, the more important it becomes over time. The Paralympics were first held in 1960 and involved 400 athletes. Today they are the second biggest summer sports event in the world.

The reasons you have identified in the discussion point in this page can be applied to any sporting event and have an effect on participants, encouraging people to take part.

Do you know anyone who has run the London Marathon?

Take it further

Can you answer the following questions about London 2012?

1 How many people took part in the Olympic Games, from how many countries, in how many sports?

2 What were the figures for the Paralympic Games?

3 How many people each day used to travel to Olympic Games events?

4 How many tickets were sold?

Assessment activity 8.1

2A.P1 | 2A.P2 | 2A.P3 | 2A.M1

You have been asked to speak to a local sports club about why they should hold a large sports event to promote their club and increase membership. Produce a handout summarising the points you will make.

1 First, you should introduce promotion in sport by considering:

- four reasons for the promotion of the sport
- the role of the media in sports promotion.

2 Next, look back at the 2012 London Olympics and another recent sporting event. What effects did the promotion of these events have on the participants and spectators?

3 What did you think of the role of the media in the promotion of the Olympics, and your other chosen event?

Tips

- For Task 2, give examples. You might consider why the Olympics were put on in East London. How has this part of London benefited as a result?
- For Task 3, consider which forms of media were used. Why do you think this was? What was good and bad about the media coverage? How was the event portrayed? What successes were reported? What problems were reported?

WorkSpace

▶ Ishmael

Aspiring professional cricketer

Ishmael is a very talented and promising cricketer who has the potential to go all the way in his sport and perhaps one day play cricket for England.

In order to improve, Ishmael needs sponsorship to help pay for equipment, travel and training. Within the public sector, Ishmael has approached his regional Sport England office and his local council. In the private sector, he has approached some local businesses including banks, building societies and supermarkets. He has also applied to a national scheme designed to help promising sports performers called the Youth Sports Trust, as they may be able to provide advice and guidance as well as a degree of funding to help support Ishmael's development.

If Ishmael eventually does play cricket for England, sponsorship will be more readily available. The England cricket team has many sponsors including the bank NatWest and the car maker Jaguar. Test match cricket in England is also being sponsored by Investec until 2021. By sponsoring the England cricket team, who will play matches both at home and abroad, Investec, which operates in a large number of different countries, will gain additional promotion and advertising of its products and services on a global scale.

Think about it

1 Why is sponsorship important to Ishmael?

2 What sources might be available to Ishmael on a local, regional or national level?

3 What are the benefits of such an arrangement to both Ishmael and a sponsor?

Sources of sponsorship for individuals, teams, organisations and events

Introduction

In this topic, you will learn about different sources of sponsorship in sport. You will study the different types of organisations that provide sponsorship to sports events, teams and individuals, as well as how to obtain sponsorship.

The term **sponsorship** is used to describe financial support that is given to an individual, team, organisation or event. Organisations generally give sponsorship to:

- promote their products or services
- raise their profile
- develop the image of their business, product or service
- improve or develop an area of sport (e.g. for international success).

Sponsorship in sport comes from a variety of sources and can be found at all levels, from a local-level team or performer, to international events such as the Olympic Games.

Key terms

Sponsorship – The financial support given to an individual, team or event for a commercial return.

Public (sponsorship) – sponsorship or funding provided by the government or public sector organisations, e.g. Sport England grants.

Private (sponsorship) – sponsorship or funding provided by companies, corporations and individuals who are not run by the government.

▶ Public and private sponsorship

The two main sources of sponsorship are from the **public** and **private** business sectors:

- The public sector is made up of organisations run by the government and other publicly funded bodies. In England, these bodies include local councils and regional offices of Sport England, with Sport Wales, SportScotland and The Irish Sports Council undertaking similar roles throughout the rest of the UK. These bodies provide funding in the form of grants that can be used by the recipient in a variety of ways, such as purchasing new equipment or paying travel arrangements to get to and from matches. Thus a team, event or individual could apply to their local council or Sports Council office for funding for equipment, travel, or other training or related expenses. This would allow the team or individual to compete or the event to go ahead.

- The Great Eastern Run is organised by Peterborough City Council (a local council). The council organises this event to raise awareness of running in the area as well as to promote Peterborough as a place to work and live. Many local organisations, including the city council, provide sponsorship because of the benefits the event brings to the city of Peterborough. The high profile of the event within the region helps to promote Peterborough as an interesting place. This might attract new businesses to the area, benefitting both local people and the city as a whole.

- The private sector is made up of organisations that are in business to make a profit for their owners or shareholders. Examples include businesses such as JJB Sports or BSkyB. Many sponsor sports events and performers. For instance, the online property finder Zoopla sponsors West Bromwich Albion FC (a Premiership football team), while Andy Murray, the UK number one tennis player, is sponsored by Adidas, Head and the Royal Bank of Scotland. Many local firms also sponsor local teams and events to raise awareness of their firm in the local area. An example of this is J Gard & Sons, a Chelmsford firm that sponsors Chelmsford City Football Club.

Regional and national sponsorship

Private sector organisations may also give sponsorship on either a regional or a national basis. For instance, Perkins Engines, a company based in Peterborough that makes diesel engines for other industries, sponsors the Great Eastern Run, which takes place in the city. Aviva, on the other hand, is a national organisation which provides a range of insurance products. Since they sell their insurance nationwide, they sponsor a national sport, athletics, and have done since 1999. To find out more, please go to Pearson Hotlinks (www.pearsonhotlinks.co.uk) and search for this BTEC First in Sport title.

Securing sponsorship

Securing sponsorship is an important activity for many sports individuals, teams and events organisers. Obtaining sufficient sponsorship is important for individuals to be able to develop and improve as performers, for teams to be able to sign new players or improve facilities, and for events organisers to be able to put on an event. Sponsorship can be obtained in many ways – for example, writing to businesses and organisations or meeting in person to discuss sponsorship needs and benefits. There are organisations whose role it is to bring together sports seeking sponsorship and sponsors seeking sponsorship opportunities.

Some events are sponsored by many well-known brands. How many sponsors in the photo do you recognise?

Ethical issues arising from sponsorship

Did you Know?

Of the tickets available for the final of the men's 100m at the 2012 Olympics, more tickets were available for sponsors than were available to the general public.

Introduction

When sponsorship takes place, it is very important that certain standards and codes of practice are followed. Organisations rarely sponsor anyone if there is no benefit to themselves. A sponsor will expect something in return for their financial commitment which, at times, may be considerable. These benefits might include access to performers, tickets for key events or linking the names of their products or services with an event or individual.

Sports marketing

The images used by sponsors in advertising must be appropriate for their target audience and legitimate. Children used in marketing campaigns by sponsors must not be exploited and must be paid for the work they do. Sponsors must also adhere to legal requirements and ensure that no inappropriate images of children are used. To prevent exploitation, a contract should be drawn up between both parties; the sponsor and those being sponsored. Sports performers who are poor role models must not be used, as their negative behaviour or attitude should not be used to sell or promote events, products or services.

Do you notice the sponsors' billboards around sports pitches?

Suitability of sponsors

Some sponsors may not be suitable for sport. For instance, sponsorship by tobacco firms is no longer permitted. Sport is an activity that is regarded as healthy and good for us. Activities such as smoking and gambling are regarded as activities that are not desirable because of their effects on health or society. On the other hand, sponsors such as Kellogg's, who make breakfast cereals for children, would be regarded as a positive sponsor.

Take it further

Visit Pearson Hotlinks (www.pearsonhotlinks.co.uk) and search for this BTEC First Sport title. Read the article 'Rory McIlroy, Nike and the $250m, 10-year sponsorship deal'.

What do you think about the content of the article? Explain, in your own words, what the benefits of this sponsorship deal are for Rory McIlroy and for Nike.

Did you Know?

English Premier League club, West Bromwich Albion, in 2012, dropped its shirt sponsor Bodog, an online gambling firm, due to concerns about the possible legal action to be taken against the firm's owner and several other individuals associated with the Bodog Entertainment Group, on alleged charges of money laundering and illegal gambling. This would clearly, if proven, have resulted in negative publicity for the club.

When a sponsorship agreement is in place, both the sponsor and recipient of the sponsorship will sign a contract. A contract is a written agreement that states the terms and conditions of the agreement on both sides, expected behaviour, and so on. Any breaches allow either party to cancel the contract.

Influence of sponsors

It is important that the sponsor does not have too much control over certain areas – changing schedules or rules, for instance. There have been negative reports about the behaviour of members of the International Olympic Committee because of their influence in deciding who is able to stage the Olympic Games. Rumours of members being offered bribes or other inducements to provide support on a bid are all too common. Members of FIFA have been banned because it has been proved that some FIFA members took inducements to support a particular bid. This is called corruption and it is illegal behaviour.

Sponsorship of major events

A major factor in sponsorship is what the sponsor will get in return. Sponsors of major events receive a range of benefits as a result of their sponsorship. For instance, sponsors can advertise and promote the fact that they are an 'official' sponsor to a certain event, or they may be the sole supplier of a particular service or product at an event.

There has been much discussion about the number of prime-time tickets that were given to sponsors in return for their financial support in the 2012 London Olympics. Do you think this is ethical?

Sponsors may receive the best tickets for an event, or tickets to particular events within a major tournament. Again, sponsors had access to tickets for the main events at London 2012, such as the men's 100 metre final, which is one of the most popular events. Sponsors may also be entitled to a certain level of access to performers at sponsors' events, such as dinners. A large part of the role of a Formula 1 driver is to help promote the products or services of their team and individual sponsors.

Local teams often find it hard to get sponsorship because they can't offer much in return.

Influence of individuals

It is important that no individual person should have too great an influence on an event or sports performer as a result of a sponsorship agreement.

For instance, the decision to award the 2018 and 2022 World Cup finals has been dogged by allegations of corruption and wrongdoing by some FIFA officials who were able to 'influence' decisions. England lost out to Russia and Qatar. Evidence suggests that the decisions were not fair and transparent and that wrongdoing might have been involved. Hosting a major sporting event can bring great prosperity to countries and businesses within those countries, which can earn huge sums of money building stadia, providing hospitality and so forth. It is thought that officials who can influence voting may sometimes accept bribes and inducements to engineer favour for a particular bidder.

Codes of practice

Many sponsors will advertise themselves using the sponsorship link. These adverts must meet set standards. The Advertising Standards Agency code of practice contains rules and marketing approaches that aim to provide responsible advertising in the UK, as well as extra consumer protection alongside current consumer protection law. Within the code of practice there are rules covering a variety of things, from environment and health and beauty claims, to use of gambling or children in adverts.

Case Study

Visit Pearson Hotlinks (www.pearsonhotlinks.co.uk) to read about alleged corruption within FIFA in respect to bidding for the 2018 and 2022 World Cup finals.

How might this situation arise? Why might a country be so keen to host an event that it allegedly pays bribes? How are the people who can influence decisions 'encouraged' to behave unethically or possibly illegally? What does this tell you about issues with sponsorship of major sporting events?

Research

Visit the European Sponsorship Association website to find out about codes of conduct in sponsorship at.

You can access this website by going to Pearson Hotlinks (www.pearsonhotlinks.co.uk) and searching for this BTEC First in Sport title.

Advertising standards

The Advertising Standards Agency has created a variety of broad codes and principles that aim to prevent advertisements from having a negative effect on audiences. Some rules are designed to prevent advertisements from misleading or offending audiences, while some ensure that adverts are created according to the principles of fair competition. No matter which product is being advertised, the principles of the Advertising Standards Agency apply.

Research

To find out more about The Advertising Standards Agency, go to Pearson Hotlinks (www.pearsonhotlinks.co.uk) and search for this BTEC First in Sport title.

These standards are in place to protect a variety of people, including those who will be involved in sponsorship and those who may be targeted by the sponsor's activities. It ensures adverts are honest and truthful, that they do not mislead people into thinking products are better than they are, and that there are no claims made about products or services that cannot be proven.

The impact of sponsorship

Positive impact

Scheduling

Many sports events are put on at a time when the largest possible audience is likely to be watching. This ensures maximum exposure of the event, and a potential sponsor knows that as many people as possible will see their name and logo.

Quality of the sporting product

Sponsorship increases the quality of the sporting product – better stadiums, television coverage and so on. London 2012, for example, depended heavily on money raised from sponsors. Premier League football teams have been able to attract the best players from all over the world because of increased income to clubs. In 2012, the owner of Manchester City FC, Sheikh Mansour bin Zayed bin Sultan Al Nahyan, had an estimated wealth of £555 billion. This staggering amount of money meant that Manchester City could afford any player they wanted to build a 'superteam'. In comparison, the owner of West Bromwich Albion was worth £40 million at the time.

Wider audiences

Increasing awareness and available methods of watching increases the number of people who watch events. Sponsors want their products and services to be advertised and promoted as much as possible and are therefore responsible for much of the raised awareness of and access to sports events.

Increased participation

As more people become aware of events and sports performers they become motivated to take part themselves. Campaigns such as Sport England's 'Active Women' have also raised the levels of participation.

Negative impact

Marginalisation

Satellite television and the internet are only available to those who can afford them. People on low incomes may be unable to afford the monthly subscription fees. Added to this, some people may not understand the necessary technology. This extends beyond individuals to whole countries, which may not be able to afford to broadcast certain sports.

Failure of clubs with no sponsorship

Smaller clubs and more unusual sports as well as less well-known sports performers often struggle to obtain sponsorship and so may find it difficult to grow and develop. The economic downturn in 2011–12 also made sponsorship more difficult to obtain.

Scheduling

A large country with a massive potential audience may demand that an event takes place at a time to suit it at the expense of another country's viewing. For instance, the men's 100 metre final at the London Olympics was scheduled for Monday 5 August between 6.50 and 9.55 p.m. However, Sydney in Australia is 11 hours ahead of London. This made it difficult for many Australians to watch this exciting event live.

Just checking

1 Ethics in sponsorship is concerned with what?

2 What benefits might a sponsor receive in recognition of their sponsorship?

3 Name three positive and three negative effects of sponsorship on a sport or event.

Assessment activity 8.2

2B.P4 | 2B.P5 | 2B.M2 | 2BM3 | 2B.D1

1 You have been asked to give some advice to:

- a promising young sports performer who could really be successful if they could take their training and competing to the next level and

- a local international performer who needs to spend more time training, which means giving up their job for some time, as they want to compete in the next Olympic Games.

They would both welcome some advice on how they might obtain some sponsorship to give them a chance to improve and achieve their goals. Your advice should include a description of the different types of sponsorship available for both athletes and an explanation of how they could secure it. You should also describe and explain the ethical issues that could emerge when an individual is being sponsored.

2 In pairs, start with one of you being the young sports performer who requires advice. The other one provides advice about the various sources of sponsorship (local, regional, national, international and global) that exist and describes how sponsorship from each source could be obtained. Give them some information on the steps they need to take to get sponsorship from each source. Once complete, swap roles but this time, provide advice for the international performer.

3 Still in your pairs, compare and contrast the impact of sponsorship on both the promising young sports performer and international performer. What are the advantages and disadvantages for each athlete?

4 Finish by now summing up, via a leaflet or similar that they could take away, the information you have given them. Provide real-life examples of two other athletes at a similar level to the one used in the activity and summarise the sponsorship they currently receive – from where and, if possible, how much.

Tips

- Before advising each athlete, you will need to think about their goals and what they need to achieve them. What specific help will they require to improve?

- To help structure your advice session, your could describe the advantages and disadvantages of each sponsorship option and explain which sponsorship option you recommend. Afterwards, justify this choice.

Planning the promotion of a sports event or scenario, then review

Getting started

Consider a sports event that has recently taken place – a fun run or charity event, for instance. In small groups, discuss what information you might have needed in order to be able to design a plan for its promotion.

Introduction

Have you heard the saying 'If you fail to plan, you plan to fail'. This is certainly true when you organise a sports event of any kind. All sports events need careful and considered planning to make sure everything is ready when the event takes place. Planning for the London 2012 Olympic and Paralympic Games took seven years. Without a huge amount of planning, the games would not have been the great success they were.

▶ Creating the plan

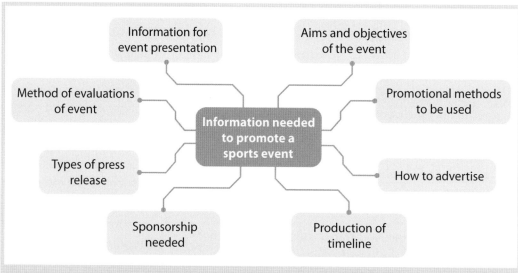

The information you would need to promote a sports event

You will need to decide and agree the following.

- What are the aims and objectives of the event – what is it for? To raise money for charity, for example?
- What method(s) are you intending to use for promotion? Newspapers? Flyers? Television? Radio?
- What format will be used for press releases?
- How are you going to advertise the event? Posters around your school or college would be fine for an internal event. But what about a large, regional event such as a county show?
- What sponsorship do you want/need? How much? For what? Which suitable sponsors are you going to approach?
- What is the timeline for the event – dates by which certain tasks must be completed and by whom.
- It is likely that you will need to prepare a presentation for your suggested sponsor, outlining the nature of the event. You will need to explain why you are asking for sponsorship and what benefits you could offer the sponsor in return.
- Prepare an evaluation questionnaire that could be used to review the plan and help provide future recommendations.

Link

This unit links well with *Unit 11: Running a Sports Event*. The plan you created above could be used to promote the sport event which occurs in Unit 11.

Discussion Point

Research the London 2012 Olympic official logo. What do you think about it? What images does it create in your mind? Why? Discuss your thoughts with the rest of your class.

In pairs, research a range of images taken from London 2012 to see if you can find images that depict the aims and objectives of the event, (e.g. raises money for charity, promote healthy life style).

Be ready to share with your class **how** and **why** you feel each chosen image does this.

Reviewing the plan

When you review the plan, you must consider three main areas.

- What elements of your plan were a success? These will be the strengths of your plan. This might be that you obtained the required sponsorship, or that the aims and objectives of the event were achieved.

- What did not go so well? These are the weaknesses or areas for improvement. Perhaps the aim of attracting 500 people to the event was not achieved, for example.

- What recommendations can be made? You might decide to advertise in a different way next time, and give reasons for this. Or perhaps the chosen date clashed with another, more established, event, and this could be avoided.

- If you implement your plan when completing *Unit 11: Running a Sports Event*, it can be reviewed in light of success of your event.

Assessment activity 8.3 *English* 2C.P6 | 2C.M4 | 2C.D2

1 In small groups decide on an event you would like to see happen in your school, college or local area – for example, a charity run, sports tournament or taster day.

2 Draw up a plan that includes the following for this event:
- aims and objectives
- media to be used for promotion and reasons for choice
- press releases
- advertising format and locations
- obtaining sponsorship, and presentation to sponsor
- meeting to evaluate planning process.

3 Explain strengths and areas for improvement.

4 Recommend ways to make improvements for the future promotion of the event.

Tips
- You will need to keep a record of everything along the way, including minutes of the meetings that take place.
- Draw up a timeline so that every task has a start and finish date.
- Make sure tasks are in the correct order and that all aspects of planning are documented, e.g. copies of advertising materials.

Introduction

For many people small changes in lifestyle can lead to positive improvements in health and happiness. Making the right lifestyle choices is important not only for athletes, so that they can perform to the best of their ability, but also for all who are keen to look after themselves.

It is essential that anyone working in the health and fitness industry understands the steps that can be taken to ensure the health and well-being of an individual. This includes exercising on a regular basis, as well as understanding the component parts of a sensible diet and how to incorporate them into what we eat in the right quantities. It is also important to know about the health risks associated with excessive alcohol consumption, smoking, and recreational and performance-enhancing drugs.

You will learn how to assess whether individuals are following guidelines and be able to recommend how they can adapt their lifestyle to improve their well-being and sports performance.

Assessment: You will be assessed by a series of assignments set by your teacher/tutor.

Learning aims

In this unit you will:

A be able to apply recommended guidelines for physical activity

B explore what makes a healthy diet and carry out dietary planning

C know the health risks associated with smoking and excessive alcohol consumption

D know the impact of drugs on health and sports performance.

" Some of my friends have smoked in the past. I have seen how this can affect them when playing sport. This is what has made me want to help people change their lifestyles to improve their health.

Tom, *16-year-old aspiring personal trainer and lifestyle coach* "

Lifestyle and Well-being

9

BTEC
Assessment Zone

This table shows what you must do in order to achieve a **Pass**, **Merit** or **Distinction** grade, and where you can find activities in this book to help you.

Assessment criteria			
Level 1	**Level 2 Pass**	**Level 2 Merit**	**Level 2 Distinction**
Learning aim A: be able to apply recommended guidelines for physical activity			
1A.1 Describe how much physical activity adults and children and young people should do to benefit their health	**2A.P1** Assess whether three selected individuals are undertaking sufficient physical activity to benefit their health **See Assessment activity 9.1, page 237**	**2A.M1** Explain recommendations for how three selected individuals could increase their physical activity levels **See Assessment activity 9.1, page 237**	**2A.D1** Justify recommendations for how three selected individuals could increase their physical activity levels **See Assessment activity 9.1, page 237**
1A.2 Summarise three ways in which a selected individual could increase their level of physical activity	**2A.P2** Make recommendations for how three selected individuals could increase their physical activity levels **See Assessment activity 9.1, page 237**		
Learning aim B: explore what makes a healthy diet and carry out dietary planning			
1B.3 Describe the functions of the essential nutrients and why a healthy diet is important for a healthy lifestyle	**2B.P3** Explain the functions of the essential nutrients and why a healthy diet is important for a healthy lifestyle **See Assessment activity 9.2, page 243**		
1B.4 Collect dietary information for a selected individual for one day, documenting via a food diary	**2B.P4** Collect dietary information for a selected individual for one week, documenting via a food diary **See Assessment activity 9.2, page 243**		
1B.5 English Design, with guidance, a healthy meal plan for a selected individual for one day, specifying the type and amount of food to be consumed	**2B.P5** English Independently design a healthy meal plan for a selected individual, for one week **See Assessment activity 9.2, page 243**	**2B.M2** English Design a healthy meal plan for a selected individual, for one week, making reference to the eatwell plate, and describing suggested recommendations for change **See Assessment activity 9.2, page 243**	**2B.D2** Justify the design of a healthy meal plan for a selected individual, for one week, justifying suggested recommendations for change **See Assessment activity 9.2, page 243**

English Opportunity to practise English skills

Assessment criteria

Level 1	Level 2 **Pass**	Level 2 **Merit**	Level 2 **Distinction**
Learning aim C: know the health risks associated with smoking and excessive alcohol consumption			
1C.6 Describe four health risks associated with smoking	**2C.P6** Describe four health risks associated with smoking and effects of smoking on sports performance **See Assessment activity 9.3, page 247**		
1C.7 Describe four health risks associated with excessive alcohol consumption	**2C.P7** Describe four health risks associated with excessive alcohol consumption and effects of alcohol consumption on sports performance **See Assessment activity 9.3, page 247**		
1C.8 Describe one technique an individual can use to stop smoking and one technique to cut down on excessive alcohol consumption	**2C.P8** Explain two techniques an individual can use to stop smoking, and two techniques to cut down on excessive alcohol consumption **See Assessment activity 9.3, page 247**	**2C.M3** Compare and contrast different techniques used to stop smoking and for cutting down on excessive alcohol consumption **See Assessment activity 9.3, page 247**	
Learning aim D: know the impact of drugs on health and sports performance			
1D.9 Describe two different types of drugs and their impact on sports performance	**2D.P9** Describe four different types of drugs and their impact on sports performance **See Assessment activity 9.4, page 249**	**2D.M4** Evaluate the impact of four different performance-enhancing drugs on performance in four different types of sport **See Assessment activity 9.4, page 249**	**2D.D3** Discuss, using relevant examples, why some individuals may resort to using performance-enhancing drugs in sport **See Assessment activity 9.4, page 249**

How you will be assessed

The unit will be assessed through a series of assignments set by your teacher/tutor. You will be expected to show an understanding of lifestyle topics including exercise, diet, alcohol, smoking and drugs. The tasks will be based on a scenario where you work in a health and fitness setting: for example you might be asked to advise a new client at a fitness centre on appropriate lifestyle changes to improve the client's fitness and well-being.

Your assessment could be in the form of:

- informational materials, such as leaflets and posters
- presentations to peers and teachers
- research collected from a real-life setting and presented appropriately.

Recommended guidelines for physical activity

Key term

Exercise – physical activity requiring exertion. It helps to maintain and improve the body's overall health and fitness levels.

Introduction

In this topic you will look at government recommendations for activity for various age groups. Understanding how much exercise we should take and how we can increase the amount of exercise we do will help us plan increases in activity that are realistic and that we are likely to continue with for more than just a short period.

 ## Government recommendations

We should all **exercise**. The current government recommendations for exactly how much physical activity we should do are shown below.

- Under-5s – physical activity should be encouraged from birth. Children who are capable of walking should be physically active daily for at least 3 hours, spread throughout the day.
- Children and young people (aged 5–18 years) – should be as active as possible, but at minimum they should do moderate to vigorous intensity physical activity for at least 1 hour every day. Vigorous-intensity activities that will help to strengthen muscles and bones should be participated in three times a week.
- Adults (aged 16–64 years) – during a week they should do at least 2½ hours of moderate intensity activity in sessions of over 10 minutes each of muscle-strengthening activities on two or more days a week that work all major muscle groups.
- Older adults (aged 65 years and older) – should try to be active daily. If possible they should aim for the same amount of physical activity as younger adults.

Ways to increase physical activity levels

There are many things in everyday life that prevent us from exercising as much as we should. Commitments such as study, work, friends and family can make it difficult for us to find time to exercise. Additionally, some people may be reluctant to spend their limited money on keeping fit. However, exercising does not need to be time-consuming or expensive. In fact, there are easy ways that can help many of us to fit more of it into our everyday lives.

Consider the following.

- Cycling – how many of us get the bus or go by car to work or school? Quite often it is not only faster but also cheaper to cycle. Cycling is a great way to keep fit and by using it as a means of transport we can easily incorporate it into our everyday lives.
- Jogging – this is another way of getting to work or school for those of us lucky enough to live close by. If that is not possible, why not get out of bed just three-quarters of an hour earlier than usual and go for a run? Make it more sociable by inviting your friends.

If you have a dog, taking it for a walk can be a fun way to exercise.

- Lunchtime exercise – there are many free outdoor gyms appearing around the UK. If you live close enough to one, perhaps you could spare a couple of lunch breaks a week to give your body some exercise?

- Dog walking – if your family has a dog, volunteer to take it for a brisk walk.

- Play active games – go outside with your friends rather than sitting in and playing computer games. Having fun with friends is both rewarding and a good way of taking exercise without really knowing it.

- Use stairs – do not take the lift or escalator; use the stairs whenever possible.

Assessment activity 9.1   2A.P1 | 2A.P2 | 2A.M1 | 2A.D1

- You have a work placement with a fitness consultant. As part of your training, you have been asked to show your ability to apply recommended guidelines for physical activity.

- Choose three friends or family, preferably of different ages. Discuss with them how much exercise they do in a week and record this information. Write a report for each, giving suggestions for ways to improve their exercise regime.

Tips

- Are your chosen individuals meeting government recommendations for exercise?
- What kinds of activities will suit their lifestyle?
- How could they incorporate these activities into their weekly schedule?
- You should be prepared to justify and support all of your suggestions.

Nutrients and food groups

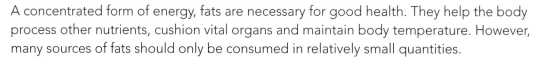

Introduction

Nutrients are found in different types of food. The different kinds are carbohydrates, proteins, fats and oils, minerals, vitamins and water. Each nutrient fulfils a different need and is essential for healthy living. Some nutrients are needed in large quantities (macronutrients), while others are needed in smaller quantities (micronutrients).

Carbohydrates

Carbohydrates are an essential fuel source for the working muscles, and are the nutrient group consumed in the largest quantity by most people.

Carbohydrates can be split into two groups.

- **Simple carbohydrates** – absorbed quickly into the body and only provide short-term energy solutions. They are high in sugars. Common examples are sweets and fizzy drinks; a healthier source would be fruit.
- **Complex carbohydrates** – absorbed more slowly into the body. As they take longer to digest the energy found in them will be released more gradually, keeping you active for longer. Examples are pasta, bread and rice.

Proteins

Proteins are essential for the growth and repair of tissues within the body. Many people think that animal products – such as meat, fish, milk and eggs – are the only sources of protein available. However, there are also high levels of proteins found in many plant sources, such as beans and nuts.

Fats

A concentrated form of energy, fats are necessary for good health. They help the body process other nutrients, cushion vital organs and maintain body temperature. However, many sources of fats should only be consumed in relatively small quantities.

Fats can be split into two groups.

- **Saturated fats** – mainly found in animal products and processed foods such as meats and dairy products, and many fast foods. Saturated fats are very thick and gooey and can clog up passages (such as blood vessels) in the body. Saturated fats are known to raise cholesterol levels, which can lead to problems such as heart disease.
- **Unsaturated fats** – found in foods such as oily fish, nuts and olives. They remain much thinner in consistency at room temperature and do not clog up blood vessels. They are actually thought to reduce the body's cholesterol levels.

Fruit and nuts are good sources of energy and are healthy snacks.

Minerals

Minerals are not organic – they are neither plant nor animal. Minerals help build and repair different areas of the body as well as maintaining the required balances in the body. Two key examples of minerals are:

- **iron** – needed to repair red blood cells and found in large quantities in meat and eggs
- **calcium** – needed to build and maintain strong bones and teeth. Milk is rich with calcium.

Vitamins

The body relies on many different vitamins to maintain balance and support many vital functions (which must continue to enable life). Vitamins are found in a wide range of foods. Many vitamins are very important, but two common examples are:

- **vitamin A** – needed to maintain strong bones and healthy skin. It is found in many fruits and vegetables.
- **vitamin B** – helps maintain healthy skin and a well-functioning nervous system. B vitamins are found in meat and wholegrains, as well as various other unprocessed foods.

Water

Water is needed to aid many processes within the body. It also helps regulate the body's temperature, carries other nutrients around the body and helps eliminate waste.

> **↗ Take it further**
>
> There are many types of vitamins, each of which is needed by the body. Carry out some research to discover what other vitamins there are. For example, can you find out what vitamin C does for the body, and where it is found?

> **? Did you know?**
>
> Water contributes to approximately 60% of an adult's body weight.

Table 9.1 Food groups

Nutrients	Benefits	Food sources
Carbohydrates	Excellent source of energy.	Simple – found in sugary foods such as sweets. Complex – found in starchy foods such as rice.
Proteins	Needed to build and repair tissues.	Found in meat, fish and dairy products as well as nuts and beans.
Fats	Another form of energy, but should be consumed only in small quantities.	Saturated – comes from animal products and processed foods. Unsaturated – comes from oily fish, nuts and olives.
Minerals	Neither animal nor plant, yet minerals are found in both. They are needed to maintain balance in the body and help it build and repair itself.	Found in various levels in different foods.
Vitamins	Support the productivity of the body's vital organs and help maintain balance.	Found in various levels in different foods.
Water	Helps us regulate temperature, transport other nutrients and dispose of waste.	Best taken pure, but also found in fruits and some other foods.

Food groups and the eatwell plate

Figure 9.1 is an image of the eatwell plate. This a visual way of explaining how much of each food group we should eat and applies to everyone over two years of age.

The eatwell plate shows that we should eat:

- plenty of fruits and vegetables, starchy foods including bread, other cereals and potatoes
- some meat, fish, egg, bean products, milk and dairy foods
- only a small amount of fatty and/or sugary foods and drinks.

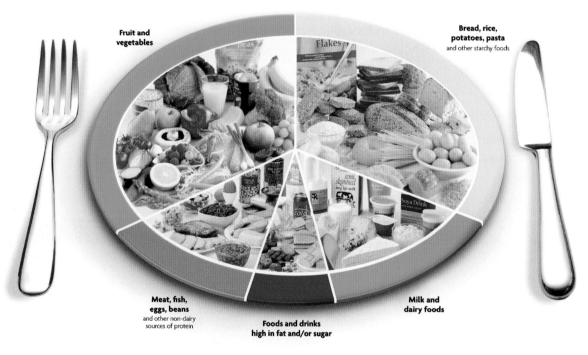

The eatwell plate

Use the eatwell plate to help you get the balance right. It shows how much of what you eat should come from each food group.

Fruit and vegetables

Bread, rice, potatoes, pasta
and other starchy foods

Meat, fish, eggs, beans
and other non-dairy
sources of protein

Foods and drinks
high in fat and/or sugar

Milk and dairy foods

Department of Health in association with the Welsh Assembly Government, the Scottish Government and the Food Standards Agency in Northern Ireland

Figure 9.1 The eatwell plate

Remember

The eatwell plate is only a guideline. People with medical requirements, those trying to lose weight and those who do a large amount of physical activity may have to vary the quantities to stay healthy.

Just checking

1 What are macro-nutrients and what are micro-nutrients?

2 Which is better for us, saturated or unsaturated fat?

3 According to the eatwell plate, which food groups should we eat most of, and which least?

WorkSpace

▶ Sarah Schippers

Self-employed dietician

On a daily basis I see a wide range of clients, some involved in the sports industry and some just wanting to lead a healthier lifestyle. I love the variety of people that I meet. I have my own office in a busy sports centre where I can see my clients privately. Some clients visit me weekly and some just every few months for a progress check. I have to be quite flexible in the times I work as I realise that many people have busy lives and seeing me can be difficult.

We spend time looking at current eating patterns. I always ask my clients to record honestly what they eat and drink over a period of a few weeks. This gives us a great starting point for beginning to make improvements. Depending what the person wants to achieve, together we adapt their eating patterns. Some people want to lose weight, some want to gain weight and some just want to feel as though they have more energy. It doesn't matter what the end goal is, though. The most important thing is to make the recommendations realistic. People need to make changes that they can stick to.

I love that my job allows me to make a real difference to people's lives. It is wonderful to see how people begin to look healthier, which in turn gives them greater confidence and improves their overall well-being.

Think about it

1. Do you think you could help people as Sarah does?
2. Why does Sarah need to be aware of the roles of different nutrients?
3. Do you think you understand the different food groups enough to help people make basic changes to their diet?

Collecting dietary information and meal planning

Introduction

When you are considering making changes to your own or another person's diet, it is vital that you have an accurate idea of current habits. Without this there is no starting point to work from. It is beneficial to gather information on types of foods eaten, in what quantities and at what times.

Maintaining a food diary

Use Table 9.2 to record your own dietary information for a week.

Table 9.2 Food diary

Day	Type of food/ drink	Food group	Quantity of food/drink*	Time of eating/ drinking	Feelings (hungry/tired/ happy/etc.)
Monday					
Tuesday					
Wednesday					
Thursday					
Friday					
Saturday					
Sunday					

*Portion sizes: e.g. one apple, one small bowl of cereal, one glass of orange juice.

Activity 9.1   Meal planning

1 Take a look at your record of the week.
2 Consider whether you are eating appropriate amounts of each food group compared with the eatwell plate.
3 Discuss with your group how you might be able to improve for next week. For example, if you were hungry at any particular time every day, maybe you should look at changing mealtimes or how much you eat at a particular meal.
4 Write a meal plan for the following week and see whether you can stick to it.

Improvements to meal plans

When making improvements to meal plans you should compare what you are actually eating with government guidelines and the eatwell plate. The eatwell plate is designed to ensure you consume the correct amounts of each nutrient type.

First, look at the food groups you should eat least of – sugary and fatty foods and drinks. If too much of this group is being consumed, the first job is to cut the amount down. You can do this by completely removing the item from the diet, reducing the amount consumed to a safe amount, and by preparing foods differently. For example, try baking chips in the oven rather than deep-frying them.

With the other food groups you need to balance consumption to fit the guidelines. For example, instead of a sandwich as a snack, have fruit to reduce your starchy food intake (often too high) and increase your fruit and vegetable intake (often too low).

Importance of healthy eating

Healthy eating is vitally important to our levels of energy and alertness. Here are just some of the ways it can improve our lives.

- Eating healthily makes you less likely to get ill, by keeping the immune system running smoothly. Diseases such as heart disease are less common in healthy eaters, as they eat fewer items that put strain on their bodies.
- Both overeating and under-eating will reduce physical and mental performance. Eating too little will leave you short of the energy you need to succeed. Overeating can leave you feeling tired and lethargic. Eating at the correct times of the day, particularly breakfast, will ensure you have enough energy throughout the day.
- Ensuring that you are **hydrated**, by drinking enough, will keep you alert and able to concentrate. It will also help your body flush out unwanted **toxins** efficiently.
- Absorbing complex carbohydrates rather than simple ones or sugary or fatty foods will keep you full of energy for longer and will often help prevent mood swings.

Remember

There are various ways to improve your diet. Here are a few suggestions:

- swap a chocolate bar for a piece of fruit
- drink fruit juice or water instead of fizzy drinks
- eat a bigger breakfast to prevent snacking during the morning
- have fast food once a week at most
- grill food instead of frying it.

Key terms

Hydrated – when the body has absorbed an appropriate amount of fluid to maintain its everyday functions.

Toxins – are poisonous substances which can cause harm to the body.

Assessment activity 9.2   *English*

2B.P3 | 2B.P4 | 2B.P5 | 2B.M2 | 2B.D2

Your local sports club is organising a training camp for their star players. One of the camp sessions will be on healthy eating to ensure players are getting the nutrients they need to perform at their best. You have been asked to:

- prepare a presentation for this session, giving the players information on nutrients and the benefits of a healthy diet

- help one of the players to review their current diet, in the lead-up to the training camp

- plan three meals a day and snacks for a week for the individual while they are on the training camp, making sure they understand the reasons why you have planned their diet the way you have.

Tips

- In your presentation, recap the food groups and the eatwell plate to ensure the players understand which items of food will be vital for optimum performance.
- Prepare engaging presentation slides – do not use too much text, use relevant images and note down the key points on each slide.
- Practise giving your presentation – you will have more confidence if you have practised and know your presentation well. Ask your teacher

how long your presentation should be (e.g. 5 minutes). Time yourself to make sure you are able to give your presentation in this time.
- When planning the players' new diet, remember that they will need plenty of energy to keep them going all day. At the end of the day the players will be tired and will need to recover – how will this affect the diet plan?

Health risks associated with smoking

Introduction

It is widely known that smoking causes diseases such as lung cancer. However, it is not as widely known just how many other diseases it is linked to. For sports performers, smoking will have a huge effect on the level at which they are able to compete. This topic covers examples of smoking-related diseases and the negative effects smoking can have on you in your daily life and while playing sport.

Smoking-related health problems

- Cancers – you will certainly be aware that smoking causes lung cancer. However, did you know it is also linked to cancer of the oesophagus, pancreas and kidneys?

- Coronary heart disease – over time our arteries harden and thin, leading to blockages and blood clots. Smoking speeds up and aggravates this process, making blood-flow problems such as thrombosis, heart attack, stroke and organ damage more of a possibility.

- Breathing-related problems – these are very common in smokers. Bronchitis causes prolonged breathing problems and coughing up of mucus. Emphysema causes difficulty in breathing due to damage to the alveoli in the lungs. Asthma is aggravated by smoking, making attacks more likely and more severe.

- Additionally, excessive smoking causes bad breath, discoloured teeth and stained fingers. This in turn can result in reduced confidence and affect your social life.

It is the law for cigarette packets to carry warning labels about the dangers to health caused by smoking.

How does smoking affect sports performance?

Smoking particularly affects cardiovascular activities such as running, cycling and swimming. This is because these activities rely on a healthy and efficient cardiovascular system, which is exactly what smoking damages.

Smoking makes the lungs less efficient, which prevents you from breathing in the additional air that you need when being active. It also thins the arteries, slowing the delivery of both oxygen and nutrients to vital organs. Smoking also involves breathing in carbon monoxide, which directly reduces the body's ability to transport oxygen around it.

Techniques to stop smoking

It takes many years for the body to repair itself after smoking. Therefore, the sooner you quit the better. It is never too late to quit, and anyone can significantly improve their life expectancy by giving up.

Here are a few ways to help smokers quit.

- Face-to-face support – talking helps. Smokers may find it useful to find a friend who also smokes and try to quit together. They can help motivate and support one another. Alternatively they may speak to their GP or use a private counsellor to help motivate them and track progress. Many people join self-help groups in which groups of smokers meet and work together towards the same goal of quitting.

- Nicotine patches and gum – nicotine is the addictive substance found in cigarettes. Patches and gum allow the body to receive the nicotine it craves without the additional damaging effects of the other components of a cigarette. Patches are usually placed on the arm and pass nicotine through the skin straight into the blood supply. Gum is chewed, and again delivers nicotine directly to the body. Over time, ex-smokers can reduce the amount of gum or patches they use and gradually break their dependence on this addictive drug.

- Hypnotherapy – more and more people are looking at alternative ways of giving up, such as hypnotherapy. Hypnotherapy uses psychological techniques to reduce or eliminate the body's need for nicotine.

Just checking

1 Describe three health risks linked to smoking.
2 What are two ways in which smoking will reduce the level at which you can physically perform?
3 Suggest two techniques that could help a smoker quit.

Health risks associated with alcohol

Getting started

Alcohol is widely available in bars, pubs and shops. The legal age for purchasing alcohol is 18. Do you think this is the right age to be allowed to buy alcohol? Why?

Did you know?

The recommended daily alcohol intake for an adult male is no more than 3–4 units (equivalent to approximately 1.5 pints of lager), and for women just 2–3 units (equivalent to approximately 1.5 shots of vodka with a mixer per day).

Introduction

You do not have to have a dependency on alcohol or be an alcoholic for it to have a serious effect on both your general health and well-being and your sports performance. In fact most people who develop drink-related problems are not alcoholics. They have just drunk over the recommended levels regularly for an extended period of time.

Alcohol-related health problems

- **Cancer** – cancers related to the consumption of alcohol include those of the mouth, neck and throat.
- **Mental health issues** – regular excessive drinking increases the chance that you will have psychological problems such as depression. It can also increase tiredness and make you argumentative.
- **Stroke** – this is more likely in people who have drunk more than recommended. Strokes are often seen in people at younger ages than normal if they have drunk heavily.
- **Weight gain** – alcohol is high in calories. Excessive drinking will cause additional weight gain. This will in turn put strain on the vital organs.
- **Ulcers** – these are more common in drinkers, and occur in the mouth, throat and stomach. Stomach ulcers in particular cause problems with digestion and can be very painful.
- **Gastrointestinal complications** – the rest of the intestine is also vulnerable to complications caused by alcohol consumption.
- **Liver complications** – the liver is used to filter out poisons found in the body. Alcohol is a poison and therefore passes through the liver to be processed. Excessive consumption puts great strain on the liver, sometimes causing a lot of damage.

How does alcohol affect sports performance?

- **Dehydration** – water is necessary to help transport vital nutrients around the body. Alcohol consumption encourages dehydration, which means there is a reduced level of water available in the body. This can cause headaches and will also slow the movement of other nutrients around the body.
- **Greater risk of muscle cramps** – due to a lack of nutrients reaching the muscles you are far more likely to suffer from cramps, aches and pains.
- **Greater risk of injury** – alcohol affects coordination and concentration, meaning that you are more likely to make mistakes. Just think of drink-driving: the same principles apply in a sport environment. Mistakes in sport performance can result in injury to yourself or others.

- **Reduced endurance** – a lack of nutrients being transported around the body combined with loss of motivation due to the psychological effects of alcohol mean that you are unlikely to be able to push yourself as hard as usual.
- **Slower reaction time** – alcohol reduces the speed at which signals travel from the muscles to the brain where they are processed and interpreted as commands for the rest of the body to follow. For example, when returning a tennis serve, our eyes send information to our brain, which in turn tells our body where to place the racket to hit the ball. Alcohol slows this process, meaning we are less likely to make the shot.

Reducing alcohol consumption

For people who develop a reliance on alcohol and become alcoholics there are self-help groups, counselling and clinics available to help with quitting.

However, for most people it is just a case of cutting down on consumption of alcohol to improve their health and well-being. Suggestions to help with this include:

- limiting the amount of drinks you have in a day
- drinking from smaller glasses
- swapping to low-alcohol or even non-alcoholic drinks
- having certain days where you drink nothing at all.

> **Remember**
>
> Ask your client to keep a log of what they drink. This will help you compare their consumption to the national recommendations and take action if you need to.

Assessment activity 9.3   2C.P6 | 2C.P7 | 2C.P8 | 2C.M3

You are assisting a health adviser who is in charge of a new government run get-healthy campaign. Design a storyboard and script for a get-healthy advert on television. In your advert you should give information about health risks associated with both smoking and alcohol and how they affect sports performance. You should also include information about the techniques people can use to stop smoking and cut down on their alcohol consumption.

Tips

- Be creative in the ways you deliver the points you are trying to make.
- Give the storyboard structure and ensure that each topic is given equal importance.
- Act out your storyboard with your classmates to get a sense of how effective it is at getting your points across.
- Remember that although smoking and alcohol are negative habits in excess, there are ways to quit or cut down.

The impact of drugs on health and sports performance

Getting started

There are many cases in the news of athletes taking drugs to improve performance. Can you name any cases? Do you think there is any justification for these athletes using illegal substances?

Introduction

Many an athlete has tested positive for taking drugs. Some are guilty of cheating while others have made innocent mistakes. Drug-taking is a complicated business. After all, many drugs are available off the shelf in the local supermarket. It can be difficult for sports performers to keep track of what they can and can not take, and how drugs may affect their performance.

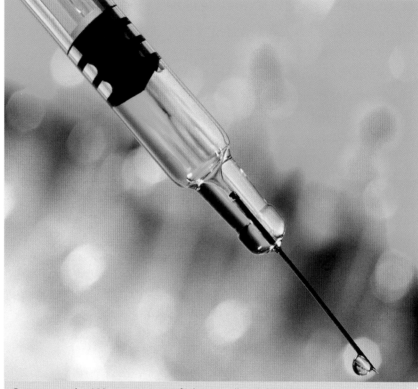

Can you ever be 100 per cent sure of what is in illegal drugs?

For most athletes the potential benefits of taking recreational drugs are far outweighed by the negative effects. However, for others the temptation is just too much. Sports performers are under ever-more pressure to succeed and push themselves to new levels. This may encourage some to look at ways of gaining an advantage. Pressure may also be applied by coaches, peers, family and fans. After all, the rewards for being the best are considerable.

Although some who cheat and take drugs do so on purpose, others may do so by mistake. Drugs are complicated and there are many legal ones that are routinely taken for medication purposes that are banned in the sporting environment. A lack of knowledge about which drugs are acceptable to take has been the downfall of many sports performers.

Table 9.3 gives a breakdown of some of the more common recreational drugs and performance-enhancing drugs that must be avoided by sports performers.

Table 9.3 Common performance-enhancing drugs that should be avoided

Type of drug	Impact of drug on sports performance	Harmful effects on the body	Use in sport
Performance-enhancing drugs			
Anabolic steroids	These are engineered versions of the male hormone testosterone. They help build muscle.	Infertility, bad skin, hair loss, aggression, and kidney, liver or prostate cancer caused by prolonged steroid use.	Power sports such as weight-lifting and rugby.
Erythropoietin	This stimulates extra growth of red blood cells, which are responsible for carrying oxygen around the body. This means increased aerobic capabilities.	Thickening of the blood, causing increased risk of heart attack and stroke. May also cause headaches and nausea.	Endurance sports such as cycling and running.
Growth hormone	Promotes the growth of bones, ligaments and tendons. In adults it also boosts the efficiency of the heart and increases the number of red blood cells available. Is naturally found within the body but can be relatively easily replicated.	Increase in size of features including the jaw, forehead and fingers. Increase in size of organs, leading to organ failure. Can lead to muscle, bone and joint pain.	Anaerobic exercises such as power lifting.
Diuretics	Reduce the amount of excess water within the body, causing weight loss. Mask the presence of other drugs in the performers system.	Dehydration, damage to liver and high blood pressure.	Sports where meeting weight requirements are important such as horse racing or boxing.
Beta blockers	Counteract the effects of adrenaline, a naturally occurring chemical released in the body when a person is under pressure. Beta blockers decrease the sports performer's heart rate, steadying their nerves and reduce the potential for shaking.	Headaches, slow heartbeat, fatigue and reduced circulation are all possible side-effects.	Sports reliant on high levels of concentration such as archery and gymnastics.

Assessment activity 9.4

2D.P9 | 2D.M4 | 2D.D3

The government campaign you were working on for Assessment activity 9.3 has been extended to cover drugs and their impact on sports performance. Design a leaflet aimed at aspiring athletes to provide information about banned performance-enhancing drugs. Include information about why some sports performers may resort to drug-taking and about the possible negative effects and dangers.

Tip
Include examples in your leaflet by linking each drug to a different sport and showing how it may affect sports performance.

Discussion point

Why do you think athletes take illegal drugs? Do you think that the reasons might include pressure to perform, financial incentives associated with winning, and lack of awareness of either health risks or the risk to their careers? What other things can athletes improve before using drugs (e.g. diet, training, rest, psychology etc)?

Introduction

Everyone who plays sport or takes part in physical activity is prone to suffer from an injury at some stage. The type of injury and the severity will vary.

Sometimes it is easy to understand how the injury occurred; other times it is not so obvious. Avoiding injury in the first place is the best way of dealing with it, but that is not always possible, so you have to be able to look at how you can recover from injury. Most sports performers do not want to miss out on participating and are often anxious to return to their sport as soon as possible. Some return too soon, others not at all.

This unit will help you identify the common causes of injury, how best to avoid them and what to do if you become injured.

It also considers how individuals react to injury and how this emotion, as well as the injury, can be taken into account during rehabilitation.

Assessment: You will be assessed by a series of assignments set by your teacher/tutor.

Learning aims

In this unit you will:

A understand risks and hazards associated with sports participation

B know about different injuries and illnesses associated with sports participation

C know about the response to injury and injury management

D know about rules, regulations and legislation associated with health and safety in sport.

This unit has taught me that you have to be really organised when coaching a group of people to make sure they are safe and no one gets injured, because it can happen easily. I now have a better understanding of what to do should an injury occur, and how to prevent an injury from happening at all!

Stefan, *15-year-old aspiring football coach*

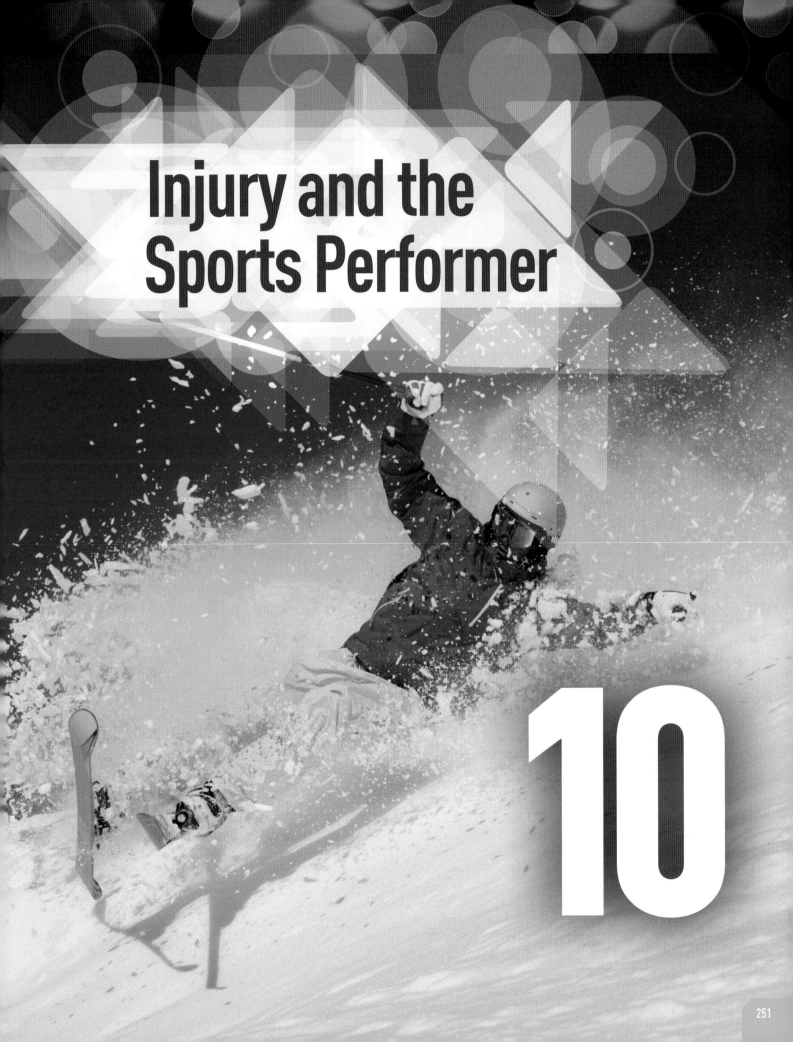

Injury and the Sports Performer

10

This table shows you what you must do in order to achieve a **Pass**, **Merit** or **Distinction** grade, and where you can find activities in this book to help you.

Assessment Zone

Assessment criteria			
Level 1	**Level 2 Pass**	**Level 2 Merit**	**Level 2 Distinction**
Learning aim A: understand risks and hazards associated with sports participation			
1A.1 Describe two different risks or hazards that relate to each topic of people, equipment and the environment, respectively	**2A.P1** Explain three different risks or hazards that relate to each topic of people, equipment and the environment, respectively **See Assessment activity 10.1, page 259**		
Learning aim B: know about different injuries and illnesses associated with sports participation			
1B.2 Outline three different physiological, and three psychological, causes of injury in relation to sport	**2B.P2** Explain three different physiological, and three different psychological, causes of injury in relation to sport **See Assessment activity 10.2, page 265**	**2B.M1** Using sport-specific examples, discuss the relationship between causes of injury and basic and complex types of injury **See Assessment activity 10.2, page 265**	**2B.D1** For a selected injury or illness give a detailed account of how it might occur, analysing the associated types and signs of injury or illness **See Assessment activity 10.2, page 265**
1B.3 Describe two basic injuries associated with sports participation	**2B.P3** Describe two different types of basic injury and two different types of complex injury associated with sports participation **See Assessment activity 10.2, page 265**		
1B.4 English Describe two types and signs of illness associated with sports participation	**2B.P4** English Explain four types and signs of illness associated with sports participation **See Assessment activity 10.2, page 265**		
Learning aim C: know about the response to injury and injury management			
1C.5 Describe the physiological and immediate psychological responses to injury in sport	**2C.P5** Describe the physiological and immediate and long-term psychological responses to injury in sport **See Assessment activity 10.3, page 271**	**2C.M2** For a selected sports injury, explain the responses and process of physiological and psychological management **See Assessment activity 10.3, page 271**	**2C.D2** Justify selected methods used to manage physiological and psychological responses to a selected injury in a sporting context **See Assessment activity 10.3, page 271**

Assessment criteria			
Level 1	Level 2 **Pass**	Level 2 **Merit**	Level 2 **Distinction**
Learning aim C: know about the response to injury and injury management			
1C.6 Describe how to manage physiological and immediate psychological responses to injury in sport	**2C.P6** Describe how to manage physiological and immediate and long-term psychological responses to injury in sport **See Assessment activity 10.3, page 271**		
Learning aim D: know about rules, regulations and legislation associated with health and safety in sport			
1D.7 English Outline reasons for having health and safety rules, regulations and legislation in sport	**2D.P7** English Discuss reasons for having health and safety rules, regulations and legislation in sport **See Assessment activity 10.4, page 278**	**2D.M3** English Explain how two selected rules, regulations or pieces of legislation help maintain the health and safety of participants in a selected sport **See Assessment activity 10.4, page 278**	**2D.D3** English Analyse the impact of two selected rules, regulations or pieces of legislation on participants in a selected sport **See Assessment activity 10.4, page 278**

English   Opportunity to practise English skills

How you will be assessed

This unit will be assessed through a series of assignments set by your teacher/tutor. You will be expected to show an understanding of the risks and hazards related to sports participation and how these can be minimised to help reduce the incidence of sports injury. In addition, you will be expected to be knowledgeable about how individuals respond to the impact of injury and how this might be managed during a rehabilitation programme. Finally, it is important that – as you prepare to either continue your studies or work within the sports industry – you are aware of the relevant legislation and regulations that help to protect sports participants from accidents and injuries. The tasks will be based on a scenario where you are working in a sports setting.

Your assessment could be in the form of:

- presentations
- information cards or leaflets on injury management
- role play
- research into a specific type of sports facility and its related legislation and regulations.

People-related risks and hazards

Introduction

No one wants to be injured – especially if you are a sports participant. Most sports people just want to take part in sport – injury is the last thing that they want or indeed sometimes admit to.

Warm-up and cool down

Pre-exercise stretching warms the muscles and makes them 'loose', enabling quicker muscle contraction, as well as improving the efficiency and effectiveness of the use of oxygen in the body.

If you do not warm up, the body is not fully prepared for physical activity and this is when injuries can occur.

A cool down will help reverse the effects of participating in physical activity and bring the performer back to a normal state of function. A thorough cool down helps to stop muscles becoming sore and stiff.

Physique

Having the appropriate **physique** for a particular sport or activity is important because it can improve a player's performance, especially in a particular role or position. For example, how many football goalkeepers or basketball players do you see who measure only 1.52 metres in height? Not many. This is because height is a physical necessity for both positions.

Having a suitable physique is also important because it can reduce the risks associated with competing in a sport or activity against someone with an unequal build. For example, a heavyset hammer thrower would not be so successful if they were a gymnast, who needs to be lighter and more flexible, and the risk of injury if a heavyset hammer thrower was to compete against a gymnast would be high.

Drugs

The use of drugs such as alcohol can not only have a negative effect on how the body functions, but can also have other side-effects that affect sports performance, including loss of controlled movement and reduced concentration. This increases chances of injury to yourself and others, particularly in contact sports.

Other recreational drugs include nicotine, which reduces lung capacity and increases the risk of heart disease and lung cancer.

Most performance-enhancing drugs are banned by governing bodies, including:

- stimulants – these make performers more alert and mask fatigue but can cause heart failure and are very addictive
- anabolic agents/steroids – these help performers to train harder and build muscle but increase aggression and can cause kidney damage.

Technique

Developing skills and perfecting techniques to perform certain sporting actions comes with time and practice. For example, hitting a good serve in tennis is a difficult technique to get right every time. If a performer does not follow a sports coach's feedback, poor technique can develop and this can increase the risk of injury, for example tennis elbow.

Skill level

It is important for performers to compete against someone of similar skill level to avoid either side getting injured. For example, a premiership football team could not compete against an under-13 school side. Not only would this be too great a mismatch physically, but the skill level would be too different for a competition, and this could result in injury.

When setting up coaching/training sessions with children, take care to match them in terms of height, weight, maturity, experience and ability, not in terms of their chronological age.

Over-training

If you train too much or too often, you will not give your body time to recover and therefore you will not be ready to perform at the level you are actually capable of. This can lead to fatigue and burn-out, which is when mistakes and injury can occur.

To prevent over-training, make sure that you and others:

- notice and are aware of the signs and symptoms of fatigue such as a lack of coordination or reduced control of movement
- have adequate rest periods between training sessions
- engage in brief periods of specific, quality training, rather than long periods of excessive training
- vary the type of training activity in terms of intensity and task
- make sure that training resembles the game situation in terms of the number of repetitions of tasks.

Link

See *Unit 9: Lifestyle and Well-being* for more information about the effects of alcohol, smoking and performance-enhancing drugs.

Activity 10.1 Avoiding injury

Imagine you are volunteering as an assistant coach for a local youth team (in a sport of your choice). What would you do to ensure that your participants did not develop an injury due to any of the reasons listed?

Think about the type of warm-up and cool-down you would take the team through and the types of skill training activities you would organise. How often would you want the team to train, and for how long?

Equipment-related risks and hazards

Getting started

Think about the sport you play – do you use specific equipment such as a racket or bat or ball during your participation? Do you use protective equipment when you take part?

Introduction

A proper warm-up and cool down, appropriate training and avoidance of risks and hazards are important to avoid injury. However, you will also need to consider the potential issues involved with using equipment.

Take it further

For further information about England and Wales Cricket Board guidelines, please go to Pearson Hotlinks (www.pearsonhotlinks.co.uk) and search for this BTEC Sport title.

Lack of protective clothing and equipment

For many sports, there are certain items of clothing and equipment that performers are required to wear, as stated in the governing body's rules and regulations.

An example of this is, in February 2000 the England and Wales Cricket Board (ECB) issued safety guidance on the wearing of helmets by young players up to the age of 18. The guidance recommends a variety of protective clothing to be worn while playing including pads, helmets with facial protection (faceguard or grille) for batters and wicket keepers, abdominal protectors (box) and protective gloves.

Sometimes, items of clothing and equipment are not specified in the rules and regulations of a game but are used by participants to protect them from injury. An example of this would be skiing and snowboarding base layers, designed to keep the body warm and dry and free from muscle pulls and tears.

Activity 10.2   Protective clothing and equipment

Carry out some research on a number of sports, including football, hockey and fencing.

1 For each sport, find out what clothes and equipment are required by the regulations to protect the performers and avoid injury.

2 What clothes and equipment are used to help protect the player but are not specified as part of the rules and regulations?

Have you ever worn a protective helmet?

Damaged equipment

How often have you seen goalposts standing at a precarious angle on a playing field in a park? This is often a result of wear and tear or damaged caused by bad weather, and if used, these goalposts could be a safety hazard. So it is vital that checks are made on all of the equipment to be used to ensure that each item is safe to use. This is normally done by a coach, teacher or, in some cases, a maintenance person responsible for assessing the risk of sports facilities. This check of equipment will be one of the first things that they do when they start work each day.

Wrong equipment

It is essential that the right-sized equipment is used for the right sport and the right age group. A full-sized tennis racket is not suitable for a young child just beginning tennis; however, a modified smaller racket will allow them to develop the basic skills correctly. The size of a normal racket could be, in some cases, almost the same size as the child and very weighty; therefore they will have difficulty controlling it to produce an appropriate shot, increasing the potential for injury.

Incorrect use of equipment

Injuries are often caused by carelessness and incorrect use of equipment: for example, trying to kick a medicine ball, or hit a golf ball with a tennis racket.

Did you know?

Other equipment that can be modified includes athletics equipment, balls of different sizes and weights for football, netball, basketball and so on.

A slightly smaller and lighter ball can allow smaller, younger people to start developing the necessary skills in line with their own body weight, without being at risk of straining or producing an uncontrolled movement which may in turn lead to injury such as a muscle strain or tear.

The equipment can then be upgraded gradually to the correct weight or size.

Just checking

1 Why is there a risk of injury with a poor warm-up and/or cool down when participating in sport?

2 What happens if you over-train?

3 Stimulants can help make athletes feel more alert and not as tired, so why are they bad for you?

4 Name a sport that requires you by law to wear protective equipment. Can you explain why?

5 Why is it important always to check that the equipment you are using is appropriate and not damaged before you start to play?

Environment-related risks and hazards

Getting started

If you are a football, hockey or rugby player, you may have warmed up inside by doing some stretching, but when you get out on to the pitch you find it is frozen solid. Why would this be dangerous to play on?

Introduction

Now you have checked the equipment and ensured an appropriate warm-up has taken place, it is time to consider risks and hazards posed by the place where you carry out your sport.

Key terms

Dehydration – an inadequate amount of fluid in the body. A person is usually considered dehydrated when they have lost more than 2% of their body weight during exercise.

Heat cramps – painful muscle contractions, mainly affecting the gastrocnemius, quadriceps and abdominals.

Heat exhaustion – when the body temperature rises as high as 40°C (104°F) with nausea, vomiting, headache, fainting, weakness and cold, clammy skin.

Heatstroke – a life-threatening emergency condition that occurs when the body temperature is greater than 40°C (104°F).

Frostbite – injury to body tissues caused by exposure to extreme cold.

Hypothermia – having an unusually or dangerously low body temperature, generally below 35 degrees, as low as 28 degrees in severe cases.

Temperature

Taking part in sport or physical activity in hot or cold weather can affect the outcome of sports performance.

Exercising in hot weather

Both the exercise itself and the air temperature can cause your core body temperature to increase. To help you keep cool, blood is diverted away from the muscles to the skin to allow heat loss leaving less blood for your muscles, which in turn increases your heart rate.

If the humidity is also high, sweat cannot readily evaporate from your skin, which can raise your body temperature further.

Your body's natural cooling systems may fail if you are exposed to high temperatures and humidity for too long, and you sweat heavily. If you do not drink enough fluids, the result may be a heat-related illness such as **dehydration**, **heat cramps**, **heat exhaustion** or **heatstroke**. To avoid these, adequate fluid intake (such as water or sports drinks) is essential before, during and after exercise.

Exercising in cold weather

A warm-up generates heat and helps prevent muscular strains, and is vital in exceptionally cold weather. It is important to be aware of the early warning signs and symptoms of cold exposure and how to prevent problems. Shivering is usually the first sign of dangerous cold exposure. As the body is trying to generate its own heat you will develop uncontrolled muscle contractions.

The two most dangerous conditions that can result from cold weather exposure include **frostbite** and **hypothermia**.

Activity 10.3   Heat- and cold-related conditions

1 Describe the difference between heat cramps, heat exhaustion and heatstroke.
2 What are the signs and symptoms of frostbite and hypothermia, and how would you treat a casualty for either of these?

Other effects of weather

The weather can also cause playing surfaces to become dangerous to play on. Care should be taken and the match or activity abandoned if the surface is not fit for play. For example, rain can cause slippery and muddy conditions, or extreme cold can cause the ground to freeze and become icy.

Taking precautions

Playing surfaces should be checked in any weather to ensure that they are in good condition before the start of a sports activity. For example, many netball and tennis courts are made of concrete, which is ideal for a ball to bounce on or for players to run on, but in a fall, it can cause grazing and cuts, or worse. AstroTurf® can give the same kind of injuries as concrete, as well as friction burns. All these injuries can later become infected if not treated appropriately.

Do you find it harder to play sports in cold weather?

Assessment activity 10.1   2A.P1

During your two-week work placement at a local sport and fitness club your supervisor has asked you to prepare a leaflet that can be used in a staff training event.

The training is to focus on the safety of clients. Staff will be asked to consider how their induction programme helps to ensure a client's safety while at the club.

Your job is to produce a leaflet that explains the possible risks and hazards that could occur if a client does not have an appropriate induction to the facility.

Tips

- Consider the areas where there is a possible cause for concern in relation to a client's health and safety: people-, equipment- and environment-related issues.
- Give three examples for each of the three areas of concern.
- Give detailed information and use examples wherever possible to make these issues clear to the staff.

Causes of injury

Introduction

While most people think first about the physiological causes of injury, there can also be psychological causes.

Physiological causes

- Overuse – some injuries are caused by repeated physical actions. Over time, conditions worsen as the affected area becomes increasingly worn or stretched.

- **Intensity** – in training or playing, this can overload the body so it is unable to function fully. 'Too much, too soon' is a sure way to pick up an injury.

- Gravity – generally a cause of injury for activities that involve balance and/or landing on the feet, for example tackling in football or a somersault in gymnastics. Bad timing can result in a performer landing badly on the ground or a piece of equipment by accident, which can cause injury.

- **Intrinsic factors** – sometimes injury can result from factors to do with a performer's own body. Examples include body type, age, skill level and experience of playing the sport.

- **Extrinsic factors** – sometimes injury can result from forces outside the body. Examples include weather conditions, footwear and type of sport (e.g. contact sports).

Weather – appropriate clothing and footwear is essential.

Psychological causes

Stress

Stress is often present, sometimes as a result of the sport we are playing, or from work, school, money worries, family problems or events such as moving house. Signs to watch out for include feeling tired and not sleeping well; illnesses such as sore throat, cold or flu; skin conditions; mouth ulcers; swollen lymph glands and weight loss. Major sources of stress that have been reported by sports performers in particular include fear of failure, concerns about social evaluation by others (particularly their coach) and lack of readiness to perform.

These sources of stress can affect concentration while participating and knock confidence. This in turn can lead to a poor performance, which ultimately makes injury more likely.

Reduced concentration

A lack of focus and concentration while playing sports can lead to injury. This may be physiologically induced, such as dehydration, or simply because the performer's mind was on something else – what happened at work or the argument they had with a friend just before they started playing, for instance. Whatever the cause, reduced concentration means less focus on the matter in hand and makes the performer more susceptible to injury.

Personality factors

Personality traits can be described as people's characteristic behaviours and conscious motives. People can be categorised as **introverts** or **extroverts**.

People who are introverted tend to be more reserved, reclusive, thoughtful, calm and rational. They are more interested in individual sports that demand concentration and precision: for example archery or golf. Some research suggests that introverted sports people tend not to be so vulnerable to sports injuries – possibly as they tend to be more focused and mindful of their actions.

People who are extroverted tend to be more excitable, outgoing, lively, sociable and impulsive. They prefer sports that are exciting and fast, such as team sports. They can sometimes display more aggression during sports performance. There may appear to be no rationale for their outbursts and this can lead to an injury being incurred, for example, during a poorly timed or overzealous tackle in football.

Case study

John plays football for his school and for a local youth team. He was involved in a cup game at the weekend, a semi-final with a local rival club. Throughout the game John never stopped trying. He had covered a lot of the pitch and had crossed the ball for the striker to score to bring the match back to 1-all. The score stood at 1 goal each with 5 minutes left to play, when he injured his right knee during a wild challenge on another player for the ball.

1 Why do you think the injury happened?

2 How might John have avoided the injury?

Types of injury

Introduction

Sports injuries can be categorised in many different ways. For simplicity we are going to look at two types – basic and complex.

Basic injuries

These are mainly injuries to the muscles or the skin.

Muscular injuries

- **Sprains** affect **ligaments** and commonly occur in the ankle, knee and wrist.
- **Strains** frequently occur near where the muscle joins the tough, fibrous connective tissue of the tendon; a similar injury occurs if there is a direct blow to the muscle.
- **Bruises** may be caused by a tackle or a piece of sports equipment such as a cricket ball.

Skin injuries

A **graze** affects only the surface layer of skin, which is scraped off, whereas a **cut** goes through several layers of skin. Grazes bleed slightly but cuts will bleed for longer because of the amount of damage done to the skin layers and their associated blood vessels.

Blisters can occur from the rubbing of clothing, such as footwear on the back of the heel, or as a result of sports equipment, such as rubbing on the hand caused by a racket grip. Over time, continued friction can cause the top layer of skin to separate from the second layer of skin.

Complex injuries

There are many types of complex injury that result from participation in sport.

Overuse injuries

These include:

- **tendonitis** – inflammation or irritation of a tendon; Achilles tendonitis is one of the most frequent tendonitis injuries in sport
- **shin splints** – pain over the front of the tibia bone (lower leg); this can be due to problems with the muscles, the bone or the attachment of the muscle to the bone
- **Osgood-Schlatter disease** – occurring in the knee and caused by inflammation of the tendon below the kneecap (patellar tendon) where it attaches to the shin bone (tibia).

Concussion

This may result from a fall in which the head strikes an object or if a moving object strikes the head. The blow causes the brain to move violently within the skull, and the brain cells all 'fire' at once, similar to a seizure. Medical attention should always be sought if someone suffers concussion, even if they do not seem badly injured. Symptoms of concussion include unconsciousness (following a severe head trauma), headache, nausea, dizziness, sickness, increased pupil size and confusion.

Dislocation

Dislocations occur at a joint, when one of the bones of the joint becomes misplaced. The bones that form a joint are normally held in place by the fibrous capsule of the joint and by ligaments that span the joint. In a dislocation, the capsule and one or more ligaments are stretched or torn.

Fracture

A fracture is a break in any bone in the body. Fractures are usually caused by trauma. This may be in the form of a fall, twist, blow or collision.

Back and spinal cord injuries

Back injuries tend to be muscle-related, such as strains or torn muscles. However, this muscle injury may impact on the function of the vertebral column, causing a lot of pain and discomfort.

A much more serious injury is when the spinal cord is damaged, causing impaired or lost function and resulting in reduced mobility or feeling, or both. This type of injury is often caused by trauma, such as a bad fall or a sports injury – diving into a shallow pool, a rugby tackle or a fall in skiing. The most extreme outcome is paralysis. Medical attention should always be sought for back injuries.

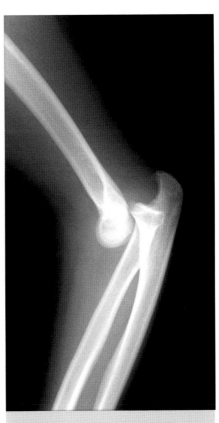

Do you know anyone who has suffered a dislocation?

Just checking

1 Give an example of an intrinsic and an extrinsic physiological cause of injury.
2 Why might reduced concentration cause injury to occur?
3 Name three types of muscular injuries.
4 What type of injury is tendonitis?

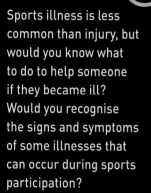

Types and signs of illness

Getting started

Sports illness is less common than injury, but would you know what to do to help someone if they became ill? Would you recognise the signs and symptoms of some illnesses that can occur during sports participation?

Introduction

Not only can injuries be a problem when participating in sports, but some illnesses can also result. This topic looks at some of the more common examples.

We are all familiar with the term 'sports injury'; however, we tend not to associate sports with illness. The sports illnesses considered in this unit are not specific to sport, but they are some of the most common illnesses that occur during sports participation.

Asthma

Asthma is a chronic inflammation of the passages (bronchi) of the lungs. Symptoms include coughing, tightening of the chest, wheezing, unusual fatigue while exercising and shortness of breath when exercising.

Exercise is a common trigger for asthma attacks. Asthma inhalers used prior to exercise can control and prevent exercise-induced asthma symptoms.

Discussion point

As a sports coach you should be used to having to deal with athletes who have minor injuries, but think about what you would do if one of your athletes started to struggle during a coaching session because of asthma.

- What would be the signs and symptoms of an attack?
- How would you deal with the situation?

Heart attacks

Heart attacks are triggered by different things, including diet and genetic factors. Fortunately a heart attack is not a common sports-related illness. A heart attack occurs when blood flow to a section of heart muscle becomes blocked. If the flow of blood is not restored quickly, the section of heart muscle becomes damaged due to lack of oxygen and begins to die. A heart attack, or myocardial infarction, can be eased by rest as this reduces the demands on the heart, but it will not help the pain. The blood supply to the affected heart muscles cannot be restored while the clot remains. Emergency help must be summoned immediately.

Common signs and symptoms of heart attack include:

- chest pain or discomfort
- upper body discomfort (arms, back, neck, jaw or stomach)
- shortness of breath.

Viral infection

This is any type of infection that is caused by a virus. For example, the common cold and flu are both viral infections. If the viral infection results in a high temperature (a fever), the sufferer should avoid exercise until this is reduced. Exercise would put too much stress on the heart, which is already beating faster as a result of the raised body temperature.

Hypoglycaemia

Hypoglycaemia symptoms develop when blood glucose levels are too low. This may be because a person has not eaten well or for a long time, or has undertaken a lot of physical activity so that their body's natural stores of blood sugar have been depleted. Symptoms can include nervousness, sweating, intense hunger, trembling, weakness, palpitations, confusion and having trouble speaking. Most people recognise the early warning signs of hypoglycaemia in themselves and counteract them by eating.

Why is it important that a sports coach has a good knowledge of common illnesses?

Assessment activity 10.2 — *English* — 2B.P2 | 2B.P3 | 2B.P4 | 2B.M1 | 2B.D1

As part of a coaching badge that you are taking you have been asked to produce a written report to show what knowledge you have in relation to sports injury. This report should have two parts.

1 Types of illness (associated with sports performance): give four detailed examples of types of illnesses and their signs.

2 Types of sports injury, and their causes.

Tips

- For part 1:

  a. explain physiological and psychological causes of injury, giving three examples of each.

  b. describe the difference between a basic injury and a complex one, giving two examples of each and discuss the relationship between causes of injury and basic and complex types of injury.

- For part 2, you should ensure you show a thorough understanding of how this injury or illness may occur and the signs and symptoms associated with it.

- Ensure that wherever possible you use illustrative material to reinforce the content of your report.

Just checking

1 What is asthma and what signs and symptoms should you look out for to be able to tell if someone is struggling with asthma during activity?

2 What causes hypoglycaemia and how can it be made better?

Responses to injury

Getting started

Imagine you have picked up an injury. You did not warm up properly and now you have pulled a muscle in your calf. Which muscle could it be? Can you name it?

Key terms

Vasodilation – widening of your arterioles (small branches of arteries).

Shock – when the body's natural balance is 'upset' due to inadequate circulation of oxygen to the vital organs. Symptoms can include: feeling sick, thirsty, weak and/or giddy; skin being cold and clammy, or pale and grey; lips, earlobes and fingernails being grey/blue; and restlessness.

Introduction

Any injury or illness has its own set of signs and symptoms to help you, and where necessary a medical professional, to identify what the injury is and then the best course of treatment for that injury.

Physiological responses

The body responds to injury in a variety of ways.

- Pain – usually accompanied by tissue injury. When cells in the body are injured or damaged, they release a chemical called prostaglandin. When prostaglandin is released, the nerve endings respond to it by picking up and transmitting the pain and injury messages through the nervous system to the brain.
- Swelling – a result of the initial bleeding caused by the trauma of injury, as well as an inflow of fluid into the area as a result of the inflammatory response of the body.
- Redness – can occur at the site of injury due to the **vasodilation** of blood vessels and/or because of damage to the blood vessels, causing blood to seep out of the vessel and into the surrounding area.
- Heat – often present as a result of the increase in blood flow to the injured area.
- Loss or partial loss of function – if there is substantial damage to the area and/or significant swelling then the normal range of movement may be impaired.

Psychological responses

Not only will the body respond physiologically, it will also respond psychologically. The type of response will depend on the extent of the injury.

Immediate response

When injury first occurs the common immediate response is to feel distressed and worried about the nature of the damage.

The suddenness of injury can cause some people to suffer from **shock** – again, dependent on the extent of injury.

If the injury is minor, reassurance and appropriate treatment will soon help the performer to deal with their initial feelings. However, if the injury is more severe there are other feelings that will soon start to take over from the initial response, such as anger – towards an opponent or even towards themselves.

Sometimes an injury may prevent you from continuing with exercise. What would you suggest this runner does to prevent further injury?

If the performer is required to take some time out from participating in sport, they may feel a lack of control over their 'sporting' future alongside the obvious pain and discomfort. This can be compounded by the impact the injury may have on goals they have set within their training programme to improve performance.

Long-term response

The immediate responses also apply in the longer term. However, in addition to these, anyone who is unable to participate in their chosen sport for a longer period of time is also likely to experience the following feelings during their rehabilitation.

- Lowered self-confidence and self-esteem – doubts may creep in about whether they will be as good when they start playing after injury as they were before they got injured, or whether they will still make the team.

- Frustration – the progress of the rehabilitation may be slower than anticipated; feelings of wanting a quicker recovery rate are not uncommon.

- Depression – for some individuals, not being able to train or play, and uncertainty over how well they will play again in future is too much, and feelings of depression are common.

Injuries obtained in sport may make you worry about participating in the future. With support from friends and teammates, trying again when fully recovered will often give you the confidence boost you need.

Just checking

1 What are the five main physiological responses to injury?

2 What are the most common long-term psychological responses to injury?

3 What is vasodilation?

Management of injuries

Introduction

In order to help a performer start to recover from an injury, it is important that you understand the types of treatment and rehabilitation necessary.

◢ Management of physiological injuries

Physiological injuries should be taken care of immediately by a professional – for example, a qualified first aider, doctor or physio/sports therapist.

Having gained an accurate diagnosis from the professionals, there is some basic treatment that can be implemented.

Injuries that cause swelling, pain and limit the range of joint motion near the injury may also have torn blood vessels, causing a bluish discoloration. The injured muscle may feel weak and stiff. To control pain, bleeding and inflammation, keep the muscle in a gently stretched position and use the PRICE formula.

- **P**rotect – protect the injured area from further harm by stopping play.
- **R**est – it is important that the injured area be kept as still as possible with no weight on it.
- **I**ce – apply ice wrapped in a clean cloth (and remove ice after 10 minutes) to reduce blood flow, pain and swelling.
- **C**ompression – lightly wrap the injured area in a soft bandage.
- **E**levation – raise it to a level above the heart.

During the first 24 to 48 hours after injury you will probably need to continue using rest, ice, compression bandages and elevation of the injured area to control bleeding, swelling and pain.

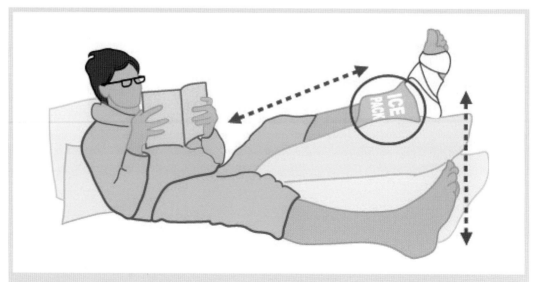

Figure 10.1 A raised limb following an injury – can you see how the PRICE formula is being applied?

If you are the one in charge of a session (or the qualified first aider), you also need to think about the immediate treatment that you should give to any casualty – SALTAPS.

- **S**top play.
- **A**sk the player – evaluate for pain and for orientation/confusion.
- **L**ook – look at the limb and evaluate the appearance of the injury.
- **T**ouch – touch the injury if the player will allow this; does there appear to be heat at the site of the injury?
- **A**ctive movement – can the player move the limb?
- **P**assive movement – if you move the limb, does it hurt; is there sufficient range of motion?
- **S**tand up – can the player really play, or are they denying the extent of the injury?

Remember, if in any doubt, seek professional advice.

Basic treatments: rehabilitation through to recovery

There are other basic treatments that you can utilise to help rehabilitation of the physiological aspects of a sports injury.

- Hot and cold – after the first 24–48 hours with a sports injury, alternating hot and cold packs is generally more effective in promoting healing than either heat or ice alone. The contrast of hot and cold acts like a local pump to bring fresh blood (carrying oxygen and nutrients) to the injury and flush out the debris from the damage (most of which is tiny scraps of protein that used to be intact muscle fibre). Apply hot then cold for 5 minutes each over a 20–30 minute period. Finish with cold to reduce blood flow, and repeat three times a day.

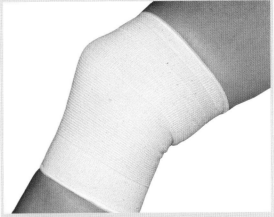

- Basic strappings – strappings such as a Tubigrip™ can also help by applying compression to the area to help minimise any swelling and by providing some support.
- Sports creams – these contain medication to help relieve pain from aches and pains and can also help to manage the injury. However, do not apply a sports cream to an injury if the skin is broken.

Have you ever needed to use a Tubigrip™? Could you feel it helping?

Take it further

- Knowledge of basic treatment procedures is a must for anyone who is involved in sport as unfortunately sports injuries can be all too common. While this BTEC qualification can give you some understanding of basic treatment knowledge and application, have you considered taking a course that might provide you with more information and skills so that as a coach or a participant, you will be well versed in how to deal effectively and appropriately with a sports injury if it should happen in your presence?
- There are lots of First Aid or Injury Management courses available nationally so there may be one running in your location. Have a look for local adverts or use the internet to identify courses that may be of use to you.

CONTINUED ▸▸

Management of psychological injuries

It is very important that the psychological effects are also considered and made a part of the rehabilitation process. There are different ways in which this can be done depending on the extent of the injury.

Goal setting

Setting performance goals is a natural part of every athlete's daily routine, so why not incorporate this into an injured phase of the routine? Injured athletes can use goal setting to facilitate their recovery. A goal is defined as a desired objective towards which effort is directed.

Short- and long-term goals could be set to help the injured performer:

- short-term goals – often daily goals that motivate by allowing the athlete to see immediate progress
- long-term goals – these provide direction and motivation to return to play in the future.

Including the athlete in the goal-setting process can help by giving them ownership of the rehabilitation goals. Goal setting can be used to identify success in rehabilitation and can increase a performer's self-confidence.

Relaxation techniques

Relaxation techniques such as mental imagery, or visualisation, can help a performer combat any frustration or depression they may be feeling as a result of their injury.

Remember

Treatment of an injury doesn't just relate to the physiological condition of the person but their psychological well-being also.

After recovering from the physical effects of an injury some people may still not be psychologically ready to return, which in turn can lead to:

- decreased confidence leading to a decline in performance
- re-injury or further injury
- feelings of stress and anxiety due to lack of confidence in their physical condition
- fear of injury and fear of returning to play.

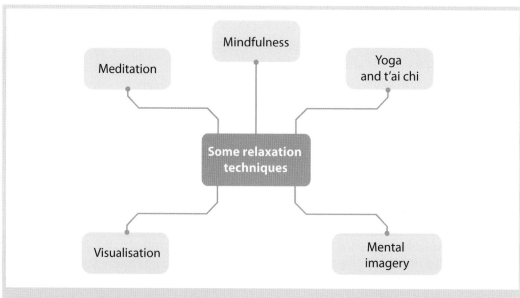

Figure 10.2 Which of these relaxation techniques do you think might work for you?

Mental imagery is a skill that involves the visualisation of an object, scene or sensation as though it were actually occurring. For example, athletes can use imagery to imagine their rehabilitation exercises before actually performing the tasks. Using this technique may improve concentration on the eventual exercises and can lead to an increase in effort throughout the rehabilitation process.

Visualisation can also help a performer think about how they might cope next time if they are in the same situation that caused the injury; they would imagine how they might avoid the tackle/contact that incurred the injury, for example.

Did you know?

Most psychologists specialise in either sport or exercise. The difference is as follows:

- Sports psychologists work with sports participants across both team and individual sports, and from amateur to elite levels of competition. Their aim is predominantly to help athletes prepare psychologically for competition and to deal with the psychological demands of both competition and training.
- An exercise psychologist is primarily concerned with the application of psychology to increase exercise participation and motivational levels in the general public. Examples of the work they do include optimising the benefits derived from exercise participation and helping individual clients with the implementation of a plan to take more exercise.

Assessment activity 10.3

2C.P5 | 2C.P6 | 2C.M2 | 2C.D2

As part of your first aid qualification you are asked to demonstrate how you would manage a casualty who had suffered a sports injury – ensuring that you not only considered the physiological aspects of injury but also accounted for any possible psychological aspects. Give a presentation to your first aid trainer describing possible responses to injury in sport and explain how to manage these responses. Illustrate your explanation by selecting a specific injury and justify your methods of physiological and psychological management.

Tips

- In your presentation you may want to use a colleague to act as your casualty in order to show how you might administer treatment.
- Make sure you select an appropriate injury to focus on in order that you can achieve across the grading grid. A basic injury will not allow you to do this.
- Ensure that physiological, immediate and long-term psychological responses to injury are described.

Purpose of health and safety

Getting started

Remember the calf muscle injury you considered earlier? You should now know the anatomical name of it and how the injury could be treated, but can you think how you might have prevented the injury happening in the first place? You know you did not warm up properly, so what could you have done specifically to prevent this injury? Explain what warm-up activities you would perform.

Key term

Risk assessment – the review of the health and safety of players and the sporting environment ahead of a planned activity. This involves identifying potential hazards (what could go wrong) and putting in place planned measures and responses to prevent/reduce risk of injury.

Introduction

Health and safety is paramount in any industry, not only for the employer and employees of a business, but also for members of the public who use the facilities and equipment. In this topic we will look at the reasons for this.

Maintaining a safe environment

In the sports industry there are very clear guidelines on what should be done to make sure that the environment is safe for sports participants and spectators.

For example:

● playing surfaces and floors in spectator areas should not be wet and slippery

● there should be adequate lighting and ventilation

● in swimming pools the appropriate chemicals must be maintained in the water for hygiene purposes

● all equipment that is to be used should be suitable for the activity and the individual, and in good repair.

People should only be permitted to participate if they:

● have appropriate and necessary protective clothing and equipment for the activity

● are fully aware of the rules of the sport.

Those in charge of the session should ensure that a full and comprehensive **risk assessment** is carried out.

Hazard	Risks *For each hazard identify the level of risk without your control measures. 1 = no risk. 6 = high risk.*	Exposure *Who might be exposed to this hazard?*	Likelihood *How likely is it that someone exposed to this hazard **without** control measures will be injured or harmed?*				Risk Rating *Risk × likelihood*	Control Measure *For each hazard list the things you will do to minimise the risk of an accident or injury occurring. You should prioritise your control measures using the risk rating score. Those with the highest rating pose the biggest risk and you should deal with them first.*
			4: Very likely (could happen at any time)	**3:** Likely (could happen sometime)	**2:** Unlikely (could happen but very rarely)	**1:** Very unlikely (could happen but probably will not)		
Example: Trip hazard – free weights left on the floor	3 Cuts, bruises, concussion	Staff and gym users		3			3 × 3 = 9	Put up signs reminding users to put weights back on the rack. Put up trip hazard signs so people are aware of the risk. Create a zone marked out on the floor where all weights must be kept.

Risk assessments are necessary when planning events. This example form outlines how you can approach this task and the types of things you will have to consider.

- There were 23,433 major injuries to employees reported in 2011–12. Over 40% were caused by slipping or tripping.
- There were 87,731 other injuries to employees causing absence from work of more than 3 days. Of these, 30% were caused by handling, lifting or carrying (28,328 reported injuries), and just under 25% were due to slipping or tripping (21,128 reported injuries).

Source: HSE (Health and Safety Executive).

Case study

We often associate sports injuries being incurred by the participant with the fact that health and safety legislation or rules have meant facilities or equipment are to blame for incidents. However what happens when the injury is to a sports official through no fault of their own?

David Nalbandian was defaulted in the Queen's Club tennis final after his kick to the front of a three-sided sponsor's advertising board struck a linesman on the shin. The Association of Tennis Professionals (ATP) rules state that any violent action will result in an automatic default. Nalbandian automatically forfeited his prize money and ranking points due to his conduct. A maximum £8,000 fine also was issued onsite by the ATP Supervisor for unsportsmanlike conduct making it a total net loss of about £44,000 that weekend.

Watch this incident on YouTube.

1 As Nalbandian's tennis coach, what aspect of his training would you look at addressing as a result of this incident?

2 Discuss with others whether you think Nalbandian was treated appropriately by the ATP after the incident.

3 Was there anything that health and safety legislation or rules for the event could have done to help prevent this injury from occurring?

Activity 10.4   Risk assessment

Carry out a risk assessment for your school's sports hall, fitness suite or outside sports area.

- What risks did you find?
- Can you identify ways in which these risks might be reduced?

Check with your teacher to see if you are right.

Legislation and regulations

Introduction

This topic looks at some of the more well-known and commonly used legislation that applies when working in a sports environment.

Health and Safety at Work (etc.) Act 1974

The basis of British health and safety law is the Health and Safety at Work (etc.) Act 1974. In 1994 the Health and Safety Commission (HSC) conducted a review of the Act and this is now the basis of all health and safety measures for employers, who are responsible for the safety of their employees and members of the public.

It states that:

Your employer has a duty under the law to ensure, so far as is reasonably practicable, your health, safety and welfare at work. Your employer must consult you or your safety representative on matters relating to your health and safety at work.

Your employer's duties include:

- making your workplace safe and without risks to health
- ensuring plant and machinery are safe and that safe systems of work are set and followed
- ensuring articles and substances are moved, stored and used safely
- providing adequate welfare facilities
- giving you the information, instruction, training and supervision necessary for your health and safety.

As an employee you have legal duties too. They include:

- taking reasonable care for your own health and safety and that of others who may be affected by what you do or do not do
- cooperating with your employer on health and safety
- correctly using work items provided by your employer, including personal protective equipment, in accordance with training or instructions
- not interfering with or misusing anything provided for your health, safety or welfare.

Source: Health and Safety at Work (etc.) Act 1974

Have you seen this poster in your school, college or place of work?

Management of Health and Safety at Work Regulations 1994

This requires employers to:

- carry out risk assessments
- make arrangements to implement necessary measures
- appoint competent people
- arrange for appropriate information and training for staff.

Health and Safety (First-Aid) Regulations 1981

This piece of legislation was reviewed in 2005. It states that:

'The Health and Safety (First-Aid) Regulations 1981 place a duty on employers to provide adequate first aid equipment, facilities and personnel to their employees.'

This is very important for people employed in sporting environments such as sports halls, sports centres and stadiums, as they will have to deal with large numbers of the public and people participating in potentially risky and hazardous activities.

Control of Substances Hazardous to Health (COSHH) 2002

COSHH requires employers to control exposure to health from hazardous substances to protect employees and those who may be exposed by work activities.

Employers must be aware of what hazardous substances are used in the workplace and their risks to health. Precautions and controls must be put in place. Employers must ensure that employees are properly trained and/or supervised when dealing with hazardous substances.

In the sports industry this is closely linked to toxic or harmful substances used while maintaining swimming pools or jacuzzis and when cleaning and disinfecting facilities. The following should be adhered to:

- correct storage and handling of substances should be closely monitored and they should be made secure at all times
- staff should be regularly trained to ensure that correct storage and use of chemicals involved in the sports environment are maintained
- protective clothing must be provided by the employer for every employee who has to handle any hazardous substance in the course of their work
- all staff should have appropriate first aid training to cope with any emergency situation that could occur while using hazardous chemicals.

 Did you know?

Health and Safety legislation is frequently reviewed and improved upon to maintain the safety and welfare of employees. 2013 saw changes to Health and Safety legislation including new regulations introduced to prevent sharps injuries from occurring in the health sector.

CONTINUED ▶▶

▸▸ CONTINUED

Safety of Sports Grounds Act 1975

The Wheatley Committee was set up in 1972 partially in response to the disaster at Ibrox Park, Glasgow. It happened because of structural failure – the steel barriers on a stairway gave way.

Did you know?

Ibrox Stadium 1971 – On Saturday, 2 January 1971, as thousands of spectators were leaving the ground by stairway 13, it appears that someone fell, causing a massive chain-reaction pile-up of people. Sixty-six people died from suffocation and over 200 other fans were injured.

Following the recommendations of this committee, the Safety of Sports Grounds Act 1975 was created. This applies to all sports grounds with accommodation for spectators and was aimed at any stadium with a capacity for 10,000 or more spectators. Safety controls are imposed through safety certificates issued by local authorities for sports grounds designated by the Secretary of State, currently:

- those grounds occupied by FA premier and football league clubs with accommodation for over 5000 spectators
- those with accommodation for over 10,000 spectators where other sports are played, which in practice means rugby, cricket and other football matches including internationals.

Despite this legislation, some accidents still occur.

Case study

Hillsborough football disaster – this occurred on 15 April, 1989. Over 500 people were injured and 96 crushed to death, many of them teenagers and children. The problems were caused by too many Liverpool fans being allowed into the back of an already full stand at the Leppings Lane end of the ground; as more fans were allowed in, those already there were pushed forward and crushed against the high, wire-topped safety fences.

Hillsborough is not the only major disaster to be linked to a sporting event or venue.

1 Can you think of any others?

2 Why do you think many are associated with football venues?

At least 500 people were injured and 96 killed in the Hillsborough disaster, 1989.

Children Act 2004

The Children Act 2004 places a duty on services to ensure that every child, whatever their circumstances, has the support they need to:

- be healthy
- stay safe
- enjoy and achieve through learning
- make a positive contribution to society
- achieve economic well-being.

As children participate in sport in so many different environments, such as summer schools, after-school clubs and coaching sessions, employers who have employees working with these children are bound by the Children Act of 2004. This means they must ensure that:

- every employee gains a police and a Criminal Records Bureau (CRB) check and clearance before they are allowed to work with children
- employees are appropriately qualified to do the work they are employed to do with the children
- they are trained to recognise signs of possible abuse.

Just checking

1 'PRICE' is the most common way to manage an injury – what does it stand for?

2 Name one way in which the psychological effects of an injury can be managed.

3 When was the first Health and Safety Act introduced?

4 Can you explain why the Safety of Sports Grounds Act of 1975 was set up?

CONTINUED ▸▸

Table 10.1 Legislation that affects sports participation

Legislation	Content	Example in the sports industry
Health and Safety at Work (etc.) Act (1974) (Amended 1994)	Employers have a duty to keep employees and visiting members of the public safe.\n\nEmployers with five or more employees must record the main findings of any risk assessments.	Vitally important to the sports industry as sport by its very nature has an element of risk.\n\nAll staff must be appropriately trained to help maintain safety within their working environment, e.g. lifeguard qualification for a pool attendant, first aid qualifications held by appropriate staff on duty, etc.
Health and Safety (First-Aid) Regulations 1981	Employers must provide adequate first aid for employees and the general public.	First-aid qualified staff on duty and first-aid facilities – first-aid box/room must be provided and checked regularly. Having basic first-aid provision is a necessity for sports environments as accidents and incidents often occur here.
Control of Substances Hazardous to Health (COSHH) 2002	Employers must ensure that all employees are protected from exposure to hazardous substances.	Training of staff to utilise chemicals for cleaning and maintaining swimming pools. Pools etc. must be kept clean for health reasons and the use of hazardous chemicals controlled.
Safety of Sports Grounds Act 1975	Building Regulations require stringent standards for all sports ground developments.	Essential to eradicate disasters such as those at Ibrox and Bradford. Sports grounds must be constructed to the highest safety specifications to protect spectators.
Children Act 2004	Children are protected by this law wherever they are.\n\nThey should be able to grow up safely and positively.	Essential that all sports coaches, teachers, etc. undergo CRB checks before they are allowed to work with children.\n\nChildren should be able to be educated, coached and allowed to play safely within a sporting environment. They should be guided by appropriately qualified people.

Assessment activity 10.4   *English*   2D.P7 | 2D.M3 | 2D.D3

As a result of your work placement you have been asked to produce a report for your supervisor on how health and safety is managed within the fitness club. The report is to help your supervisor ensure that all staff have had adequate training and are aware of the need for health and safety regulations.

Discuss the reasons for health and safety rules, regulations and legislation. Then, give detailed information on two of these that you feel are essential for all staff to know about.

Tip
Consider a range of rules, regulations and legislation at the start of your report in relation to health and safety at the club. Then, focus on two specific rules, regulations or pieces of legislation, analysing why these are of particular importance.

WorkSpace

▶ Catherine

Squash coach

Catherine has always been a keen and successful squash player, representing her school, local club and county in the under-16 age group.

Her parents have supported her throughout by helping transport her to different fixtures around the country. Now 17, Catherine has recently passed her driving test and is working at a local sports centre, which employs her not only as a sports attendant and supervisor but also as a squash coach.

She has been struggling to play recently after slipping on court and twisting her ankle. Her coach made sure she went to the hospital and that an X-ray was taken. The doctor whom she saw said that it was just an ankle strain and that nothing was broken. However, he advised that she should take it steady for the next few weeks until she was able to walk and run normally on it again without pain. While she has continued to work, she has taken time off her own training in order to help rest her ankle, but she is feeling very low and worried that if she takes too long off she will lose her place in the club rankings and her seeding at county level. Her coach has tried to reassure her and encourage her to concentrate on recovery but she is starting to lose sleep and worry so much that she is becoming impatient. She has started to try to train again even though she is in a lot of pain and there is still swelling and bruising around the joint.

Think about it

1 What sort of treatment would you suggest Catherine tries to alleviate her ankle problem?

2 How might her coach help her understand why it is important to recover properly and not to rush back?

3 What would you recommend in order to help Catherine start to relax and be able to sleep properly again?

Introduction

When participating in a sports event we very rarely consider the amount of time that has gone into the organisation and planning of it. And as participants we very rarely think about the people who support the running of an event, often volunteers. Within this unit you will work as a group on the planning and delivery of a sports event of your choice.

Through completing this unit you should further develop your leadership skills and develop an ability to work as part of a team.

You will develop an idea from scratch and be responsible for making the idea work successfully.

The attributes of sports leadership and the ability to plan an event are valuable transferable skills. Through completing this unit you will develop a wide range of skills that will support your development.

Assessment: You will be assessed by a series of assignments set by your teacher/tutor.

Learning aims

In this unit you will:

A plan a sports event

B contribute to the organisation of a sports event

C assist with running and leading a sports event

D review your own contribution to running a sports event.

I always loved school sports day when I was at school. I never realised the planning and organisation that went into such an event. When we were asked to plan a school sports day I thought this would be easy and take a matter of minutes. How wrong was I? This unit was such a great experience… The rewards of planning our sports day were worth every second.

Charlotte, *16-year-old sport student*

Running a
Sports Event

11

Assessment Zone

This table shows what you must do in order to achieve a **Pass**, **Merit** or **Distinction** grade, and where you can find activities in this book to help you.

Assessment criteria			
Level 1	**Level 2 Pass**	**Level 2 Merit**	**Level 2 Distinction**
Learning aim A: plan a sports event			
1A.1 English Produce, with guidance, a plan for running a given sports event	**2A.P1** English Produce a plan for a selected sports event, outlining the planning process to meet event aims and objectives **See Assessment activity 11.1, page 290**	**2A.M1** English Produce a plan for a selected sports event, describing the planning process to meet event aims and objectives **See Assessment activity 11.1, page 290**	**2A.D1** English Justify the plan for a selected sports event, explaining the planning process **See Assessment activity 11.1, page 290**
Learning aim B: contribute to the organisation of a sports event			
1B.2 Contribute, with guidance, to the organisation of a given sports event	**2B.P2** Contribute to the organisation of a selected sports event **See Assessment activity 11.1, page 290**		
Learning aim C: assist with running and leading a sports event			
1C.3 English Contribute, with guidance, to the running and leading of a given sports event	**2C.P3** English Contribute to the running and leading of a selected sports event, demonstrating the application of leadership attributes **See Assessment activity 11.2, page 297**	**2C.M2** English Contribute to the running and leading of a successful sports event, demonstrating the application of leadership attributes **See Assessment activity 11.2, page 297**	
Learning aim D: review your own contribution to running a sports event			
1D.4 Collect qualitative or quantitative feedback from participants using two different methods	**2D.P4** Collect qualitative and quantitative feedback from participants using four different methods **See Assessment activity 11.2, page 297**		
1D.5 Maths Review feedback obtained, identifying strengths of the event and areas for improvement	**2D.P5** Maths Review feedback obtained, describing strengths of the event and areas for improvement. **See Assessment activity 11.2, page 297**	**2D.M3** Maths Assess feedback, evaluating strengths of the event and areas for improvement, providing recommendations for future events. **See Assessment activity 11.2, page 297**	**2D.D2** Analyse strengths of the event and areas for improvement, justifying recommendations for future events. **See Assessment activity 11.2, page 297**

English / Opportunity to practise English skills

Maths / Opportunity to practise mathematical skills

How you will be assessed

This unit will be assessed through a series of assignments set by your teacher/tutor. You will be expected to show your involvement in the planning of a sports event. You will also be required to demonstrate your ability to contribute to the organisation of the event. You will then be observed assisting the leadership of the planned event and on completion of the event you will be required to review it using a variety of different methods of feedback, commenting on the strengths and also the areas for improvement. You will then provide further recommendations for the development of future events.

The following could form part of your assessment:

- agendas and minutes of meetings
- an event plan
- evidence of organisation of the event
- observation checklists of you leading the event and contributing to the planning of the event
- visual evidence of you assisting in the leadership of the event
- a report of the outcomes of the event and a review session including strengths, areas for improvement and recommendations for future event planning.

Planning a sports event

Introduction

The organising and running of a sports event can be a very time-consuming and demanding project. However, if done effectively and meticulously it can be one of the most rewarding outcomes within the sports industry. The success of any event always relies on the planning process and obviously the larger the event the more planning is required.

The sports event

There is a wide range of sports events for you to choose from. The formats that these events take will direct the basis of the planning process. It is therefore important that you consider a number of factors before considering which event you are going to offer.

- Who is your target audience?
- What is your budget?
- What facilities, equipment and resources do you have access to?

The event that you select may focus on a particular purpose; this will differ depending on the event you choose. Within your own organising committee it will be important that you decide on this purpose. It might be to:

- educate the target audience
- aid personal development of the target audience
- provide enjoyment for the target audience
- raise funds for a charity
- provide the target audience with a focus away from crime and antisocial behaviour.

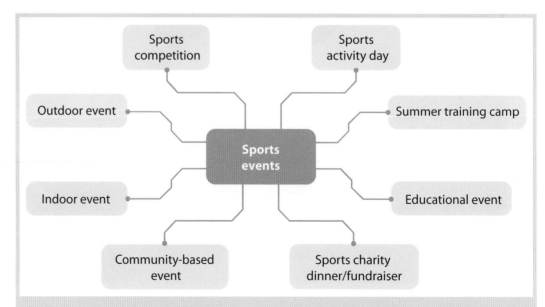

Figure 11.1 The range of events you might choose from; it is very important that you decide on the type of event you want to host before the serious planning starts

Which 2012 Olympic events did you enjoy? Why did you enjoy them?

The planning process

Most of your time and effort will be spent on the planning of the sports event. It is important to follow a specific protocol and it is essential that all those involved in the delivery of the event are involved in the planning process from the start.

It is a requirement that the planning committee have regular meetings, so decisions can be shared and discussed in a democratic way. For every meeting there should be an **agenda**; these points should be the focus of the meeting. In order to keep accurate records of the progress of every meeting it is important that **minutes** are taken to document what was said, by whom, and what the main outcomes of the meeting were.

It is important that you agree on the frequency of the meetings. The number of times you meet and how often you meet will depend on the amount of time you have to plan the event. Once agreed, these dates of future meetings should be recorded in the minutes of the meeting.

After every meeting the minutes should be distributed to all attendees and any people who sent their apologies (who were unable to attend) to ensure that everyone is aware of the outcomes of the meeting.

 Key terms

Agenda – a list of items to be covered in each meeting.

Minutes – a written record of what was discussed in each meeting.

CONTINUED ▶▶

▶▶ CONTINUED

Maintaining a personal diary

Throughout each stage of the planning process for your event, you should keep your own diary or logbook to record your group's progress towards its desired outcomes. In this log you should also include the minutes of team meetings, meeting outcomes, and any actions arising for the entire group. In particular you should note those that you may have to complete for the next meeting as part of the preparation for your sports event.

It is important to consider the following questions as a group from early on.

- What are the aims and objectives of the event? A sports event will require specific aims (what you want to achieve) and objectives (how you are going to achieve those aims).

- What is the nature of the event? You need to choose a type of event with a particular purpose. You will also need to consider the size of the event and the location.

- Who is your target audience? Do you have a specific audience that you have to cater for, for example primary school children or a local sports club?

- What are the timings of the event? How much time do you have for the entire event? How much time will you require for each of the components that will make up your event?

- What budget do you have? In most instances this will be very small.

- What are the costings for your event? You will be required to provide a costing sheet for your event to show all your expenditure during the planning process (though some events are planned at no cost).

- What constraints will you encounter when planning your event? You need to be aware of the factors that might prevent your event from taking place – for example, bad weather, lack of equipment, double-booking.

- What are your back-up plans? It is important to consider **contingency planning** for each of the possible constraints. This can reduce stress and ensure that the event can continue whatever happens. Details of these contingency plans should be recorded and discussed at every meeting.

- What resources are required to deliver your event? You will need to provide a detailed list of all the equipment and resources required for your event, including such items as refreshments, equipment for each activity, first aid kit, staff clothing, register and public announcement system.

- What are the procedures in the event of an emergency? You will be required to provide emergency procedure protocols for major and minor injuries, you will need contact information for all parents and carers, and this information will need to be gathered before the event takes place. You will need to have qualified first aiders and to make all participants aware of where they are located.

- What are the staffing roles and responsibilities for each member of the planning team? These roles should be established very early on in the planning of the event.

Activity 11.1   Team roles

1 For each of the following roles, make a list of their responsibilities.

- Coordinator
- Chairperson
- Secretary
- Finance officer
- Publicity officer
- Marketing officer
- Steward
- Specialist coach or trainer

2 Allocate everyone within your planning team at least one of these roles – there can be more than one person doing one role and in some instances some people may have more than one role.

Key terms

Contingency planning – planning what to do in the event of the unexpected occurring.

Disclaimer – a statement intended to make the participant aware of and partly responsible for the risks.

Informed consent form – a form listing any injuries or other concerns that may affect their performance. If the participant is under 18, a consent form must be completed by a parent or carer.

- Have you completed a risk assessment of the venue and the activities for your event? Clearly identify what actions will be taken to minimise the risks.

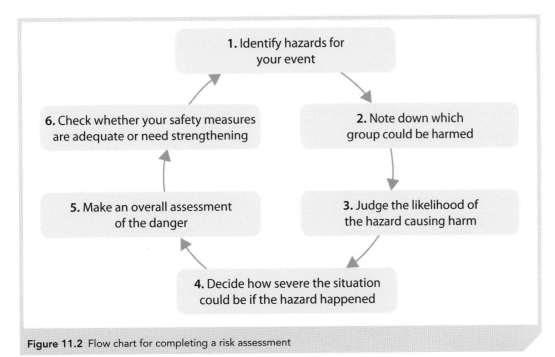

1. Identify hazards for your event

2. Note down which group could be harmed

3. Judge the likelihood of the hazard causing harm

4. Decide how severe the situation could be if the hazard happened

5. Make an overall assessment of the danger

6. Check whether your safety measures are adequate or need strengthening

Figure 11.2 Flow chart for completing a risk assessment

- Have all participants (or their parents/carers) completed a **disclaimer** and an **informed consent form**? These must be completed before the event takes place to ensure that you have all the necessary details documented and to hand. It is also important that participants sign a photograph consent form if it is likely that photographs will be taken during the event.
- What promotional materials and activities will you use to market the event to the participants and public? These may include posters, leaflets, pre-event presentations and post-event presentations (certification events, etc.).
- What methods for obtaining feedback will you use for those who take part in your event, and those who observe it? These might include questionnaires, comment cards or interviews with participants during the event, or after it.

Just checking

1 List the different types of sports events that could be run by a group of sports leaders.

2 List the different staff roles required to run a sports event.

3 For two of the members of staff from your list, consider the responsibilities that they will hold in the planning of a sports event.

Contribute to the organisation of a sports event

Getting started

Consider an event that you have supported in the past. Did you simply turn up on the day of the event, or did you have to contribute to some pre-event planning? Share your findings with the rest of the group.

Introduction

When all members of the team have been given defined roles it is then important that the team works together. The larger the event the more important it is that deadlines are met and that each member of the group pulls their weight towards the end goal. At this stage of the organisation of an event you will need to consider all eventualities and plan for each of them. A good sports leader should be prepared for every eventuality on the days of a sports event, which could include anything from bad weather to loss of equipment.

Event organisation

When you have identified the type of event, target audience and venue, you will then need to ensure that the event meets the needs of the performers who will participate in it.

Clear aims and objectives should be set for the event. It is these which will give the event a focus, and they might include:

- fundraising
- providing information
- education
- raising awareness
- health and fitness
- well-being.

When the aims and objectives of the event have been agreed, as a team you will also need to discuss the resources that will be required for the event to run successfully.

A primary school sports day – do you remember yours?

Activity 11.2   School sports day

Look at the image of a primary school sports day. At some point in your education you may have taken part in one of these events.

Make a list of all the resource requirements that the teacher in charge will have to consider to ensure an event like this runs smoothly.

When contributing to the running of a sports event as a sports leader or an assistant sports leader, you have responsibility for the health and safety of the participants.

You must also consider the health and safety of people other than the participants, such as other members of your team. For example, when supporting a road cycling race, as well as the safety of the cyclists, the race marshals' safety must be assured.

The safety of the spectators during a sports event is also your responsibility. It must be carefully planned before the event and put into practice on the day.

It is important that the team members are aware of what is expected of them and the timings of the event. Everyone should be aware of their roles and duties throughout the event and especially what to do in the event of any unforeseen circumstances arising, for which clear contingency plans should be made.

> **? Did you know?**
>
> Race marshals always wear high-visibility safety vests and have to undergo training before marshalling at such an event.

> **💬 Discussion point**
>
> For a large event such as the BUPA Great North Run, consider the safety measures that are put in place for:
> - performers participating in the event
> - staff supporting the event
> - spectators.

Have you seen race marshals in action at sporting events?

CONTINUED ▸▸

Participant requirements

Before the event it is important that your group has considered all of the requirements of those who will be participating in the event. For example, it may be a requirement that you obtain informed consent and a health screening questionnaire from the parents/carers, or the performers themselves if they are old enough.

A health screening questionnaire involves collecting information about a performer's current physical activity level, dietary habits, lifestyle and general health. From this you should be able to find out any particular needs of the sports performers who will be taking part in your event.

Before the event you should also think about the methods you are going to use during and after the event to measure the satisfaction of the participants.

Assessment activity 11.1   *English*   2A.P1 | 2A.M1 | 2A.D1 | 2B.P2

Your school has been contacted by a local primary school, asking if a group of your students could plan and deliver a sports day for their Year 6 students.

As part of the group of sports leaders selected, you have been asked to produce a plan for a sports day event. You must explain the planning process for the teachers from both schools, justifying how the plan will meet the event aims and objectives. For each of the activities you have selected within your plan, provide an explanation as to why you have selected each particular one.

Tips

- Ensure that you record each stage of the planning process, keep a log of all meetings and keep a personal diary that informs you and the reader of the developments at each stage of the planning process.
- Ensure that each member of the team has a clear, defined role. They should feed back the progress towards their agreed targets at each meeting.
- Ensure that you have a clear plan for the event, including the content of the event and the health and safety considerations.
- Consider methods of developing feedback from a variety of people (participants, sports leaders, observers and assessors).

WorkSpace

◤ Frances Orla

Sports hall athletics event organiser

I have been a sports hall athletics event organiser for over a year. I first started as a sports athletics leader through completing the Level 1 Leadership award through England Athletics. I then supported the delivery of some events for my school and really enjoyed the experience. After this, I wanted to get more involved in the organisation of the events within schools and at other clubs.

My move towards organising sporting events began when I first started supporting the under-12 sprinters' senior coach. As my confidence developed, the coach would let me coach small parts of the sessions. I used the session plans I learnt when completing my own leadership course and the more coaching I did, the more impressed the coach became.

As a response to my strong progression, the coach asked it if would organise a taster event for younger children, in an attempt to increase the number of children who joined the club. I worked as part of a team to deliver the introductory session. It was a great success. We had 25 young athletes who attended the mini sports hall athletics event. I found it amazing what experience and confidence can do for you when working with young children.

The club's coaches were so impressed with my ideas and ability to lead the event that I now coordinate two sports hall athletics events for young adults every year and help run other smaller tester sessions.

Think about it

1   What are the planning processes that will need to be considered when organising a sports hall athletics event?

2   Can you identify the methods that Frances could use to assess the effectiveness of the event?

3   Design some promotional materials that could be used to promote the sports hall athletics event for new members to the club.

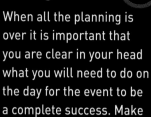

Assist with running and leading a sports event

Introduction

When a plan has been created, the next stage is very often putting the plan into action. For sports events, this often means all of the planning team coming together and delivering the event. As a group, it is important that you support every member. You will need to develop an understanding of not only your own role but of the roles of the other people you are working with, as in some cases a member of the group may be unable to attend the event. In situations such as this, you will need to demonstrate excellent leadership and organisation skills at all times to make sure that everything is going ahead as planned and that the missing group member's work is covered.

Running a sports event

When running a sports event it is important that you and the rest of the team fulfil all your roles and responsibilities as you have previously agreed. Everyone in the group will have specific jobs and should also be prepared to support other members of the team in their roles when needed.

Table 11.1 Roles and responsibilities

Timings	Examples of roles and responsibilities
Setting up	Signs, sports equipment (including equipment checks and ensuring equipment is set up safely and securely), drink service areas, food service areas, seating
During the event	Communicating with participants/customers (e.g. supporting and supervising, motivating), responding to participant/customer queries, responding to emergencies/accidents/other issues, refereeing, instructing, officiating, monitoring
After the event	Signs, sports equipment (including correct and safe storage), waste disposal, seating, cleaning/tidying, collecting feedback

Leading a sports event

When leading a sports event, it is important that your contribution is effective and appropriate. You should demonstrate the appropriate skills, qualities and responsibilities of a sports leader in your chosen sport.

Activity 11.3

It is important that as a sports leader you contribute to the sports event in a positive way. Consider the skills and qualities you need to demonstrate in order to be an effective sports leader on the day of your event.

For example, if you are delivering the warm-up to the sports performers you should ensure that you communicate effectively throughout to each of the performers. When it is appropriate, you should demonstrate the activities to the performers so that they are aware of what is required. The level of communication and support applied by a sports leader will depend on a number of different factors.

- Stage of development of the sports performers, for example beginner, intermediate or advanced.
- Age of the performers – toddlers, children, teenagers, adults, elderly people.
- Ability of the sports performers – able-bodied or disabled sports performers?

When leading a sports activity session you should make sure that you take account of all of the responsibilities – including the wider responsibilities – required to be a successful sports leader. You should ensure that you demonstrate excellent professional conduct and a thorough and effective approach to the health and safety considerations of all the performers, spectators and staff throughout the event. It is your responsibility to see that rules, regulations, ethics and values are put into practice throughout the event by you as well as others when appropriate.

It is important for sports leaders to measure the success of the event that they deliver. These methods can take many different forms.

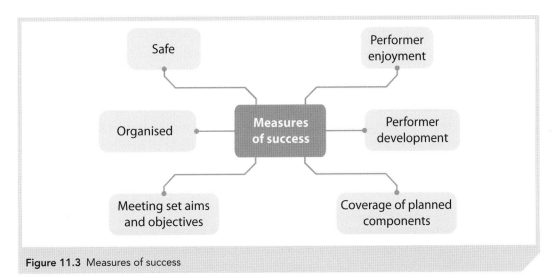

Figure 11.3 Measures of success

Within your plan it is important that you clearly state which measures of success you will be using for your event.

Leadership attributes

The sports leader should ensure that the event flows and provides a variety of activities for the sports performers, while ensuring that they are safe at all times. This should be measured through effective planning and preparation, through pre-activity checks, and through the sports leader monitoring the performance of the athletes during the session. An appropriate display of leadership qualities and skills should ensure success of the event. These qualities and skills will be observed by participants and those watching the event.

Link

This topic links to *Unit 6: Leading Sports Activities*.

Discussion point

Considering the factors above (relating to the age of sports performers) develop a warm-up that you would deliver to toddlers, children, teenagers and adults. Discuss what factors you had to consider when developing each warm-up and why?

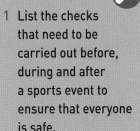

Just checking

1 List the checks that need to be carried out before, during and after a sports event to ensure that everyone is safe.

2 List all the attributes required to be a successful sports leader.

TOPIC D.1

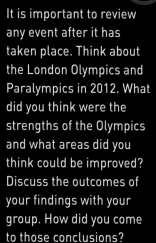

Reviewing the running of a sports event

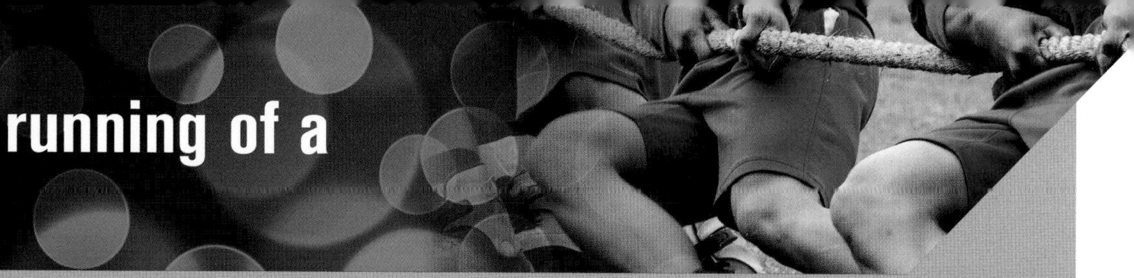

Getting started

It is important to review any event after it has taken place. Think about the London Olympics and Paralympics in 2012. What did you think were the strengths of the Olympics and what areas did you think could be improved? Discuss the outcomes of your findings with your group. How did you come to those conclusions?

Introduction

It is important that on completion of a sports event, you take time out to reflect on what went well and what could be done to make the event better should it run again in the future. All sports events teams go through this process and this is why every time after a large event such as the Olympics takes place, the media compare it to previously successful games. Do you think London 2012 was the greatest games of all time?

Review the event

When you are considering how to review an event as a sports leader it is very important to think about where the information will come from. The feedback should come from participants who supported the delivery of the session, the assessor (teacher), the sports performers who participated in the session, spectators, other witnesses who observed the event and, finally, you.

Qualitative and quantitative feedback

You will receive feedback that is based on the opinions and words of other people. For example, your teacher may inform you that your communication was excellent, although your demonstrations during the event were poor. This is **qualitative feedback**, taken from opinions and words. However, within your review you should also have some **quantitative feedback**; this is the use of data and statistics to assess performance. For example, from the questionnaires you produced you may have the results that show that 25 participants rated the warm-up as 'good', that is gave it 5 out of 6 on a six-point scale, whereas 30 participants only rated the cool down as fair, giving it 2 out 6 on a six-point scale. You can interpret quantitative data to draw firm conclusions.

Key terms

Qualitative feedback – the use of opinions and words to assess performance.

Quantitative feedback – the use of data and statistics to assess performance.

Table 11.2 Methods of feedback that can be used to support the gathering of information

Method of feedback	Description
Questionnaires	A questionnaire is a group of printed questions used to collect information from the people who answer them.
Surveys	A survey is a data collection tool used to gather information about individuals. Surveys are carried out on a number of people.
Observation sheets	The completion of a particular sheet after the observation of someone. The information on the sheet should summarise the findings.
Witness statements	A witness statement is a statement summarising the oral evidence of what a witness has observed. This can then be used as evidence to support the outcomes.
Participant comment cards	A comment card is used to obtain the views of customers in a confidential manner. These cards can include questions but also request general comments.
Interviews with participants (during and after the event)	An interview is a conversation between two people (the interviewer and the interviewee) where questions are asked by the interviewer to obtain information from the interviewee.

Have you found questionnaires useful in terms of feedback before?

When conducting your review you will draw from both sources of feedback, as you should have a variety of both from a range of participants.

Just checking

1 What is qualitative feedback?
2 Provide five examples of qualitative feedback.
3 What is quantitative feedback?
4 Provide five examples of quantitative feedback.
5 Identify five methods that you can use to measure the success of a sports event.

Activity 11.4   What kind of feedback?

For each of the following methods of feedback, identify whether you think the source will be used to obtain qualitative or quantitative feedback:

- questionnaires
- surveys
- observation sheets
- witness statements
- comment cards
- interviews with participants (during and after the event).

Link

This unit links to *Unit 14: Carrying Out a Sports-related Project, Topic B.3.*

When reviewing the event it is important that you review your performance against each of the following questions.

- Did the event meet the original aims and objectives that your group set out to meet?
- Did you meet the overall target budget for the event?
- What were the actual costings for each component of the event? Did you overspend?
- Did anything prevent you from meeting your aims and objectives?
- Did you need to use your contingency planning?
- How effective were your meetings?
- Was there enough planning time to organise the event and keep to schedule?
- How was your performance in your specific role?
- How did your team perform?
- Were your team, participants and observers satisfied?

When answering these questions you should provide a detailed response and justification for each.

CONTINUED ▶▶

Strengths and areas for improvement

After receiving feedback from participants and observers, you should then conclude, using the feedback and your own thoughts, what you felt were the strengths (what went well) of the event and what parts of the event you would like to develop and improve on for future sessions. Once you have gathered all of the feedback from the session you should consider the following components and complete your review of the session.

- Were event aims and objectives met?
- Where event outcomes did not meet planned aims and objectives, what could be done to ensure this did not happen in the future?

After you have considered what the strengths and areas for improvement are when leading your sports event, you should then set a series of targets to support your own development as a sports leader and to support the development of your team.

SMARTER targets

When setting yourself targets you should use the SMARTER model.

- **S**pecific – make the target as precise and detailed as possible.
- **M**easurable – set achievement targets and consider the methods used to measure your performance against the targets.
- **A**chievable – goals should be attainable within a set period of time and relevant to the sports performer.
- **R**ealistic – appropriate targets that can be met within the timescales set by you; the targets you set for yourself should be achievable but not too easy.
- **T**imed – ensure you set yourself a timescale for each target.
- **E**xciting – the targets that are set should motivate and challenge the individual/team.
- **R**ecorded – progress towards the attainment of each target should be documented.

Remember

When reviewing a sports event, it is important that you consider how to measure success. People measure success in different ways, including: performer enjoyment, performer development, coverage of planned components featured in the event plan, safety of the session, organisation of the event, and most importantly whether the event met the planned aims and objectives. You should develop your SMARTER targets around the particular parts of the event that you feel were not as successful as they could have been.

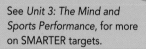

Link

See *Unit 3: The Mind and Sports Performance*, for more on SMARTER targets.

Recommendations for future events

To conclude your review you should make recommendations for future events, justifying your suggestions. These could be about particular parts of planning that need development, or the process of running the event, for example. You could also include goals for future development, opportunities and training that would support the group's ability to plan future events, such as gaining relevant qualifications. You should also consider the potential barriers that could prevent your group from meeting the recommendations detailed in the review.

In what ways do you think recommendations might improve the running of future events?

Assessment activity 11.2   *Maths English*   2C.P3 | 2C.M2 | 2D.P4 | 2D.P5 | 2D.M3 | 2D.D2

After evaluating your plan of the Year 6 sports day, the primary school has asked that your group host the event.

They would like your group to deliver the sports day and to complete a review of the event once finished. Once the review has taken place, the feedback will provide an insight into how successful the event was and the primary school will use it to help them consider whether or not to run future events.

- You must contribute to the running and leading of a successful sports day, demonstrating the application of leadership attributes.
- You should ensure that once the sports day event has finished, you collect qualitative and quantitative feedback from participants using four different methods.
- Using the feedback obtained, you should examine the strengths and areas for development of the sports day and justify recommendations for development if you and your group were to deliver future events.

Tips

- Ensure that you lead the sports event, demonstrating effective leadership skills and qualities consistently.
- On completion of the event, ensure that you obtain feedback from the participants using at least four different methods of feedback (two qualitative and two quantitative).
- Ensure that you analyse the strengths of the event – say what was good about the event and why it was successful (evidence).
- Ensure that you discuss the parts of the session that were not as successful, and explain why you think this was the case. Provide alternatives to what you did, so that the session could be improved on in the future.

Introduction

The sport and active leisure industry is one of the fastest-growing employment sectors in the UK. More than half a million people were employed in the sector in 2011, and this figure is expected to continue to grow (State of the Industry Report, 2012, SkillsActive). This does not include the ever-increasing number of volunteers required to support the growth of the sector over the next ten years.

In the first part of this unit you will investigate different organisations in the sport and active leisure industry and occupations that are available in the sector. You will focus on specific occupations, deciding on the advantages and disadvantages of each.

In the second part of the unit you will examine current trends in sport and seek to understand people's reasons for participation in sport and active leisure. You will also explore reasons why some people take part in sport and why others do not.

Finally you will investigate how key issues affect sport and active leisure today.

Assessment: You will be assessed by a series of assignments set by your teacher/tutor.

Learning aims

In this unit you will:

A investigate organisations and occupations in sport and active leisure

B recognise current trends in sport and sports participation

C know about the impact of key issues on sport and active leisure.

I had always wanted a job in sport, but I was never quite sure of what I wanted to do. Investigating occupations in sport and active leisure opened my eyes to the opportunities available. The information I found about the best places to look for sports employment helped me to gain my current job.

Zachary, *17-year-old pool lifeguard*

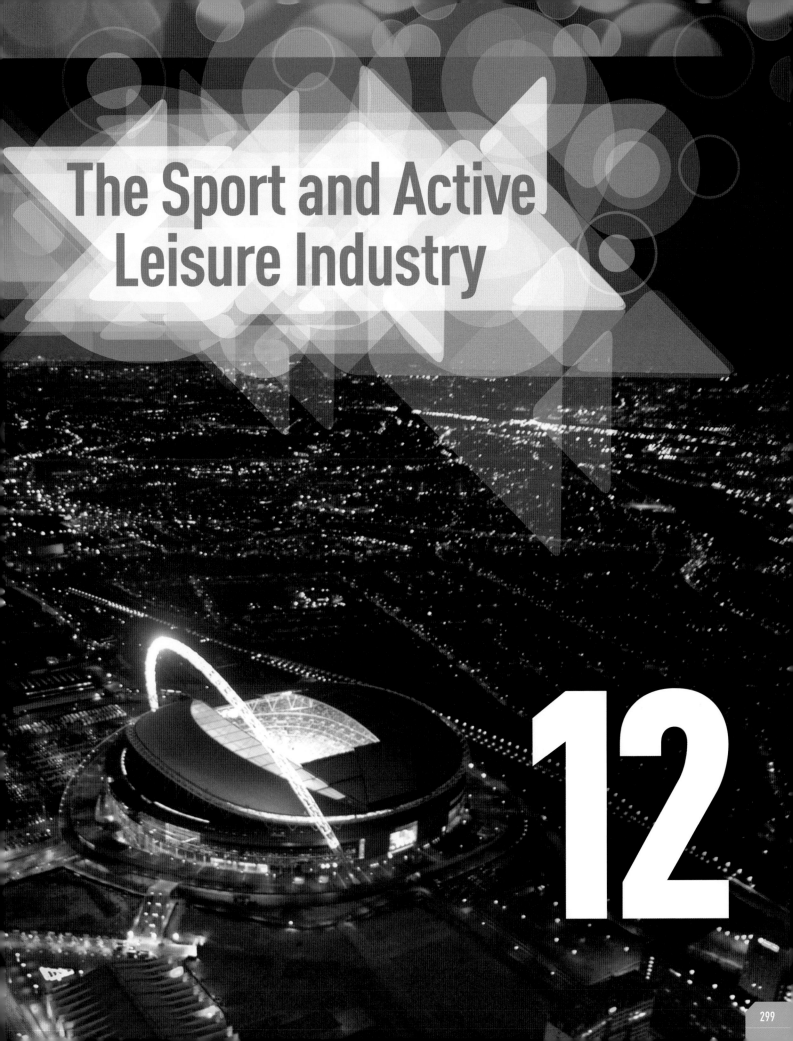

The Sport and Active Leisure Industry

12

BTEC
Assessment Zone

This table shows you what you must do in order to achieve a **Pass**, **Merit** or **Distinction** grade, and where you can find activities to help you.

Assessment criteria			
Level 1	Level 2 **Pass**	Level 2 **Merit**	Level 2 **Distinction**
Learning aim A: investigate organisations and occupations in sport and active leisure			
1A.1 Outline the different types of organisations in sport and active leisure	**2A.P1** Describe the different types of organisations in sport and active leisure, and the benefits of each **See Assessment activity 12.1, page 307**	**2A.M1** Explain, using relevant examples, the benefits of each of the different types of organisations in sport and active leisure **See Assessment activity 12.1, page 307**	**2A.D1** Compare and contrast the benefits of each different type of organisation in sport and active leisure **See Assessment activity 12.1, page 307**
1A.2 English Using information from given sources, outline the responsibilities of, and skills required by, two occupations in sport and active leisure	**2A.P2** English Using information from selected sources, describe the requirements for, responsibilities of, and skills required by, two occupations in sport and active leisure **See Assessment activity 12.1, page 307**	**2A.M2** English Summarise selected information about occupations in sport and active leisure, describing the advantages and disadvantages of each **See Assessment activity 12.1, page 307**	**2A.D2** English Explain the advantages and disadvantages of occupations in sport and active leisure **See Assessment activity 12.1, page 307**
Learning aim B: recognise current trends in sport and sports participation			
1B.3 Maths Outline reasons for participation in sport and active leisure	**2B.P3** Maths Using relevant information, describe reasons for, and growth in, participation in sport and active leisure **See Assessment activity 12.2, page 313**		
1B.4 Describe four factors that can affect participation in sport and active leisure	**2B.P4** Describe six factors that can affect participation in sport and active leisure **See Assessment activity 12.2, page 313**	**2B.M3** Explain using relevant examples, how different factors can affect participation in sport and active leisure **See Assessment activity 12.2, page 313**	
1B.5 Maths Describe two different trends that can affect participation in sport and active leisure	**2B.P5** Maths Describe six different trends that can affect participation in sport and active leisure **See Assessment activity 12.2, page 313**	**2B.M4** Maths Explain trends in participation in sport and active leisure **See Assessment activity 12.2, page 313**	**2B.D3** Maths Compare and contrast trends in participation in sport and active leisure **See Assessment activity 12.2, page 313**

Assessment criteria			
Level 1	Level 2 **Pass**	Level 2 **Merit**	Level 2 **Distinction**
Learning aim C: know about the impact of key issues on sport and active leisure			
1B.6	2C.P6	2C.M5	2C.D4
Describe four different key issues and their impact on sport and active leisure	Describe six different key issues and their impact on sport and active leisure **See Assessment activity 12.3, page 316**	Explain, using relevant examples, the impact of key issues on sport and active leisure **See Assessment activity 12.3, page 316**	Analyse the impact of key issues on a selected sport and active leisure activity or business **See Assessment activity 12.3, page 316**

English Opportunity to practise English skills

Maths Opportunity to practise mathematical skills

How you will be assessed

This unit will be assessed through a series of assignments set by your teacher/tutor. You will be expected to investigate organisations in sport and active leisure and show your understanding of responsibilities and skills required for job roles in this sector. You will also need to show that you can recognise trends in sports participation, and have knowledge about key issues. Your tasks will be based on a scenario that will involve research into real issues and businesses in the sport and active leisure sector.

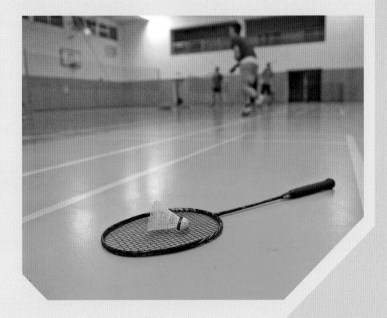

Your assessment could be in the form of:

- a job advertisement portfolio
- a written report
- a presentation that includes relevant case studies
- a mixed-media product such as a display.

Organisations in sport and active leisure

Introduction

Thanks to the growing awareness of the need to keep fit and healthy, more people are actively taking part in sport and active leisure. This growth has led to a massive expansion of the fitness industry and a huge increase in the sale of sports clothes and equipment.

Sports-related products and services are generally provided by four different types of organisations, as shown in Table 12.1.

Table 12.1 Organisations in sport and active leisure

Type of organisation	Examples	Benefits
Public	Facilities or services that are provided by local councils or authorities in an attempt to improve the standard of living for people in the local community. For example, local leisure centres, swimming pools, parks and outdoor pursuit centres.	• Easily accessible • Reasonably priced to be affordable for the whole community • You are usually allowed to pay per visit, rather than purchasing a membership
Private	Organisations that provide facilities, activities and services with the aim of making a profit for the organisation. For example, private health clubs (such as Virgin Active, Bannatyne's) or private golf/tennis clubs.	• Offer the latest equipment • Often have modern, attractive facilities that are appealing to the general public • Sometimes they will be specialised, such as tennis or squash centres • Offer membership schemes
Voluntary	Organisations that offer sports activities, often to small groups who share similar interests, such as cricket, netball, cycling, running or martial arts. For example, a Sunday morning football club.	• Charge a low fee to take part in activities as they are not run for profit • Usually cover their costs by collecting subscriptions each week • Generally sport-focused, offering specialist skills and knowledge of the sport on offer • Run by volunteers

continued

Table 12.1 Organisations in sport and active leisure (continued)

Type of organisation	Examples	Benefits
Joint/dual-use	For example, school or college sports centres being used by members of the local community outside of school hours, or a public leisure centre being used by a school or college during school hours.	• Facilities are used throughout the whole day • Allows links to be formed between schools, colleges, leisure centres and the local community • Joint use also allows schools to gain extra revenue during evenings, weekends and holidays

Case study

The City of Salford Community Stadium is a dual-use facility. It is the home of Salford Rugby League Club. Salford City Council formed a joint venture company with Peel Holdings to develop and deliver the £16 million stadium, which will also be used by community groups.

1 What are the benefits for Salford Rugby League Club of their ground being a dual-use facility?
2 What are the benefits for the local community of a dual-use facility?
3 Are there any dual-use facilities in your local area?

The City of Salford Community Stadium.

Activity 12.1   Matching facilities

For the following facilities, decide which of the four kinds of organisations they are (public, private, voluntary or joint/dual-use):

• council-used sports stadium
• Anfield – Liverpool football stadium
• leisure centre
• water-based activity centre
• London Soccer Dome
• amateur football club
• school with leisure centre
• amateur running club.

Discussion point

Think of places where you have taken part in sporting activities and then decide which of the four types of organisations they were. Discuss with other members of your group which type of organisations provide most of your sporting activities.

Just checking

1 Name the four different types of organisation in sport and active leisure.
2 Give two examples of a public organisation in the sport and active leisure sector.

Occupations in sport and active leisure

Getting started

Make a list of occupations in sport and active leisure that interest you and identify what it is about each occupation that appeals to you.

Discussion point

Figure 12.1 provides you with some examples of occupations in sport and active leisure. Can you think of others? Consider the employment opportunities that were created during the London hosting of the 2012 Olympic and Paralympic Games, including those that involved organising and holding the Games, as well as roles that involved preparing and supporting the athletes.

Introduction

There are many different opportunities for employment in the sport and active leisure industry. Some require further education or training; other opportunities allow employees to work their way up the organisational ladder. Figure 12.1 gives some examples of occupations in the sport and active leisure industry.

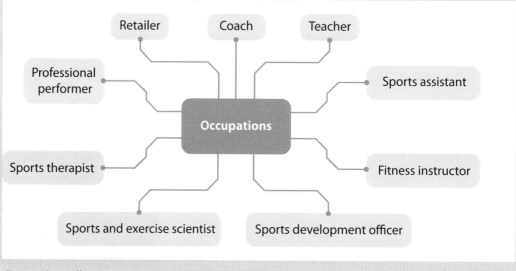

Figure 12.1 Different occupations in the sport and active leisure industry

Activity 12.2 Find the organisation

For each occupation shown in the spidergram (Figure 12.1), decide in which of the four types of organisations listed in Table 12.1 it would mainly be found.

▶ Responsibilities of different occupations

As an employee in sport and active leisure, you will have certain responsibilities to your clients or customers and the people you work with.

Customer care

Many jobs in sport and active leisure involve interacting with customers or clients. It is the responsibility of the employee that a high level of customer care is provided and that the customer or client is satisfied with how they are treated. For example, you would expect a personal trainer to be punctual and polite during a session.

Health and safety

It is the responsibility of a person running a coaching or training session to ensure the safety of the participants during the session. For example, a coach would have to be aware of risks and hazards that could cause injury to performers throughout the session.

Child protection

Child protection is essential in sport. It is the responsibility of anyone delivering sessions to children to complete child protection training. This training will help to ensure that you are fully aware of the issues surrounding coaching sports performers under the age of 18.

Skills required for different occupations

There are generic skills that are required for most occupations in sport and active leisure. These include the following.

- Communication – it is important to be able to communicate effectively with customers or clients to ensure that you are understood.
- Organisational skills – if you are working in more than one venue you will need to be organised in order to fulfil your duties in all of them.
- Interpersonal skills – if you are working closely with clients as a personal trainer or coach, you need to be able to talk to people that you have never met before.
- Time management – in all occupations it is essential that you are punctual and that other people can rely on you to turn up and manage your time effectively.
- Motivation – if people are paying you to coach or teach them, they will expect you to be motivated yourself and also to be able to motivate them.
- Leadership skills – if you are in charge of a team of workers, they will look to you to lead them and provide them with instructions.

Particular occupations will also require specific skills; for example, a fitness instructor will be required to be able to use their own initiative and work well with others of different backgrounds and needs. A sports coach will require a good knowledge of different training principles and methods. A professional performer will require an exceptional talent in a sport as well as commitment and dedication.

Why do you think personal trainers and coaches need public liability insurance?

CONTINUED ▶▶

Advantages and disadvantages of different occupations

Working in sport and active leisure can have advantages and disadvantages; see Table 12.2.

Table 12.2 Advantages and disadvantages of working in sport and active leisure

Advantages	Disadvantages
• Allows flexible hours of work • Work outside in the summer is often a requirement • Opportunity to work with elite athletes • Helping people improve their sports performance • Teaching people new skills	• May be required to work evenings or weekends • Work outside in the winter is often a requirement • Not always highly paid • People expect instant results • Work is not always full-time

Qualifications and training

Some occupations in sport and active leisure require you to hold relevant qualifications. All sports coaches, for example, must have a recognised qualification in coaching. This may be gained directly through a sport's National Governing Body, or as part of a college or university course. Although there are no set entry qualifications to become a sports development officer, this is increasingly becoming a graduate profession. As well as holding relevant academic qualifications, anyone who will be working closely with children will require Criminal Records Bureau (CRB) clearance. Personal trainers and coaches are required to have public liability insurance to cover themselves in the event of a claim from a client.

Activity 12.3 | Job match

Make a list of all of the qualifications you will have obtained by the end of the academic year. Then, using the sources listed, find different jobs that match with the qualifications you will have, as well as your skills and experiences.

For the purpose of this activity you can search for jobs anywhere in the UK, rather than just in your local area.

Sources of information

When seeking employment you need to know where to find the relevant information. Organisations often advertise their jobs in magazines, on websites and in industry journals. Sport and active leisure job advertisements can also be found in local and national newspapers. The following sources of information may help you when you are trying to gain employment in sport and active leisure:

- Institute for the Management of Sport and Physical Activity (IMPSA)
- local and national press
- specialist publications and periodicals
- SkillsActive (the Sector Skills Council)
- sports-specific recruitment agencies.

Assessment activity 12.1   *English*   2A.P1 | 2A.M1 | 2A.D1 | 2A.P2 | 2A.M2 | 2A.D2

You have been asked by your teacher to produce a 'Working in Sport and Active Leisure' portfolio that can be used by students who may be considering a career in sport and active leisure. The portfolio should provide information about the different types of organisations and the different occupations available in sport and active leisure.

1 Within the 'Organisations' section you are required to produce four information sheets, one for each of the different types of organisations in sport and active leisure, giving their features and benefits.

2 Produce a fifth information sheet to compare and contrast the benefits of each of these organisation types, so that students have an overview when they are considering which part of the sector they would like to work in.

3 Within the 'Occupations' section you are required to produce two information sheets for two occupations in sport and active leisure. Each information sheet should:

- cover the requirements for, responsibilities of and skills required for the occupation
- summarise selected information describing the advantages and disadvantages of the occupation

4 Finally, produce a summary sheet that explains the advantages and disadvantages of occupations in sport and active leisure.

Tips

When producing your information sheets you should:

- make sure the information is engaging for the reader. Provide photographs and use tables to present the information where appropriate
- give examples of each type of organisation (Task 1)
- choose two occupations where information is readily available. Use a variety of sources to research these occupations, including job adverts and careers websites (Task 3)
- when explaining advantages and disadvantages of occupations in sport and active leisure, ensure that you provide relevant examples to support your work (Task 4).

Participation in sport

Getting started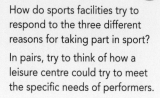

Try to list as many reasons as you can why a person might take part in sporting activities. Then, separate your list into three sections – health and fitness benefits, social benefits and developmental benefits.

Introduction

The reasons why people get involved in sport are varied. Lots of things can affect the decision to participate in sport and which sport you might choose.

◢ Reasons for taking part in sport and active leisure

People generally take part in sport for one or more of the following reasons.

- Health and fitness benefits – people may take part in sport to lose weight, improve posture, improve flexibility or prepare for an event (such as Race for Life).
- Social benefits – taking part in sport can provide an opportunity to meet new friends or to spend time with current friends.
- Development benefits – some people discover that taking part in sport raises their self-confidence and self-esteem.

Do you find social benefits in sport?

Discussion point

How do sports facilities try to respond to the three different reasons for taking part in sport?

In pairs, try to think of how a leisure centre could try to meet the specific needs of performers.

- Developmental benefits – playing a sport regularly allows you to develop your skills in the activity and grow as a performer.

Activity 12.4 / Participation in sport research

You were asked above to consider the reasons why you thought people might take part in sport. You now need to research whether the reasons you thought of were correct and to identify whether there are any other reasons why people might take part in sport that you did not think of.

Prepare a questionnaire that asks people why they do or do not participate in sport and active leisure, and for those that do, how often they participate. When you have completed the questionnaire, you should then use it with a variety of people. This could include your friends, family and peers. Once you have completed the questionnaires, answer the following questions.

1 Did you think of all of the reasons that you found from your research for why people take part in sport and active leisure?

2 What was the most popular reason given for taking part in sport and active leisure?

3 What was the most popular reason given for not taking part in sport and active leisure?

4 Did the age of the person you conducted your questionnaire with affect their answers? (Did young people participate more often in sport and active leisure?)

Reasons for growth in participation

Sports participation continues to grow in the UK for a number of reasons.

- Research by Sport England suggests that a growing number of people see participating in sport as an everyday need, rather than a luxury. These people are happy to spend their disposable income on sports participation.

- The time of year can affect sports participation. Every January memberships in gyms and fitness clubs increase – why do you think this is? And during the summer, people are more likely to be cycling or jogging than they would be in winter – why do you think this is?

- Major high-profile events, such as the Olympics, being hosted by a country tend to increase interest in sporting activities.

Discussion point

Why do you think that London hosting the 2012 Olympic and Paralympic Games led to an increase in sports participation? Try to justify your answer.

Did the rise in participation continue after the games? Explain your thoughts.

Case study

Race for Life is the largest women-only fundraising event in the United Kingdom. Women run either 5K or 10K to raise money for cancer research. Race for Life started in Battersea Park in 1994 with 680 women taking part in the event. Since 1994 over 6 million participants have taken part in the events, raising over £493 million for cancer research.

1 Why do you think that participation in the Race for Life events has grown so dramatically?

2 What do you think are some of the main reasons for women taking part in the Race for Life events?

3 What 'knock on' effect will participation in Race for Life events have for the sport and active leisure industry?

To find out more about Race for Life, go to Pearson Hotlinks (www.pearsonhotlinks.co.uk) and search for this BTEC First in Sport title.

CONTINUED ▶▶

▶▶ CONTINUED

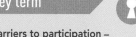

Factors that affect participation

While participation in sport is growing, there are still many people in the UK who do not participate in sporting activities. Here are some of the main factors that are seen as **barriers to participation** in sport and active leisure in the UK.

- Provision – sports participation in certain activities is dependent on the facilities being available to use. For example, if someone lives in a rural area, they may not have access to certain sports facilities.

- Disability – although new buildings are designed for ease of access, many sports facilities are not easily used by or accessible to those with a disability.

- Cost – the equipment required to take part in an activity may be very costly. For example, to take part in skiing a person requires a number of expensive items, such as skis, gloves and goggles.

- Ethnicity – one of the main factors contributing to low levels of participation for black and minority ethnic (BME) communities is a lack of role models in some sports.

- Location – a person's location can affect their ability to take part in certain sports. For example, if someone wanted to ski, they may have to travel a long distance to access facilities.

- Age – a young person may be unable to afford the cost of an activity, or another may be too old to play.

- Gender – stereotypical views have led to barriers that deter women from participating in some sports. For example, rugby is much less accessible to girls than boys.

- Time – lack of time is the most commonly used excuse for non-participation. Young people may want to participate in sport but have other time pressures, such as part-time jobs, homework or social commitments. Older people may work full-time and have family or carer responsibilities.

Key term

🔑

Barriers to participation – factors that prevent participation or make it more difficult.

Wheelchair basketball is one of the most popular sports in the paralympic games. As its popularity grows facilities increase, allowing more people to participate.

Activity 12.5 Barriers

List five activities that you would like to take part in as a competitor, or watch as a spectator, but cannot do so.

Suggest reasons why you cannot take part in or watch these activities. Look at Table 12.3 for examples.

Table 12.3 Examples of barriers to participation

Reason	Example
Provision	No lacrosse teams or clubs in the local area.
Disability	Participant requires adapted game or equipment to take part in the activity.
Cost	Financial commitments, for example mortgage, car loan and insurance.
Ethnicity	Not being able to take part in sport during religious festivals.
Location	Having to travel to the seaside to take part in sand surfing.
Age	The time spent taking part in sport becomes less and the nature of the sport changes due to this factor.
Gender	No women's rugby teams or clubs in the local area.
Time	Work commitments, for example studying at college full-time and a part-time job.

It is important to recognise that these factors will affect people in different ways; performers may be affected by one or more of them.

A person with a disability may have both the money and time to participate in sporting activities, but may find that sports facilities in their local area do not provide the types of activities or specialist equipment that they need.

Someone with a full-time job that requires them to work shifts or weekends may have the money to participate in sporting activities, but not the time. However, an unemployed person may have the time, but not the money.

Individuals interested in sports that have specific requirements, for example, skiing, rock climbing or sailing, may have to travel long distances to be able to participate in these activities. The time taken and also the cost of travel to take part in the activity may make it difficult to access for many.

Discussion point

One of Sport England's key strategic targets is to reduce the drop-off rate in sports participation among 16- to 18-year-olds.

Why do you think there is such a large drop-off rate when young people leave school, and what do you think could be done to try to prevent it?

Just checking

1 Name five factors that can affect participation in sport and active leisure.

2 How can the time of year affect rates of participation in sport?

Trends in participation

Introduction

Participation in sport can be affected in many ways; for example, perhaps someone from your country has won a gold medal recently, or there may be a high-profile competition being held. In this topic you will look at factors that can have an influence on the type and number of people who are attracted to sport.

New/emerging sports activities

Extreme endurance sports, such as open-water swimming and triathlons, are growing in popularity.

People are keen to challenge themselves physically, and marathons, ultramarathons and triathlons provide that challenge. Emerging sports activities are often adapted versions of traditional sports, which open them up to new audiences. Sports such as cyclo-cross, which is a cross between mountain biking and road cycling, and kitesurfing, which is a cross between kite flying and surfing, have grown in popularity in recent years.

Team GB modelling the kit designed by Stella McCartney.

Influence of sport on fashion

Sports clothing has progressed from clothing worn just to play sport in. It now plays an important role in influencing fashion trends. Fashion designers now produce designer sportswear ranges – think, for example, of Stella McCartney's collaborations with Adidas. Trainers that were once designed for sport are now everyday wear.

Activities with increasing/decreasing participation

Participation in both running and cycling on a weekly basis has increased in recent years. The number of those running has increased due to a growing network of informal running groups across the country. Increased numbers of people cycling could be linked to many factors: for example, the success of the Great Britain cycling team and the Cycle to Work scheme.

However, the Active People Survey 6 completed by Sport England indicates that weekly participation in a number of sports, such as cycling and athletics, has increased compared to cricket which decreased between October 2010 to October 2011.

Changing expectations of participants and spectators

Gym-goers may expect immediate results and can become demotivated when physical adaptations do not appear immediately. Spectators expect to be entertained and see positive results, and when these are not delivered changes are called for. For example, when a football team is not doing well the fans may demand that the manager or chairman is sacked.

Technological developments

Sportswear companies are constantly designing new clothes and footwear that they claim will help improve your performance. Equipment required to participate in sports, such as a tennis racket, is constantly adapted in an attempt to improve performance.

Camera technology has developed and is used to help referees and umpires to make accurate decisions. Technology is used in many sports: think of the Hawk Eye in tennis, Hot Spot in cricket and the video referee in rugby league. Also, in April 2013, FIFA and premier league clubs signed up to use goal-line technology in all premier league matches.

Discussion point

How often do you wear sports clothing? Do you only wear it to play sport?

Try to think of as many companies as you can who make sports clothing and accessories.

Take it further

Access the Active People Survey 6 and see whether weekly participation in your favourite sport has increased or decreased.

To access the report go to Pearson Hotlinks (www.pearsonhotlinks.co.uk) and search for this BTEC Sport title.

Assessment activity 12.2   *Maths*   2B.P3 | 2B.P4 | 2B.M3 | 2B.P5 | 2B.M4 | 2B.D3

A local company looking to set up a new fitness centre has approached your teacher to see if your group can help them complete some research focused on participation in sport and active leisure.

1 Design a questionnaire that can be used to find out why people do and do not participate in sport, and then ask your friends and family to complete it. Try to collect as many responses as possible. Use your findings from this questionnaire and relevant research to produce a poster that describes reasons for growth in participation. Highlight six factors that affect participation.

2 The company has been impressed with your research, and has asked you to prepare a presentation about different trends in sports participation to help it develop ideas for the new fitness centre. You will need to submit your presentation slides and speaker notes.

Tips

Task 1

- Make sure that you use examples from your findings.
- Try to make you poster eye-catching by using relevant images.
- Prepare to present your poster to the group by writing some speaker notes, so you remember to mention all of the key points.

Task 2

- Talk to your peers, family and friends about current trends. Research other sport and active leisure facilities in the area, and use the internet, newspapers and magazines.

- Prepare eye-catching presentation slides including information on six different trends that can affect participation.
- Think about the order that you want to present things, and the key points for each slide.
- Practise giving your presentation – this might be to your friends, parents or even to a family pet!
- Find out from your teacher how long your presentation should be (for example, 5 minutes).

Key issues

Getting started

Think about two major issues that affect sports: Do male and female sports events get the same coverage in the media? Do you think holding major sporting events here has a positive effect on the UK, or could the money be spent on better things?

Key term

Impact – an effect or influence on something or someone; to have an effect or influence.

Introduction

The **impact** of key issues on the sports industry has become much more prominent due to the mass coverage of sport in the media. Satellite television and the internet mean that sports can be viewed around the world as they happen.

Some of the issues that currently affect sport and active leisure are shown in Figure 12.2.

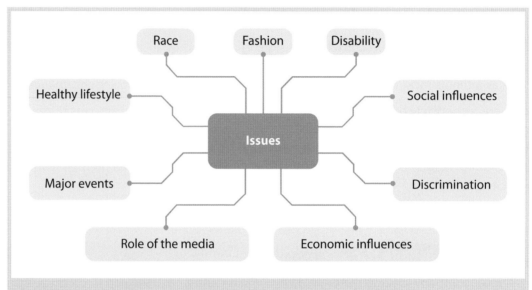

Figure 12.2 Issues that impact on participation in sport and active leisure

Positive and negative impact of key issues

Case study

The UK hosting the 2012 Olympic and Paralympic Games was a key issue in relation to participation in sport. Holding the Games in London had many benefits for the local community, including regeneration and the legacy of world-class sports facilities that were left behind. Thousands of jobs were created before, during and after the games in a variety of sectors. Tourists visited London and spent money in hotels, restaurants and shops and provided a major boost to the economy. However, hosting the Games and building new sports facilities and accommodation also cost the country millions of pounds.

One of the key elements of the successful bid had been that the Games would lead to increased participation in sport. However, no host country has yet been able to demonstrate a direct benefit from the Olympic Games in the form of a lasting increase in sports participation.

- Do you think hosting the Olympic Games was worth the investment?
- Prepare an argument for and against a country holding the Games in the future, and have a debate to decide if your group is for or against holding the Olympics.

Media coverage

Most forms of media are involved with sports coverage: sport can be read about in newspapers or magazines, listened to on the radio or watched on the television, computer or mobile phone. The media coverage (or lack of coverage) of sport can have a major impact on participation in sport and active leisure. It can affect the way that a sport is perceived by the general public – fair or unfair, clean or doped, exciting or boring … Unfortunately, not all sports receive the same coverage, and without coverage it is very difficult for sports to develop and gain sponsorship or advertising rights; for example, women's football is not given the same exposure as men's football and is consequently much less developed.

Activity 12.6 Media coverage

1 Which sport do you think gets the most coverage in the media?

2 Look at a national newspaper and record how many sports are covered and how much coverage each sport receives.

3 Are you surprised by the sports that are covered? How many sports with female participation were covered in the newspaper?

4 Why do you think some sports get so much coverage?

Role models

A key factor in encouraging participation in sporting activities is role models. It is important that people have someone to look up to and inspire them to take part in the activity. Sports performers can usually link their participation in a sport to a performer who inspired them or whom they wanted to be like. It is important for athletes to realise that they are representing their sport as a role model and to understand the importance of appropriate behaviour at all times. This is especially important with today's high levels of media coverage.

Activity 12.7 Role models

1 Who are your role models? Who inspired you to start taking part in your sport?

2 Can you think of five sports performers whom you see as 'good' role models and five sports performers whom you would describe as 'bad' role models? Justify your answers.

CONTINUED ▸▸

Obesity

In the UK an estimated 60.8% of adults and 31.1% of children are overweight. It is estimated that almost a quarter of adults in England were classified as obese (a BMI of 30 or over). These figures highlight the need for people to live a healthier lifestyle, which involves not only eating well, but also being active. Schemes such as Change4Life have attempted to raise awareness of the importance of healthy living, by providing advice on the many different ways that people can become active and participate in sport and active leisure.

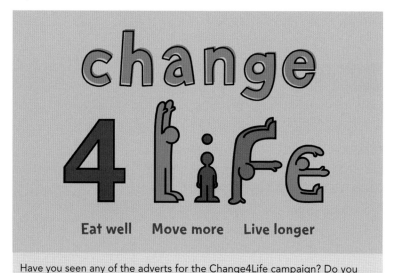

Have you seen any of the adverts for the Change4Life campaign? Do you think that they are effective in delivering the healthy lifestyle message?

Assessment activity 12.3   2C.P6 | 2C.M5 | 2C.D4

Your local sports development officer has approached your school and asked your group to produce a presentation that can be shown to other schools to:

* raise awareness of the key issues in sport and their impact on sports participation
* look at the impact of these issues on a selected sport and active leisure activity or business.

You will need to submit your presentation slides and speaker notes.

Tips

When producing your presentation you should consider the following.

* Think about how you might be able to find out more about the key issues so you have enough information for your presentation. If you know people with jobs in the sports industry, prepare a list of questions to ask them. Is there any information on the websites of sport organisations such as SkillsActive? If so, select six issues of key interest and summarise these in your own words. Are key issues being reported in the local or national newspapers?

* Your selected activity or business could be for your own sport or one that you are less familiar with participating in, but that has been affected by a key issue that you have managed to collect a lot of research on. Are there people associated with the sport you can talk to for more information?

* Once you have collated your research, decide on the main points you would like to include in your presentation, and the order you are going to present these in.

* See Assessment activity 12.2 for more guidance on giving presentations.

WorkSpace

▼ **Mia-Esme Gardner**

Sports development officer for women's cricket

I work for a county cricket board. I joined the team as a cricket development administrator and was then appointed as the women's and girls' cricket development officer. My main responsibilities include:

- developing women's and girls' cricket across the county
- coaching on the Chance to Shine project in the county
- organising and running Asda Girls' Kwik Cricket Festivals
- increasing the number of girls and women developing as cricket leaders, coaches and officials.

My day is rarely 9 to 5; it often involves evening and weekend work. I spend time working in my office during the morning and am usually out during the afternoon and evening. Luckily, I can be quite flexible about the hours that I work. In the office I usually catch up with my paperwork and write reports. I may be developing or reviewing an action plan – this could involve reviewing the participation rate of women and girls playing cricket in the county and the level at which they play. In the afternoon I usually visit primary and secondary schools, where I deliver the Chance to Shine project. As part of the project, I deliver assemblies to introduce the MCC Spirit of Cricket campaign, which aims to reinforce the message of fair play. I also support the schools in organising an intra-school competition, which is scored and umpired by the children in an attempt to reinforce the rules of the game.

The best thing about my job is the fact that I can create opportunities for girls and women to play cricket. I really enjoy seeing people watching a session and being surprised by the high standards of some of the players. I also love seeing young girls in primary schools joining in the game and having a lot of fun. I get the most satisfaction from knowing that I am contributing to an increase in participation and providing opportunities for girls and women to play cricket.

Think about it

1 Can you think of any advantages and disadvantages of Mia-Esme's occupation?

2 What skills do you think Mia-Esme requires to be successful in her role?

3 Can you think of some barriers to participation for girls and women who want to play cricket?

4 Is women's cricket given as much coverage as men's cricket in the media? Why do you think this is the case?

Introduction

How often do you look back over your own sports performance and consider how you performed and where you might need to improve your game or technique? Performance profiling is used to determine a sports performer's current profile, strengths and areas for improvement.

Elite sports performers have their performance analysed on a regular basis and from this their training programmes for short- and long-term development are designed and implemented. For these sports performers the identification of a particular weakness can be the difference between winning and losing. Behind every great team or sports performer is a great coach who has the knowledge and experience to carry out this performance profiling and give effective feedback.

As a sports performer, you must develop the ability to assess your own performance and that of others. In this unit you will be introduced to the components of a sports profile. You will learn how to carry out performance profiling for a sports performer or team and use this information to set goals for further development.

Assessment: You will be assessed by a series of assignments set by your teacher/tutor.

Learning aims

After completing this unit you should:

A understand the performance profile of sports

B be able to analyse and profile sports performance

C review the performance profiles and set goals for further development.

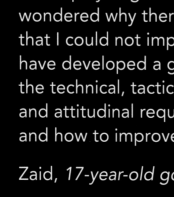

I have played golf for over 7 years and always wondered why there were parts of my game that I could not improve. Through this unit I have developed a greater understanding of the technical, tactical, fitness, psychological and attitudinal requirements for my own sport and how to improve elements of my game.

Zaid, *17-year-old golfer*

Profiling Sports Performance

This table shows what you must do in order to achieve a **Pass**, **Merit** or **Distinction** grade, and where you can find activities in this book to help you.

Assessment Zone

Assessment criteria

Level 1	Level 2 **Pass**	Level 2 **Merit**	Level 2 **Distinction**
Learning aim A: understand the performance profile of sports			
1A.1 Identify the technical, tactical and fitness profiles required to successfully participate in a selected sport	**2A.P1** Describe the technical, tactical, fitness, psychological and attitudinal profiles required to successfully participate in two selected sports **See Assessment activity 13.1, page 329**	**2A.M1** Compare and contrast the technical, tactical, fitness, psychological and attitudinal profiles required to successfully participate in two selected sports **See Assessment activity 13.1, page 329**	**2A.D1** Justify the technical, tactical, fitness, psychological and attitudinal profiles required to successfully participate in two selected sports **See Assessment activity 13.1, page 329**
Learning aim B: be able to analyse and profile sports performance			
1B.2 English Design and complete a performance profile to assess performance of a team or individual in a selected sport, with guidance	**2B.P2** English Independently design and complete performance profiles to assess performance of a team or individual in two different selected sports **See Assessment activity 13.2, page 333**	**2B.M2** Evaluate the qualities, traits and attributes for a team or individual in two different selected sports **See Assessment activity 13.2, page 333**	**2B.D2** Justify the completed performance profiles for a team or individual in two different selected sports **See Assessment activity 13.2, page 333**
1B.3 Use the completed performance profile to describe the qualities, traits and attributes for a team or individual in a selected sport	**2B.P3** Use the completed performance profiles to describe the qualities, traits and attributes for a team or individual in two different selected sports **See Assessment activity 13.2, page 333**		
Learning aim C: review the performance profiles and set goals for further development			
1C.4 Review the performance profile for a team or individual, outlining goals and recommendations for future performance	**2C.P4** Review the performance profiles for a team or individual in two different selected sports, summarising goals for future performance and development planning **See Assessment activity 13.3, page 337**	**2C.M3** Explain set goals for future performance and development for a team or individual in each selected sport, describing the development plans **See Assessment activity 13.3, page 337**	**2C.D3** Justify the selection of activities within the development plans for the performers in each selected sport **See Assessment activity 13.3, page 337**

English Opportunity to practise English skills

How you will be assessed

This unit will be assessed through a series of assignments set by your teacher/tutor. You will be expected to show that you understand the qualities, attributes and traits required to participate successfully in two selected sports. You will then be required to design and carry out performance profiles for sports performers or teams in two selected sports, and design development plans, recommending improvements for future performance.

Your assessment could be in the form of:

- performance profile outlines for two sports
- a review of the outcomes of the performance profiles
- development plans.

Performance profiles and sporting activities

Introduction

A performance profile is used by sports coaches and sports analysts to assess the qualities, attributes and traits of a sports performer, such as their technical and tactical abilities. The profile of the performer is then compared to a model or standard.

Performance profile

When carrying out a profile of a 100-metre sprinter, the assessor will look at the performance relating to key points in the race:

- reaction time
- block clearance
- drive phase
- transition
- maximum velocity
- maintenance
- final acceleration
- finish.

When carrying out a profile of a footballer the assessor may compare each quality, attribute and trait against that of an elite footballer. For example, when assessing the technique of dribbling, the assessor may have the ideal model in their mind of the world's best footballer carrying out this skill and will compare the application of the skill performed by an individual with this model.

There are two ways to make judgements when preparing a performance profile for an individual or team: subjective and objective assessments.

Subjective assessments

Subjective assessments are based on personal interpretations and opinions. For example, a sports coach will observe a sports performer or team and make a judgement about their effectiveness and overall performance. When making a subjective assessment the observer compares their observations against their view of an ideal performance.

Objective assessments

Objective assessments involve the measurement and comparison of performance data. For example, the ability to perform a netball shot could be assessed objectively by counting how many shots a netball player scores out of ten. During a competitive situation this is often done using observation checklists and tally charts. The tally chart may count the number of:

- shots on target
- shots off target
- fouls committed
- completed passes
- unsuccessful passes
- interceptions made
- interceptions missed.

Key terms

Qualities – necessary standards required by a sports performer to perform competently within a selected sport.

Attributes – features regarded as invaluable components of being a successful sports performer within a selected sport.

Traits – particular personality requirements for sports performers.

Statistics – data, which can then be used to assess the outcome of an observation, survey, etc.

Notational analysis and statistical data

Notational analysis involves the use of data that have been collected during live or recorded performance to analyse performance. On completion of the performance the data can be converted into **statistics**, which will summarise the outcomes of the observation.

These statistics are used by sports coaches or performers to identify strengths and areas for further development. For example, if a basketball coach is provided with statistics on the points his team scored within each quarter of a game, it may be revealed that the team scored least points in the final quarter. The coach may then carry out further analysis to find out the reason for this and develop a training programme around the results.

Link

See *Unit 2: Practical Sports Performance* for more information on observation checklists and analysis of sports performance.

Psychological profiles

We often associate performance profiling with the technical and tactical requirements of a sport. However, it is also important to assess the psychological skills of a sports performer.

To carry out a psychological profile you will need to identify the psychological qualities required for a selected sport. For example, team sports performers are usually more aggressive than those sports performers who play individual sports. Once you have identified the required qualities, you should rate the sports performer against each of these qualities. This should give you an idea of the psychological skills a sports performer needs to improve.

When doing this for the first time, you should seek advice from an experienced sports coach or sports psychologist. Because this type of profiling often relies on observation of a performer's behaviour and personality, it is best done using subjective assessment methods.

Link

See *Unit 3: The Mind and Sports Performance* for further information on psychological profiles.

Coaches give advice and help you to improve your sporting performance – how do your coaches or teachers/tutors help you improve in sport?

CONTINUED ▶▶

Sporting activity

When carrying out a performance profile you will be looking at a sports team or individual sports performers. It is therefore important to know the difference between a **team sport** and an **individual sport**.

Curling is a team sport.

Fencing is an individual sport.

Activity 13.1   Individual or team sport?

1 Make a list of five individual sports.

2 Make a list of five team sports.

3 Make a list of five different individuals from within a team sport.

Just checking

1 What is a trait?

2 What is a quality?

3 What is an attribute?

4 What are subjective assessments?

5 What are objective assessments?

6 What is a tally chart?

7 What is notational analysis?

8 What are statistics?

9 Provide examples of psychological differences between team and individual sports.

10 What is a team sport?

11 What is an individual sport?

WorkSpace

► Malcolm Thorburn

Tennis coach

I have been a tennis coach at my local tennis club for the last three years. My team has experienced a mixture of results over the last couple of seasons.

I played tennis as a very young child and represented my school and county in various championships. My coach was very strict and developed my ability through repetitive practice. Although my game developed, I struggled with boredom within his sessions, which eventually led me to quit playing tennis. It was only after I finished studying at college that I decided to play again. I enjoyed it so much that I decided to start coaching and supporting the development of young people through tennis.

As my skills have improved as a sports coach, I have managed to develop more technical and tactical knowledge of the sport. Through working with a variety of abilities, levels and age groups, I have gained a greater understanding of the attitudinal and psychological attributes required to be a very good player in this sport.

To date, my greatest success was supporting a 14-year-old girl through coaching to win the regional championship. I worked with her for such a long time that I completed a variety of assessments of her performance and provided her with specific development opportunities. Together, we worked on these improvements and were able to see the outcomes of all the hard work. The progress that I made with this particular player motivated me to continue to coach players at the club.

Think about it

1   What are the physical, technical, tactical, attitudinal and psychological requirements for a tennis player?

2   Can you identify the methods of assessment that Malcolm may have used to support the development of the young girl?

3   Design a performance profile that Malcolm could use to analyse the performance of the young girl in the future.

Qualities, traits and attributes

Link

In *Unit 2: Practical Sports Performance* you were introduced to the skills, techniques and tactical demands in one team and one individual sport.

Introduction

When carrying out a performance profile of a sports performer or team it is important to be aware of all the qualities, traits and attributes required to perform successfully within the sport and the correct application of these, including technical, tactical, psychological, attitudinal and fitness requirements.

Technical requirements

Technical requirements are the physical skills that are needed for participation in a sport. For example, in basketball the technical requirements include running, catching and jumping, as well as more complex requirements and skills such as shooting, dribbling, passing, tackling, pivoting and receiving.

These can be classified as:

- continuous skills – skills that have no clear beginning and end, e.g. running, walking or dribbling
- serial skills – skills that use a linked series of movements, e.g. lay up, (dribble, run, jump, shoot)
- discrete skills – skills with a clear beginning and end, e.g. a basketball free throw.

Activity 13.2 List of technical demands

Categorise each of the technical demands of a sport of your choice into serial, discrete and continuous skills in a table like this:

Serial skills	Discrete skills	Continuous skills

Tactical requirements

In sport, tactics are the decisions a team or sports performer make when playing in a competitive situation – for example who to pass to, where to run or who to mark. In each situation the action taken by the sports performer can have an impact on the overall outcome of a game or match.

Tactical demands relate to various components of a sport, such as:

- attack and defence – what methods to use when you have control of the ball, court or race
- the situation a performer or team is in – if winning or losing; the time/distance left until the end of the competitive situation
- the performer's or team's preferred style of play or performance – their own strengths and weaknesses

- the opposition – strengths and weaknesses of the opponents and what strategies you or your team will adopt to overcome or exploit them.

Activity 13.3   Tactical demands

Create a list of the different tactics used by sports performers in three sports to achieve success. Consider methods of defence and attack for each sport.

Defensive tactics	Attacking tactics

Fitness requirements

Different sports have different fitness requirements depending on the technical demands, duration of play and/or competitive environment. For some sports there may be individuals within the team who have different fitness requirements from other members of the team. For example, in rugby union a winger will need to have excellent levels of speed and agility whereas a front row forward will need great strength and power.

Link

See *Unit 1: Fitness for Sport and Exercise* for more information about physical and skill-related fitness.

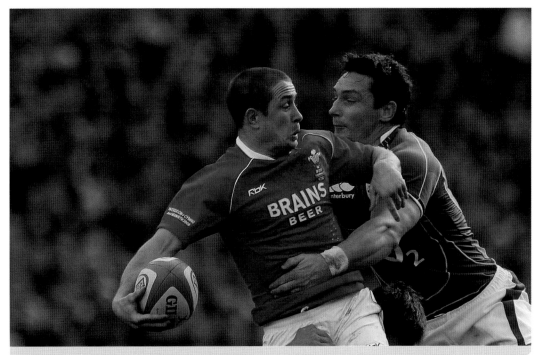

Rugby requires speed, agility and the ability to control the ball in difficult situations.

Activity 13.4   Fitness requirements

1 Make a list of the fitness requirements for a sport of your choice.

2 For a team sport, consider two positions and consider the fitness requirements for each position.

CONTINUED ▶▶

Psychological requirements

In recent years the importance of sports psychology in competitive sports has grown. Most elite sports performers have access to sports psychologists and the link between psychological well-being and successful sports performance is well recognised. Figure 13.1 summarises the psychological requirements of sports performance. In team sports such as football and rugby, psychologists believe that sports performers tend to have a strong urge for competition, and a strong desire to be successful. It is also believed that personality types can be linked to the sports that sports performers choose.

Link

See *Unit 3: The Mind and Sports Performance* for more information about sports psychology.

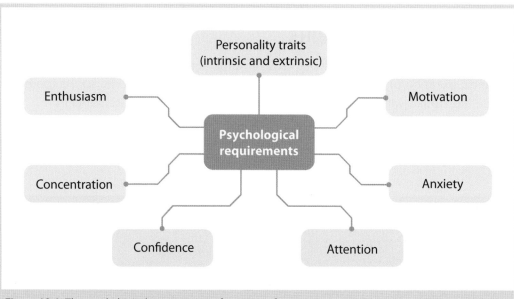

Figure 13.1 The psychological requirements of sports performance

Attitudinal requirements

Attitudinal requirements are the emotions, drive or state of mind a performer needs to increase their chances of success. For example, when playing snooker, it is not only very important that players have the desire to win, and are competitive when at the table, but they must also be calm and collected to ensure that they build a game-winning break or a defensive safety strategy. Similarly, when a rugby team takes to the field it is important they demonstrate their desire to win by channelling their competiveness and determination through positive aggression, a positive attitude and a willingness to take on anybody to win the match outright.

For some Olympic sports, the chance to compete at the highest levels comes only once every four years. Within these sports, it is especially important that sports performers demonstrate dedication and commitment to their training and personal development.

In snooker and rugby some attitudinal factors are very similar, although the methods in which these are displayed by the performers in each sport are very different.

Can you think of any other sports that share similar attitudinal requirements that are demonstrated very differently by the sports performers?

Assessment activity 13.1

2A.P1 | 2A.M1 | 2A.D1

You are on a work placement at a local secondary school and have been asked to produce training materials containing information about the technical, tactical, fitness, psychological and attitudinal profiles required to be a successful sports performer within two sports. These will be used to recruit new players for the school's teams.

You could produce a training booklet or a presentation (for this you will be recorded and will need to submit slides and speaker notes for assessment).

Tips

- Observe people playing your two selected sports and think about why each profile is required for performance at an elite level.
- Find examples of successful performers within your chosen sports.
- Include a table that shows the similarities and differences between the technical, tactical, attitudinal and psychological requirements for each sport. Summarise your findings, stating why you think certain requirements for these sports are the same and why others are different.

Analysing sports performance

Introduction

Analysis of performance in competitive situations enables coaches to monitor the progress of the team or sports performer, compare them with other players and assess their strengths and weaknesses. Performance profiling is also used to plan the next phase of development for the performer or team.

Observing performance

Profiling begins with the observation of performance, either live or through video analysis.

Video analysis involves the coach or sports performer playing back a video recording to observe performance in real time and, when required, slow motion. Video analysis allows the coach or sports performer to review the physical application of skills and techniques many times in detail.

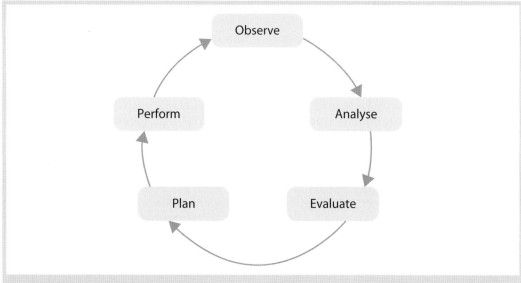

Figure 13.2 Performance analysis model

Establishing current profile

The performance analysis model (Figure 13.2) illustrates the different stages of performance profiling.

The planning stage of this model should be decided by both performer (or team) and sports coach. At this stage they should agree aims and objectives for further development. The targets should be set using the SMARTER target method (see page 335). Without this, a performer's development may falter. After the planning stage, learners should undertake the required action and training and then be observed performing in a competitive situation again so further analysis can take place. After this cycle has been completed it is expected that it will start again.

A performance profile should be carried out against each of the pre-selected qualities, traits and attributes that have been highlighted as necessary for successful performance within the selected sport.

See Table 13.1 for a performance profile of the technical ability of a rugby player, which has been completed by an observer.

Table 13.1 Using the data from the table, can you identify Luke's strengths and areas for development?

Performance profile – Techniques of rugby – Subjective assessment
Luke Benjamin – Hull Ionians Rugby Union Club Under-15s
Observer: Jonathan Leighton – Assistant manager

Tactics	1	2	3	4	5	6	7	8	9	10
Handling							✓			

Comments: Luke demonstrated some excellent handling and was very competent at taking the high ball throughout the game. However, he did knock the ball on once when attacking in the opponents' third, which cost the team possession.

| **Passing/receiving** | | | | | | ✓ | | | | |

Comments: Luke showed some excellent passing ability throughout the game and at times his attacking flair with the ball in his hand caused the opponents a great many problems. However, Luke tried to play the killer pass on too many occasions and twice the opposition predicted his pass and intercepted. He should consider varying his passing throughout the game.

| **Running with the ball** | | | | | | | ✓ | | | |

Comments: Luke had four runs within the game, three of which resulted in tries. His ability to spot holes within the defence was excellent and threatened the opponents considerably. However, on one occasion Luke ran the ball from within his own 20-metre line and this resulted in his team losing possession and the opponents gaining the ball. Luke should always ensure that he only runs with the ball when appropriate.

| **Intercepting** | | | | | ✓ | | | | | |

Comments: Luke tried to intercept on a number of occasions, and when he did this he committed himself to the attacking line. When he did not intercept the ball (on all but one occasion within the game) he caused excess pressure on his teammates and he was out of the line of defence.

| **Setting up a ruck** | | | | | ✓ | | | | | |

Comments: As a back, Luke only did this twice within the game. His technique was poor and he needs to work on this.

| **Retaining possession within a ruck** | | | | ✓ | | | | | | |

Comments: The only time Luke set up a ruck with other members of the team they lost possession. Luke needs to develop his ability to protect the ball in the ruck.

| **Retaining ball in maul** | | | | | | | ✓ | | | |

Comments: Luke did this well on two occasions and when in a maul always ensured that the ball made it out to the supporting player on his own team.

| **Tackling** | | | | | | ✓ | | | | |

Comments: Luke is a very strong defender and as the last line of defence on a number of occasions had to make some crucial tackles. His tackling technique is exemplary. However, at times he tackled the legs of the player rather than attempting to smother the ball. On these occasions the player who was stopped by Luke released the ball to another player. Luke should develop this method of defence.

CONTINUED ▶▶

Profiling

The person completing the performance profile should award the sports performer(s) with a grade for each target or goal.

Methods of rating a sports performer can vary. Some use a scale of 1–10, with 1 being very poor and 10 being elite level (see Table 13.2). Others award stars (one star being the lowest and five stars being the highest rating) or A–F grades (with F as the lowest and A as the highest).

Activity 13.5   Skills rating

Use Table 13.2 to rate the skills of sports performers in your group for a selected sport. Focus on a basic skill and provide each member of the group (including yourself) with a mark out of 10 for this skill. Compare your results with the rest of the group and discuss your reasons for awarding each mark to each member of the group.

Table 13.2 Analyse and profile sports performance

1	No success at all when applying the skill. Technique non-existent.
2	Some success when applying the skill. Major technical flaws in the execution of the skill.
3	Some success when applying the skill. Flaws within the technical application of the skills but parts applied correctly.
4	Some success when applying the skill. Some flaws within the application of the technique .
5	An equal amount of success and failure when applying the skill. Some flaws within the application of the technique.
6	More success than failure in the application of the skill, although still a lot of failure. Some flaws within the application of the technique.
7	Satisfying levels of success of the application of the skill and a limited number of failures. A sound application of the technique.
8	High levels of success and a limited number of failures of the skill. Good application of the technique.
9	Very high levels of success of the skill with only few failures. Very good application of the technique.
10	Application of the skill is always successful. Perfect application of the technique.

It is important that those observing draw conclusions about the performance and produce a list of identified strengths and weaknesses. These should relate to each of the relevant qualities, traits and attributes that have been previously identified as requirements for the selected sport.

For example, when observing the performance of a rugby team, the observer could draw conclusions about the technical requirements of the sport through assessing the number of completed passes, tackles, successful attacking plays and so on, and could make generalisations regarding individuals' or the team's technical ability through assessing the number of set plays successfully converted, the success rate in the attacking third and quality of defence in their own third. As well as using notational analysis, the observer should award a rating for each of the areas.

It is important that each quality, trait and attribute that has been identified as important for success in the sport (technical, tactical, fitness, attitudinal, and psychological) is assessed. You should use subjective and/or objective assessment when completing a profile.

See Table 13.3 for different methods of measuring success using objective assessment methods.

Table 13.3 Methods used to measure success

Methods for measuring success	Methods for measuring failure
• Overall victory	• Losing the competitive situation
• Completed passes	• Incomplete passes
• Completed tackles	• Missed tackles
• Number of assists	• Shots off-target
• Shots on target	• Goals/points conceded
• Goals/points scored	

Assessment activity 13.2 *English* 2B.P2 | 2B.P3 | 2B.M2 | 2B.D2

The coach at your school has asked you to complete a performance profile of a team or individual in two different sports of your choice, to demonstrate to others in these sports how performance can be profiled.

1 Design and complete performance profiles for each team/individual (two sports).

2 What did you learn about the qualities, traits and attributes for your selected performers? Present your findings.

Tips

• To complete your performance profiles, you will need to observe the team/individual in a competitive situation.

• What are the strengths of the performers? Are there areas where they can improve?

Remember

Attitudinal measures include: desire to win, discipline, competitiveness, determination, willingness to take on anybody, positivity, aggression, dedication.

Psychological measures include: focus, emotional control, concentration, level of relaxation, ability to cope with pressure, confidence.

Setting goals for further development

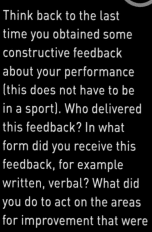

Getting started

Think back to the last time you obtained some constructive feedback about your performance (this does not have to be in a sport). Who delivered this feedback? In what form did you receive this feedback, for example written, verbal? What did you do to act on the areas for improvement that were highlighted to you?

Introduction

After the performance profiling has taken place it is very important that the performer(s) obtain feedback from the observer, which can then be used to create a training programme to support the whole development of the sports performer(s). Feedback should be clear and concise, and should make performers aware of which areas of their performance are their strengths, and which areas they need to improve. Feedback may also include practical instruction for developing performance, such as guidance on specific activities and drills.

Reviewing the performance profile

After completion of the performance profile you are required to review this and form conclusions to help inform future training. You will need to make judgements regarding the strengths and areas for improvement of the sports team or individual performer.

Setting goals

All sports performers want to develop their areas for improvement and enhance their strengths to maximise their performance in a sport. Performance profiling gives athletes a base from which to start this development. Once you have identified the individual's or team's strengths and areas for improvement you will need to make recommendations to improve their future performance. These recommendations may be linked to specific qualities, attributes and traits.

Visualising yourself achieving your long-term goals can be highly motivating.

Goals

The observer and the sports performer(s) should agree on a set of goals for future development, to increase motivation and confidence for future sports events. Each goal should have a realistic timescale (see Table 13.4).

Table 13.4 Goals of a professional golfer, with timescales

Goal	Timescale	Example
Short-term goal	To be achieved within 1 month	Improve average putts per green from 4 to 3 by the next tournament.
Medium-term goal	To be achieved within 1–3 months	Develop close approach play by next championship evidenced by a one shot reduction.
Long-term goal	To be achieved within the entire season, or longer	Win the British Open championship by the end of career.

◤ Development plan

Areas for improvement, goals and suggested timescales are written down to form a development plan for the team or individual. Without a development plan, an individual's or team's performance might fail to improve.

Aims and objectives

Before formulating a plan for future performance development, a team/athlete and coach should agree clear aims: things they would like to achieve by the start of the next season.

In order to achieve their aims, a team or athlete will also need to agree on a set of objectives: actions they are going to take to meet each of their aims. Each aim needs a matching objective.

SMARTER targets

Whenever objectives and goals are set for teams or individuals, they should be SMARTER.

- **S**pecific – the goals set should be as precise and detailed as possible for the team or individual.
- **M**easurable – the goals set should define a method of measuring the success of the team or individual.
- **A**chievable – the goals set should be possible to attain within a set period of time and should be relevant to the team or individual.
- **R**ealistic – appropriate for the team or individual.
- **T**ime-bound – the goals set should have an agreed timescale (short-, medium- and long-term goals).
- **E**xciting – the sports performer or team needs to remain motivated and enthused about their goals.
- **R**ecorded – each target, and the progress towards achieving also it, should be written down to track progress.

Targets for the development of specific qualities, traits and attributes should be clearly set out within the development plan.

CONTINUED ▶▶

Opportunities

Formulating a plan for future development can open up new doors for teams' and individuals' personal development as well as success within the sport. The plan could include:

- attending a course – to develop knowledge about a specific area of a sport
- obtaining qualifications – to learn new skills and techniques
- joining a local sports clubs – to learn from other sports enthusiasts
- observing more advanced performers in action – to observe the correct application of skills, techniques and tactics
- working with a personal trainer – to seek help with particular fitness areas for development
- meeting with a sports psychologist – to get support with the development of psychological and attitudinal areas.

By accessing these opportunities, a sports performer or team may improve their performance in particular situations.

Other elements of the development plan between the coach and the team may introduce the team to new methods of training and, possibly, new coaches. This may freshen up the methods used previously and develop further motivation. It may also provide an opportunity to develop the team's overall performance.

Possible barriers

Although the development plan may cover almost every possible eventuality and provide some excellent opportunities, unforeseen circumstances may arise and hinder progress towards attaining the set goals.

When participating in a training programme, performers should be given every opportunity to meet their goals and targets. A coach and performer/team can only do a certain amount of planning. Performers can seek support from within their club, or from their sport's National Governing Body if appropriate.

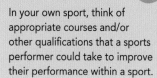

Take it further

In your own sport, think of appropriate courses and/or other qualifications that a sports performer could take to improve their performance within a sport.

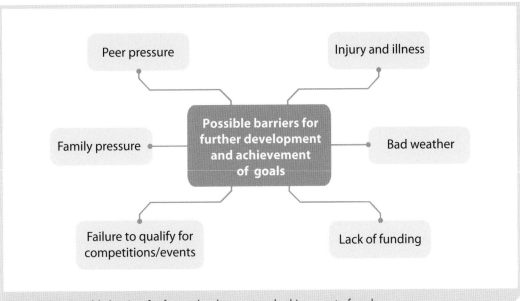

Figure 13.3 Possible barriers for future development and achievement of goals

---

Assessment activity 13.3   2C.P4 | 2C.M3 | 2C.D3

You have completed performance profiles for individuals or teams in two sports. You have been asked to use the results to provide the participants with feedback. The information you provide will be used to further develop their training programmes.

Prepare a set of goals for each team/individual to help them develop and improve their performance, Next, prepare development plans for each team/individual to help them achieve these goals. You will need to be prepared to present these plans to your teacher.

Tips

- State the strengths of the players, and then state why the players need to improve certain areas of their performance.
- Set specific short-, medium- and long-term goals.
- Make sure your development plans include aims, objectives and SMARTER targets for specific qualities, traits and attributes.
- Include suggestions for potential opportunities to support further progression.
- When giving feedback to the players, make sure they understand why you have included certain activities in their development plans.

Answers to Assessment Practice questions

Unit 1, Assessment practice 1.1

1. Which component of fitness can have kgm/s as its unit of measurement? Select the correct answer. [1]

Answer: A Anaerobic power

2. Give three reasons why speed is an important component of physical fitness for basketball players. [3]

Any three answers from:

- Speed is needed so that the basketball player can move quickly and efficiently around the court
- Speed will enable players to get away from opponents
- Whilst gaining/retaining possession of the ball
- Quickly moving into advantageous positions e.g. to score baskets.

Unit 1, Assessment practice 1.2

Malcolm is 30 years old and Vivienne is 48 years old.

1. Calculate their maximum heart rates. [4]

Answers: **Malcolm:** 220 – 30 = 190 bpm

Vivienne: 220 – 48 = 172 bpm

2. Calculate their lower and upper heart rate training zones for cardiovascular health and fitness. [4]

Answers: **Malcolm:** Lower heart rate training zone: 0.6 x 190 = 114 bpm
Upper heart rate training zone: 0.85 x 190 = 161.5 bpm

Vivienne: Lower heart rate training zone: 0.6 x 172 = 103.2 bpm
Upper heart rate training zone: 0.85 x 172 = 146.2 bpm

Unit 1, Assessment practice 1.3

1. Frida is 33 years old and exercises in the gym. She records her RPE during the following activities:

Exercise	RPE	Heart rate (bpm)
Exercise bike	13	
Free weights	15	
Treadmill	16	

a) Complete the table to show Frida's heart rate (bpm) for these three activities. [3]

Answers:

Exercise	RPE	Heart rate (bpm)
Exercise bike	13	130
Free weights	15	150
Treadmill	16	160

b) Frida wants to work at 70% HRmax. Using the table above, work out which type of exercise would give her this HR training zone? [1]

Answer: Exercise bike

2. Describe how the Borg RPE Scale can be used to determine exercise intensity. [2]

Answer: Using the scale, the higher level of perceived exertion means the higher the exercise intensity. If the RPE is 15, it can be determined that the level of exercise intensity is hard (heavy).

Unit 1, Assessment practice 1.4

Rudi has joined his local gym with the aim of improving his strength and muscular endurance.

1. Which fitness training method should Rudi follow to help him achieve his aim? [1]

Answer: Circuit training

2. Explain why Rudi should increase progressive overload and give an example of how he could do this in circuit training. [2]

Answer: Progressive overload could be used in circuit training by increasing the number of stations in the circuit so that the body adapts to the level of demand, improving Rudi's performance.

Other answers for how progressive overload could be applied in circuit training could include:

- Reduce rest periods
- Increase workout time at each station
- Increase target intensity
- Increase the number of circuits performed per session
- Increase the number of training sessions per week.

3. Rudi wants to train for maximum strength. What % 1–RM and reps should he be working at? [2]

Answer: 90% 1–RM and 6 reps.

Unit 1, Assessment practice 1.5

1. Give two reasons why fitness testing is important. [2]

Answer: Fitness testing is important for a number of reasons. Firstly, fitness testing can highlight areas where the performer needs to improve, allowing for the coach to design a base training programme and determine if training programmes work effectively. Secondly, fitness testing provides a performer with clear goals.

2. With reference to fitness testing, which term is defined as 'the consistency' of fitness test results? [1]

Answer: B Reliability

Unit 1, Assessment practice 1.6

1. Rob is 18 years old. He reached Level 12 Shuttle 12 in the multistage fitness test. Use Table 1.16 on page 29 to predict Rob's VO2 max. Then use Tables 1.14 and 1.15 on page 28 to interpret Rob's aerobic endurance test result. [2]

Answer: Level 12 Shuttle 12 = 57.1 ml/kg/min (VO2 max). Interpretation of aerobic endurance is 'Good', and compared to elite performers, Rob's result shows he is 'Trained'.

2. Ana has just completed the Forestry step test. Her 15 second pulse count is 33. Ana is 15 years old and weighs 59kg. Use Tables 1.17b–d on pages 32–33 to work out and interpret Ana's VO2 max (ml/kg/min). [2]

Answer: Non-adjusted aerobic fitness (ml/kg/min) = 41 Age-adjusted fitness level (ml/kg/min) = 43 Interpretation of aerobic endurance is 'Good'

3. Pablo weighs 84kg and is 1.84m tall. Calculate and interpret Pablo's BMI (kg/m.) using Table 1.25 on page 38. [2]

Answer: $1.84 \text{ m} \times 1.84 \text{ m} = 3.3856 \text{ m}^2$ $BMI = 84\text{kg} \div 3.3856\text{m}^2 = 24.8\text{kg/m}^2$ This can be interpreted as desirable.

Unit 1, Assessment Zone

1. Body fat can be predicted using the Jackson-Pollock (J-P) Nomogram method. This method uses three skinfold sites for females.

Select the three correct skinfold sites for females from the list below [3].

Answer: Suprailiac, Thigh, Triceps.

2. Fitness testing can play an important part in an athlete's training cycle.

a. Name the piece of fitness testing equipment shown in the photograph [1].

Answer: Sit and reach box.

b. State the component of fitness this piece of equipment is used to test. [1]

Answer: Flexibility.

c. State the units of measurement [1].

Answer: Centimetres (will also accept inches).

3. Describe how a greater range of movement is achieved using the PNF technique. [2]

Answer: The sports performer stretches the muscle to the upper limit of its range of movement.

A partner helps to hold the muscle in an isometric contraction for approximately 6–10 seconds. The performer then relaxes the muscle and with the help of their partner performs a static (passive) stretch.

This enables them to make the muscle stretch even further by inhibiting the stretch reflex.

Unit 7, Assessment practice 7.1

1. Which of the following descriptions best describes antagonistic muscles. [1]

Answer: B Muscles that work together to produce a movement and its opposite movement.

2. Name two types of muscle found in the human body. [2]

Answers could include:

- Skeletal
- Smooth
- Cardiac

Unit 7, Assessment practice 7.2

1. Slow twitch oxidative fibres are relied upon for which type of exercise. [1]

Answer: C Low intensity events such as long distance swimming.

2 What are the single cells or fibres found in muscle embedded in? [1]

Answer: Collagen

Unit 7, Assessment practice 7.3

1. Where are flat bones found in the body? [1]

Answer: B Protecting vital organs.

Unit 7, Assessment practice 7.4

1. Name two of the main types of bone. [2]

Answers could include:

- Long
- Short
- Flat
- Irregular
- Sesamoid

2. The vertebral column provides structural support and balance to maintain an upright posture and enable flexible motion. Identify one other function of the vertebral column. [1]

Answer: Protect the spinal cord.

Unit 7, Assessment practice 7.5

1. What is the other name for the hyaline cartilage? [1]

Answer: A Articular

2. State the role synovial fluid plays within the synovial joint? [1]

Answer: Reduces friction during movement.

Unit 7, Assessment practice 7.6

1. Which of the following definitions best describes the septum [1]

Answer: A It separates right and left side of the heart.

2. Complete this sentence. Blood vessels with single cell walls are known as... [1]

Answer: B capillaries

Unit 7, Assessment practice 7.7

1. The body is exceptionally good at regulating its temperature. What temperature is the norm for the human body? [1]

Answer: C 37°

Unit 7, Assessment practice 7.8

1. Describe the function of the cilia and where they are found. [2]

Answer: They are found in the nose and filter air for small particles.

2. What helps to keep the trachea open? [1]

Answer: C Hyalene cartalidge.

Unit 7, Assessment practice 7.9

1. Describe what we mean by gaseous exchange. [1]

Answer: The process in which oxygen and carbon dioxide move in opposite directions between the air and our body.

2. What is the waste product of gaseous exchange? [1]

Answer: B Carbon Dioxide

Unit 7, Assessment practice 7.10

1. What system are the heart and lungs otherwise known as? [1]

Answer: C The cardiorespiratory system.

2. During exercise, explain how the body responds to the need to remove a greater amount of carbon dioxide from the red blood cells. [2]

Answer: The respiratory rate increases so you breathe more frequently, expelling more carbon dioxide and taking in more oxygen.

Unit 7, Assessment Zone

1. There are three different classifications of joints in the human skeleton.

   a. Which of the following would be classified as a slightly moveable joint? [1]

   Answer: Between vertebrae

   b. When we are born our skull is made up of smaller sections of bone. Over time these fuse together to form one. Which joint classification can be applied to this new bone formation? [1]

   Answer: Immovable

2. a. Identify two muscles found in the upper arm. [2]

   Answer: Bicep and triceps.

   b. Which joint do these muscles cross? [1]

   Answer: Elbow

3. The heart is found in a cavity between the sternum and lungs. It consists of atria, ventricles and the septum. Identify the parts of the heart labelled A, B and C. [3]

Answers:

A Atria   B Ventricles   C Septum

4. Describe two differences between arteries and veins. [4]

Answer: Arteries have thick muscular walls and carry blood away from the heart where as veins have thinner walls and carry blood towards the heart.

Glossary

1-RM – the maximum amount of weight that you can lift in a single repetition.

A

Abduction – movement away from the midline of the body such as when the legs go out during a star jump (abduction at the hip joint).

Achievement motivation – an individual's motivation to master a task and achieve excellence.

Acromion process – the outer end of the scapula, forming the highest point of the shoulder.

Active stretching – stretches performed by a sports performer on their own. The performer applies force to stretch and lengthen the muscles.

Adaptation – changes made within the body to increase its ability to cope with training loads.

Adduction – movement towards the body, such as when the arms are pulled back together during breaststroke in swimming (adduction at the shoulder joint).

Adenosine triphosphate (ATP) – a molecule that is the only useable form of energy in your body.

Adrenaline – a hormone that prepares your body for exercise.

Adversity – an unfavourable or negative experience that can happen during sport.

Aerobic endurance – the ability of the cardiorespiratory system to work efficiently, supplying nutrients and oxygen to working muscles during sustained physical activity.

Aerobic – using oxygen.

Agenda – a list of items to be covered in each meeting.

Agility – the ability to move quickly and precisely or change direction without losing balance or time.

Agonist or prime mover – the muscle that is directly involved in the initial contraction to produce a movement.

Aims – what you want to achieve in your session or by the end of the training programme.

Alveoli – air sacs that allow gas exchange within the lungs.

Anaerobic exercise – exercise that doesn't use oxygen as the main way of releasing energy.

Anaerobic – not dependent on oxygen.

Antagonist – a muscle that opposes the agonist muscle during a movement.

Antagonistic muscles – a pair of muscles working together to produce movement; one muscle works and the other opposes the action.

Anterior auxiliary line – the crease at which the top of your arm, when hanging down, meets the chest.

Anticipatory rise – an increase in your heart rate before you start exercising.

Anxiety – the level of worry or nervousness an individual experiences.

Appendicular skeleton – consists of the pectoral (shoulder) girdles, upper extremities (arms), pelvic girdle and lower extremities (legs).

Areas for improvement – areas where training outcomes did not meet planned goals.

Arteries – thick muscular-walled vessels that carry blood away from the heart.

Arterioles – these branch from arteries and are smaller in diameter. The arterioles branch and lead to even smaller blood vessels called capillaries – they allow for the passage of oxygenated blood.

Articular cartilage or **hyaline cartilage** – a shiny, firm type of cartilage that is flexible and elastic. It is found on the articulating surfaces of bones that form joints and also in the trachea.

Asthma – inflammation of the lungs and its airways.

Atria – are the two upper chambers of the heart – they pump blood to the ventricles which pump blood out of the heart.

Attitude – how positive or negative you generally feel about something.

Attributes – features regarded as invaluable components of being a successful sports performer within a selected sport.

Autocratic – a leader who makes all decisions, and tells sports performers what to do and how to do it.

Axial skeleton – consists of the skull, sternum (manubrium, body, xiphoid process), vertebral column, and ribcage.

B

Balance – the ability to maintain centre of mass over a base of support. There are two types: static balance and dynamic balance.

Ballistic stretching – involves making fast, jerky movements, usually in the form of bouncing or bobbing through the full range of movement.

Barriers to participation – factors that prevent participation or make it more difficult.

Bioelectrical impedance analysis (BIA) – method used for measuring body composition.

Blister – a friction injury to the skin.

Blood plasma – the water-based component of blood.

Blood pooling – the process in which blood is no longer forced to return to the heart after exercise has stopped suddenly and so stays in the legs.

Blood pressure – the force exerted by blood against the walls of the blood vessels.

Body composition – the relative ratio of fat mass to fat-free mass (vital organs, muscle, bone) in the body.

Bone density – the amount of minerals (such as calcium) in your bone, sometimes referred to as bone mineral density.

Bradycardia – a decreased resting heart rate.

Bronchioles – these branch from the bronchi and link to the alveoli. They are responsible for controlling air distribution and airflow resistance in the lungs.

Bronchi – the trachea divides into two bronchi that allows air to pass in to the lungs.

Bruise – when tiny blood vessels are damaged or broken as the result of a blow to the skin.

Bursa – fluid-filled sac that helps reduce friction at a synovial joint.

C

Calcium – a mineral that is important for maintaining bone health.

Cancellous bone – Spongy connective tissue forming the ends of bone.

Candlestick technology – video software which shows a sports performance in slow motion.

Capillaries – very thin vessels that allow oxygen and carbon dioxide exchange.

Capillarisation – new capillaries developing and existing capillaries becoming more efficient to help the movement of blood.

Cardiac hypertrophy – increasing size and strength of the heart muscle.

Cardiac or heart muscle – found only in the heart and used to force blood into the circulatory vessels. This type of muscle has a fairly rapid and sustained contraction and is controlled unconsciously by the heart's pacemaker

Cardiac output – the amount of blood pumped out per minute.

Cardiorespiratory system – a combination of the cardiovascular and respiratory systems.

Cartilage – a tissue that protects the ends of bones.

Cervical vertebrae (seven unfused bones) – these support the weight of the head by enabling muscle attachment through each of the vertebrae. The top two vertebrae, the atlas and the axis, enable the head to move up and down and from side to side respectively.

Cilia – microscopic hair-like structures that vibrate to trap particles from the air.

Circuit training – moving from one exercise to another at a series of stations.

Circumduction – movement in which flexion, abduction, extension and adduction movements are combined in sequence, for example in the shoulder joint during an over-arm bowling action in cricket.

Cognitive anxiety – the mental effects of anxiety.

Collagen – a fibrous protein that connects and supports other bodily tissues, such as skin, bone, tendons, muscles and cartilage.

Compact bone – hard, rigid connective tissue forming the shaft of the bone.

Competitive situations – events where more than one sports performer competes to achieve a set goal.

Complex carbohydrates – absorbed more slowly into the body. As they take longer to digest the energy found in them will be released more gradually, keeping you active for longer. Examples are pasta, bread and rice.

Component – a part of something.

Concentric contraction – muscle contraction in which the muscle shortens in length and develops tension as it contracts e.g. when lifting weights.

Conditioned game practices – game practices with special rules or restrictions that support the development of a skill, technique or tactic in a natural, game-like scenario.

Consent form – used to obtain permission to participate in a physical activity session.

Constant-resistance exercises – exercises in which the amount of resistance for a muscle/muscle group remains the same throughout the repetition.

Constrict – become narrower.

Contingency planning – planning what to do in the event of the unexpected occurring.

Continuous skills – skills that have no obvious beginning or end and can be continued for as long as the performer wishes.

Continuous training – training method that involves keeping a steady pace over a long distance.

Coordination – the ability of parts of the body to work together to move smoothly and accurately.

Core muscles – muscles that are responsible for maintaining good posture.

Costal cartilage – layers of cartilage between each pair of ribs.

Creatine phosphate (CP) – a molecule that can quickly be converted to ATP for energy.

Criteria – a standard by which a sports performer is judged.

Cut – an injury that goes through several layers of skin.

D

Dartfish technology – video software which shows a sports performance in slow motion.

Dehydration – an inadequate amount of fluid in the body. A person is usually considered dehydrated when they have lost more than 2% of their body weight during exercise.

Democratic – leader who involves sports performers in the decision-making process, but makes the final decision on what is to be delivered in the session.

Depression – movement of a part of the body downwards, such as lowering the shoulder blade when pulling down on a pulley-system weights machine.

Diastolic pressure – pressure that results when the heart relaxes and fills with blood.

Diffusion – movement of gases between the alveoli and red blood cells.

Dilate – become wider.

Disclaimer – a statement intended to make the participant aware of and partly responsible for the risks.

Discrete skill – a skill that has a clear beginning and end.

Dominant side – an individual's dominant/preferred side of the body.

Dorsiflexion – moving the foot upwards, towards the tibia, such as when preparing to land in long jump.

Dynamic balance – maintaining balance whilst in motion.

Dynamic stretching – performing activities that are similar to the sporting movements and will be needed during a game or event.

E

Eccentric contraction – muscle contraction in which the tension increases as the muscle lengthens e.g. when lowering weights.

Elastic cartilage – gives support with some degree of flexibility.

Elastic strength – ability of a muscle to contract quickly and overcome resistance.

Elevation – movement of a part of the body upwards, for example, when serving in tennis or raising the shoulder blade when lifting weights.

Energy system – method of converting nutrients to energy.

Environment – the surroundings or conditions in which a sports leader delivers a session.

Enzymes – the catalyst for chemical reactions that release energy for exercise.

Epiglottis – a flap of cartilage that covers the windpipe when swallowing (to prevent food and liquid entering).

Epiphyses – growth plates at the end of bones.

Equality – fair treatment of everyone.

Evaporation – process by which a liquid turns into vapour.

Exercise adherence – how well you stick to your exercise programme.

Exercise – physical activity requiring exertion. It helps to maintain and improve the body's overall health and fitness levels.

Expiration – process of breathing out.

Extension – straightening the joint, such as when the angle at a joint, is increased decreased when shooting in basketball.

Extrinsic factors – factors outside the body.

Extrinsic motivation – external factors that influence motivation, such as trophies.

Extroverts – people who are outgoing and comfortable in the company of other people.

F

False ribs – the next three (8–10) pairs of ribs which connect at the back to the thoracic vertebrae but only connect at the front by costal cartilage to the rib above.

Fartlek training – Swedish training method involving a variety of intensities and terrains.

Fatigue – tiredness.

Fatty acids – produced from the breakdown of fat. Fatty acids are converted to ATP for energy.

Feedback – the information you obtain from yourself and others which reflects on your performance.

Fibrocartilage – highly fibrous cartilage found in places where shock absorption is key.

Fibrous tissue – connective tissue that has a specialised function.

FITT principle – Frequency, Intensity, Time, Type.

Fixed or immoveable – joints where there is no movement.

Fixed-resistance machines – weight training equipment where a weight/fixed amount of resistance is used.

Flexibility – having an adequate range of motion in all joints of the body.

Flexion – the bending of a limb at a joint.

Floating ribs – last two (11–12) pairs of ribs that do not attach to anything at the front of the ribcage but attach to the thoracic vertebrae.

Freely moveable or **synovial** – joints that have a large degree of movement.

Free weights – a weight that is not attached to another machine or device.

Frequency – the number of training sessions you complete over a period of time.

Frostbite – injury to body tissues caused by exposure to extreme cold.

G

Gaseous exchange – the exchange of oxygen and carbon dioxide between the lungs and blood.

Glycogen – a form of carbohydrate stored in the liver and muscles.

Glycolysis – the process of converting glycogen/glucose to ATP for energy.

Goal – something that you want to achieve.
Graze – an injury to the surface layer of skin.

H
Heart rate – the number of times the heart beats per minute.
Heart rate training zone – the lower and upper heart rate you should be training between.
Heat cramps – painful muscle contractions, mainly affecting the gastrocnemius, quadriceps and abdominals.
Heat exhaustion – when the body temperature rises as high as 40°C (104°F) with nausea, vomiting, headache, fainting, weakness and cold, clammy skin.
Heatstroke – a life-threatening emergency condition that occurs when the body temperature is greater than 40°C (104°F).
Height stadiometer – equipment used for measuring height.
Hyaline cartilage – cartilage found on joints that absorbs synovial fluid.
Hydrated – when the body has absorbed an appropriate amount of fluid to maintain its everyday functions.
Hypertension – high blood pressure (greater than 140/90 mmHg).
Hypertrophy – an increase in the size of skeletal muscle.
Hypothermia – having an unusually or dangerously low body temperature generally below 35 degrees, as low as 28 degrees in severe cases.

I
Imagery – a technique used to enhance self-confidence by picturing yourself being successful.
Imaginal experiences – imagining personal performances are successful.
Impact – an effect or influence on something or someone; to have an effect or influence.
Incline press-ups – a press-up exercise where the hands are placed on a raised surface.
Individual differences/needs – each individual's different ability levels, goals, physical attributes, medical history and training activity preferences.
Individual sport – a sport in which a sole performer works towards a set goal.
Inequality – social unfairness, e.g. inequality between the rich and the poor.
Informed consent form – a form listing any injuries or other concerns that may affect their performance. If the participant is under 18, a consent form must be completed by a parent or carer.
Inspiration – process of breathing in.
Insulate – protect from heat loss.
Intensity – how hard training for or playing a sport is.

Intention – planning to do something.
Interactional view – the explanation that suggests behaviour and motivation are shaped by a combination of traits and the social environment.
Interaction – when sports performers communicate effectively with the aim of attaining a joint goal.
Intercostal muscles – muscles laying between the ribs. The external intercostal muscles help with inhalation, while the internal intercostal muscles help force expiration.
International Governing Body (IGB) – an organisation responsible for the promotion and development of a particular sport at an international level.
Interval training – training method that involves alternating work periods with rest and recovery periods.
Intrinsic factors – factors within the body.
Intrinsic motivation – internal factors that influence motivation, such as enjoyment.
Introvert – a person who does not to actively seek excitement and prefers calm environments and tasks that require lots of concentration.
Invasion games – a game in which teams have to get into their opponents' area in order to score.
Iron – needed to repair red blood cells and found in large quantities in meat and eggs
Isolated practices – training drills and skill-specific exercises.
Isometric contraction – when there is tension on the muscle but no movement.
Isometric – muscular action in which tension develops but there is no change in muscle length and no joint movement.

J
Joint capsule – fibrous tissue that encapsulates a synovial joint.

L
Lactic acid – a waste product, that builds up in the body during intense bouts of physical activity.
Laissez-faire – sports leader who lets performers make decisions and helps them when appropriate.
Ligament – thick, tough, fibrous tissue that connects bones together.
Long-term (LT) goals – what you want to achieve in the long term.
Lumbar vertebrae (five unfused bones) – these are the largest of all the individual vertebrae. They offer a great deal of weight-bearing capacity, and secure the attachment of a number of muscles. This, together with the intervertebral discs of cartilage, enables flexion of the trunk.

Lungs – main respiratory organ where gas exchange takes place.

M

Macronutrients – nutrients that are required in large quantities, such as carbohydrates, proteins and fats.

Marrow – the soft, vascular tissue that fills most bone cavities and is the source of red blood cells and many white blood cells.

Maximal fitness test – requires the participant to make an 'all-out' maximal effort.

Medium-term (MT) goals – goals that give progressive support towards achievement of long-term goals.

Metabolic activity – the body's way of releasing energy so that it can be used for exercise.

Micronutrients – nutrients that are needed in much smaller quantities, such as minerals.

Micro-tears – tiny tears in muscles that are necessary 'damage' for a muscle to get bigger and stronger.

Minutes – a written record of what was discussed in each meeting.

Mitochondria – the part of the muscle that produces energy aerobically.

Motivation – the internal mechanisms and external stimuli that arouse and direct behaviour.

Motive to achieve – achievement motivation that means you will eagerly accept challenges and strive for success.

Motive to avoid failure – an individual's efforts to avoid failure.

Mucus – a slippery secretion produced by, and covering, mucous membranes.

Muscle – a tissue made up of fibres that are capable of contracting to produce movement.

Muscle contraction – shortening of the muscle length.

Muscular endurance – the ability of muscles contract over a period of time against a light to moderate fixed-resistance load.

Muscular strength – the maximum force that a muscle or muscle group can produce.

Musculoskeletal system – a combination of the muscular and skeletal systems.

Myofibrils – the contractile elements of the muscle fibre.

N

Nasal cavity – is a large air-filled space above and behind the nose in the middle of the face.

National Governing Body (NGB) – an organisation responsible for the promotion and development of a particular sport at a national level.

Nomogram – special chart used to process data and obtain the correct units of measurement for the interpretation of test results.

Non-verbal communication – communication without using words, e.g. facial expressions and bodily gestures.

Normative data table – data table that presents the usual results given from testing a specific group of people.

O

Objectives – how you are going to achieve your aims in the session.

Observing – watching people to see which traits or behaviours they display.

Official – a representative of a National Governing Body who applies the rules of a specific sport in competitive situations.

Officiate – to administer the rules and control the game, race or match.

Olecranon process – bony projection at the elbow.

Optimal – the best, or most favourable.

Osteoporosis – a condition in which you have brittle bones.

Outcome goals – goals that focus on the outcome of an event, such as winning a race.

Outcome – the results of the session.

P

Passive stretching – requires another person or object applying an external force, which causes the muscle to stretch.

Performance accomplishments – previous accomplishments that increase your belief in future performances.

Performance goals – objectives that focus on the athlete developing their own performance, and that make comparisons with their own performance.

Personality – the sum of characteristics that make a person unique.

Physique – the physical shape, size and muscular development of a person's body.

Plantarflexion – moving the foot downwards, away from the tibia, such as pointing the toes in a gymnastic move.

Pliable – able to stretch and change shape without breaking.

Pliant – can be easily bent.

Plyometric – training that develops sport-specific explosive power and strength.

Posture – a position that the body can assume.

Power – the work done in a unit of time. It is calculated in the following way: Power = Force (kg) × Distance (m) / Time (min or s).

Practicality – how easy a fitness test is to carry out in terms of the costs involved, time available and equipment requirements.

Prejudice – intolerance or dislike of people of a specific race, religion, sexual orientation, age, disability, etc.

Principles of training – factors that you must take into account to ensure that your training will be successful.

Private (sponsorship) – sponsorship or funding provided by companies, corporations and individuals who are not run by the government.

Process goals – goals that focus on what needs to be done to improve performance.

Progressive overload – increasing your training workload gradually so that your body keeps adapting.

Proprioceptive Neuromuscular Facilitation (PNF) – an advanced form of passive stretching that inhibits the stretch reflex that occurs when a muscle is stretched to its full capability, so that an even greater range of movement can occur.

Psychological core – the most stable and innermost, 'real' part of the personality.

Public (sponsorship) – sponsorship or funding provided by the government or public sector organisations, e.g. Sport England grants.

Pulmonary network – system connected to the lungs.

Pulmonary – relating to the lungs.

Q

Qualitative feedback – the use of opinions and words to assess performance.

Qualities – necessary standards required by a sports performer to perform competently within a selected sport.

Quantitative feedback – the use of data and statistics to assess performance.

R

Radiation – heat energy given off from the body in waves.

Reaction time – time taken for a sports performer to respond to a stimulus.

Regulations – rules in sport that are controlled by an authority (a National Governing Body).

Reliability – consistency of fitness test results.

Repetition maximum (1-RM) – the maximal force that can be exerted by a muscle or muscle group in a single contraction.

Repetitions – the number of times you perform a single exercise such as a biceps curl; often abbreviated to 'reps'.

Resilient – able to return to original state after stress such as stretching or being compressed.

Rest and recovery – time to allow the body to repair and adapt, and for the renewal of body tissues.

Re-synthesise – to reproduce ATP.

Reversibility – the reversal of training effects if you stop training, or the intensity of training is not sufficient to cause adaptation. Also known as de-training.

Risk assessment – the review of the health and safety of players and the sporting environment ahead of a planned activity. This involves identifying potential hazards (what could go wrong) and putting in place planned measures and responses to prevent/reduce risk of injury.

Role-related behaviours – the least stable part of the personality, which is influenced by the environment.

Role – the actions and activities assigned to or required or expected of a person.

Rotation – a circular movement of part of a girdle or a limb outwards or inwards, such as when the hip moves towards the body during a drive shot in golf.

S

Sanction – a penalty which is awarded against a sports performer for breaking a rule.

Saturated fats – mainly found in animal products and processed foods such as meats and dairy products, and many fast foods. Saturated fats are very thick and gooey and can clog up passages (such as blood vessels) in the body. Saturated fats are known to raise cholesterol levels, which can lead to problems such as heart disease.

Self-confidence – the belief that a desired behaviour can be performed.

Self-efficacy – self-confidence in a specific situation.

Self-talk – a technique used to improve self-confidence by telling yourself that you will be successful.

Septum – is muscular tissue which separats the two sides of the heart or the ventricles.

Serial skill – a series of individual skills that together produce an organised movement.

Sets – a group of repetitions; for example, an experienced strength trainer may complete three sets of six reps.

Shock – when the body's natural balance is 'upset' due to inadequate circulation of oxygen to the vital organs. Symptoms can include: feeling sick, thirsty, weak and/ or giddy; skin being cold and clammy, or pale and grey; lips, earlobes and fingernails being grey/blue; and restlessness.

Short-term (ST) goals – goals set over a short period of time, between 1 day and 1 month.

Simple carbohydrates – absorbed quickly into the body and only provide short-term energy solutions. They are high in sugars. Common examples are sweets and fizzy drinks; a healthier source would be fruit.

Sino-atrial node – located in the right atrium – is the heart's pacemaker.

Situational view – the explanation that suggests behaviour is shaped by our social environment.

Situation-centred view – the view that motivation is determined by the situation we find ourselves in.

Skeletal or voluntary muscle – striated muscle tissue used primarily for movement of the skeleton, for example the biceps or hamstrings. They produce rapid and powerful contractions brought about by a conscious thought process.

Skill – something that we learn how to do.

Slightly moveable or **cartilaginous** – joints that have a small degree of movement.

Smooth or involuntary muscle – found in the stomach and intestines, this has several functions, including forcing food through the digestive system (by peristalsis) and squeezing blood throughout the circulatory system. It comprises about 40% of the body mass in the human body. This muscle type produces a slow and rhythmic contraction that is controlled unconsciously by the nervous system.

Somatic anxiety – the physical effects of anxiety.

Specificity – how specific training is to the individual's preferred sport, activity, or physical/skill-related fitness goals.

Spectator – someone who watches a sporting event or activity.

Speed – distance divided by the time taken, measured in metres per second (m/s).

Spinal cord – protected by the vertebral column, is a long, thin bundle of nervous tissue transmitting nervous impulses/messages from the brain to the rest of the body.

Sponsorship – The financial support given to an individual, team or event for a commercial return.

Sport – an activity involving physical exertion, skill, competition and rules.

Spotter – a person who watches/helps a participant during a particular weight training exercise.

Sprain – an injury to a ligament.

Stable – people who are not easily affected by their emotions.

State anxiety – temporary anxiety due to the nervous system becoming activated.

Static balance – maintaining balance in a stationary position.

Static stretching – slowly stretching a muscle to the limit of its range of movement and then holding the stretch still for 10 to 20 seconds.

Statistics – data, which can then be used to assess the outcome of an observation, survey, etc.

Sternum – the large, flat bone in the centre and at the front of the cage.

Strain – when a muscle is stretched beyond its limit, tearing the muscle fibres.

Strength endurance – a muscle's ability to perform a maximum contraction and repeat over a long period of time.

Strengths – areas in which performance is consistently successful

Stroke volume – the amount of blood pumped by the heart in one beat.

Submaximal – exercising below an individual's maximal level of physical effort.

Submaximal fitness test – fitness test in which the participant performs the test at less than their maximal effort.

Synovial fluid – a fluid that lubricates and nourishes a joint.

Synovial membrane – soft tissue that protects joints from wear and tear.

Systemic – the non-pulmonary part of the circulatory system.

Systolic pressure – pressure that results when the heart contracts.

T

Tactics – strategies or actions planned to achieve a desired goal.

Target audience – the people a product or service is aimed at.

Team sport – a sport in which more than one player work together towards a set target or goal.

Tendon – a tough band of fibrous connective tissue that usually connects muscle to bone and is capable of withstanding tension.

Thermoregulation – maintaining a constant temperature.

Third umpire – an off-field umpire who makes the final decision in questions referred to him by the two on-field umpires.

Thoracic vertebrae (12 unfused bones) – these allow for the attachment of the ribs. These bones, together with the ribs, form the ribcage, which protects the heart and lungs.

Thorax – the part of the body that lies between the neck and the abdomen.

Tidal volume (TV) – the amount of air inhaled and exhaled with each breath.

Time – how long you train for.

Toxins – are poisonous substances which can cause harm to the body.

Trachea – often called 'the windpipe', and has a primary function of bringing air to your lungs. It contains strong rings of hyaline cartilage that prevent the passage from the collapsing.

Trait anxiety – a personality factor that is characterised by consistent feelings of tension and apprehension due to the nervous system being continually activated.

Trait-centred view – the view that motivation is determined by our personality, needs and goals.

Traits – personality characteristics that can be used to predict or understand behaviours in different settings.

Trait view – the explanation that suggests our behaviour is based on personality traits.

Trigger – something that starts off a particular behaviour.

True ribs – top seven (1–7) pairs of ribs that attach at the back to the thoracic vertebrae and at the front to the sternum.

Type A personalities – people with a high competitive drive who are quite prone to anger and hostility.

Type B personalities – people who are generally laid back and of a quiet disposition.

Typical responses – the way that we usually respond to different situations.

U

Umbilicus – belly button.

Unsaturated fats – found in foods such as oily fish, nuts and olives. They remain much thinner in consistency at room temperature and do not clog up blood vessels. They are actually thought to reduce the body's cholesterol levels.

Unstable – people who have a relatively changeable mood and is easily affected by their emotions.

V

Validity – the accuracy of the fitness test results.

Valves – heart valves ensure blood flows in the correct direction through the heart, preventing back-flow.

Variation – variety in your training programme to prevent boredom and maintain enjoyment.

Vasoconstriction – narrowing of the arterioles.

Vasodilation – widening of the arterioles.

Veins – non-muscular vessels with valves that carry blood towards the heart.

Ventricles – are the two lower chambers of the heart – they receive blood from the atria.

Venules – these branch from veins and are smaller in diameter. They lead to even smaller braches called capillaries – they allow for the passage of de-oxygenated blood.

Verbal communication – communication using words, e.g. team talks.

Verbal persuasion – used by teachers, coaches and peers to persuade you that you can be successful.

Vertebral column – also known as backbone or spine, consists of 33 vertebrae.

Vicarious experiences – using modelling or demonstrations to develop self-efficacy.

Video analysis – using video footage to review practices and games, and improve performance.

Video referee – replaying footage in sports before making or revising a decision.

Views of personality – explanations that have been given to help us understand why we behave in particular ways.

Vital capacity – the amount of air that you can forcibly expel from the lungs.

Vitamin A – needed to maintain strong bones and healthy skin. It is found in many fruits and vegetables.

Vitamin B – helps maintain healthy skin and a well-functioning nervous system. B vitamins are found in meat and wholegrains, as well as various other unprocessed foods.

VO$_2$ max – the maximum amount of oxygen uptake.

Index

353